Technology Assessment of Dual-Use ICTs

Thea Riebe

Technology Assessment of Dual-Use ICTs

How to Assess Diffusion, Governance and Design

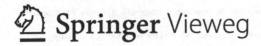

Thea Riebe
Offenbach, Germany

Dissertation approved by the Department of Computer Science of the Technical University of Darmstadt for the award of the academic degree Doctor rerum naturalium (Dr. rer. nat.) submitted by Thea Riebe, M. A. (born in Eisenhüttenstadt)
First examiner: Prof. Dr. Dr. Christian Reuter
Second examiner: Prof. Dr. Alfred Nordmann
Date of submission: 20.09.2022
Date of disputation: 07.11.2022

ISBN 978-3-658-41666-9   ISBN 978-3-658-41667-6   (eBook)
https://doi.org/10.1007/978-3-658-41667-6

This Springer Vieweg imprint is published by the registered company Springer Fachmedien Wiesbaden GmbH, part of Springer Nature.
The registered company address is: Abraham-Lincoln-Str. 46, 65189 Wiesbaden, Germany

Foreword of the Supervisor

The dual-use concept sounds promising at first. Innovations can be used in different contexts and thus have a great impact. However, the term traditionally tends to refer to the unintended use of civilian research results in military contexts; specifically, the danger that research for the benefit of humanity (e.g. for energy production) promotes potential for misuse (e.g. for use in weapons systems). As early as 1979, the THD Initiative for Disarmament was founded at the Technical University of Darmstadt with the aim of demonstrating the interconnection between science/technology and armament and to strengthen the sense of responsibility in this regard among scientists and students, to clarify the global threats to peace and to counteract the deployment of medium-range missiles and cruise missiles in Europe and to publicly advocate for further disarmament. This led to the establishment of the Interdisciplinary Working Group on Science, Technology and Security (IANUS) at the TU Darmstadt in 1988, which dealt with this topic. IANUS was transformed into a network of researchers in 2017, the year my research group Science and Technology for Peace and Security (PEASEC) was founded and Thea Riebe began her doctorate under my supervision.

Although IANUS focused strongly on the classical natural sciences, especially physics, dual-use issues are also important in computer science. In some discourses dual-use is associated with use and misuse, while others distinguish between civilian and military actors or fields of application. Research on dualuse in computer science is not yet available to a sufficient extent, which is a compelling motivation to conduct a doctorate in that field. Thea Riebe's dissertation addresses this research area and explores how dual-use risks of ICT can be assessed. Her thesis contributes to dual-use technology assessment of ICTs in the areas of diffusion and monitoring in the case of artificial intelligence, a reflection on the governability and proliferation regulation of ICTs as dual-use goods in the case of Lethal Autonomous Weapon Systems (LAWS) and cryptography, and the design of Open Source Intelligence (OSINT) for cybersecurity by analysing values and value conflicts.

The methodological range of the work, from qualitative and quantitative empirical to technical contributions to computer science (esp. human-computer interaction as well as cyber security and privacy) should be emphasised: Thea represents an original approach to measuring spillover effects (which is otherwise done via patent citations) with LinkedIn. This can also be measured via job changes in the sample presented, but in a simpler way. She also presents an approach to measuring diffusion between the civilian and military sectors using patent networks. The thesis also analyses the discourse of LAWS using values from Meaningful Human Control and looks at the evolution of US regulation of cryptography from 1990 to the present. She examines OSINT for cybersecurity and explores popular acceptance of OSINT using a representative study. Also, part of the work is the investigation of organisational structures, technology use and collaborative practices of Computer Emergency Response Teams as well as the development of a Twitter-based system for the generation of cyber alerts. The individual studies were published as eight peer-reviewed publications.

Thea Riebe has demonstrated that she is capable of independent scientific work. Thus in November 2022, her dissertation was accepted by the Department of Computer Science at the Technical University of Darmstadt for the degree of Dr. rer. nat. – as the second PhD thesis in our research group PEASEC. I would like to see more research on this important topic. Thea, thank you for allowing me to accompany you on this journey towards your PhD. I wish you the very best and as much success in the future.

Christian Reuter
Professor for Science and Technology
for Peace and Security (PEASEC)
Technical University of Darmstadt
Darmstadt, Germany

Acknowledgements

My research activities have been possible with the support of many people, projects and organisations. I am deeply grateful for the constant and encouraging feedback from by doctoral advisor *Prof. Christian Reuter*. Christian helped me to navigate through the adventurous process of interdisciplinary research. I want to further thank my second advisor *Prof. Alfred Nordmann*, who I have had the luck to assist as a student working for the interdisciplinary working group Science Technology and Security (IANUS) at the Technical University of Darmstadt, and who has been a patient and inspiring facilitator to my journey and dissertation. Further I want to thank *Prof. Max Mühlhäuser, Prof. Gunnar Stevens and Prof. Arjan Kuijper* who kindly agreed to join the doctoral committee.

My work has been made possible by the Technische Universität Darmstadt, in which I was lucky to work within the research group Science and Technology for Peace and Security (PEASEC) since October 2017. Here, I received the opportunity and funding for successful projects, such as the "IT Research of Concern: Assessment of Dual-Use Risks in Software Development" (FIF-IANUS) funded by the Forum for Interdisciplinary Research at TU Darmstadt. The interdisciplinary project has brought together *Prof. Alfred Nordmann* and the perspective of the philosophy and history of technology and technoscience with the perspective of peace informatics at the research group PEASEC. Further, the project "Strategy and Technology Development for Cross-Platform Cyber Situational Awareness and Actor-Specific Cyber Threat Communication (CYWARN)" (No. 13N15407) led by *Dr. Marc-André Kaufhold* and funded by the German Federal Ministry for Education and Research (BMBF) which focuses on the strategy and technology development for cross-platform cyber situational awareness and actor-specific cyber threat communication (2020–2023) has been an important facilitator for my research on technology assessment of Open Source Intelligence Systems (OSINT) for cybersecurity.

Equally, I want to thank my colleagues at the Universität Siegen in which I worked as part of the independent research group "Civic Societal and Business Continuity Through Socio-Technological Networking in Disaster Situations" (KontiKat) (2017–2021), funded by the BMBF (No. 13N14351) first led by *Prof. Christian Reuter,* and later led by *Dr. Marén Schorch.*

I truly appreciate the exchange and collaboration with my co-authors on my conference and journal papers, as well as on the project proposals. Especially, I would like to express my gratitude to my supervisor *Prof. Christian Reuter,* my colleagues *Dr. Marc-André Kaufhold, Stefka Schmid, Philipp Kühn, Markus Bayer, Tom Biselli* and my former students *Tristan Wirth and Philipp Imperatori* and further collaborators *Dr. Volker Knaute and Dr. Stefan Guthe.*

Further, I want to thank my student assistants, especially *Hannah Appich, Julian Bäumler, Anja-Liisa Gonsior, Clarissa Neder, Lilian Reichert,* and *Josefine Süpke* who have contributed to the publications in many different ways, such as proofreading, formatting and many more supportive activities. Also I want to express my gratitude towards all the participants of our interview studies and survey, which have taken time to answer our research questions patiently.

Additionally, I want to express my appreciation towards the anonymous reviewers, who have provided me with constructive feedback and helped to greatly improve my research endeavours.

Finally, I want to express my deep gratitude towards my family, friends, and my partner *Marc,* who enabled this endeavor with patience, support and love.

Abstract

Technologies that can be used in military and civilian applications are referred to as dual-use. The dual-use nature of many information and communicationstechnologies (ICTs) raises new questions for research and development for national, international, and human security. Measures to deal with the risks associated with the various dual-use technologies, including proliferation control, design approaches, and policy measures, vary widely. For example, AutonomousWeapon Systems (AWS) have not yet been regulated, while cryptographic products are subject to export and import controls. Innovations in artificial intelligence (AI), robotics, cybersecurity, and automated analysis of publicly available data raise new questions about their respective dual-use risks.

Dual-use risks have been systematically discussed so far, especially in the life sciences, which have contributed to the development of methods for assessment and risk management. Dual-use risks arise, among other things, from the fact that safety-critical technologies can be easily disseminated or modified, as well as used as part of a weapon system. Therefore, the development and adaptation of robots and software requires an independent consideration that builds on the insights of related dual-use discourses. Therefore, this dissertation considers the management of such risks in terms of the proliferation, regulation, and design of individual dual-use information technologies. Technology Assessment (TA) is the epistemological framework for this work, bringing together the concepts and approaches of Critical Security Studies (CSS) and Human-Computer Interaction (HCI) to help evaluate and shape dual-use technologies.

In order to identify the diffusion of dual-use at an early stage, the dissertation first examines the diffusion of dual-use innovations between civilian and military research in expert networks on LinkedIn, as well as on the basis of AI patents in a patent network. The results show low diffusion and tend to confirm existing

studies on diffusion in patent networks. In the following section, the regulation of
dual-use technologies is examined in the paper through two case studies. The first
study uses a discourse analysis to show the value conflicts with regard to the regulation of autonomous weapons systems using the concept of Meaningful Human
Control (MHC), while a second study, as a long-term comparative case study,
analyzes the change and consequences of the regulation of strong cryptography
in the U.S. as well as the programs of intelligence agencies for mass surveillance.
Both cases point to the central role of private companies, both in the production
of AWS and as intermediaries for the dissemination of encryption, as well as
surveillance intermediaries. Subsequently, the dissertation examines the design
of a dual-use technology using an Open Source Intelligence System (OSINT)
for cybersecurity. For this purpose, conceptual, empirical, and technical studies
are conducted as part of the Value-Sensitive Design (VSD) framework. During
the studies, implications for research on and design of OSINT were identified.
For example, the representative survey of the German population has shown that
transparency of use while reducing mistrust is associated with higher acceptance
of such systems. Additionally, it has been shown that data sparsity through the
use of expert networks has many positive effects, not only improving the performance of the system, but is also preferable for legal and social reasons. Thus,
the work contributes to the understanding of specific dual-use risks of AI, the
regulation of AWS and cryptography, and the design of OSINT in cybersecurity.
By combining concepts from CSS and participatory design methods in HCI, this
work provides an interdisciplinary and multi-method contribution.

Zusammenfassung

Technologien, welche in militärischen und zivilen Anwendungen verwendet werden können, werden als Dual-Use bezeichnet. Durch den Dual-Use-Charakter vieler Informations- und Kommunikationstechnologien (IKT) ergeben sich für die Forschung und Entwicklung neue Fragen für die nationale, internationale und menschliche Sicherheit. Maßnahmen zum Umgang mit den Risiken bei den verschiedenen Dual-Use-Technologien, u. a. die Verbreitungskontrolle, Gestaltungsansätze sowie politischen Maßnahmen sind sehr unterschiedlich ausformuliert. So sind Autonome Waffensysteme (AWS) bisher nicht reguliert, während kryptographische Produkte Export- und Importkontrollen unterliegen. Innovationen im Bereich der Künstlichen Intelligenz (KI), Robotik, Cybersicherheit und der automatisierten Analyse öffentlich zugänglicher Daten werfen neue Fragen zu ihren jeweiligen Dual-Use-Risiken auf.

Systematisch wurden Dual-Use-Risiken bisher insbesondere in den Biowissenschaften diskutiert, die dazu beigetragen haben, Methoden zur Beurteilung und zum Risikomanagement zu erarbeiten. Dual-Use-Risiken ergeben sich u. a. dadurch, dass sicherheitskritische Technologien einfach verbreitet oder verändert, sowie als Teil einerWaffe verwendet werden können. Die Entwicklung und Anpassung von Robotern und Software benötigt deshalb eine eigenständige Betrachtung, die auf den Erkenntnissen verwandter Dual-Use-Diskursen aufbaut. Deswegen betrachtet die vorliegende Dissertation den Umgang mit solchen Risiken in Form von Verbreitung, Regulierung und Gestaltung von individuellen Dual-Use-Informationstechnologien. Technikfolgenabschätzung (TA) ist der epistemologische Rahmen für diese Arbeit, in der die Konzepte und Ansätze der Kritischen Sicherheitsforschung (CSS) und der Mensch-Computer Interaktion (HCI) zusammengeführt werden und dazu beitragen die Dual-Use-Technologien zu bewerten und zu gestalten.

Um die Verbreitung von Dual-Use frühzeitig erkennen zu können, untersucht die Dissertation zunächst die Diffusion von Dual-Use-Innovationen zwischen ziviler und militärischer Forschung in Expert*innennetzwerken auf LinkedIn, sowie anhand von KI-Patenten in einem Patentnetzwerk. Die Ergebnisse zeigen geringe Diffusion und bestätigen dabei in der Tendenz vorhandene Studien zur Verbreitung in Patentnetzwerken. Im darauffolgenden Abschnitt wird die Regulierung von Dual-Use-Technologien in der Arbeit durch zwei Fallstudien untersucht. Die erste Studie zeigt in einer Diskursanalyse die Wertekonflikte im Hinblick auf die Regulierung von Autonomen Waffensystemen mithilfe des Konzeptes Meaningful Human Control (MHC) auf, während eine zweite Studie als Langzeit-vergleichende Fallstudie den Wandel und die Konsequenzen der Regulierung von starker Kryptographie in den USA sowie der Programme von Geheimdiensten zur Massenüberwachung analysiert. Beide Fälle deuten dabei auf die zentrale Rolle der privaten Unternehmen hin, sowohl bei der Produktion von AWS als auch als Intermediäre zur Verbreitung von Verschlüsselung sowie als Überwachungsintermediäre. Darauffolgend untersucht die Dissertation das Design einer Dual-Use-Technologie anhand eines Open Source Intelligence Systems (OSINT) für die Cybersicherheit. Dafür werden als Teil des Value-Sensitive Design (VSD)-Framework konzeptuelle, empirische und technische Studien durchgeführt. Bei den Studien wurden Implikationen für die Forschung zu und die Gestaltung von OSINT herausgearbeitet. So hat die repräsentative Befragung der deutschen Bevölkerung gezeigt, dass Transparenz der Maßnahmen bei gleichzeitigem Abbau von Misstrauen mit einer höheren Akzeptanz solcher Systeme assoziiert wird. Zusätzlich hat sich gezeigt, dass Datensparsamkeit durch die Verwendung von Expert*innennetzwerke viele positive Effekt hat, nicht nur die Verbesserung der Performanz des Systems, sondern auch aus rechtlichen und sozialen Gründen vorzuziehen ist. Damit leistet die Arbeit einen Beitrag zum Verständnis von spezifischen Dual-Use-Risiken von KI, die Regulierung von AWS und Kryptographie, sowie der Gestaltung von OSINT in der Cybersicherheit. Durch die Kombination der Konzepte aus der CSS und den Methoden der partizipativen Gestaltung in der HCI stellt diese Arbeit hier einen interdisziplinären und multimethodischen Beitrag dar.

Contents

Abbreviations

AI	Artificial Intelligence
AVs	Autonomous Vehicles
AWS	Autonomous Weapons Systems
CERT	Computer Emergency Response Team
CCW	Convention on Certain Conventional Weapons
CSCW	Computer Supported Cooperative Work
CSS	Critical Security Studies
CTI	Cyber Threat Intelligence
DURC	Dual Use Research of Concern
ELSI	Ethical, Legal, Social Impacts
HCI	Human-Computer Interaction
ICT	Information and Communication Technology
IR	International Relations
LAWS	Lethal Autonomous Weapons Systems
MHC	Meaningful Human Control
NSABB	National Science Advisory Board for Biosecurity
OSINT	Open Source Intelligence
RRI	Responsible Research and Innovation
TA	Technology Assessment
VSD	Value Sensitive Design

List of Figures

List of Tables

Part I
Synopsis

Introduction

1.1 Motivation and Problem Statement

In 2016, the American Academy of Arts and Sciences published a report on the Governance of dual-use technologies, in which the dual-use risks of Information and Communication Technology (ICT) were recognized (Harris, 2016):

> "Today, questions are being raised about how to manage the potential threat posed by information technology, whose growth and spread some believe may position cyber weapons alongside nuclear and biological weapons in the elite club of technologies capable of unleashing massive harm."

The quote captures the common exaggeration that derives by comparing the possible harm caused by ICTs to weapons of mass destruction. The benign or malicious impact of individual ICT innovations differs regarding the area of application as well as its features, and thus cannot be generalized or evaluated in an isolated manner. Ethics committees and advisory boards such as the German Joint Committee of the DFG and Leopoldina have issued the need for research regarding such dual-use ICTs (Diekmann et al., 2020; Fritsch, 2019). The JRC Report on horizon scanning on dual-use civilian and military research, which was produced for the European Commission, has identified relevant trends in innovation linked to dual-use areas (Bordin et al., 2020). Among the 14 issues, seven are linked to ICT and security, such as Artificial Intelligence (AI) in decision support, enhancing humans, brain-imaging and simulations including brain-computer interfaces. These research areas are expected to have an impact on both military systems and civilian applications, for which close monitoring regarding possible harm is necessary.

T. Riebe, *Technology Assessment of Dual-Use ICTs*,
https://doi.org/10.1007/978-3-658-41667-6_1

Research and technologies are considered *dual-use* when they are "intended to provide a clear benefit, but which could easily be misapplied to do harm" (WHO, 2020), provide military and civil applications (Rath et al., 2014, p. 771), or can be part of a weapon system (Forge, 2010). The dual-use of such research and technologies has impacted the public discourse on the security and benefits of technologies which we regard as highly important for our society. For example, in 1910, Haber and Bosch invented the large-scale synthesis of ammonia, which both helped to create the explosive industry and is still the basis of most fertilizers for food production for half of the world's current population (Kavouras & Charitidis, 2020). Both, synthetic fertilizer and explosives are important for the industrial production of crops, while explosives have both military relevance and civilian use. In the 1940s, nuclear physics made nuclear weapons and nuclear reactors possible (Kavouras & Charitidis, 2020). Nuclear deterrence is still at the center of military strategies, and scholars are discussing the technological change of nuclear weapons and the effects of emerging technologies on strategic stability (Sechser et al., 2019). Since many countries consider nuclear power an essential energy source for the future, the number of new plants has been steadily growing (IAEA, 2022). These examples of technological innovation illustrate that dual-use innovations cannot simply be banned or ignored, as their benefits are seen as too essential for society, while the risks demand careful consideration and a deliberate discourse.

This demonstrates that studying the duality of technological innovation is not a new research endeavor. Research on the assessment of these dual-use risks is strongly, but not exclusively, driven by contributions within life sciences and recently neurological sciences, which have worked on the risks of biological hazards, gene drives and gene engineering, as well as human enhancement (Evans, 2014; Forge, 2010; Harris, 2016; Oltmann, 2015). Biological safety and security faces similar challenges compared to information and communication security: biological weapons are difficult to attribute, they have a multi-use nature in medical and biological research, they are attractive for weaker non-state and militarily actors, and they are to some extent unpredictable in their potential for collateral damage (Koblentz & Mazanec, 2013). To prevent accidental harm or collateral damage through such necessary research, the community has agreed on preventive measures, and defined the term Dual Use Research of Concern (DURC) (WHO, 2020), which refers to research that is intended to provide a benefit, but which could easily be misapplied to do harm. Some ICTs share the characteristics of biological weapons, such as malicious software (Koblentz & Mazanec, 2013), while other research areas in computer science produce different dual-use risks. For example, in robotics and autonomous systems, their risks are discussed from multiple perspectives of dual-use, such as their relevance as part of weapon systems (Altmann & Sauer, 2017), their relevance in military and civilian applications (Verbruggen, 2019), and their ability to be misused and to do harm (Bode, 2019). Therefore, the approaches created in the discourse on DURC cannot capture all aspects of dual-use in ICT.

Computer science and its sub-disciplines have reflected on the design and development of information and communication systems. In particular, the interdisciplinary field of Human-Computer Interaction (HCI) deals with the design of systems and their interaction with the user (Dix, 2017). In HCI, approaches for technology assessment have already been established, such as Value Sensitive Design (VSD) (Friedman et al., 2013; van den Hoven & Manders-Huits, 2020) and Ethical, Legal, Social Impacts (ELSI) assessments (Büscher et al., 2018; Liegl et al., 2016). Many approaches focus on the values and needs of users (Mueller and Heger, 2018; Mueller et al., 2018) or an a combination of social, ethical and legal requirements (Liegl et al., 2016).

The field of Critical Security Studies (CSS) deals with the deconstruction of security as a tool, which frames the certain issues as "security-relevant" (Wæver et al., 1993). Information technology with implications for the national or human security has increasingly been discussed in the field (Hansen & Nissenbaum, 2009; Nissenbaum, 2005). Thus, the use of the concept of dual-use as a category to regulate certain research and artifacts can be analysed with the help of CSS (Rychnovská, 2016; 2020). To do so, case studies provide empirical insights into use cases and risks, and contribute to the understanding of dual-use ICTs. As researchers from the life sciences have noted, a research gap can be found in understanding the phenomena of dual-use in other fields to broaden the awareness of dual-use risks (Evans, 2014; Oltmann, 2015). The Technology Assessment (TA) of dual-use ICT aims to inform the democratic and public discourse on dual-use governance (Grunwald, 2018; Nordmann, 2014), and is a valuable source for dual-use education (Nordmann & Vida, 2022; Riebe & Reuter, 2019). Additionally, the discourse in HCI benefits from methodological perspectives on the design and evaluation of ICTs.

1.2   Aims and Objectives

This thesis contributes to the methodological and empirical discourses regarding the assessment of dual-use ICT to mitigate dual-use risks. To do so, the thesis examines the *monitoring, governance and design of dual-use ICT* in eight studies (Part II). The thesis investigates the monitoring of innovation and knowledge diffusion between industrial sectors in two studies, it analyzes the norms and regulations of dual-use ICTs in two studies, as well as the values and implications for design in four studies. Thereby, risks to international, national, human, and infrastructure security are studied, bridging approaches from CSS and HCI. The main research question of the thesis is: **How can dual-use risks of ICT be assessed for monitoring, governance as well as design?**

For the assessment of dual-use ICTs, it is relevant to systematize related dual-use risks, as well as the technology's characteristics (Tucker, 2012). One characteristic, which is relevant to dual-use, is the diffusion of innovation between civilian and military-industrial sectors. To measure the diffusion, expert networks and their outputs (e.g., publications in form of patents, and social media content) can be used to assess indicators for the diffusion of dual-use research and technology between industrial sectors and application areas. Therefore, as a first step, this dissertation seeks to understand the diffusion of dual-use innovation, and how the diffusion can be measured in the social network LinkedIn as well as in the case of patent citation networks concerning AI innovations. To study the diffusion of knowledge within social networks like LinkedIn is a promising addition to patent and bibliographic approaches (Acosta et al., 2011; 2017), as experts connect, publish and communicate with each other. Based on a patent network analysis, the following research paper addresses diffusion between civilian and military AI innovations, as AI is seen as highly adaptive ICT research (Horowitz et al., 2018). Therefore, the first research question addresses this gap: **RQ1: What are suitable methods to monitor the diffusion of dual-use ICT innovations?** This question is mainly answered in the chapters 8 and 9.

Due to the spread of ICTs in all areas of life, governmental measures concerning dual-use ICTs can influence the access and use of everyday life technologies. This makes any regulation challenging and requires careful cost-benefit analysis. Therefore, the second research question sheds light on the trade-offs of dual-use governance with two case studies: First, the case of Lethal Autonomous Weapons Systems (LAWS) and the approaches for their risk governance, such as Meaningful Human Control (MHC) is interesting from the perspective of conflicting norms, values and requirements. While LAWS are not yet legally regulated, the second case of cryptography is interesting due to the historical development of the dual-use regulation in the US. The study sheds light on the regulation's consequences for the access to strong encryption between 1990 and 2021. Therefore, the second research question asks: **RQ2: How are dual-use technologies governed in light of trade-offs for different concepts of security?** This question is mainly answered in the chapters 10 and 11.

After investigating the monitoring and governance of dual-use ICT, the assessment of dual-use ICT is complemented by studies on the design implications. Therefore, taking into consideration the discourse on VSD, four studies investigate the case of Open Source Intelligence (OSINT) using social media platforms, such as

Twitter, for the development of an alert generation system for cybersecurity events (CySecAlert) for Computer Emergency Response Teams (CERTs) (Kassim et al., 2022; Pastor-Galindo et al., 2020). OSINT is a framework, which aims to collect and analyze public data utilizing a range of gathering, prepossessing and analytical approaches. It touches on social, ethical, legal implications, and can be misused for surveillance (Casanovas, 2014). Therefore, the studies in this part consider stakeholders' perspectives and investigate organizational and collaborative structures, as well as stakeholder interests and value-conflicts in the case of OSINT in cybersecurity. Thus, the third research question is: **RQ3: How can VSD support the assessment of dual-use ICT to prevent the harmful use?** This question is mainly answered in the chapters 12–14 as well as in the design of the artifact in chapter 15.

Through the investigation and synthesis of the three research questions, this thesis seeks to address the research gap in conceptualizing and monitoring dual-use ICTs, as well as the trade-offs in their governance by normative concepts and laws. In addition, the organizational and structural, and stakeholder perspectives are empirically investigated to inform the design of an event detection system. All three individual questions contribute to the understanding of the TA of dual-use ICT.

1.3   Structure of the Work

This dissertation consists of two parts: a synopsis (I) and the research publications (II).

Part I: Synopsis
The synopsis presents the theoretical foundations for this research and contextualizes it in light of the scientific fields which are elaborated in the related work section. Further, the research design and the results of the empirical contributions are summarized and discussed in light of the related work. The work concludes by describing the limitations and future work.

Chapter 1   (Introduction) presents this work's motivation regarding the assessment of dual-use ICT, its aims to identify methods and indicators for the assessment as well as its objectives and structure.

Chapter 2   (Related Work) will provide an overview of CSS, TA and HCI discourses, which builds the foundation to this thesis and further provides relevant terms and definitions regarding the assessment of dual-use in the categories monitoring, governance and design. The the field of CSS provides analytical categories to systematize dual-use definitions, TA provides a framework for the assessment of technology, while participatory design approaches in HCI add tools for dual-use technology design. Lastly, the research gap will be derived from the areas of research.

Chapter 3 (Research Design) will present the overall methodological foundations and the research design of this dissertation. After introducing the epistemological and conceptual background of Technology Assessment, the research approach of the dissertation will be discussed followed by the individual study design which will be described in detail. This chapter further provides the context in which the research has been conducted.

Chapter 4 (Results) will present a comprehensive overview of the contributions of the published papers and provide a synthesis of the results. Thus, the results will summarize the findings of the individual papers on the dual-use case studies on (1) military and civilian applications and the monitoring of the diffusion of innovation between them, (2) on weapon and non-weapon classified systems and the governance of such technologies, as well as (3) on ICT research and development of concern focusing on the VSD case studies, its design implications, and the technological artifact.

Chapter 5 (Discussion) will discuss the research questions and related work in light of the results, focusing first on the contributions towards the monitoring of emerging dual-use ICTs and second on their governance, while the third part discusses the design methodology and design implications for dual-use sensitive design. This will be followed by the limitations and future work.

Chapter 6 (Conclusion) will provide a summary of the synopsis. This includes the research relevance for the fields of peace and security studies and HCI, the research gap and questions regarding the assessment of dual-use ICTs, as well as the methodology to assess different kinds of dual-use ICTs.

Chapter 7 will provide an overview over all of my publications. Among the overall 31 publications, there are eight publications as part of the dissertation, from which two are CORE-A, two CORE-B, and four which have an impact factor of 1.109, 2.36, 2.80 and 3.52.

Part II: Publications
This part of the dissertation consists of the publications which provide the empirical and theoretical findings to answer the research questions. The first question investigates the diffusion of dual-use innovations between sectors. To assess the diffusion, expert networks, their publications, patents and social media networks can thus be used to monitor innovation spillovers into new sectors or areas of application.

Chapter 8 (Measuring Spillover Effects from Defense to Civilian Sectors—A Quantitative Approach Using LinkedIn), drawing on the importance of experts for early technology assessment and risk monitoring, the paper reviews and compares methodological approaches, such as patent citation analysis and social network analysis, to measure innovation spillovers between civilian and military research. Further, the paper introduces an approach to identify innovation spillovers in career networks. This chapter has been published in the *Journal of Peace and Defence Ecnomomics* (Riebe, Schmid, & Reuter, 2021) (Paper A).

Chapter 9 (Dual-Use and Trustworthy? A Mixed Methods Analysis of AI Diffusion Between Civilian and Defense R&D) identifies innovation diffusion within the European patent network using a mixed-method approach analyzing 804 patents regarding AI and arms production. In the second part, the paper investigates 13 papers and documents conducting dual-use research on AI regarding the diffusion of regulative concept of Trustworthy AI. Both parts of the study provide an insight into the diffusion of AI innovation as dual-use research. This paper has been published in the Journal *Science and Engineering Ethics* (S. Schmid et al., 2022) (Paper B).

The second research question investigates which trade-offs and value conflicts arise for dual-use governance in the cases of LAWS, as well as in the case of cryptography products as dual-use items.

Chapter 10 (Meaningful Human Control of LAWS: The CCW-Debate and its Implications for Value-Sensitive Design) analyzes the regulative debate on lethal autonomous weapons within the United Nations Convention on Convention on Certain Conventional Weapons (CCW) by analyzing statements and documents by national representatives and NGOs. The study follows the VSD approach to anticipate stakeholders perspectives and values towards a certain technology and anticipates value conflicts. Based on the value assessment, the study offers

research and design implications for autonomous systems which com-
ply to MHC. This paper has been published in the journal *IEEE
Technology and Society Magazine* (Riebe, Schmid, & Reuter, 2020)
(Paper C).

Chapter 11   (U.S. Security Policy: The Dual-Use Regulation of Cryptography and
its Effects on Surveillance) is a historical analysis of the dual-use regulation policies of the United States since the 1990s until today. The
chapter compares the changes in dual-use regulation to the surveillance programs of the US secret and intelligence agencies, thereby
showing how dual-use regulations and surveillance programs have
influenced encryption in mass communication and by intermediaries.
This paper has been published in the *European Journal for Security
Research* (Riebe et al., 2022) (Paper D).

The third research question, which is concerned with the design of a dual-use ICT,
is answered by the chapters of this part. First, the conceptual investigations in the
Chapters 12 identify relevant stakeholders and use cases, while the empirical investigations identify the values, and value conflicts of the same (Chapter 13 and 14).
Lastly, Chapter 15 develops and evaluates an OSINT system for cybersecurity event
detection, taking the design implications into account.

Chapter 12   (Values and Value Conflicts in the Context of OSINT Technologies
for Cybersecurity: A Value Sensitive Design Perspective) investigates
value conflicts that arise from using OSINT systems for cybersecurity. This first conducts a systematic literature research to provide a
complete overview of the state of research and technology, as well
as the ethical, social, and legal implications that are discussed in the
relevant studies (N=73). This is followed by a focus group analysis (N=7) and interviews (N=9) to gain insights into stakeholders'
perspectives. Taking the empirical results into consideration, design
implications are derived. This paper has been published by the Journal *Computer Supported Collaborative Work* (Riebe, Bäumler, et al.,
2023) (Paper E).

Chapter 13   (Computer Emergency Response Teams and the German Cyber
Defense—an Analysis of CERTs on Federal and State Level) analyzes
the need to support the German public CERTs with (semi)automated
OSINT for cybersecurity to improve the collaboration of German
CERTs. The study, in which 15 interviews and 25 documents were
analyzed, illustrates the existing collaborative practices and derives

implications for the design of a (semi)automated system for cyber-security monitoring. The paper has been published in *Human Computer Interaction (PACM): Computer-Supported Cooperative Work and Social Computing (CSCW)* (Riebe, Kaufhold and Reuter, 2021) (Paper F).

Chapter 14 (Perceptions of the German Population regarding the Impacts of OSINT in Cybersecurity) presents another part of the technology assessment of OSINT systems for cybersecurity. This paper considers the perspective of the German population by using a representative survey (N=1,093), asking for factors that are associated with the acceptance of OSINT systems and the analysis of publicly available social media. Factors that are associated with acceptance of such systems are privacy concerns, as well as the perceived need for OSINT, and the fear of crime and terrorism. Further, we tested the awareness of OSINT as an interactive factor. This paper has been published in the proceedings of the conference *Privacy Enhancing Technologies Symposium* (Riebe, Biselli, et al., 2023) (Paper G).

Chapter 15 (CySecAlert: An Alert Generation System for Cyber Security Events Using Open Source Intelligence Data) develops a near real-time system to detect cybersecurity threats early on, by using expert networks on the social media platform Twitter. The system uses uncertainty sampling to reduce ad-hoc work of classifier training, making the tool easily and rapidly adaptable to the specific context, while also supporting data minimization for OSINT. This paper has been published in the conference proceedings of the *International Conference on Information and Communications Security* (ICICS21) (Riebe, Wirth, et al., 2021) (Paper H).

1.4 Underlying Publications and Contributions of the Author

The thesis consists of works which have been previously published as research articles in peer-reviewed journals and conferences. Therefore, most parts of this dissertation were written in collaboration with several authors. This section outlines the independent academic contributions, which have been confirmed by all authors.

Paper A in Chapter 8: **Thea Riebe**, Stefka Schmid, Christian Reuter (2021) Measuring Spillover Effects from Defense to Civilian Sectors—A Quantitative

Approach Using LinkedIn, Defence and Peace Economics; 32(7):773–785.
doi:10.1080/ 10242694.2020.1755787 [Impact Factor 2.361]

As corresponding and leading author, Thea Riebe led the overall research design,
and management. Thea developed the research relevance as an additional approach
for the TA (Introduction). Stefka Schmid and Thea worked closely together on the
state of research, in which Stefka focused on the research on knowledge economy,
and Thea contributed to the state of research regarding TA and dual-use. As a collaborative work, Thea and Stefka developed the methodological approach (Methodology), as well as the LinkedIn data set and codes, while Stefka coded the data.
Thea developed the operationalization of the categories for civilian and defense
R&D to measure the spillover effect. Further, Thea led the detailed presentation
and analysis of the results (Empirical Results) and the discussion of the results
to other approaches to measure spillover effects (Comparison of the Approaches).
However, all the chapters were written in close coordination between Stefka and
Thea. Christian Reuter supported the work as supervisor, especially regarding the
paper's publication process, research design development, and overall presentation
and readability.

Paper B in Chapter 9: Stefka Schmid, **Thea Riebe**, Christian Reuter (2022) Dual-
Use and Trustworthy? A Mixed Methods Analysis of AI Diffusion between
Civilian and Defense R&D, Science and Engineering Ethics; 28(12):1–23.
doi:10.1007/s11948-022-00364-7 [Impact Factor 3.525]

As corresponding and leading author, Thea Riebe led the overall research design
and management. The initial research idea was based on a former joint publication between Thea and Stefka Schmid (Riebe, Schmid, & Reuter, 2021), and was
iteratively refined. Thus, Stefka and Thea identified the research relevance in close
exchange (Introduction). Related Work was discussed and developed in exchange
between Stefka and Thea, in which Thea introduced the literature on responsible
research and development of dual-use technologies and Stefka focused on the literature on Trustworthy AI. Stefka and Thea developed the research question and
design in an iterative approach in which the former identified the data and documents,
developed the codes, and conducted the coding of the documents for the patent and
document analysis (Research Design), which was then refined and supervised by
Thea, especially regarding the conjuncture of the mixed method analysis, as well as
the coding of the dual-use patents. Stefka made an initial draft of the presentation
of Results, which was then revised and refined in close collaboration and led by
Thea. In the Discussion, Thea derived implications for dual-use assessment of AI

innovations, while Stefka focused on the implications for Trustworthy AI. Christian Reuter advised the entire research process from the idea until the submission.

Paper C in Chapter 10 : **Thea Riebe**, Stefka Schmid, Christian Reuter (2020) Meaningful Human Control of Lethal Autonomous Weapon System: The CCW-Debate and its Implications for Value-Sensitive Design, IEEE Technology and Society Magazine; 39(4): 36–51. doi:10.1109/MTS.2020.3031846 [Impact Factor 1.109]

As corresponding and leading author, Thea Riebe led the overall research design and management. Stefka Schmid and Thea identified the research relevance (Introduction). Related Work was discussed and developed in exchange between Stefka and Thea, in which Thea introduced the framework of VSD and Stefka focused on the literature on autonomy and Autonomous Weapons Systems (AWS). Stefka and Thea developed the research question and design in an iterative approach, in which Stefka identified the data and documents, developed the codes, and coded the documents for the discourse analysis (Research Design). This was supervised by Thea regarding the data set and research quality. Stefka led the presentation of the results. In the Discussion, Thea derived implications for MHC based on the VSD-perspective. Christian Reuter supported the paper by supervising the publication process, especially regarding the readability, quality, and presentation of the research paper and its findings.

Paper D in Chapter 11 : **Thea Riebe**, Philipp Kuehn, Philipp Imperatori, Christian Reuter (2022) U.S. Security Policy: The Dual-Use Regulation of Cryptography and its Effects on Surveillance, European Journal for Security Research. doi:10.1007/s41125-022-00080-0

As the corresponding and leading author, Thea Riebe developed the initial research idea, which then has been iteratively refined by Thea and Philipp Imperatori in close exchange. Thus, Thea led the Introduction, highlighting the relevance of this paper. Thea contributed the section Related Work, which focused on surveillance studies, as well as the governance of cryptography as a dual-use good. Further, Philipp I. drafted the research design and hypothesis which was refined and revised by Thea. Philipp I. conducted the literature research of the comparative material, and drafted the presentation of the Results, which have been added to and refined by Thea and Philipp Kühn. Lastly, Thea performed the Discussion in exchange with Philipp K., where she focused on the interpretation of the results considering the surveillance and dual-use discourse, while Philipp K. contributed the discussion on cryptographic innovations. Christian Reuter advised the whole research process from the idea until the submission.

Paper E in Chapter 12 : **Thea Riebe**, Julian Bäumler, Christian Reuter (2023) Values and Value Conflicts in the Context of OSINT Technologies for Cybersecurity: A Value Sensitive Design Perspective, Computer Supported Cooperative Work (CSCW): The Journal of Collaborative Computing and Work Practices. doi:10.1007/s10606-022-09453-4 [CORE-B, Impact Factor 2.800]

As the corresponding and leading author, Thea Riebe developed the initial research idea, which she iteratively refined in close exchange with Julian Bäumler. Julian wrote the Introduction, which was supervised and refined by Thea. The Related Work was discussed and developed in exchange between Julian and Thea, in which Julian introduced the framework of Value-Sensitive Design (VSD) and Thea focused on the context of OSINT for cybersecurity. Following, Julian and Thea developed the research question and design in an iterative approach. While Julian identified the data and documents, developed the codes, performed the coding of the documents for the systematic literature review, and conducted the semi-structured interviews and focus group workshop (Research Design), Thea supervised the process iteratively regarding the data set and research quality. Julian wrote the Results and developed the illustrations in exchange with Thea, who focused on the cohesion of the presentation and refined the interpretation of the results. In the Discussion, Thea, and Julian derived implications for OSINT systems for cybersecurity based on the VSD perspective. Marc-André Kaufhold and Christian Reuter advised the whole research process from the initial idea until paper submission.

Paper F in Chapter 13 : **Thea   Riebe**,   Marc-André   Kaufhold,   Christian Reuter (2021) The Impact of Organizational Structure and Technology Use on Collaborative Practices in Computer Emergency Response Teams: An Empirical Study, Proceedings of the ACM: Human Computer Interaction (PACM): Computer-Supported Cooperative Work and Social Computing; 5(CSCW2). doi:10.1145/3479865 [CORE-A]

As corresponding and leading author, Thea Riebe developed the initial research idea to investigate the collaborative practices and organizational structure of German state-level CERTs. Marc-André Kaufhold and Thea refined the research question in an iterative approach. Thea drafted the state of research, in which Marc-André added the focus on crisis informatics and computer-supported collaborative work. Thea led the research design and developed the codebook for the qualitative analysis. Thea collected and analyzed the first round of data collection (Interviews=10, documents=25) while Marc-André analyzed the second round of interviews which added among others, the perspective of civilian protection (N=5). Thea drafted the presentation of results, which was revised by Marc-André and Thea in collaboration in the final version of the manuscript. Thus, the discussion was written by Marc-André and Thea in close exchange to derive implications for policy and design of a collaborative system for CERTs. Christian Reuter advised the entire research process from the idea until the submission.

Paper G in Chapter 14 : **Thea Riebe**, Tom Biselli, Marc-André Kaufhold, Christian Reuter (2023) Perceptions of the German Population regarding the Impacts of OSINT in Cybersecurity, Proceedings on Privacy Enhancing Technologies (PoPETs). doi:10.56553/popets-2023-0028 [CORE-A]

As the corresponding and leading author, Thea Riebe developed the initial research idea, which then has been iteratively refined by Thea and Tom Biselli in close exchange. Thea wrote the Introduction, highlighting the relevance of this paper within the research field. Thea wrote the section Related Work, which focused on surveillance studies, surveillance technologies privacy research and the factors associated with the acceptance of surveillance technologies. The research constructs and hypotheses were developed both by Thea and Tom in close collaboration, where Tom focused more on methodological aspects and Thea more on content aspects. Thea drafted the questionnaire in exchange with Tom and Marc-André Kaufhold. Thus, Thea, Tom and Marc-André contributed the Research Design, in which Thea focused on the survey design, Marc-André on the questionnaire and Tom on the statistical analysis and ethics. Thea and Tom presented the results, while Thea focused on the descriptive statistics and Tom on the inference statistics. Lastly, Thea wrote the Discussion in exchange with Tom, with a focus on the interpretation of the results considering the factors associated with the acceptance of surveillance technology and deriving implications for technology design. Christian Reuter advised the whole research process from the idea until the submission.

Paper H in Chapter 15 : **Thea Riebe**, Tristan Wirth, Markus Bayer, Philipp Kühn, Marc-André Kaufhold, Volker Knauthe, Stefan Guthe, Christian Reuter (2021) CySecAlert: An Alert Generation System for Cyber Security Events Using Open Source Intelligence Data, Proceedings of Information and Communications Security. Cham: Springer International Publishing, pp:429–446. doi:10.1007/ 978-3-030-86890-1_24 [CORE-B]

As corresponding and leading author, Thea Riebe led the overall research design, management, and introduction, as well as discussion of the paper. Thea developed the initial research idea to support CERTs with a social media-based threat detection system, then Tristan Wirth, Marc-André Kaufhold, and Thea refined the research question in an iterative approach (Introduction). Tristan drafted the state of technology and research and the technology concept (Concept), which I improved regarding the research context. Tristan implemented the system. For the evaluation, Tristan developed the ground truth data set and coded it for the process of evaluation (Evaluation), which Thea then refined and supervised. Further, the Related Work and Discussion was performed by Tristan and Thea, in which both worked in close exchange. During this process, Philipp Kühn supported the improvement of the work regarding cyber threat intelligence approaches and Markus Bayer especially helped to improve the discussion of related approaches of supervised learning and state-of-the-art machine learning. Christian Reuter advised the entire research process from the idea until the submission. Volker Knauthe and Stefan Guthe advised the overall structure and presentation of the paper as part of an internal peer review.

Theoretical Background and Related Work   2

This chapter introduces the domains and fields relevant to the thesis. First, as this dissertation contributes to computer science peace research, it introduces the field (Section 2.1). The field of CSS is introduced (Section 2.1.1) as well as the discourse on dual-use (Section 2.1.2). To build a theoretical bridge from computer science peace research to methods of TA and design approaches in HCI, Section 2.2 introduces the theory and discourse in TA, the dimensions of assessment (Section 2.2.1) and how technology and design are evaluated in HCI (Section 2.2.2). Further, Section 2.3 summarizes the related research, and derives the research gaps and potentials, some of which are addressed in this dissertation.

2.1   Peace and Conflict Studies

Peace and conflict studies has emerged as an interdisciplinary field from the social, psychological, political and historical sciences in the late 1950's and 1960's to promote peace and to develop "quantitative, mathematical, and behavioral approaches to the study of their discipline and linking it to general social science" (Kelman, 1981, p. 99). However, the interdisciplinary nature of the research subject "peace", what it is and how it can be achieved, has even led to the discourse if peace and conflict studies is a separate discipline at all (Alger, 2014). Galtung (1964, p. 2) defines peace as the absence of armed conflict (negative peace) or structural violence (positive peace). The field of peace and conflict studies researches the conditions of peace, peaceful conflict transformation (Alger, 2014, 312f.), relevant stakeholders (state and non-state actors), the local, national or international system and the institutional setting and its norms and rules, (violent) conflict prevention, the transformation of violent conflicts into more non-violent forms, as well as transitional justice in post-conflict societies (Alger, 2014).

© The Author(s), under exclusive license to Springer Fachmedien Wiesbaden GmbH,   17
part of Springer Nature 2023
T. Riebe, *Technology Assessment of Dual-Use ICTs*,
https://doi.org/10.1007/978-3-658-41667-6_2

In all these research topics covered by peace and conflict studies, ICT gains relevance and influences the conditions of peaceful conflict resolution and co-existence. ICTs shape the human condition and therefore can be studied both, from the perspective of normative research aiming to promote peace as well as from the empirical perspective to develop new quantitative approaches. The field of IT peace research deals with the role of information technology in conflicts as well as the development of artifacts for conflict prevention or resolution (Reuter et al., 2019, p. 24). IT peace research is an interdisciplinary field which connects peace and conflict studies with computer science and cybersecurity research (Reuter et al., 2019, p. 24). Thus, the study of security as the protection against threats is a central part of peace and conflict studies and IT peace research.

2.1.1 Critical Security Studies

Security is referred to as an "essentially contested concept" (Buzan, 2008, p. 7) because security evokes different meanings and understandings, all of which cannot necessarily be encompassed within a universally agreed-upon definition. Instead, the very definition of security depends on the chosen referent object, issue dimension, geographical focus, and danger dimension, and can accordingly change over time (Schlag et al., 2015). The realist school of thought of International Relations (IR), which is seen as the "traditional" school, understands security as national and military security against the threats posed by other states (Floyd, 2007, p. 334). In the 1980s, constructivist understandings and conceptualizations of security challenged the traditional notion and discussed additional referent objects, such as humans, communities, or the environment (Floyd, 2007, p. 334). Constructivist approaches challenged the neo-realist assumption of security being focused solely on states. Constructivist approaches aim to deconstruct security and security threats as socially and discursively constructed (Wæver et al., 1993). Thus, saying something is a matter of security can change society's or government's perception thereof and consequently the necessity to provide any possible means to deal with such new security issues and threats (Buzan et al., 1998). This discursive construction of security is referred to as "securitization" (Buzan et al., 1998). However, Buzan et al. (1998) viewed securitization as something negative, for which regular political means have failed (Floyd, 2007, p. 328). Among the constructivist school, the Welsh School of security scholars (Booth, 1991a, 1991b; R. W. Jones & Jones, 1999) follow the critical theory of the Frankfurt School and conceptualize security as an emancipation from fear and the deterministic dynamics of deterrence (Floyd, 2007, p. 332). Floyd (2007) points out that this approach has its limitations in practice, emphasizing that if there are no limits on the definition of security, everything could be defined as security. Thus, she proposes to complement both perspectives on understanding security, both as a powerful linguistic tool and as an emancipatory term.

Like the Welsh School, the focus on the individual has been strengthened by Kaldor (2011) and her concept of human security. Both approaches criticize that national security has prioritized military concerns over individual concerns and has consequently contributed to an overall increase in human insecurity. The claim that national security comes at the cost of human security, that people have to be protected from their governments, or that power should be removed from the same is usually derived from the increase in insecurity linked to the increase in nuclear proliferation, as well as the related risk and threat of possible accidents at military bases during the Cold War (Booth, 1991a, 1991b). Nevertheless, human security does not rule out the use of force. As Kaldor (2011, p. 446) states:

> "Human security is a means as well as a goal. It may involve the use of force and thus can be regarded as a hard security policy but the use of force has to be directed towards protection rather than fighting or revenge. It means using the military in a different way, more like policing than war fighting [...] the aim of any human security approach is to dampen down violence and not support one side or another militarily".

Therefore, this thesis follows the post-positivist approach to not only study socio-technical phenomenon's empirically from the perspective of states as main actors but incorporates the constructivist notion of security as in the concept of human security. In the following section, the dual-use terms and their relevance for different conceptions of security are discussed.

2.1.2   Technology Ambivalence and Dual-Use

The role of ICT for peace and security has increased, and guided many interdisciplinary research endeavours, leading to a intersection of technology, science and (security) politics (Dunn Cavelty & Wenger, 2020). While Banta (2009) defines technology as "science or knowledge applied to a definite purpose", Hubig (2014) has noted how technology is the product of human agency and human skills. Further, Jonas (1979, p. 41) is making humans responsible for the impacts of technology on the environment and other humans: "How in short can [human] freedom prevail against the determinism [they have] created for [themselves]?" During the research and development of technology, in which technologies are called "emerging", their implementation might already have consequences. These so-called *Emerging Tech-*

nologies are technologies that have not been fully developed or implemented. Rotolo et al. (2015) found that emerging technologies combine the following features: "(i) radical novelty, (ii) relatively fast growth, (iii) coherence, (iv) prominent impact, and (v) uncertainty and ambiguity".

The ambiguity of technology has been named *dual-use* (Forge, 2010; Oltmann, 2015). Liebert and Schmidt (2018, p. 54) define dual-use or the Ianus-faced ambivalence [1] as "a dichotomy of effects, impacts and opportunities that [...] occur simultaneously and that are intrinsically linked to a technology". It is noteworthy that studies on the ambivalence of technology focus on more than dual-use, (see Bauman, 1990; Lösch, 2012). However, the term dual-use is itself far from universally agreed-upon and used in various contexts and meanings (see Table 2.1). Rath et al. (2014, pp. 779-783) lays out the evolution of dual-use concepts, identifying five definitions: (1) civilian versus military use, (2) benevolent versus malevolent purpose, (3) peaceful versus non-peaceful purpose, (4) legitimate versus illegitimate purpose, and the (5) good military and good civilian purpose. However, Rath et al. (2014) misses out to include the definition by Forge (2010) which defines dual-use items as possible parts of (improvised) weapon systems. The definition by Forge (2010) further includes the possible violent use of the dual-use non-weapon-items as improvised weapons, as well as the possibility that weapons are used by non-state actors. Both aspects aim to include terrorist appropriation of any technology. Therefore, this work draws on three definitions which focus on areas of application (civilian versus military, weapon systems and non-weapons systems) and its consequences (beneficial and harmful).

In the field of the life sciences[2], an intense debate on dual-use research and risks on biological safety and security took place in the 2000s and 2010s (Evans, 2014; Oltmann, 2015; Resnik, 2009; Tucker, 2012). With advances in life sciences, e.g. regarding new methods for gene editing and research on viruses since the 2000s, the related disciplines have ignited a fruitful discourse on risks by researching and developing relevant, yet dangerous technologies and items. In 2007, the U.S. National Science Advisory Board for Biosecurity (NSABB) defined dual-use as "research yielding new technologies or information with the potential for both benevolent and malevolent applications" (NSABB, 2007, p. 2). The NSABB has further defined the threats in more detail as "life sciences research that, based on current understanding, can be reasonably anticipated to provide knowledge, products, or technologies that could be directly misapplied by others to pose a threat to public health and safety,

---

[1] Ianus-faced refers to the Latin god IANUS with two faces.

[2] Life sciences are concerned with research on life forms, such as human, animal, or plant microbial pathogens (viruses, bacteria, fungi) and toxins (Oltmann, 2015, p. 329).

agricultural crops and other plants, animals, the environment or material" (NSABB, 2007, p. 17). The WHO (2020) has based its definition of DURC on the NSABB's definition. This definition is the result of an intense debate within life sciences in which the scientific community has developed guidelines for working with DURC (Evans, 2014).

In the field of computer science, there have been some contributions on the issue of dual-use, however, the discourse in the field remains fragmented. Even Oltmann (2015) has not particularly included computer science in her investigation across multiple disciplines. Although she includes "engineering and technology", it remains unclear to what extent this includes the various sub disciplines of computer science which are highly relevant for today's dual-use discourse, e.g. regarding (lethal) autonomous systems or (social) big data. In engineering, students and researchers have demanded to increase awareness about dual-use. In her study 11% of senior editors of peer-reviewed journals in engineering and technology reported that they had to consider dual-use questions (Oltmann, 2015, p. 333). However, Oltmann (2015) criticizes that although non-life science editors of surveyed journals have had contact with dual-use research, the definition of dual-use with a strong focus on life sciences might create the impression that dual-use only occurs within the life sciences. Thus, she postulates "a need for a broader or new definition of dual use that explicitly applies to non-life sciences" (Oltmann, 2015, p. 338). Further, Lin (2016, pp. 119-120) highlights that ICT should not be considered a dual-use technology in the same way that physics, biology, and chemistry are because communication and information are considered general-purpose, and, thus, meaningful governance like in established dual-use control regimes is hard to imagine.

The definitions of dual-use all refer to a threat due to the use of technology, implying a referent object which needs to be secured. Therefore, the definitions of dual-use can be categorized according to their referent objects (Rychnovská, 2016; 2020) (see Table 2.1). The first definition (military versus civilian use) highlights the relevance of a certain good for military superiority and deterrence. Technologies, such as AI and AWS are seen as a possible threat to national security, deterrence and stability (Altmann & Sauer, 2017; Horowitz et al., 2018). For the definition by Forge (2010) which focuses on (improvised) weapon systems and its components, deterrence and superiority are still relevant, but non-state actors might use a certain technology to their advantage as well. Thus, it also draws the focus away from the state as the sole referent object of security. This definition can be applied for the legitimization of the dual-use regulation of cryptography, which was justified by the "war on terror" (Vella, 2017). The third definition of dual-use, which is based on the DURC understanding, emphasizes the human as a referent object, which have to be protected from harm, and is thus human-centered (WHO, 2020). Consequently, the

Table 2.1 Definitions of dual-use and its security concepts

Category	Dual-use Definitions	Security Concept
Goods, which can be used for military or civilian applications	"[...] research and goods, software and technology that can be used for both civilian and military applications and/or can contribute to the proliferation of Weapons of Mass Destruction (WMD)" (Alavi & Khamichonak, 2017; European Commission, 2018; Wassenaar Arrangement Secretariat, 2021)	National security (Waltz, 1990)
Goods, which can be used as part of a weapon system	"(knowledge, technology, artifact) [...] if there is a (sufficiently high) risk that it can be used to design or produce a weapon, or if there is a (sufficiently great) threat that it can be used in an improvised weapon, where in neither case is weapons development the intended or primary purpose" (Forge, 2010).	National security (Waltz, 1990)
Research with either harmful or beneficial outcomes	"Dual use research of concern (DURC) is life sciences research that is intended for benefit, but which might easily be misapplied to do harm." (WHO, 2020)[a]	Human security (Kaldor, 2011)
Composite Definitions	"Research, teaching and studies at Technische Universität Darmstadt exclusively pursue peaceful goals and serve civilian purposes; research, particularly relating to the development and optimisation of technical systems, as well as studies and teaching are focused on civilian use." (Utz et al., 2019)	Combination of the concepts

[a]For a further overview on dual use definitions in the life sciences see (Oltmann, 2015).

definition also resonates with other emancipatory concepts of security, such as the concept of human security (Kaldor, 2011). Human security-centered definitions of dual-use can be connected to emancipatory discourses on ethical AI (Floridi et al., 2018) and OSINT or big data analytics (Rajamäki & Simola, 2019). The relevance of the approaches towards DURC for other disciplines is considerable, as stated by Resnik (2010, p. 4). If the scope of the dual-use definition is too wide, it might be also applied in benign areas of science and thus become irrelevant to identify possibly harmful technologies. In the other case, if the definition is too narrow, it might lead scientists and policy makers to overlook technologies outside of the definition (Resnik, 2009, 3f.).

2.2   Technology Assessment and Design

Technology Assessment (TA) is a socio-epistemic practice which aims to make methods available which help to anticipate the effects of innovations, to prevent trial and error-approaches, especially when innovations would be irreversible (Grunwald, 2018). From the perspective of conflict and security studies, emerging security-relevant technologies can have impacts on human security, and might be misused with malicious intent. TA was developed in the United States in the 1960s, which was the first nation to open the Office of Technology Assessment (OTA), which published studies regarding the impacts of technologies on society between 1972 and 1995. The work of the OTA provided the democratic bodies and the public with an analysis of "complex scientific and technical issues" ("The OTA Lagacy", 2022). This service has become necessary to provide insights for the societal and democratic discourse on the use and governance of certain technologies. Thus, TA is both a theoretical and a practical approach, in which the scientific endeavour is driven by the practical challenges of the emergence of technology for society, which will then induce the theoretical reasoning (Grunwald, 2018, p. 1). The three practical aims of TA are (1) policy advice, (2) engaging in public debate, and (3) contributing to the making of technology (Grunwald, 2018, p. 92). TA theory aims to facilitate the reflexivity of technology design and development (see Figure 2.1).

There is no universal definition for TA, but some shared understandings of its aim can be summarized as "a wide category encompassing an array of policy analytic, economic, ethical, and other social science research that attempts to anticipate how research and research-based technologies will interact with social systems" (Guston & Sarewitz, 2002, p. 94f). Furthermore, it is sometimes understood as technology evaluation or technology foresight (Grunwald, 2018, p. 4). However, the evaluation of technology is no end in itself, but it should serve "to contribute to the formation of public and political opinion on societal aspects of science and technology" (Decker et al., 2004, p. 14). Therefore, Grunwald (2018, p. 100) defines TA as a socio-epistemic practice with institutions, projects, and methods which is embedded in a societal framework:

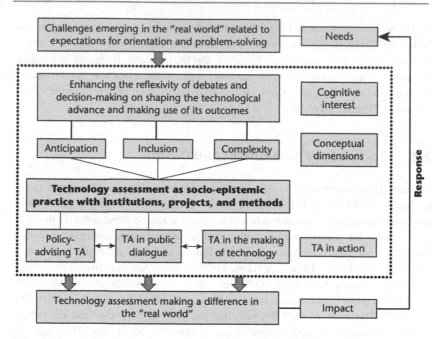

Figure 2.1 A general model of technology assessment by Grunwald (2018, p. 89)

"The complexity of socio-technical systems, their diverse interlacing, and their con-
nectivity with many areas of human life beyond technology increase the difficulties of
anticipating and assessing the consequences of actions or decisions, which is a major
epistemological challenge to technology assessment." (Grunwald, 2018, p. 25)

2.2.1 Dimensions of Technology Assessment

With the advancement of sciences and technologies which would have irreversible
impacts on ecosystems and societies, the need to evaluate technology before implementation, even before conducting experiments, has become a driver of TA. Grunwald (2018, p. 91) even states that TA is an approach to facilitate reflexivity as it
"provides a counter-model to 'trial and error' approaches, to 'wait and see' strategies and to 'quick and dirty' decisions with respect to technological advance."
Unintended effects of technologies on human health or the ecosystems might not be

visible early on but appear many years or even decades later, thus making it much more difficult or expensive for societies to abandon certain technologies.

Therefore, these unintended effects on the environment and the society have made philosopher Hans Jonas emphasize the precautionary principle as the guiding principle to the ethics of responsibility (Jonas, 1980). As the boundaries of human actions can no longer be regarded as limited to time and space, humanity must take the needs of future generations as well as those of the biosphere into account (Coyne, 2018, p. 230). As such, Jonas has been an influential thinker for the environmental movement as well as for the legitimization of research governance by, e.g., the European Union and the concept of Responsible Research and Innovation (RRI) (von Schomberg, 2011). Von Schomberg defines RRI as

> "a transparent, interactive process by which societal actors and innovators become mutually responsive to each other with a view on the (ethical) acceptability, sustainability and societal desirability of the innovation process and its marketable products (in order to allow a proper embedding of scientific and technological advances in our society)." (von Schomberg, 2011, p. 11)

While the academic debate has struggled to identify a practical process (Burget et al., 2017, p. 14), even though it has been integrated into research projects (Spruit et al., 2016), Burget et al. (2017, p. 9) conclude in their systematic study of RRI that it is mostly seen as an "attempt to govern the process of research and innovation with the aim of democratically including, early on, all parties concerned in anticipating and discerning how research and innovation can or may benefit society."

To anticipate the effects of research, technology and innovation, TA allows for a systematic discourse as it differentiates between the following effects and consequences (Grunwald, 2018, p. 17):

- intended and unintended effects
- desired and undesired consequences
- main and side effects
- expected and unexpected effects

In this categorization, the dual-use of technology is seen as part of the unintended side effects (Liebert & Schmidt, 2018). A technology which functions well and is safe to use may still have undesirable effects which only occur or can be recognized later on when the technology is used. Examples of this can be found in infrastructural or environmental innovations, such as the reliance on fossil fuels and private transportation (Grunwald, 2018, p. 18). Technologies, which are dual-use can be applied to more contexts than to only those that they are created for. Thus, evaluating their dual-use, i.e. unintended side effects, is especially crucial when they can cause harm to people, or are relevant in security contexts. Thus, Liebert and Schmidt (2018) argue for developing and performing a TA which focuses on this kind of ambivalence of technologies by characterizing the technological core. Doing so, the aim is not to dissolve the dual-use, which would not be possible as ambivalence is seen as the result of the modern societies creation of order (Liebert & Schmidt, 2018, p. 53). Moreover, TA would help to analyze certain dual-use scenarios and design choices, while taking these unwanted side effects into account. Thus, they propose the categorization of types of ambiguities and technologies.

Dual-use issues are conjoined with the *Collingridge Dilemma*, which describes that in the process of research and development, potential harmful outcomes cannot be easily predicted, as this requires predicting any potential application and the consequences thereof. However, in early stages of development, during which such predictions are difficult, changes would be easiest to implement in contrast to later stages where changes and adjustments may come at a higher cost: "When change is easy, the need for it cannot be foreseen; when the need for change is apparent, change has become expensive, difficult and time consuming" (Collingridge, 1980, p. 11). In many areas, especially in basic research, both civilian and military research can contribute towards the application of the research to the other area known as spillover effects (Liebert, 2013, p. 244). Nordmann (2010, p. 14) questions, that instead of following the logic of the Collingridge Dilemma ("when can we get hold of the future such that it is neither too early nor too late for meaningful TA?") to consider "what are the best sites for a forensics of wishing?" This includes a variety of sites, such as cultural imaginaries, technology and political bodies. These venture points of TA inquiry help to understand the visions of socio-technical futures. Thus, TA of socio-technical futures needs to be reflected as a design practice by itself in offering alternative visions of possible futures (Lösch et al., 2019, p. 302).

2.2.2   Human-Computer Interaction: From Technology Assessment to Participatory Design

Within the TA discourse, the "participatory turn" has led to the inclusion of relevant stakeholders and public dialog as a central paradigm of technology design (Boden et al., 2018, p. 85). This has resulted in many approaches for stakeholder engagement and iterative, experimental and more participatory design. The design of technologies influences the socio-technical futures (Lösch et al., 2019) and practices (Stevens et al., 2018). Thus, design is seen as an *enabler* of possibilities

(Grunwald, 2018, p. 25). Van den Hoven (2010, p. 75) even described ICTs' architects as "choice architects, who have responsibilities for organizing the context in which people make decisions." Therefore, ICT artifacts interfere with and even change socio-technical practices, which is why socio-technical interactions are the subjects of participatory design research (Wulf et al., 2011). Stevens et al. (2018) propose the Grounded Design Approach, which accounts for the societal relevance of computing by including the "context specificity of local knowledge and appropriation of information and communications technology". It uses a practice-based constructivist paradigm which aims to study IT artifacts over time in the context of use (Stevens & Pipek, 2018). These participatory design approaches have been particularly discussed in the field of HCI, and its sub-discipline Computer Supported Cooperative Work (CSCW), which focuses on the collaborative and cooperative practices between individuals and in organizations (Wallace et al., 2017). Thus, deliberate forms of participation in the design process have become especially relevant in design of technology for the health and public sector (Callon, 1999; Van der Velden, Mörtberg, et al., 2015).

And while the role of peace and security has entered HCI research (Hourcade & Bullock-Rest, 2011; Leal et al., 2021), they explore the possibility for a normative approach in HCI, and reflect on the ways in which research methods can support justice-oriented interaction design (Dombrowski et al., 2016), how collaboration and computing can promote peaceful co-existence (Hourcade & Bullock-Rest, 2011), or how to use design to "do good" and what it means (Light et al., 2017; Pal, 2017). Leal et al. (2021) state that

> "design, by definition, is a form of changing the world and making new ones. But given the systematic exclusion of specific perspectives, we would argue that as researchers in general and HCI researchers and designers in particular, we need a critical sensibility to question our situated understanding of the world from which we set out to design."

Thus, approaches in HCI have included critical theories to enable design in support of social change, such as feminist HCI (Bardzell & Bardzell, 2011), HCI for social good (Pal, 2017), or sustainable HCI (Bates et al., 2017). All these approaches work towards the support of socio-technical change and conceptualize how their values can be accounted for in the technology design. Methodologically, participatory approaches have worked towards reflecting, accounting and including values in the technology design, such as Value Sensitive Design (Friedman et al., 2013) or ELSI-Co Design (Liegl et al., 2016). In VSD, doing "good" means to include the relevant values into the design (Friedman et al., 2013, p. 2). The question of what is considered to be "good" ICT is answered empirically, in the form of a user-centered design approach or forms of collaborative design which accounts for the users' values. Moreover, the identification of conflicts between these values allow for a reflection on possible design solutions (Friedman et al., 2013).

To conduct VSD-studies, conceptual, empirical and technical investigations should be conducted as iterative steps (Friedman et al., 2013; Winkler and Spiekermann, 2021). In a meta-study of VSD projects, Winkler and Spiekermann (2021) note that, out of 17 identified projects, only four projects allowed for iterations to enhance the design. Further, it is criticized, that "[m]any studies did not employ a good methodical approach for stakeholder identification" and that the methodology to derive values and design solutions are often not well described (Winkler & Spiekermann, 2021, p. 19). However, to translate values into design decisions, values are organized in a hierarchy of higher and lower-level values, for example in the context of work, human well-being would be the higher and working conditions the the lower level values (van de Poel, 2013, 257f). Then these values need to be translated into general norms (or rules), from which the specific design requirements can be derived (Poel, 2013, p. 262). This approach allows for the explicit documentation and deliberation of value-based design decisions, making design more transparent to outsiders (Poel, 2013), allowing for the democratic and transparent discourse of design e.g. as part of citizens science and participatory transformation of technology (Preece, 2016).

2.3   Research Gap

The related works regarding dual-use assessment in ICT offer some venture points for research and research gaps. There are different concepts of dual-use and they have been discussed with corresponding security scenarios (see Table 2.1). Dual-use has been discussed as a question of military and civilian applications of research and development (Vella, 2017), as possible parts of weapons systems or classified as a dual-use good to control the proliferation of certain technologies (Forge, 2010), or as harmful and beneficial (WHO, 2020). Looking at dual-use cases in ICT, all three definitions of dual-use are relevant, considering technologies which have relevance for military applications and civilian contexts (Dunn Cavelty & Wenger, 2020), as well as ICTs which are relevant as parts of weapon systems as in the case of LAWS (Gill, 2019; Verbruggen, 2019). Then, there are ICTs which are rather discussed from the perceptive of their beneficial and harmful potential, such as (social) big data analytics (Rajamäki & Simola, 2019) and decision support systems (Burmeister, 2016; Zweig et al., 2018).

All the named technologies have been identified as dual-use, however aside from a few exceptions regarding cryptography (Vella, 2017), LAWS (Schulzke, 2019; Verbruggen, 2019) and AI (Brundage et al., 2018), the assessment of dual-use ICTs has not yet been conducted. These risks include the fast diffusion between research and industrial sectors, approaches towards the governance of dual-use risks, as well as approaches for dual-use responsible design. As Oltmann (2015) and Evans (2014) have suggested, there is a lack of understanding of dual-use outside the life sciences, such as of ICT. In sum, a systematic approach towards the different dual-use concepts and corresponding case studies, as well as, analytical tools for the monitoring, assessment and the design is needed.

Much research has been conducted on the diffusion of knowledge between military and civilian sectors in general (Acosta et al., 2011; 2013; 2019). At the same time, foresight studies and real-time TA have increasingly included methods for trend identification (Lösch et al., 2019). Innovations in machine learning and social media analysis have contributed methods for hot topic detection (Atefeh & Khreich, 2015). However, case studies regarding dual-use diffusion of ICT are lacking. This is even more relevant, as it is assumed that certain multi-use technologies such as machine learning and AI could adapt to many sectors rapidly (Brundage et al., 2018; Favaro, 2021; J. Schmid, 2017). However, the basic research on the spillover of dual-use has contradicted this hypothesis and has instead suggested a limited diffusion of dual-use innovations between the industrial sectors (Acosta et al., 2017). Therefore, investigating actual cases of innovation diffusion between military and civilian research is a research gap. Further, it could be explored how new approaches from topic detection or social media analytics could support existing approaches. The diffusion of innovation between civilian and military sectors can, however, be measured in the form of citations, e.g. patents, but innovation diffusion might also be seen using the approaches of social media analytics and OSINT, which can be summarized as the first research gap.

The control of dual-use technologies and their proliferation bears challenges when technologies are already being used or when they have many civilian applications, but could also be used for weapons systems (Bode, 2020). As Lin (2016) argues, due to the multi-purpose nature, dual-use ICT artifacts seem difficult to govern in terms of distribution and use. This becomes apparent, when looking at the discourse on the regulation of autonomous weapon systems, and how to distinguish the functionalities both from the design and regulative perspective (Amoroso & Tamburrini, 2019; Bode & Huelss, 2018). The governance and control of proliferation of technology can also be seen in the case of cryptography export control regulations as a dual-use good (Vella, 2017). Digital communication and its cryptography has shifted to be a dominantly civilian infrastructure, thus the dual-use regulations have affected the accessibility of certain cryptography. The effects of the regulation have been part of an over-30 year public discourse on the state's power and its access to surveillance (Monsees, 2019). Both case studies show that the regulation of commercially relevant dual-use technologies is in need of a thorough assessment of the ambivalence both by ICT and its regulation. Therefore, understanding the divergent values and interests of stakeholders, visions for human-computer interaction, and the stakeholders practices can support a normative and responsive approach towards technology governance informed by historical experience (Nordmann, 2014). As a result, the research on the ambivalent effects dual-use governance of ICTs is the second research gap.

To the author's best knowledge, the assessment of dual-use ICT artifacts from the perspective of HCI design research has not been conducted yet. Even though, value sensitive and participatory approaches directly aim at preventing harm by including the values of direct and indirect stakeholders, the third research gap can be found in the consideration of the ambivalence of technology and design (Liebert & Schmidt, 2018). In the field of HCI, the theory and method of VSD (Friedman et al., 2013) has been applied to many security-relevant cases, such as health care technologies (Mueller and Heger, 2018; Mueller et al., 2018) and crisis informatics (P. Hayes & Kelly, 2018). Many VSD studies lack the iterations for actual design improvement, the methodological documentation and description of how values and design solutions are derived (Winkler & Spiekermann, 2021). However, designing dual-use ICTs raises questions regarding the ethics and security, which require a transparent and deliberate process. For example, in their study on big data and OSINT for health care surveillance A. Ioannou & Tussyadiah (2021) have shown, that acceptance of surveillance of citizens depend on factors like trust and the perceived legitimacy of the cause. OSINT, as it uses public data, is a perfect case for a tripartite and iterative VSD study, which aims at making the design process transparent, deliberate and accessible. Therefore, not only is there a lack of VSD studies, which are conducted with extensive documentation (Winkler & Spiekermann, 2021), all relevant indirect and direct stakeholders, but also the perspective of dual-use is missing in the existing studies.

Research Design

3

This chapter presents the overall methodological foundations and the research design of this dissertation. Based on the epistemology and conceptual background of the field (Section 3.1), the research approach (Section 3.2) explains the methodology of the dissertation in greater detail. The following Section 3.3 describes this work's research context in three research projects. In Section 3.4, the methods used in this dissertation are described.

3.1 Conceptual Background

This dissertation is interdisciplinary, both in the methods and the topics of research. Thus, its contributions are made at the intersection of TA, CSS, and HCI. TA provides the epistemological framework for technology assessment (see Figure 2.1). The assessment needs conceptual dimensions, which are derived from the security model of the dual-use concepts. For the deconstruction of security, CSS provides the analytical framework to understand dual-use as a practice (see Table 2.1). The context of technology, its design and use practices are provided by the case studies and the field of HCI which has contributed to the methodology of participatory technology design and assessment (Friedman et al., 2017; Stevens et al., 2018).

The field of TA is a socio-epistemic practice which aims to make methods available that help to anticipate the effects of innovations. As described in Section 2.2, TA includes institutions, projects, and methods and is not limited to one scientific discipline. Thus, TA has many different aims and approaches and the methodology helps to connect the different kinds of knowledge from the fields (see Table 3.1). In this epistemological practice, HCI and CSS provide different forms of knowledge on the socio-technical systems (system knowledge), on possible future developments of the systems (prospective knowledge), criteria for social, legal

© The Author(s), under exclusive license to Springer Fachmedien Wiesbaden GmbH, part of Springer Nature 2023
T. Riebe, *Technology Assessment of Dual-Use ICTs*,
https://doi.org/10.1007/978-3-658-41667-6_3

and ethical evaluation (normative orientation), knowledge of the specific context (hermeneutic knowledge), as well as an understanding for possible tools for interventions (instrumental knowledge) (Grunwald, 2018, 112f,). Therefore, TA

Table 3.1 Classification of knowledge involved in technology assessment (Grunwald, 2018, p. 112)

Knowledge in TA	Functions	Attributes	Objects	Disciplines (exemplary list)
System knowledge	Understanding the functionality of the system and considering its boundaries	General, descriptive, and empirics-based in the form of causal or statistical knowledge	Empirical natural and social systems, socio-technical constellations	Natural, social, and engineering sciences, Earth systems analysis, STS studies
Prospective knowledge	Illustrating the space of possible or plausible future developments for enabling consequentialist reflection	Explorative and extrapolative projections based on present knowledge systems involving different assumptions	Development of specific parameters or indicators in the future	Futures studies in different fields, simulation, foresight, systems analysis
Normative orientation	Provide criteria of evaluation and assessment and targets of transformation	Normative, based on ethical or legal reasoning	Action and decision-making, weighing up alternative options, trade-offs	Ethics, legal sciences, political theory
Hermeneutic knowledge	Understanding the specific case and its social as well as epistemic configuration	Interpretative and reconstructive, based on empirical data of the context	Tools of current debates, actors' motives, narratives, pieces of art, movies	Hermeneutic sciences and humanities such as sociology, linguistics
Instrumental knowledge	Provision of a "toolkit" for action and decision-making	Know-how about measures and instruments	Opportunities for intervention, governance of the system considered	Economic and political sciences, engineering sciences, law, medicine

helps to connect the forms of knowledge from the fields of CSS and HCI as part of the technology assessment and design.

The field of CSS, which studies the security as a contested concept (Buzan et al., 1998; Schlag et al., 2015), follows a post-positivist approach towards social research (Salter & Mutlu, 2013). In opposition to positivist social science, post-positivist and interpretivist methods focus on "discourse, field analysis, ethnography, the study of affect and the somatic, and neomaterialist object analysis" (Salter & Mutlu, 2013, p. 3). Therefore, post-positivist research is reflective of its own construction of "the world". Within the realm of CSS, the influence of ethnography, sociology, linguistics and philosophy have produced methodological "turns" of their own: such as the "practice turn", the "discursive turn", the "corporeal turn" and the "material turn". These turns have brought individual methodological reflections into the field, such as focusing on practices, identity performance and habitus (Bigo, 2011; Bourdieu, 1990; Butler, 2011), on discourse, agency, networks and power (Foucault, 1982; Latour, 2007). The used methods are based on qualitative interpretation of (participatory) observations, content and discourse analysis and mapping (Salter & Mutlu, 2013).

The field of HCI is "concerned with the design, evaluation and implementation of interactive computing systems for human use and with the study of major phenomena surrounding them" (Hewett et al., 1992, p. 5). Wobbrock and Kientz (2016) have outlined research contributions to HCI to be empirical (to which the survey contribution can be added), methodological, theoretical, artifact, dataset and opinion. In the field of participatory human-computer interaction design, VSD was developed as a theory and method and is "a theoretical and methodological framework with which to handle the value dimension of design work" (Friedman et al., 2013). It aims to provide a deliberate process to include values such as "what a person or group of people consider important in life" into the technology design (Friedman et al., 2013, p. 2). These values often include "privacy, ownership and property, physical welfare, universal usability, informed consent, autonomy and trust" (Boden et al., 2018, p. 84). VSD as a research and design framework follows three steps: (1) conceptual investigations, (2) empirical investigations, and (3) technical investigations. In conceptual investigations, stakeholder groups affected by the envisaged technical artifacts are identified, and values expected to be important to them are conceptualized (Friedman et al., 2013). In empirical investigations, social science methods are used to revise and extend these findings with a focus on the opinions of direct and indirect stakeholders, as well as the anticipated usage contexts of the technical artifacts (Manders-Huits, 2011). During both conceptual and empirical investigations, potential value conflicts may be identified (Friedman et al., 2013). Finally, in technical investigations, design choices that support the identified and prioritized values are derived (Manders-Huits, 2011). Methods for the identification of stakeholders, values and the design are outlined by Friedman et al. (2017) and are based on hermeneutic understanding through observations, interviews and scenario development. Repeated iterations, however, allow for reflexive design, which anticipates change in the socio-technical system.

3.2   Research Approach

For the technology assessment in his decision framework, Tucker (2012, p. 69) proposes the three steps of monitoring, technology (risk) assessment and governance. In contrast to Tucker (2012), in this thesis, the term assessment is used as the higher category, while monitoring, governance and design are sub-categories. To decide if a certain technology is considered dual-use is already the result of its assessment. All named steps involve the assessment of the technology, its innovations, as well as the assessment of risks, the assessment of governance approaches, as well as of design choices. Further, this thesis adds the study of ICT design to the framework to account for its societal influence (Grunwald, 2018, pp. 79–82). Therefore, the methods were selected according to the steps (1) monitoring, (2) governance and (3) design (see Table 3.2).

Monitoring of dual-use diffusion contributes to the prospective knowledge, finding indicators for the spillover of innovation between different sectors. This is done using the methodological toolkit of knowledge economy (Acosta et al., 2013; 2019) and foresight studies (Grunwald, 2011; Shibata et al., 2011). The discourse on knowledge diffusion has considered mostly methods from bibliometric analysis to identify trends in research and development (Nazarko, 2017), as well as patent analysis (Acosta et al., 2017). Both sources can be analyzed for networks through citations, as well as, for their features or associated values through content analysis. However, advances in machine learning have made topic detection and explorative methods more accessible (Atefeh & Khreich, 2015). While at the same time, social media platforms have made new data sources for network, hot topic and content analysis available. Therefore, this thesis explores network analysis both on social media platforms (LinkedIn in Chapter 8 and Twitter in Chapter 15), as well as patent analysis with regard to AI diffusion (9).

Research on the **governance** of dual-use ICTs contributes to three knowledge categories: hermeneutic and instrumental knowledge as well as to normative orientation (see Table 3.1). As governance as a security practice is studies from the perspective of CSS, dual-use is deconstructed as a political "tool" of securitization. Therefore, methods from discourse analysis and historical comparative analysis are chosen to shed light on two divergent cases. In the first case, the discourse on the regulation of LAWS uses a discourse analysis to identify the value conflicts, which result in divergent regulative approaches and interpretations of MHC (see Chapter 10). The case study on the dual-use regulation of cryptography uses the 30-year history of legal regulation and its effects on the accessibility of encryption (Chapter 11).

The research approach towards the **design** of dual-use ICTs contributes to the system knowledge, as it helps to understand the functionality of the system and its boundaries, as well as to the instrumental knowledge, as it helps to refine the VSD approach for dual-use. The contributions are thus the three investigations of the VSD framework, consisting of the (1) conceptual (Chapter 12), (2) empirical (Chapter 13 and 14) and (3) technical investigations (Chapter 15). Thus, the methodological approach is based on mixing qualitative and quantitative methods (Friedman et al., 2017). The identification of direct and indirect stakeholders and use contexts was done with a systematic literature review as well as interviews. The values and value conflicts the methods ranged from small-n semi-structured interviews and a focus group to a large-n representative survey and the large-n artifact evaluation. While the small-n surveys were analyzed with interpretative methods and coding (Kuckartz, 2016), the large-n survey was analyzed with descriptive and analytical statistics using multiple linear regression.

Table 3.2 The research approach towards dual-use assessment in ICT

Assessment	Research Object(s)	Method	Technology
Monitoring	Innovation diffusion	Network and content analysis	AI
Governance	Discourse, norms and regulations	Discourse analysis longitudinal comparative study	LAWS Cryptography
Design	Technological artifacts and anticipated use contexts	VSD	OSINT in the context of cybersecurity

3.3   Research Context

This dissertation comprises empirical and methodological studies, which have been conducted in the three research projects KontiKat, Dual-Use and CYWARN. Within the projects, I was able to interview experts and conduct empirical studies, which provided the context for this research. In the following, the three projects and their aims will be introduced:

The research project "Civic-Societal and Business Continuity through Socio-Technical Networking in Disasters" (KontiKat)[3] was funded by the Federal Ministry of Education and Research (No. 13N14351) and carried out between 01/06/2017–31/12/2021. The project aimed at maintaining and restoring social life after major damage events and disasters. To this end, empirical studies were carried out to record the social networking of the population and of small and medium-sized enterprises. The results help to promote self-organization, assistance and emergency communication in crisis situations. I worked on the project as a doctorate candidate between 2017–2021, focusing on the evaluation of technology for self-help of citizens in crisis situations.

The research project "IT Research of Concern: Assessment of Dual-Use Risks in Software Development" (Dual-Use)[4] was carried out between the 01/02/2019–31/12/2021 and founded by the Forum for interdisciplinary research (FIF-IANUS) at the Technical University of Darmstadt as a joint project of the disciplines of computer science (Prof. Reuter) and philosophy of technology (Prof. Nordmann). The project investigated dual-use potentials in research and development of ICT to prevent misuse. These approaches to dual-use assessment are systematized in this project and their transferability from classical natural sciences and engineering to computer science, with a special focus on the process of software development. In working for the project during its entire duration, I, together with my co-authors, conceptualized dual-use for ICT, and also worked on the methods to monitor the diffusion of technologies between military and civilian research and development.

The third research project "Analysis and communication of the situation picture in cyberspace" (CYWARN)[5] was funded by the Federal Ministry of Education and Research (BMBF) and aims to support CERTs with new strategies and technologies in analyzing and communicating cyber situations (No. 13N15407–13N15410). During the funding period (01/10/2020–01/09/2023), a demonstrator is being created that will enable automated collection of public and closed data sources, as

---

[3] www.kontikat.peasec.de

[4] https://www.fif.tu-darmstadt.de/foerderung/foerderung_details_19201.en.jsp

[5] https://cywarn.peasec.de

well as data mining with credibility analysis and information prioritization. With a high degree of automation, the demonstrator empowers teams to more efficiently identify, analyze, and communicate cyber threats. The results are incorporated into recommended actions, awareness activities, situation reports and alerts, which are then used by teams to communicate with the public, authorities or CRITIS operators. Acceptability and user-friendliness are taken into account during development, as are ethical, legal and social frameworks. In the long term, it is conceivable that the system will also be used by other authorities and organizations with security tasks, or by companies that operate their own CERT. I have been involved in this project since 2020 and focus on the ethical, social and legal assessment of the demonstrator and its related artifacts using the VSD approach.

3.4 Methods

To contribute to the discourse on dual-use in ICT, this dissertation consists of two studies on the monitoring of innovation and work force diffusion in dual-use industry sectors (Section 3.4.1). The governance of dual-use ICTs is studied in two case studies concerning the regulation of LAWS and cryptography as dual-use goods (Section 3.4.2). Lastly, the VSD framework has been used to conduct conceptual, empirical and technical investigation for the development of an OSINT artifact for cybersecurity event detection (Section 3.4.3). The overview of all cast studies and its methods can be found in Table 3.3.

Table 3.3 Empirical Case Studies Overview

No.	Method	N	Time Period	Chapter
1	social media network study	512	01/2009–03/2019	8
2	patent network analysis	2,438	01/01/2008–01/06/2018	9
3	qualitative content analysis	13	2014–2020	9
4	qualitative discourse analysis	42	09/04/2018–31/08/2018	10
5	longitudinal two-case causal analysis	3	1990–2021	11

(Continued)

Table 3.3 (Continued)

No.	Method	N	Time Period	Chapter
6	systematic literature review	73	until 2021	12
7	semi-structured interview	7	04/02/2021–06/08/2021	12
8	focus-group	9	28/06/2021	12
9	semi-structured interview	7	29/01/2019–28/03/2019	13
10	document analysis	25	2014–2020	13
11	representative survey	1,093	09/2021	14
12	machine learning evaluation	151,861	01/01/2019–31/07/2020	15

3.4.1   Monitoring

In general, some papers conduct method triangulation, combining two methods to achieve a combination of qualitative and quantitative insights or to gain insight into different data bases for the same topic. Especially the methodological approaches are combined with empirical studies.

To measure the dual-use nature of technologies, the flow of innovations between industry sectors has been studied and operationalized in economics (Acosta et al., 2017; 2019). In our papers, we operationalized dual-use following the three definitions (Table 2.1 in Section 2.1.2). In Chapter 8, the spillover between military and civilian industry sectors is operationalized following the SIPRI list of arms producing companies (Fleurant et al., 2017) and using *social network analysis* to study the churn rate of employees between different sectors using LinkedIn profiles (N=513).

To study the diffusion of AI into the sector of arms production, as well as the concept of Trustworthy AI (see Chapter 9), a triangulation was conducted. First, in a *patent network analysis* the flow of mutual citations between AI and weapon patents is studied. For this, we used the European Patent Database, in which we identified relevant patent citations (N=2,438) and their citation network. Further, to add to the citation network, we studied academic dual-use papers in dual-use AI research done by the Fraunhofer IOSB (N=13), to understand the diffusion of the normative concept of Trustworthy AI.

3.4.2 Governance

The empirical studies combine data collection methods which helped to analyze the perspective of the respective stakeholders, their discourses and values with regard to the regulation of dual-use technologies. In Chapter 10, a *discourse analysis* was conducted using the statements, working papers, governmental documents and press releases (N=43) in the Convention on Certain Conventional Weapons Group of Governmental Experts (CCW GGE) between April and August 2018. The goal of this analysis was to develop a deep understanding of the discourse, value conflicts and arguments regarding the assessment of technologies, particularly the use of the concept of MHC of autonomous weapons systems. The divergent understandings of human-LAWS interaction are deconstructed by choosing the theoretical perspective of VSD as well as a through the investigation of CCW-relevant socio-technological values and their inter-relatedness.

A policy analysis to investigate the development and legal regulation of cryptography as a dual-use good was conducted (Chapter 11) in the form of a *longitudinally two-case causal analysis* (Gerring & Cojocaru, 2016) in three different time periods between 1990 and 2021. For this, the history of the dual-use regulation of cryptography by the U.S. government and the surveillance practices as a reaction to this policies by the NSA were analyzed. The policy process approach puts its focal point on political processes and the involved stakeholders, while the scope is on the broader meso-scale. In this context, it aims at determining what processes, means, and policy instruments, e.g., regulations, legislation, or subsidies, are used. Within this policy process, the role and influence of stakeholders was discussed (Hult, 2015). Against the background of our selected policy field, the stakeholders were chosen based on an examination of the dual-use export politics and their related practices as well as the policies of the security agencies.

3.4.3 Design

In the CYWARN project, multiple studies on the technology assessment of OSINT in cybersecurity were conducted which followed the VSD approach by Friedman et al. (2013). In this three step approach, first conceptual data on the stakeholders and threat scenarios were collected. This was done with a *systematic literature study* on OSINT systems in cybersecurity (in Chapter 12). The study was done to gain a systematic overview on the field of OSINT for cybersecurity and how ELSI or dual-use issues are considered. The review followed the reproducible method by vom Brocke et al. (2015). For the search, the literature databases ACM

Digital Library, IEEE-Xplore, Science Direct, and Springer Link were used with the following search expression using Boolean operators: *("cyber security" OR cyber-security OR "information security" OR cybercrime) AND (OSINT OR SOCMINT OR WEBINT OR "open-source intelligence" OR "social media intelligence" OR "web intelligence")*. The search resulted in 1,419 preliminary results, of which after applying the exclusion criteria 73 remained and were analysed with Excel. In the second step of VSD, empirical studies were conducted, which survey the context in which the technology is used. Thus, a *focus group workshop* (N=9) and additional *interviews* (N=7) helped to identify relevant risk scenarios, as well as values and value conflicts of stakeholders.

Further, to include the perspective of the population, a *representative survey* was conducted with the German population to receive insights into perceptions on the use of OSINT for cybersecurity, and as a tool for incident monitoring by authorities. The panel (N=1,093) was questioned in September 2021 by the certified provider GapFish and was representative in terms of age, gender, education, income, and state (represented by ISO 3166-2 codes). The questionnaire was constructed as a result of two workshops with relevant stakeholders in the CYWARN project (for more details, see Chapter 14.3). The questionnaire consisted of 20 questions in total, from which their threat perception, their privacy behavior, their evaluation of statements regarding the prevalence, use, and impact of OSINT, as well as OSINT activities by security agencies was surveyed. The items were combined into five factors which were analyzed with regression analysis, as well as with and without an interaction factor (awareness). For a summary of the survey, see Table 3.4

Table 3.4 Representative Survey of Perceptions towards the Use of OSINT for Cybersecurity

Panel	GapFish
Inquiry	September 2021
Sample Size	1,093
Population	Germany
Representation with regard to	age, gender, education, income, and state
Topics	current and future threat situation and possible protective measures in cyberspace, prevalence, use, and impact of OSINT, as well as OSINT activities by security agencies, citizens' communication and information needs and behaviors
Analysis	Regression Model, Interactive Factor

As the third part of VSD, the technical investigations aim at the implementation of a technology in a particular context (Friedman et al., 2013). Therefore, the implications of design have been derived from the empirical studies and implemented in the system CySecAlert (see Chapter 15). From the state of technology and the requirements in the Chapters 12, 13 and 14, the concept was developed, implemented and evaluated regarding its ability to detect cyber threats in near real time in Twitter for incident response teams. For the *evaluation* of the system, 350,061 English Tweets (151,861 Tweets excl. retweets) were gathered, published by 170 Twitter accounts of leading cybersecurity experts in the time period between 1st January 2019 and 31st July 2020.

Results

4

This chapter provides a summary of the papers' research results, mapping them on the dual-use and underlying security concepts. In the following subsections, the results are structured following the concepts of dual-use as a diffraction between civilian and military applications (Section 4.1), as possible parts of weapon systems (Section 4.2), and as an ICT of concern (Section 4.3). In the Section 4.4 the results are summarized.

4.1 Monitoring Perspective: Military and Civilian Applications

Dual-use technologies are based on research and innovations, which can be applied to both civilian and military applications and systems. Therefore, understanding how innovations both from civilian and military R&D influence each other, how innovation in one sector might spillover to another sector, is relevant for the governance of these dual-use technologies. Further, Stowsky (2004) argues that ICT has transformed both civilian and military systems in a way which makes them much more exchangeable and commercial as well as civilian off-the shelf solutions much more interesting for military systems. The shift towards commercial R&D alone would create new security challenges (Stowsky, 2004). Therefore, it is necessary to investigate the spillover of innovation within the recent past, as well as exploring the diffusion regarding individual case studies.

Supplementary Information The online version contains supplementary material available at https://doi.org/10.1007/978-3-658-41667-6_4.

T. Riebe, *Technology Assessment of Dual-Use ICTs*,
https://doi.org/10.1007/978-3-658-41667-6_4

The empirical results of the churn rates between defense and civilian job positions in LinkedIn of 513 persons showed that the fewer people changed the industry, the less they changed job positions (see Chapter 8). Thus, spillovers are less likely between defense and civilian sectors. This even indicates that churn rates in the defense sector are much lower than in the civilian sector. In the sample, a high rate of people only worked in the defense sector (50%, Group D, see Figure 4.1), while the other half of the sample had a higher percentage of positions in defense companies (group DC, equal and more than 50% of their positions) and the other had a lower percentage (group C, less 50% of their positions). Comparing our results of reluctant flow of defense innovation into the civilian sector to the patent study of Acosta et al. (2017), the results are similar: Germany has the second-highest rate of military registered patents (22% of all patents) worldwide. At the same time, the civilian use of these patents is rather low, with 16.8% of citations by other patents in civilian classifications (Acosta et al., 2011).

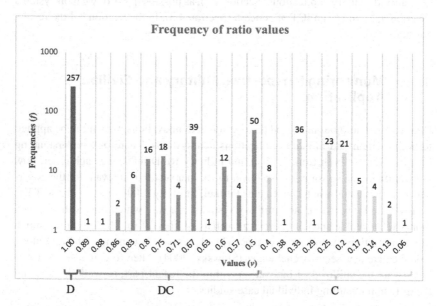

Figure 4.1 Frequency of ratio values v (N_{total} = 513, $M_{DC\ and\ C}$ = 0.49, $SD_{DC\ and\ C}$ = 0.17)

After looking at the possible knowledge spillovers within LinkedIn, investigating a particular technology and its patent citation networks was interesting. AI has been discussed from the ethical perspective (Floridi et al., 2018) and has been identified as multi-purpose and adaptive which would make it diffuse more easily (Zambetti et al., 2018), as well as relevant for the defense sector and its research on automation (Taddeo et al., 2021). Thus, the European patent citations regarding the spillover of AI innovations in the defense and armament production was studied (see Chapter 9). In our data set of 2,438 patent citations, 524 patents are cited by AI patents and 1,890 patents are cited by weaponry patents. The citations mostly stayed within the same CPC class, indicating no diffusion.[1] Therefore, for knowledge transfers across the fields of weapons and ammunition (F41, F42) and special computational systems (G06N), there is no indication of such transfer-representative patent citation. Among AI patents, however, 14.6% of the patents cited other G06N patents, constituting the biggest group comparatively. Looking at weaponry patents, citation links exist frequently to other weapons and ammunition technologies. Considering responsible R&D as illustrated by the EU's guideline *Trustworthy AI*, no frequent and widespread knowledge transfer among civilian and defense actors through their technologies can be observed. Consequently, we could not find evidence supporting the hypothesis of emerging technologies such as AI being applied primarily for civilian purposes and subsequently for military purposes (S. Schmid et al., 2022, Verbruggen, 2019). The analysis of the patent citation shows almost no diffusion between civilian and military companies, and most AI patents are based on interactions between civilian entities, with only one citation pair among defense companies. However, three patent pairs with civilian actors that cite patents from defense companies and another 72 pairs of citing and cited weaponry patents are from companies that usually produce for civilian markets To sum up the citation network, the most active applicants rely on actors of the same type or mostly on their own inventions. For example, Rheinmetall has cited 231 of its own patents.

In the case of AI, the concept of Trustworthy AI has been coined by the EU to promote value-driven AI research. But how does such a concept translate into civilian and military contexts? In the second part of the study, 13 research documents of the Fraunhofer IOSB were analyzed concerning the values which correspond to the concept of Trustworthy AI. For military purposes, it was found that robustness, accuracy, and information quality seem to be prevalent values. However, this does not mean that these norms are entirely absent when it comes to civilian AI application (see Table 4.1). The value of *robustness* is comparatively more significant in the context of military (D11) applications (D10). Further, *accuracy* has been found to be particularly important in the context of military applications, including transparency on problems of inaccuracy (D12).

---

[1] The patent network can be viewed in Appendix 16.1 in the electronic supplementary material.

Table 4.1 Frequency of word stems representing values in civilian and military corpora

Values	N_{Mil} (Word Occurrences)	N_{Civ} (Word Occurrences)
Focus on data	190	96
Focus on information	77	32
Focus on input	29	23
Awareness: geography	21	0
Awareness: space	96	276
Awareness: time	65	231
Robustness	13	1
Accuracy	50	25
Obscurity	51	3
Information quality	16	11
Awareness: adaptivity	5	6
Awareness: object	38	107
Awareness: target	15	2
Awareness: movement	23	26
Explainability	7	76
Human centrism: Assistance to humans	76	601
Health	0	2
Safety, security	32	29
Intelligence of systems	26	103
Modelling, reconstruction	133	178
Automation	56	97
Autonomy	16	16
Self-consciousness, reasoning	28	97
Behavior	5	72
Gestures	1	22

In alignment with this finding, the EU guideline stresses the importance of robustness and accuracy, as they both relate safety and security. Military AI applications may support standards of Trustworthy AI, paying special attention to robustness and accuracy (European Commission, 2019). This reflects the potential to ensure security as proposed by the EU guideline   (European Commission, 2019), while also indicating the technology's possible normative ambiguity regarding general human and environmental well-being. *Information quality* has also been found to be relatively more important for military (D1) applications. Given the high stakes of a military operation, errors due to low information quality may have a greater impact on people, e.g., by mistaking civilian infrastructure for military bases or by falsely identifying civilians as combatants (Wilcox, 2017).

At the same time, focusing on civilian projects, there is a comparatively stronger interest in *awareness*. For example, SPARC, a project on autonomous driving in urban traffic, relies heavily on orientation in the context of moving and directing surrounding objects, opting for a "holistic representation" (D3), while at the same time training data is focused on "eventful [...] and [...] unique situations" (D13). Whether in terms of space, time, or speed, there is a strong reference to environmental information. This is surprising, as situational awareness is not only stressed by the EU (European Commission, 2019) but is mostly apparent in military contexts.

Overall, civilian applications emphasize the relevance of *explainability,* which is referred to as "retaining many of the advantages of variational trajectory optimiza-tion methods, in particular *expressiveness*" (D11; own emphasis). This highlights the ambivalence of explainability as a normative concept. While it may be defined as the ability to explain, interpretability—namely the ability to provide (grounds for) an interpretation - is often associated with the concept of explainability, as it is also the case in the *Trustworthy AI* guide (European Commission, 2019).

It should be noted that both *security and safety* were also qualitatively deduced regarding military applications, indicating human-centric approaches albeit in dif-ferent terms. Human dignity, implying human-centric approaches, represents one of the core values of *Trustworthy AI* (European Commission, 2019). Such statements are more common in the context of civilian applications; as they apply AI applica-tions that focus on human reasoning, hand gestures, or the human body.[2] Military applications accordingly reflect less interest in a precise analysis of the social or intimate environment. Yet, a strong focus on people's movements or behavior does not necessarily imply the implementation of a human-centric AI in terms of human dignity or personal rights.

To summarize, diffusion of knowledge and innovation between the military and civilian sectors happen less often with low churn rates of job changes between the military and civilian sector, in general and with no diffusion in the specific case of the European patent network of AI and weapon patents. Further, companies mostly cited their own patents. Additionally, the use of normative concepts for the development

---

[2] The values associated with trustworthy AI data can be viewed in Appendix 16.1 in the electronic supplementary material.

of AI showed dual-use specifications, as human-centric values are more often seen in civilian research, while values regarding safety have been more often addressed in military research. Therefore, this can be a venture point for vision-assessment (Lösch et al., 2019), technology governance (Tucker, 2012) and value-sensitive design research (Friedman et al., 2013; Umbrello & Van de Poel, 2021).

4.2   Governance Perspective: Weapons and non-Weapon Systems

The governance of dual-use technologies is not able to "solve" the Collinridge Dilemma, but is anticipating its ambivalence and its consequences (Liebert & Schmidt, 2018), as well as societal values like freedom of research and security (Rychnovská, 2016). Following Rychnovská (2016), this process also distributes responsibility towards researchers, developers and companies, making them actors of security. Therefore, dual-use governance can be analysed as a form of security politics (Rychnovská, 2020). The multi-purpose nature and accessibility of many ICTs makes the governance of them especially challenging. Therefore, two case studies are particularity interesting: first, the discourse on the regulation of Lethal Autonomous Weapons Systems (LAWS) (Chapter 10), and second the regulatory history of cryptography export restrictions in the US (Chapter 11). In order to link the normative requirements for the government of AWS, from 9 to 13 April 2018 and from 27 to 31 August 2018, 43 documents [3] from the *2018 Group of Governmental Experts on Lethal Autonomous Weapons Systems (LAWS)* (GGE on LAWS) were analyzed. This helped to understand the values associated with *Meaningful Human Control*, and how the human-computer interaction is conceptualized, as well as how implications for design can be derived.

The discourse on autonomous weapons systems focuses on the question which functions should not be fully autonomous, and which ones could be. The role of the human is either "in the loop", "on the loop" or "outside of the loop" of decision making. Thus, the code "autonomy" was found 168 times, often with references to humans no longer being in the loop. Concerning the general problem of defining and differentiating between autonomy and its various degrees, one can notice a recurrent focus on autonomy as a function. Autonomy was used 56 times to specifically refer to selecting and targeting as critical functions. The International Committee of the Red Cross (ICRC) noted that a "weapon system with autonomy in its critical

---

[3] The list of the documents can be viewed in Appendix 16.2 in the electronic supplementary material.

functions" is one "that can select (i.e. search for or detect, identify, track, select) and attack (i.e. use force against, neutralize, damage or destroy) targets without human intervention" (WP5-BR, ICRC). Here, detection or identification is seen as a synonym or subcategory, respectively, for selecting. This statement implies the significance of an autonomous identification of a target with respect to its actual, fixating selection and it becomes clear that the identification of targets is another critical function which is to be distinguished from the ultimate selection of a target. Often, autonomy of a system meant automating processes, but references to artificial intelligence and machine learning, indicating self-learning capabilities and independence, were also prevalent (WP2-ES/FI).

The envisioned relationship between human operators and autonomous systems was portrayed within a spectrum. Statements indicating hierarchical relationships of humans and subordinated technology were found almost twice as much as statements supporting the autonomy of technology (49% vs. 27%). At the same time, "interaction", as a rather neutral or non-hierarchical position, made out roughly a quarter (27%) of the respective human-LAWS interaction statements. This indicates that perceiving humans to be superior to technology is the dominant view within the CCW GGE forum. The values which were associated with the use of AWS showed a strong economical perspective. The codes "time", "predictability", and "reliability" appeared often (77, 74, and 70 codings). References coded as statements regarding "productivity" (n=64), "accountability" (n=58), "explainability" (n=53), or "safety" (n=50) appeared at a relatively high frequency, while CCW documents surprisingly referred to issues of (human) "intervention" (n=21) or an accurate flow of information (n=14) only at a relatively moderate rate. However, ethical questions were also present, with "ethics" as a structuring discourse of MHC coded almost 400 times across CCW documents. The frequency shows how ethical vocabulary serves as a dominant frame for discussion. The relevance of ethics as a guiding discourse is also illustrated considering respective sub-codes "hum_responsibility" (n=121) or "HL_principles" (n=205), with the latter clarifying the close link between ethics and law ("intern_law" n=349) (see Figure 4.2).

As for the second case study on dual-use regulation, we investigated the regulation of cryptography as a dual-use good in the US between 1990 and 2021 (see Chapter 11). In the 1990s, the dual-use regulations were adapted to the increasing access to cryptography as part of the commercial internet (see Table 11.4). This was acknowledged by changing the legislation from the United States Munition List (USML) to the Commerce Control List (CCL), while also enforcing the implementation of key escrow for symmetrical encryption. However, with the rising use of encryption, the exceptions and key lengths accelerated until 2000. In the 2000s, the use of end-to-end encryption increased, which made the key escrow approach

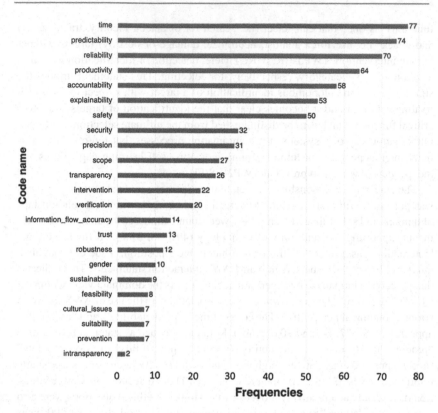

Figure 4.2 Occurrences of socio-technological values with regard to the MHC of LAWS

impractical. The products for mass-marked communication have been excluded from the dual-use export restrictions, which were still in place for other exports with market encryption at up to 64-bits following a technical examination. However, the bureaucracy was further removed, requiring only self-reports and many exceptions, or even supporting the use of end-to-end encryption for military goods and information since 2016 (Eichler, 2018). Today, the export of cryptography with key length of 128 bits or more is considered dual-use. Within the U.S., the import, or domestic sales of cryptography, however, have never been restricted.

The surveillance policy in the 1990s (see Table 11.5), in alignment with the dual-use policy, was developed to ensure a key escrow mechanism with the Clipper Chip initiative. In the 2000s, mass communication services became popular, as well as the first possibilities to implement end-to-end encryption for end-users. To retrieve data, security agencies made a bilateral agreement between ICT companies and exploited weak encryption standards or software vulnerabilities. Consequently, intelligence organizations, like the NSA, profited from the export restrictions in two ways: first, from the increased and global use of social media platforms and other commercial services for mass communication which did not use strong encryption. And second, from the data provided by these companies to law enforcement agencies.

Besides the key length, other factors also impact the security of cryptographic algorithms (Paterson, 2015). One such factor is the actual implementation of the cryptographic algorithm. It might be implemented with vulnerabilities compromising the algorithm otherwise mathematically proven to be a secure. Another factor is the system itself, which is used for cryptographic operations since it might be compromised. However, these organizational factors of security can be created or unknowingly taken advantage of by companies which are forced to implement access to their data by the government to prevent users to "go dark" (Murphy, 2020). Many states, e.g., in the EU have evoked ideas of legal state hacking, however, without paying enough attention to the safeguards towards these methods (B.-J. Koops & Kosta, 2018). In addition, there is a growing industry which offers "surveillance as a service", in which law enforcement agencies and secret services outsource the technological hacking capacities or to exploit software vulnerabilities when needed, instead of building the capacity themselves (Kirchgaessner et al., 2021). This makes the use of "surveillance as a service" more flexible for organizations. However, the proliferation and use of such services is difficult to safeguard, as the U.S. has put the NSO Group on a trade blacklist because it has conducted "transnational repression [..] targeting dissidents, journalists, and activists" (Clayton, 2021).

When looking at the regulation of LAWS, the distinction of the selection and targeting as automated functions has shown to be difficult to separate from other functions, such as identification of targets. The existing automation, e.g. in air defense systems is putting operators in use of force-situations already under pressure, as their capacity has been diminished (Bode & Watts, 2021, p. 62). The gradual increase of automation further allows for the "creeping in" of unwanted loss of human autonomy (Verbruggen, 2019). Here, the vision of the human-computer or machine interaction relationship provides an entry point for a vision assessment for future research. However, while there is not yet a regulation for LAWS, the proliferation of cryptography has been regulated for decades. This impacts the access to technology and is especially relevant when the technology is commercial successful and used by many people and organizations. The spread of online mass communication has transformed the relevance of encryption and has shown the limits of governance through export control for non-proliferation.

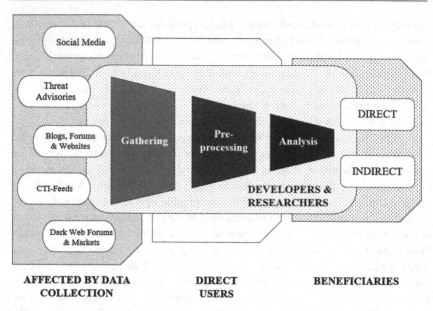

Results

AFFECTED BY DATA   DIRECT   BENEFICIARIES
COLLECTION   USERS

Figure 4.3 Main stakeholder groups of the prospective OSINT framework and their interaction with OSINT artefacts. (Source: own research)

4.3 Design Perspective: ICT Research and Development of Concern

Future-oriented TA has moved the assessment from the finished socio-technical system towards the focus on the vision (Nordmann, 2010) and design of the same (Lösch et al., 2019). Therefore, the TA of dual-use technologies should account for the technology ambivalence and respective threat scenarios. The case of OSINT, as a framework with multiple different technologies to gather, preprocess and analyze public data, i.e. from social media platforms, is especially interesting. OSINT touches on ethical, legal and social discourses on privacy, proportionality and different security referent objects, such as health (A. Ioannou & Tussyadiah, 2021) and IT systems (Kassim et al., 2022). Kassim et al. (2022) have shown, that the use of OSINT systems is on the rise for Computer Emergency Response Teams (CERTs). Therefore, all three steps of the VSD framework for an OSINT system for the CERT context are conducted. First, the conceptual studies provide the relevant stakeholders (Figure 4.3).

For the development of Open Source Intelligence (OSINT) system for cybersecurity, the first study captured the state of the art in a systematic study, identifying the direct and indirect stakeholders, as well as possible value conflicts which might arise between their conflicting interests (see Chapter 12). In the systematic literature review (N=73), the intended scenarios of 74% of the systems were the gathering of Cyber Threat Intelligence (CTI). The most common named user groups of such systems, were law enforcement agencies (58 times). Founding projects was mostly done by civilian institutions (38 times) and military organizations in 11 instances. The technological features mainly aimed to gather public data (in 44 publications), and aimed to detect new cyber threats (in 36 publications). While the classification or filtering was also relevant in 26 publications, visualization of the information was not common in the systems (in 15 publications). Interestingly, the most common sources for data gathering was Twitter (20 times), followed by cybersecurity blogs, forums and websites. Combining different data sources was rare (only 15 instances), as well as gathering data from vulnerability databases (5 times), and software vendor websites (2 times). Only 11 publications made assessments of ethical, social or legal impacts, focusing mostly on risk assessment and mitigation systems, which aim to profile individuals rather than CTI. In the second part of the mixed-method study, interviews (N=9) and a focus group (N=7) workshop helped to identify possible value conflicts which might lead to conflicting requirements for the system. Here, the most important values identified were accuracy, security, and efficiency (see Table 12.3). Further, the role of human-AI expertise was elaborated. Especially, for the gathering, pre-processing and credibility, criticality and relevance analysis, the ML-expertise should be complementary to increase the effectiveness of CERTs (see Figure 12.7) (Figure 4.4).

To understand the future use context in CERTs, an interview (N=15) and document study (N=25) was conducted which focused on the federal organizational structure of CERTs in Germany, as well as their needs, collaborative practices, and requirements (see Chapter 13). The organizational structure is driven by federal characteristics, directives and laws, while the states have different structures for their CERTs either as part of the ministry or as part of an IT service provider. Thus, the resources, and daily routines, as well as regulations for the CERTs differ. Therefore, any system would need to be modular enough, to be able to be customized. The technology used for collaboration, mainly for sharing information in chats, could be improved by automation, as well as a support for the increasing demand to monitor different sources for cybersecurity threats. In addition, privacy-preserving cross-platform monitoring and incident analysis was identified as an area for improvement. However, collaboration has been mostly bilateral between CERTs, based on personal connections due to the asymmetries of resources and

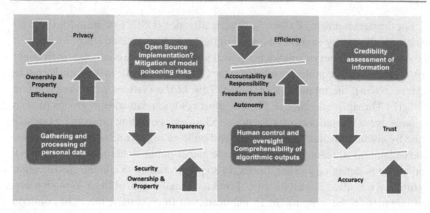

Figure 4.4 Value conflicts and associated design issues identified in the empirical material. (Source: own research)

lack of liabilities for inter-organizational exchange. Thus, the (semi)automation of monitoring and customized cyber threat information sharing are seen as desirable.

Another stakeholder for an OSINT system using publicly available data are non-expert citizens, which have privacy concerns as well as threat perceptions, which are associated with the acceptance of surveillance and monitoring of technology for security (SOSTs) (see Chapter 14). Thus, a representative survey (N=1,093), in which non-expert citizens were asked about their acceptance of OSINT systems, their perceived need for open source surveillance, as well as their privacy behavior and concerns was conducted. The survey tested if the awareness of OSINT is an interactive factor that changes the dynamic of privacy behavior, privacy concerns, perceived need for OSINT and threat perception and the acceptance of OSINT. The results indicate, that cyber threat perception and the perceived need for OSINT are positively related to acceptance, while privacy concerns are negatively related. The awareness of OSINT, however, has only shown effects on people with higher privacy concerns. Here, particularly high OSINT awareness and limited privacy concerns were associated with higher OSINT acceptance. Based on the results, approaches for individual steps of OSINT can be selected and combined to adhere to data minimization and anonymization as well as to leverage improvements in privacy-preserving computation and machine learning innovations.

Based on the requirements for OSINT for CTI, a system was developed which applies a supervised classifier, based on active learning, that detects tweets containing relevant information (see Chapter 15). The approach reduces the number of accounts and tweets that are needed for the classifier training using uncertainty sampling, thus making the tool easily and rapidly adaptable to the specific context while also supporting data minimization for OSINT. Relevant tweets are clustered by a greedy stream clustering algorithm in order to identify significant events (see Figure 4.5). The proposed system is able to work in near real-time within the required 15-minute time frame and detects up to 93.8% of relevant events with a false alert rate of 14.81%.

Summing up, four studies were conducted as part of a VSD approach to identify (1) direct and indirect stakeholders and use contexts, (2) central values and value conflicts which are relevant for the implementation of a system, as well as (3) one cycle of technical investigation. However, as noted by Winkler and Spiekermann

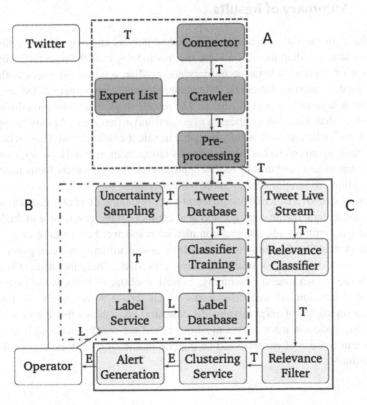

Figure 4.5 Architecture of proposed Information and Communication Technology (ICT) illustrating the information flow for [T]weets, [L]abels and [E]vents. The ICT is divided into Tweet Retrieval (A), Relevance Classifier Training (B) and Real-Time Event Detection (C)

(2021), the iterative approach works best with multiple cycles of investigations. Dual-use issues were accounted for in all three investigations, since the systematic literature review took account of ethical and social implications as well as application area and civilian and military funding. The interviews and focus group also highlighted both the need for automation and cross-platform collaboration as well as privacy-preserving and data-minimizing approaches, which are further developed in the project CYWARN. The CySecAlert system already helped to support the use of expert networks for event detection in cybersecurity, rather than gathering all available data.

4.4   Summary of Results

The results of the eight studies provide methodological and empirical insights for the assessment of dual-use ICTs. First, the methodology for the monitoring of the diffusion of innovation between military and civilian was studied, using both the social media analytics (Stieglitz, Mirbabaie, Ross, & Neuberger, 2018) as well as patent analysis (Acosta et al., 2017). The results show, that innovation diffusion between civilian and military research in general and in the case of AI either happens at a low rate, which at least is not yet visible in patent citations, and when, it occurs first within organisations (as they are mostly citing themselves). However, looking at different values attributes to AI R&D projects, military projects focus more on safety, while civilian projects are more human-centric.

Second, the governance of two different cases of dual-use technologies was studied, shedding light on the consequences and conflicts of the governance of dual-use technologies with a multi-use and commercial relevance. For the case of LAWS, this was done using discourse and document analysis, utilizing position papers and statements to identify the positions and visions for MHC. There are different visions towards the human-machine hierarchy, as well as obstacles towards the particular automated functions of weapon systems which should be regulated. As for the dual-use regulation of cryptography, the case study has shown that the increasing use of encryption in mass communication shifted the regulation towards an non-transparent politics of exceptions, making communication platforms surveillance intermediaries.

Third, the design of a dual-use relevant OSINT system was approached using VSD. First, for the conceptual investigation using a systematic literature review the the use cases, stakeholders, technological features as well as ethical, social and legal impact and funding organizations were identified and discussed. The empirical investigations in the form of interviews, a focus group and a representative study, helped to identify central values, value conflicts for the use context of OSINT in public CERTs in the German federal system. The design requirements were derived, the CySecAlert system developed and evaluated.

Discussion 5

The discussion is organized as follows: In Section 5.1, approaches for the monitoring of dual-use ICTs are discussed, while Section 5.2 reflects the results of dual-use governance ICTs. Furthermore, Section 5.3 considers dual-use and its implications for design, followed by the discussion of the main research question (Section 5.4), the limitations of this thesis and avenues for future work (Section 5.5).

5.1 Monitoring of Dual-use ICTs

The first research questions **RQ1: What are suitable methods to monitor the diffusion of dual-use ICT innovations?** is answered in the Chapters 8 and 9. In the case studies, dual-use ICTs are analysed and methods for the diffusion of innovation are applied. Oltmann (2015, p. 388) has identified the lack of non-life science research on dual-use, as such cases in computer science research might be overlooked. Thus, to monitor dual-use ICTs, there needs to be an understanding of dual-use in the research and development processes of ICT. This has been done on the basis of underlying security concepts in Chapter 2.1.2. By monitoring the emergence of possible dual-use ICTs, innovations in the scientific and industrial community could be assessed regularly. For the innovations in the life sciences, this is already institutionalized by bodies like the NSABB and the German Joint Committee on the Handling of Security-Relevant Research. Both have also addressed some dual-use ICTs, like in the case of governance of cyberweapons (Lin, 2016), AI for deep fakes, and autonomous systems (Diekmann et al., 2020).

T. Riebe, *Technology Assessment of Dual-Use ICTs*, https://doi.org/10.1007/978-3-658-41667-6_5

Scientists and experts are a valuable source to monitor the diffusion of innovations between different scientific or industrial sectors. Their output, in the form of publications, patents, or as social media content, can be analysed as a barometer for innovation spillovers (see Chapter 8) and diffusion (see Chapter 9). In the field of knowledge economy, these networks have been utilized as a measure for the production of revenue due to dual-use products (Acosta et al., 2011, 2017). Such citation networks have great potential for monitoring innovation diffusion of dual-use technologies, as they indicate trends and central actors or networks for innovation (Acosta et al., 2017). In their study on the cross-sector knowledge diffusion in the case of drones, Meunier and Bellais (2019, p. 12) conclude that diffusion is limited as "[m]any sectors appear to function in silos." Their conclusion matches the results on the career churn rate on LinkedIn and on the citation networks in the European Patent Network on AI of this dissertation. While drones consist on many different software and hardware components, organisational similarities of sectors are most important for diffusion to take place: "As the structural analysis of patents demonstrates, architectural knowledge can predominate over component knowledge in innovation choices" (Meunier & Bellais, 2019, p. 12).

The data which is retrieved by the discussed methods can be used to support the assessment of emerging dual-use technologies in the following ways (see Table 5.1): Since the number of publications doubles every 17.3 years (Bornmann et al., 2021), keeping track of the scientific landscape has helped bibliometric and machine learning approaches. Here, trends and hot topics can be detected (Allan, 2012), as well as the networks in which dual-use diffusion takes place. However, as a source of research, patents and publications differ, e.g. in their technical features and their use by the publisher.[1] Additionally, the diffusion of innovation can also be analysed in discourse and content analysis, understanding the particular values, requirements and use cases of military contexts or weapon systems, as it was done in Chapter 9. In the case of AI, underlying values which were associated with the technology development showed a different profile than the values which were associated with civilian AI innovations. Therefore, the combination of certain values, visions of socio-technical futures (Grin, Grunwald, et al., 2000; Lösch, 2017) and requirements for an innovation could be used for dual-use monitoring (Lösch et al., 2019).

---

[1] On the differences between patent and bibliometric analysis see Belderbos and Mohnen (2013).

Table 5.1 Methods for Dual-use Monitoring

Source	Data	Method	Approaches (selection)
Scientific publications	Patent, authors and citation networks	Bibliographic, trend and network analysis	Shibata et al. (2011)
Patents	Citation networks, owner, features	Network analysis, qualitative analysis	Acosta et al. (2011, 2013, 2017), Meunier and Bellais (2019), and S. Schmid et al. (2022)
Social media and blogs	Text and images	Network and content analysis	Riebe, Schmid, and Reuter (2021)

5.2   Governance of Dual-use ICTs

The second research question inquires the ambivalence within governments' policies on dual-use by asking **RQ2: How are dual-use technologies governed in light of trade-offs for different concepts of security?** While regulation for LAWS does not exist yet, the proliferation of cryptography has been regulated for decades (Vella, 2017) (see Table 5.2). This impacts the access to technology when it becomes more relevant for online mass communication. In the case of cryptography as a dual-use good, the discourse has shown the limits of the use of export controls as the spread of online mass communication has transformed the relevance of the technology for civil society and businesses. The trade of cryptographic products has been regulated as a dual-use technology in the Wassenaar Arrangement (Wassenaar Arrangement Secretariat, 2021) and in the export restrictions of the 40 member countries, and many more worldwide (Vella, 2017). The dual-use regulation of cryptography in the US (see Chapter 11) highlights how control of proliferation is securitized and a powerful regulative tool, with effects on many commercial areas and the security of end-users.

The limits of dual-use as an governmental concept for R&D in neuroscience and brain research has been criticized by Mahfoud et al. (2018). They point out that some innovations emerging from the field may be of high importance for the military, e.g. noninvasive brain-computer interfaces (BCIs) in the area of human enhancement, which also yield medical advances for neurological diseases such as dementia. Regarding the dual-use concept, the authors criticize: "Current treaties and regulatory frameworks that focus on export controls are not designed to deal with the complex and far-reaching consequences that future brain research will have at the intersection of technological advance, or with the broad arenas where government and nongovernment actors seek to advance their interests" (Mahfoud et al., 2018, p. 78). Instead, the notion of "responsibility" by the self-regulation of "industry, universities, and philanthropic organizations, especially in relation to artificial intelligence, machine learning, and autonomous intelligent systems" is suggested. This argument has been central to the creation of the DURC concept, which has led to a system of self-commitment, soft norms and awareness raining (Tucker, 2012). Thus, the idea of RRI has been supported to strengthen self-governance in R&D (Owen et al., 2012; Rychnovská, 2016; von Schomberg, 2011).

This demands, however, stronger self-regulation in form of institutional oversight mechanisms. These mechanisms in turn require additional work from researchers, developers and their organizations, even reshaping institutions and the ways in which science is organized (Evans, 2014). Rychnovská (2020, p. 174) calls this development the "responsibilization of researchers", making them agents of security. This might even apply to all researchers, as the "unpredictability of research and innovation development and the broadening threat scenarios, [...] it becomes impossible to draw a clear line between secure and insecure research" (Rychnovská, 2020, p. 122).

When looking at the discourse to regulate LAWS, no agreement can be seen so far (Barbé & Badell, 2020). The vision of the human-computer or machine interaction and relationship, however, provides an entry point for a vision assessment for future research. In their interviews with engineers in the civilian sector of Autonomous Vehicles (AVs), Schwartz et al. (2022) analysed the awareness for dual-use issues within the industrial sector and found out that there is awareness, but a lack of discourse and procedures to discuss the matter among the developers. As the automation of functions is increasing, and diminishing the capacity of the human operators (Bode & Watts, 2021), the engagement with the industry to provide knowledge, enable standards and norms is crucial (Verbruggen, 2019). Furthermore, this exchange could help to shed light on the value conflicts of military-planning and design ethics (Umbrello, 2021).

Tucker (2012, p. 74) has identified five factors which influence the governability of technologies, i.e., the embodiment, maturity, convergence, rate of advance, and international diffusion. However, as the case of cryptography has shown, the diffusion and its relevance might change due to the emergence of technology, such as the emergence of mass online communication and the implementation of end-to-end encryption has shown. However, the two investigated cases share the following characteristics: they certainly have a strategic importance, either in the protection of sensitive information or in the battlefield, while their basic research has a relevance for a wide range of civilian researchers, developers, and users. Therefore, the spectrum of governance measures need to focus on forms of "participatory-governance", based on education, self-commitment and industrial norms which emerge from the discourse between civil society, research and industrial sectors contributing knowledge and defining norms (Tucker, 2012; Verbruggen, 2019). Non-governmental organizations and approaches to citizens science need to be included in the research and development process (Eames & Egmose, 2011).

Table 5.2 Governance of Dual-use ICTs

Technology	Chapter	Type of regulation
LAWS	10	Self-commitments and declarations
Cryptography	11	Export controls

5.3 Design of Dual-use ICTs

The third research question inquires the implications for design and the values associated with use cases of cybersecurity, by asking **RQ3: How can VSD support the assessment of dual-use ICT to prevent the harmful use?** The TA discourse (Liebert & Schmidt, 2018) has emphasized that the ambivalence of technology cannot be dissolved. Instead, Liebert and Schmidt (2018, p. 53) proposes to include such an ambivalence to the method of TA to incorporate the assessment of different kinds of ambiguities to enable a reflective technology design: First, the technical and scientific causalities, followed by the effects in societies and its dynamics are to be evaluated. In the field of HCI, in the participatory turn, design and participation of users and stakeholder groups has been developed to account for the societal relevance of technology and its potential to change socio-technical systems (Manders-Huits, 2011; Stevens et al., 2018). For the assessment of dual-use, the methodology and theory of VSD (Friedman et al., 2006) is a valuable approach because it does not only allow for the analysis of functional values like usability, but it further allows to include ethical and higher values in an iterative and inclusive deliberation within the design process (van Der Hoven & Manders-Huits, 2020). To do so, conceptual, empirical and technical investigations are proposed, which have been outlined in detail in Chapter 12.2.2. These three steps have been conducted in this thesis with regard to OSINT in the context of cybersecurity (see Table 5.3). In the conceptual investigations, direct and indirect stakeholders and ethical scenarios have

been identified (see Chapter 12). Empirical investigations helped to further anticipate the future use context of an possible OSINT system for cybersecurity event
detection and warning infrastructure (see Chapter 13 for the collaboration among
CERTs and Chapter 14 for the perspective of the citizens).

As the VSD chapters of this thesis contributed more than the dual-use risk assessment, they also show that dual-use issues can be integrated of the research and design
approach: In all of the investigative steps, the question of harmful consequences and
unintended use was discussed, and even raised by the researchers and designers in the
focus group workshop (Chapter 12.4). The systematic literature study showed that
ELSI has only been discussed in 11 of the 73 relevant papers which designed OSINT
systems for cybersecurity. To complement existing research, Chapter 12.4.2 details
the identified value conflicts and the ambivalence of the possible design choices,
offering venture points for approaches which are developed to optimize conflicting requirements, e.g., conflicts with regard to privacy, transparency or accuracy of
such an OSINT system. Dual-use assessment categories can be integrated into the
conceptual and empirical investigations, helping to develop dual-use scenarios, use
cases and threat models (Friedman et al., 2017). Higher-level values, like freedom
from harm and human security (Kaldor, 2011) can be translated into norms and
requirements (Poel, 2013; Umbrello & Van de Poel, 2021). Similar to the approach
on OSINT, Umbrello & Van de Poel (2021, p. 291) have shown how to map values from the AI4People initiative (Floridi et al., 2018) on the VSD process and
develop the respective norms and requirements. The identification of values and
value conflicts helps to reflect on the ambivalent design choices within the research
and development team.

The use context in the case of OSINT for cybersecurity by public CERTs adds
another layer of legal and organizational requirements (Liegl et al., 2016), because
the direct stakeholders are part of the public administration (see Chapter 13). CERT
members agreed, that they would benefit from the semi-automation of cyber threat
intelligence, but also need to comply with the norms and rules of public administration. Further, as indirect stakeholders and social media users, the representative
study (Chapter 14) added factors which are associated with the acceptance of social
media surveillance for cybersecurity, such as high awareness and low privacy concerns. The results seem to indicate the need for an engagement in a public dialog to
inform both the design and governance decisions (Grunwald, 2018, p. 89).

As a result of the context and stakeholder value analysis, a system was developed
which applies a supervised classifier, based on active learning, that detects tweets
containing relevant information (see Chapter 15). The approach reduces the number
of accounts and tweets that are needed for the classifier training using uncertainty
sampling, thus making the tool rapidly adaptable to the specific context while also

supporting data minimization for OSINT. In the design, relevant tweets are clustered by a greedy stream clustering algorithm in order to identify significant events which could be used to inform the CERTs on a new threat. The proposed system is able to work in near real-time within the required 15-min Twitter time frame and detects up to 93.8% of relevant events with a false alert rate of 14.81%. Therefore, using expert networks, the systems combines the requirement to use social media data within its context of publication (Nissenbaum, 2018), data-minimization (B. J. Koops et al., 2013) as well as near-real time performance.

Table 5.3 Implications for Design and Development

VSD Iteration	Chapter	Implications
Conceptual Investigation	12	Dual-use risks have been identified: Value conflicts emerge with regard to use-case, privacy, transparency and accuracy
Empirical Investigation	13	Transparency and awareness for OSINT CERTs would benefit from inoperable and modular architectures for which would reduce costs for cyber situational awareness by OSINT, privacy-preserving cross-platform monitoring of incident data and events
Empirical Investigation	14	High threat perception and the perceived need for OSINT and high awareness of OSINT in combination with low privacy concerns also associated with the acceptance of OSINT for cybersecurity
Technical Investigation	15	Data minimization by account-based architecture, uncertainty sampling enables rapid training of ML algorithm and near real-time event detection

5.4   Towards Dual-Use Assessment of ICTs

The main research question asks: **How can dual-use risks of ICT be assessed for monitoring, governance as well as design?** In short, the assessment of dual-use ICTs comprises of a combination of three steps. For this the contributions (C) of the dissertation are summarized in the following paragraphs and in Table 5.4. First, knowledge on the diffusion of innovations between military and civilian use contexts is crucial to identify the need for forms of governance. Further, an understanding of possible part of weapon system is crucial to monitor on a regular basis. The continuous development of autonomy and the automation of dull and dangerous military tasks lead to the "creeping in" of AI into weapon systems. As Verbruggen (2019, p. 341) argues, there "will be no water-shed moment when systems unambiguously definable as LAWS will suddenly be deployed". Therefore, continuous monitoring using social network (C1) and patent analysis (C2), as well as values and visions has shown to be a contribution (C3).

Second, technologies and goods which have a high commercial relevance, and can be accessed by a large spectrum of actors, such as citizens, researchers and organizations, make the control of proliferation, use and adaption difficult. The thesis contributed to the discourse of regulating LAWS by identifying values and value conflicts between human-centered values and economic and performance oriented values, while also shedding light into the spectrum of hierarchical relationships in human-machine interactions (C4). Further, the changes in dual-use regulation of cryptography in the US and the surveillance practices has shown how mass communication and end-to-end encryption have challenged the regulation (C5), while also supported the role of surveillance intermediaries (C6).

Third, the design of dual-use technology can utilize the dual-use definitions, the referent objects and threat scenarios for the development of assessment categories, as it was done in the VSD case studies regarding OSINT for cybersecu-

Table 5.4 Contributions

Aspect	Contributions (C) and Description
Monitoring	• C1: monitoring approach for expert networks (in Twitter und LinkedIn)
	• C2: dual-use monitoring approach for AI innovations using patent citation network
	• C3: monitoring of values which are associated with either military or civilian application
Governance	• C4: identification of values, value conflicts and visions of human-machine interaction and hierarchy for the regulation of LAWS and MHC
	• C5: identification and analysis of the effects of dual-use export governance and surveillance practices in the US
	• C6: identification of the role of communication intermediaries as stakeholders in dual-use governance of cryptography
Design	• C7: utilization of the VSD approach to include dual-use assessment categories in the conceptual and empirical investigations regarding OSINT for cybersecurity
	• C8: empirical investigations regarding the use contexts, values and value conflicts of OSINT for cybersecurity in public CERTs
	• C9: the development and evaluation of the artifact CySecAlert

rity (C7). Thus, the thesis identified the relevant direct and indirect stakeholders, as well as values and value conflicts of relevant technologies and use contexts (C8). Further, based on the value-informed design decisions, the CySecAlert artifact was developed and evaluated as part of the technical investigations of VSD (C9). The deliberation of value-conflicts can furthermore be important as documentation, as transparency-enabling measure and public information for ICT development with societal relevance (Leal et al., 2021). All in all, the dual-use assessment of ICT should make use of the mulit-use nature and accessibility of ICT artifacts and systems, as well as take contributions of participatory design research in HCI as a venture point for participatory dual-use assessment and design.

5.5   Limitations and Future Work

There are some limitations to this thesis: First, assessment of risks can only go so far, as to take into account the known unknowns, while there will always be consequences which cannot be known (unknown unknowns) (Beck, 2004). Therefore, the unknowns will grow in the same way the knowledge on technology increases. Further, the dynamics of technoscience make the issue even more pressing, as the dichotomy between basic and applied research is vanishing (Liebert & Schmidt, 2010). Thus, more case studies on dual-use ICTs needs to be conducted, especially as some of the technologies studied in this work are emerging and will be developed further and on more contexts, for example, in the application fields for AI, such as decision support systems (P. Hayes & Kelly, 2018; Zweig et al., 2018), big and social data analytics (R. Bernard et al., 2018) and in life science research and simulation (Urbina et al., 2022). Additionally, highly active fields are autonomous systems and robotics (Winfield & Jirotka, 2018), which have many applications, such as in medical care (Misselhorn, 2020), and in military systems (Umbrello, 2021). New methods in machine learning can further help to improve expert network analysis, e.g., as in the cases of bibliometric or patent analysis, as well as social media analytics (D. R. Hayes & Cappa, 2018). Never the less, these approaches need carefully assessment to avoid illegitimate surveillance (A. Ioannou & Tussyadiah, 2021).

The societal assessment and values to use and regulate a certain dual-use ICTs can change, as the technologies themselves are further developed and applied to new contexts. Therefore, dual-use TA needs to be conducted to assess the visions of technology design (Grin, Grunwald, et al., 2000; Lösch, 2017). Especially, when combining different dual-use technologies, the risks might evolve, e.g., as in the case of AI and automated drug discovery (Urbina et al., 2022). The dynamics in both fields lead to a complex challenge for the assessment, which is why authors in such disciplines recommend raising awareness among scientists through relevant conferences, institutional review boards, and funding bodies (Urbina et al., 2022, pp. 2-3).

Further, assessment of dual-use is not enough to mitigate risks. A responsible culture has to be supported with teaching and educational materials, which supports the individual and organization responsibility (Evans, 2014; Nordmann & Vida, 2022). Further, TA aims to provide input into the public discourse on security-relevant technologies. This needs a communication and translation of scientific research for the public. The participation of citizens in forms of participatory design is an important research contribution not only for the technology development, but also for education and democratic opinion-building.

Conclusion

6

The scientific discourse on dual-use has been driven by efforts for non-proliferation of nuclear, biological and chemical weapons, as well as by ethical and security concerns regarding threats by terrorism since 9/11, in which everyday items have been used as weapons or to used to harm people. The latter discourse was mostly held in the field of the life sciences, because their research and development offers many technologies which which have become more accessible. For a few years, science oversight boards have issued dual-use risks by research and development of ICTs, regarding autonomous systems, AI, big data, and assistant systems. However, ICT dual-use risks need more systematic assessment. Although ICT artifacts can be assessed with approaches from the life sciences, some dimensions of dual-use risks are not captured, e.g., military or national security interests in autonomous systems or surveillance-oriented security policies. Thus, this thesis uses CSS to deconstruct the security concepts of the three dual-use concepts (military and civilian use, part of a weapon system, and beneficial or harmful use) and derives the threat scenarios and indicators. To develop an approach of the TA of ICT cases, this thesis combines constructivist approaches from CSS and HCI to assess the monitoring, governance and design of dual-use ICTs.

The results of the case studies (Chapter 8-15) contribute to the assessment of dual-use regarding ICT artifacts and research in three ways. First, as ICT is versatile and ubiquitous, it is assumed that the diffusion of innovation might happen easily between civilian and military sectors. Thus, Chapters 8 and 9 investigate the spillover of knowledge in general in the first and the diffusion of AI innovation in particular in the second. Both studies conclude that innovation diffusion between the civilian and military-industrial sectors in general and in particular only occur in a very limited way, and that is more likely within a company or organization. The following part of the thesis investigates the proliferation and governability of two cases of dual-use technologies: LAWS (Chapter 10) and cryptography (Chapter

T. Riebe, *Technology Assessment of Dual-Use ICTs*, https://doi.org/10.1007/978-3-658-41667-6_6

11). The results show how the versatility and universal use affect the governance on proliferation. In both cases, the role of companies either as producer of autonomous systems, or as surveillance intermediaries needs to be more accounted for regarding governance approaches. To assess the design of dual-use ICT, OSINT in the context of cybersecurity is investigated using VSD. The four studies conduct conceptual, empirical and technical investigations. First, the state of the technology and research as well as the direct and indirect stakeholders are identified (Chapter 12). Further, the value conflicts from the perspective of the stakeholders, such as the CERTs (Chapter 13), and the citizens (Chapter 14) are identified. Further, implications for the design are derived, which have been used in the development of the CySecAlert system for cybersecurity event detection (Chapter 15).

The thesis contributes to the dual-use technology assessment of ICT in the areas of diffusion and monitoring in the case of AI, a reflection of governability and proliferation regulation of acict as dual-use goods in the cases of LAWS and cryptography, as well as the design of OSINT for cybersecurity, by analyzing the values and value conflicts. However, this work has limitations and offers many venture points for future work, such as more case studies on dual-use relevant ICTs, e.g., at the intersection to the life sciences and health care. In addition, due to the advances in each technology, the results of the assessment from stakeholders will change, as well as the public perception of a technology. Therefore, TA approaches like vision assessment and participatory design should be applied and developed further for the assessment dual-use ICTs.

List of the Author's Publications

In sum, 30 publications have been published in the context of the authors work. The publications are ranked according to the CORE (Computing Research and Education Association of Australasia, 2022) and the Journal Impact Factor (JIF) The following 8 publications are published as chapters of this dissertation.

1. **Thea Riebe**, Tom Biselli, Marc-André Kaufhold, Christian Reuter (2023) Perceptions of the German Population regarding the Impacts of OSINT in Cybersecurity, *Proceedings on Privacy Enhancing Technologies (PoPETs)*. https://doi.org/10.56553/popets-2023-0028 [CORE-A]
2. **Thea Riebe**, Julian Bäumler, Christian Reuter (2023) Values and Value Conflicts in the Context of OSINT Technologies for Cybersecurity: A Value Sensitive Design Perspective, in revision for *Journal Computer Supported Cooperative Work (CSCW)*. http://dx.doi.org/10.1007/s10606-022-09453-4 [CORE-B, Impact Factor 2.800]
3. **Thea Riebe**, Philipp Kuehn, Philipp Imperatori, Christian Reuter (2022) U.S. Security Policy: The Dual-Use Regulation of Cryptography and its Effects on Surveillance, *European Journal for Security Research*. http://dx.doi.org/10.1007/s41125-022-00080-0
4. Stefka Schmid, **Thea Riebe**, Christian Reuter (2022) Dual-Use and Trustworthy? A Mixed Methods Analysis of AI Diffusion between Civilian and Defense R&D, *Science and Engineering Ethics*; 28(12):1–23. http://dx.doi.org/10.1007/s11948-022-00364-7 [Impact Factor 3.525]
5. **Thea Riebe**, Marc-André Kaufhold, Christian Reuter (2021) The Impact of Organizational Structure and Technology Use on Collaborative Practices in Computer Emergency Response Teams: An Empirical Study, *Proceedings of the ACM: Human Computer Interaction (PACM): Computer-Supported*

T. Riebe, *Technology Assessment of Dual-Use ICTs*, https://doi.org/10.1007/978-3-658-41667-6_7

Cooperative Work and Social Computing; 5(CSCW2). http://dx.doi.org/10.1145/3479865 [CORE-A]

6. **Thea Riebe**, Stefka Schmid, Christian Reuter (2021) Measuring Spillover Effects from Defense to Civilian Sectors—A Quantitative Approach Using LinkedIn, *Defence and Peace Economics*; 32(7):773–785. http://dx.doi.org/10.1080/10242694.2020.1755787 [Impact Factor 2.361]

7. **Thea Riebe**, Tristan Wirth, Markus Bayer, Philipp Kuehn, Marc-André Kaufhold, Volker Knauthe, Stefan Guthe, Christian Reuter (2021) CySecAlert: An Alert Generation System for Cyber Security Events Using Open Source Intelligence Data, *Proceedings of International Conference on Information and Communications Security.* Cham: Springer International Publishing, pp: 429–446. http://dx.doi.org/10.1007/978-3-030-86890-1_24 [CORE-B]

8. **Thea Riebe**, Stefka Schmid, Christian Reuter (2020) Meaningful Human Control of Lethal Autonomous Weapon System: The CCW-Debate and its Implications for Value-Sensitive Design, *IEEE Technology and Society Magazine*; 39(4): 36–51. https://ieeexplore.ieee.org/document/9288888 [Impact Factor 1.109]

The following papers are not included in the dissertation, although their findings are supplementary to it.

9. Christian Reuter, **Thea Riebe**, Jasmin Haunschild, Thomas Reinhold, Stefka Schmid (2022) Zur Schnittmenge von Informatik mit Friedens- und Sicherheitsforschung: Erfahrungen aus der interdisziplinären Lehre in der Friedensinformatik, *Zeitschrift für Friedens- und Konfliktforschung (ZeFKo)*: 1–12. https://doi.org/10.1007/s42597-022-00078-4

10. Malte Göttsche, Sibylle Bauer, Anja Dahlmann, Friederike Frieß, Filippa Lentzos, Götz Neuneck, Irmgard Niemeyer, **Thea Riebe**, Jantje Silomon, Christian Reuter, Jakob Brochhaus, Lukas Rademacher (2022) *Conference Proceedings: Science, Peace, Security '21*, 8–10 September 2021 Aachen: RWTH Aachen University. http://dx.doi.org/10.18154/RWTH-2022-02256

11. **Thea Riebe**, Stefka Schmid, Christian Reuter (2021) LinkedIn als Barometer: Austausch zwischen ziviler und militärischer F&E, *Wissenschaft & Frieden*. https://peasec.de/paper/2021/2021_RiebeSchmidReuter_LinkedInalsBarometer_WuF.pdf

12. Marc-André Kaufhold, Jennifer Fromm, **Thea Riebe**, Milad Mirbabaie, Philipp Kuehn, Ali Sercan Basyurt, Markus Bayer, Marc Stöttinger, Kaan Eyilmez, Reinhard Möller, Christoph Fuchß, Stefan Stieglitz, Christian Reuter (2021) CYWARN: Strategy and Technology Development for Cross-Platform Cyber Situational Awareness and Actor-Specific Cyber Threat Communication,

Workshop-Proceedings Mensch und Computer, Bonn. https://doi.org/10.18420/muc2021-mci-ws08-263

13. **Thea Riebe**, Christian Reuter (2021) Neue Technologien und Resilienz, *Wissenschaft und Frieden*. https://wissenschaft-und-frieden.de/artikel/neue-technologien-und-resilienz/

14. **Thea Riebe**, Jasmin Haunschild, Felix Divo, Matthias Lang, Gerbert Roitburd, Jonas Franken, Christian Reuter (2020) Die Veränderung der Vorratsdatenspeicherung in Europa, *Datenschutz und Datensicherheit—DuD*; 44(5):316–321. http://dx.doi.org/10.1007/s11623-020-1275-3

15. Philipp Imperatori, **Thea Riebe**, Christian Reuter (2020) Verschlüsselungspolitik der USA: Vom Clipper-Chip zu Edward Snowden, *FIfF-Kommunikation*; 37:77–80. https://www.fiff.de/publikationen/fiff-kommunikation/fk-2020/fk-2020-1/fk-1-20-p77.pdf to https://tuprints.ulb.tu-darmstadt.de/20060/1/fk-1-20-p77.pdf

16. Philipp Kuehn, **Thea Riebe**, Lynn Apelt, Max Jansen, Christian Reuter (2020) Sharing of Cyber Threat Intelligence between States, *S+F Sicherheit und Frieden / Peace and Security*; 38(1): 22–28. http://dx.doi.org/10.5771/0175-274X-2020-1-22

17. **Thea Riebe** (2020) Umgang mit Killerrobotern, *Wissenschaft & Frieden*; 2. https://wissenschaft-und-frieden.de/artikel/umgang-mit-killerrobotern/

18. Marc-André Kaufhold, Arne Schmidt, Fabienne Seifert, **Thea Riebe**, Christian Reuter (2019) SentiNet: Twitter-basierter Ansatz zur kombinierten Netzwerk- und Stimmungsanalyse in Katastrophenlagen, *Mensch und Computer 2019—Workshopband*; Hamburg, Germany. http://dx.doi.org/10.18420/muc2019-ws-133-04

19. **Thea Riebe**, Marc-André Kaufhold, Tarun Kumar, Thomas Reinhold, Christian Reuter (2019) Threat Intelligence Application for Cyber Attribution, *SCIENCE PEACE SECURITY '19—Proceedings of the Interdisciplinary Conference on Technical Peace and Security Research*, Darmstadt, Germany. https://tuprints.ulb.tu-darmstadt.de/id/eprint/9164

20. **Thea Riebe**, Amanda Langer, Marc-André Kaufhold, Nina Katharina Kretschmer, Christian Reuter (2019) Werte und Wertekonflikte in sozialen Medien für die Vernetzung ungebundener Helfer in Krisensituationen—Ein Value-Sensitive Design Ansatz, *Mensch und Computer 2019—Workshopband*, Hamburg, Germany. http://dx.doi.org/10.18420/muc2019-ws-133-05

21. **Thea Riebe**, Christian Reuter, Christian Reuter, Jürgen Altmann, Malte Göttsche, Mirko Himmel (2019) Accessing Dual Use in IT Development, *SCIENCE PEACE SECURITY '19—Proceedings of the Interdisciplinary Con-*

ference on Technical Peace and Security Research, Darmstadt, Germany: TUprints, 46–49. https://tuprints.ulb.tu-darmstadt.de/id/eprint/9164

22. Stefka Schmid, **Thea Riebe**, Christian Reuter (2019) Meaningful Human Control of Lethal Autonomous Weapon Systems, In: Christian Reuter, Jürgen Altmann, Malte Göttsche, Mirko Himmel: *SCIENCE PEACE SECURITY '19— Proceedings of the Interdisciplinary Conference on Technical Peace and Security Research*, Darmstadt, Germany: TUprints, 196–200. https://tuprints.ulb. tu-darmstadt.de/id/eprint/9164

23. Christian Reuter, **Thea Riebe**, Larissa Aldehoff, Marc-André Kaufhold, Thomas Reinhold (2019) Cyberwar zwischen Fiktion und Realität— technologische Möglichkeiten, In: Ines-Jacqueline Werkner, Niklas Schörnig: Cyberwar—die Digitalisierung der Kriegsführung. Springer VS, 15–38. http:// dx.doi.org/10.1007/978-3-658-27713-0

24. Christian Reuter, Konstantin Aal, Larissa Aldehoff, Jürgen Altmann, Johannes Buchmann, Ute Bernhardt, Kai Denker, Dominik Herrmann, Matthias Hollick, Stefan Katzenbeisser, Marc-André Kaufhold, Alfred Nordmann, Thomas Reinhold, **Thea Riebe**, Annette Ripper, Ingo Ruhmann, Klaus-Peter Saalbach, Niklas Schörnig, Ali Sunyaev, Volker Wulf (2019) The Future of IT in Peace and Security, In: Christian Reuter: Information Technology for Peace and Security—IT-Applications and Infrastructures in Conflicts, Crises, War, and Peace. Wiesbaden, Germany: Springer Vieweg, 405–413. http://dx.doi.org/10. 1007/978-3-658-25652-4_19

25. Christian Reuter, Larissa Aldehoff, **Thea Riebe**, Marc-André Kaufhold (2019) IT in Peace, Conflict, and Security Research, In: Christian Reuter: Information Technology for Peace and Security—IT-Applications and Infrastructures in Conflicts, Crises, War, and Peace. Wiesbaden, Germany: Springer Vieweg, 11–37. http://dx.doi.org/10.1007/978-3-658-25652-4_2

26. **Thea Riebe**, Christian Reuter (2019) Dual Use and Dilemmas for Cybersecurity, Peace and Technology Assessment, In: Christian Reuter: Information Technology for Peace and Security—IT-Applications and Infrastructures in Conflicts, Crises, War, and Peace. Wiesbaden, Germany: Springer Vieweg, 165–184. http://dx.doi.org/10.1007/978-3-658-25652-4_8

27. Marc-André Kaufhold, Christian Reuter, **Thea Riebe**, Elmar von Radziewski (2018) Design eines BCM-Dashboards für kleine und mittlere Unternehmen, *Mensch und Computer 2018: Workshopband*, Dresden, Germany. https://dl.gi. de/bitstream/handle/20.500.12116/16796/Beitrag_453_final__a.pdf

28. Marc-André Kaufhold, **Thea Riebe**, Christian Reuter, Julian Hester, Danny Jeske, Lisa Knüver, Viktoria Richert (2018) Business Continuity Management in Micro Enterprises: Perception, Strategies and Use of ICT, *International Jour-*

nal of Information Systems for Crisis Response and Management (IJISCRAM);
10(1): 1–19. http://dx.doi.org/10.4018/IJISCRAM.2018010101

29. **Thea Riebe**, Katja Pätsch, Marc-André Kaufhold, Christian Reuter (2018)
From Conspiracies to Insults: A Case Study of Radicalisation in Social
Media Discourse, *Mensch und Computer 2018: Workshopband*, Dresden,
Germany. https://dl.gi.de/bitstream/handle/20.500.12116/16795/Beitrag_449_
final__a.pdf

30. **Thea Riebe**, Alfred Nordmann, Christian Reuter (2018) Responsible Research
and Innovation: Interdisziplinärer Workshop von IANUS und Schader-
Stiftung, *Wissenschaft & Frieden*. http://www.peasec.de/paper/2018/2018_
RiebeNordmannReuter_RRI_WuF.pdf

Part II
Publications

Measuring Spillover Effects from Defense to Civilian Sectors: A Quantitative Approach Using LinkedIn

8

8.1   Introduction

Progress in science and technology influences the dynamics of peace and security (Reuter, 2020). Among other scientific and technical disciplines (physics, biology, chemistry) many areas of computer science (e.g., artificial intelligence) are currently of rising importance (Reuter, 2019) due to the disciplines' involvements into the research and development of dual-use technologies. Dual-use technologies have an impact on the assessment of international and national security, as do their spillover effects (Acosta et al., 2011, 2017). The measurement of technological and innovation spillover is relevant for the effective regulative control of certain high-risk industries. Dual-use, in more general terms, is on the one hand all items that can either be used in a beneficial or harmful way or have civilian or military applications (Oltmann, 2015). our research is motivated by industrial spillovers, focusing on German companies most active in conventional arms sales.

Public funds for research and development (R&D) in the defense sector are often argued to lead to a backflow of know-how in the form of spillover effects in the civilian sector (Acosta et al., 2017; Brzoska, 2006). Other scholars have assumed that innovation from the defense sector diffuses less due to idiosyncratic factors, such as the culture, market structure, and policy environment of the defense industry (Molas-Gallart, 1997; J. Schmid, 2017).

ORIGINAL PUBLICATION Riebe, T., Schmid, S., & Reuter, C. (2021). Measuring Spillover Effects from Defense to Civilian Sectors–A Quantitative Approach Using LinkedIn. Defence and Peace Economis, 32(7), 773–785. https://doi.org/10.1080/10242694.2020.1755787

On the other hand, developing and producing emerging dual-use technologies for both potential civilian and defense applications can lower production costs and is therefore in many fields desirable for companies. Even though spillover effects on an economic productivity scale are difficult to measure (Sempere, 2018).

Naturally, measurement of spillovers depends on the item's operationalization; for example, it is based on patents (Acosta et al., 2017), or labor mobility (Fujiwara, 2017). The location of the R&D industry has shown to be an important factor regarding the spillover of technology (Keller, 2004), reflected by a geographical concentration in Western countries (Jaffe et al., 1993; Keller, 2004) and more recently Asian countries like China (WIPO, 2019).

While patent citation analysis has many advantages, it also has limitations (for a discussion see Belderbos & Mohnen (2013)). Especially regarding emerging technologies, which may not have developed an established output of patents yet, other indicators of the spillover of innovations may prove necessary. Additionally, not all innovations lead to patents; thus, some spillovers might not be measurable by patent citations, but rather by focusing on knowledge transfer via workforce mobility and local networks. Social media, for instance, is currently used in many different ways, ranging from personal conversations to business networking—and emerging data is analyzed for business purposes, but also in context for crises and conflicts (Reuter & Kaufhold, 2018). Social Media Analytics (SMA) (Russel, 2018; Stieglitz, Mirbabaie, Fromm, & Melzer, 2018) provides a set of approaches taking advantage of the evolution of networks, work biographies, skills, accomplishments, and interests. Furthermore, SMA, more specifically, Social Network Analysis (Leistner, 2012) can provide insights into the centrality of actors and the density of a network, giving additional insight into skills of highly educated employees (Geyik et al., 2018; Ha-Thuc et al., 2015; Russel, 2018) involved in the research and development of dual-use technologies and related (informal) knowledge transfers among individual users (Havakhor et al., 2018; Leistner, 2012).

Emerging and high-technologies are developed in interdisciplinary teams, which involves the exchange of ideas and information. As part of job changes, the knowledge is used in other teams and companies (Branstetter et al., 2017). Measuring spillover based on individual behavior, this approach does not focus on patents or technologies, but rather on individuals as they transfer knowledge between companies and job positions using a career network analysis (Russel, 2018; Stieglitz, Mirbabaie, Fromm, & Melzer, 2018). Thus, we are interested in the methodological and empirical question: **What are the spillover effects that can be measured using career-network analysis?** Assuming SMA can be used to investigate spillover effects, similar effects should be measured that confirm studies which focused on knowledge spillovers based on patent data. J. Schmid (2017, p. 3) argues that "the distinctive culture, policy environment, and market structure of the defense-servicing sector impede the diffusion of technologies developed therein", thereby functioning as a limitation to the flow of knowledge from the defense industry to the civilian sectors. Therefore, we assume that the spillover of knowledge is lower from the defense to the civilian sector (H1).

Counting nearly 675 million users, of which 211 million are in Europe, LinkedIn is the career network with the highest number of users worldwide (LinkedIn, 2020) and thus selected as a data source for professional networks. However, due to LinkedIn's purpose of matching companies and employees, its matching algorithm is steadily adjusted (Geyik et al., 2018). This imposes limitations due to access restrictions and data protection policy (LinkedIn, 2020).

The work is structured as follows: Section 8.2 describes our theoretical background, referring to related work of knowledge economics (Section 8.2.1), and patent analysis (Section 8.2.2). Section 8.3 then introduces the method of our SMA approach, the data collection (Section 8.3.1), and the coding of the companies (Section 8.3.2). In Section 8.4, the data is analyzed in terms of their churn behavior (Section 8.4.1). Subsection 8.4.2 describes the limitations of the approach. Put in relation to the traditional methodological approach of patent analysis, Section 8.5 discusses the results of this work in comparison to other approaches. The conclusion and outlook on the further development of the research approach are presented in the last section (Section 8.6).

8.2   State of Research

Scholars of knowledge economics have focused on economies, knowledge, and technology transfer and conducted theoretical work with respect to spillovers, knowledge transfer in social networks, or innovation by industrial districts (Audretsch & Vivarelli, 1996; Cayford & Potì, 2009; Costantini et al., 2013; Tappi, 2001). Thus, this section presents related work of knowledge economics and sheds light on research regarding the measurement of spillover effects by patent analysis.

8.2.1   Knowledge Economics and the Italian School

Works of knowledge economics (Westeren, 2012) may be associated with the contemporary "industrial society" experiencing a "profound transformation" which has been reflected by "increasing importance of intellectual property rights, [...] 'human capital'", or the erosion of former sources of growth (Stehr & Mast, 2005). Within this context, various scholars focus on knowledge or technology spillovers as innovation-inducing factors (Aghion & Jaravel, 2015). Conceptually, spillover grasps the process of transferring (technological) knowledge, often originating within companies and subsequently published by, e.g., patents or passing it on to other actors (Aghion & Jaravel, 2015; van Oort & Raspe, 2012). Additionally, there has been a focus on labor mobility as initiating knowledge spillover (Audretsch & Keilbach, 2005). In this regard, the measurement of knowledge transfers has been discussed in more detail, differentiating between codified and tacit knowledge and focusing on geographical proximities as well as on transfers of informal knowledge across social networks (Audretsch & Keilbach, 2005; Panahi et al., 2013). Departing from the work of the economist Alfred Marshall, the so-called Italian School coined the industrial district as a unit of analysis, characterized by a variety of firms, which may share relationships with each other (Morrison, 2008; Tappi, 2001). The network of respective firms is embedded in a social system (Tappi, 2001), taking personal relationships into account as well (Carbonara, 2018; Owen-Smith & Powell, 2004).

We take the perspective of connectedness among firms through people, i.e., individual agents which are socially embedded, into account. While the individuals may not personally know each other, their paths may be connected by working for the same firm, conducting similar working activities, learning or transferring the same tacit or explicit knowledge (Belussi & Pilotti, 2002; Robertson & Jacobson, 2011). Our work does, in contrast to approaches of the Italian School, not specifically focus on human beings' sociability or socio-economic laws of productivity increase (Becattini, 2002). LinkedIn does not constitute a typical industrial district (Becattini, 2002). Yet, our sample based on LinkedIn profile data reflects the most important companies of the German defense industry, comprised of various individuals of different working positions. Furthermore, these individuals are connected by their employing firm(s) and reflect the importance of humans' economic force and neighboring industrial clusters, defined by other commodities (Becattini, 2002). In our view, LinkedIn (profiles) partly represent the network characteristics of the Italian School's propagated industrial districts and thus allow for studying linkages among network-relevant firms with a focus on spillovers from the defense to the civilian industries, initiated by job changes of individual agents, entailing knowledge transfer.

Table 8.1 Distribution of defense company in the sample

Frequency of job positions	1,926	100%
Hensoldt	336	17.45
Krauss-Maffei Wegmann	65	3.37
Rheinmetall	406	21.08
Total	**807**	**41.90**

8.2.2   Measuring Spillover Effects by Patent Referencing and Labor Mobility

To distinguish between defense and civilian R&D is challenging due to some companies being active in both areas, especially when producing dual-use items (Acosta et al., 2017). Spillover effects describe the process in which a company gains benefits from the R&D activities of another company and obtains an economic advantage (Jaffe et al., 1993).

A method for examining and quantifying spillover effects uses citations of patents or references of scientific literature in patents of interest to understand the relationships between technological inventions (Acosta et al., 2011, 2017; Kim et al., 2016).

Approaches that focus on patent citation focus on technologies that are already fully developed and therefore easier to assess. Technologies, on the other hand, that are in earlier stages of their research and development need an early assessment for tailored and informed policy risk assessment (Tucker, 2012). Using the data provided by SMA yields insight on social networks and relevant knowledge spillovers that may precede patent publication. Using the data provided by SMA yields insight on social networks and relevant knowledge spillovers that may precede patent publication. Due to the rise of social networks such as Facebook and LinkedIn, the field of SMA has emerged, which intends to combine, extend, and adapt methods for the analysis of social media data (Stieglitz, Mirbabaie, Fromm, & Melzer, 2018). Taking advantage of SMA is an exploratory approach to measure spillover effects, as applied in a study of cyber-military capabilities of the US Cyber reserve using keyword search for skill analysis in LinkedIn profiles of a selected population (Porche et al., 2017). Skill analysis is an often-used approach of SMA in LinkedIn, mostly to match the supply and demand of the employers and employees (Geyik et al., 2018; Ha-Thuc et al., 2015; Ramanath et al., 2018). At the same time, SMA based on LinkedIn data allows grasping employed users' job change histories, indicating occurrences of knowledge transfer (Audretsch & Keilbach, 2005).

8.3   Analyzing the LinkedIn Profile Data

8.3.1   Sample and Case Selection

To analyze spillovers from the German defense to civilian industry using SMA, data from LinkedIn was retrieved manually. Therefore, a profiling account was used. We analyzed 513 profiles of employees, working or having worked for the three arms companies with the highest revenue in Germany[1] (Table 8.1) over the last ten years. The companies have been selected based on the SIPRI Arms Industry Database Top 100 from 2002–17 (Fleurant et al., 2017). From the 1,100 results on LinkedIn, the first 513 have been coded. Only job positions that have been held for longer than six months were counted, excluding internships. To ensure the possibility of job change(s), the sample comprises solely profiles of people who have graduated their latest educational program until 2016. Within the last ten years (from January 2009 until March 2019), the 513 sample employees held 1,926 different positions in 113 companies, including the subsidiary companies. Incomplete profiles were excluded from the dataset. In general, profile information showed rare spelling errors and career-interruptive blank spots. Thus, it is plausible to assume that the profile information has been chosen carefully and represent the actual career paths of respective individuals. Due to the sensitivity of the data, we anonymized profile information and summarized companies which occurred only once across the entire sample under the labels civilian or defense for reasons of clarity. Personalized descriptions of freelancers were also anonymized instead of being excluded from the sample. The manual process of data retrieval allowed for a well-thought assessment of the data's saturation with respect to our research interest. Choosing a European country with a comparatively strong defense industry legitimizes the case selection of Germany. At the same time, focusing on respective firms allows for a suitable representation of the relevant actors of the German defense market. The German case stresses the plausibility of our way of conduct with regards to our interest in spillovers induced by knowledge transfer through individuals' job changes within the context of a network of companies (in contrast to concentrating on governmental defense funding or RF&D policies with a strong focus on the defense industry as initiators of innovation).

---

[1] ThyssenKrupp has been ranked as the second most active German company in arms sales (Fleurant et al., 2017). Yet, as its share of arms sales in relation to total sales makes out "only" 4% percent, the company mainly has a civilian profile. Hence, the sample was saturated before such additional inclusion, and we aimed for Hensoldt, Rheinmetall, and Krauss-Maffei Wegmann, representing the German arms market in SIPRI's Top 100.

8.3.2   Coding the Companies

The unit of analysis is the job position, which is coded as civilian or defense based on the company's business model (Fleurant et al., 2017). In case numbers were not accessible online, companies' profiles were qualitatively assessed with reference to declared industries of activity, partners, as well as the range of products with respect to their field of application (defense or civilian). Extracting data from LinkedIn was done manually, selecting the first 513 profiles from the selected companies which are located in Germany (LinkedIn, 2020). LinkedIn users can assign an industry sector to their current position. The distribution of the sectors is shown in Figure 8.1. 69% of the sample work in Defense and Space at the time of the inquiry. However, professionals might work for defense R&D, but assign themselves to other industry sectors, such as Aviation & Aerospace (11%), Machinery (4%), and Automotive (4%), and others. To review the results of the LinkedIn search, a control group was sampled (n = 62). The control group was selected searching for civilian R&D companies in Germany.

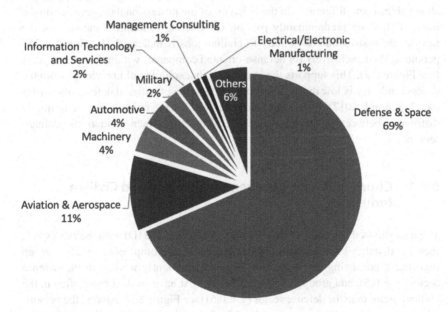

Figure 8.1 Industry sector distribution in sample in 2019

Table 8.2 Job mobility between 2009–2019

Number of jobs between 2009–2019	1,926
Professionals	513
Average position change pP	3.75
SD	1.76
Median	3

8.4   Empirical Results

The professionals changed their jobs on average 3.75 times between 2009 and 2019, with a standard variation of 1.76 and a median of 3 (see Table 8.2). The standard variation is relatively high, being a result of the individual differences in the position changes in the sample. the sample consists of 70.92% job positions in the defense industry and 29.08% civilian positions. Data regarding job changes shows significant differences in the behavior of the professionals depending on the industry they are predominantly part of. Conducting descriptive statistics of the sample, the distribution of military to civilian jobs is indicated, showing that 257 people worked exclusively for defense-oriented companies within the last ten years (see Figure 8.2). This supports the hypothesis that spillover of knowledge from the defense industry is low due to idiosyncratic features of national defense industries (see J. Schmid, 2017). Figure 8.2 further shows that the ratio-values are normally distributed between the people who have changed between civilian and defense sectors.

8.4.1   Churn Behavior between the Defense and Civilian Industries

The data shows three groups within the sample: group one (D) with the ratio $v = 1$, meaning that they have exclusively worked for defense companies (N = 257), group two (DC,), consisting of people that have predominantly worked in the defense sector ($v \geq 0.5$), and group three (C) of people that have worked more often in the civilian sector than the defense sector ($v < 0.5$) (see Figure 8.2). Among the persons who have worked at least once outside of the defense industry ($v < 1$), the values are almost normally distributed with a mean M of 0.49 and a standard deviation (SD) of 0.17 with a tendency towards positions in the civilian sector (see Figure 8.2). Thus, for further detailed analysis of significant variables on job changes, we categorized three groups: v(D) =1 (100% positions in the defense sector), v(DC) ≥ 0.5 (50% or more positions in the defense sector) and v(C) < 0.5 (more than 50% positions in the civilian sector). To test the hypothesis (H1), t-Tests for job changes and the ANOVA—in combination with post-hoc tests (Tukey's HSD-Test with Bonferroni correction) were conducted using R (Bühner & Ziegler, 2007; M. Luhmann, 2011). Testing for the significance of these differences, the ANOVA showed a significant result ($F(3,509)=18.13$, $p = 0.0071$, $\alpha = 0.05$). Thus, the job changes and the groups 1–3 correlate significantly overall. In line with the mean values for v(D) 3.242, v(C) 4.608, and v(DC) 4.019, the subsequent Tukey's test showed significant differences in job change behavior of group 1 (D) to both group 2 (DC) and 3 (C) ($p < 0.05$). Professionals change their jobs less often, the more positions they have had in the defense industry than in the civilian sector (Table 8.3).

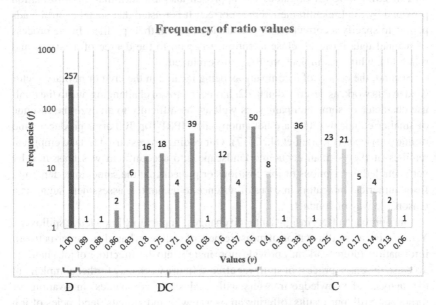

Figure 8.2 Frequency of ratio values v (N_{total} = 513, $M_{DC\,and\,C}$ = 0.49, $SD_{DC\,and\,C}$ = 0.17)

Table 8.3 Means and results of Tukey's test

D	DC	C	Variables	Difference	p
M = 3.24	M = 4.02	M = 4.61	C-D	1.37***	0.000
			DC-D	0.78***	0.000
			DC-C	−0.59*	0.031

8.4.2   Limitations of the Approach

The sample is focused on German companies and thus only representative for simi-larly structured economies (Verspagen, 1997). In addition, it is not known how many employees of the investigated companies are logged in to LinkedIn. To counteract this problem, only companies of which several thousand employees had profiles on LinkedIn, were investigated. The approach also assumes that the information provided by the LinkedIn members is correct. It is trusted that social control leads people to specify a correct employment biography in their profiles. In the process of manual data retrieval, close attention was paid to the degree of accuracy and reliability, while incomplete profiles were excluded.

Second, the coding of a company as being located in the civil or military sector used in this work, as described in 8.2.2, has been proven challenging due to the dual-use character of some companies, as well as the difficulty to analyze the revenue of smaller companies, that are not among the SIPRI Top 100 arms producers and military services (Fleurant et al., 2017). Our coding process tried to take empirical realities of the German economic landscape into account and was reassured by very detailed descriptions of job positions or projects. At the same time, departing from numerical indicators in cases of absence to qualitative assessment suggests a reasonable way of conduct.

Our approach offers insights into job changes, implicating knowledge spillovers. Yet, offering a first illustration of measurement of spillovers based on career-network information, future work may provide more insight into the directions of job changes. To grasp the entire process of spillover effects, future work may further complement the analysis of knowledge transfers with analysis of companies' innovations or turnovers. Still, our results, offering an overview of individuals' tendencies of job types as well as insights into correlations of groups and frequency of job changes, indicate that there is little evidence for spillovers from defense to civilian industries. Further, despite LinkedIn profiles showed standardized information regarding skills, it is not possible to derive points of time when an individual's knowledge, i.e., skills, did expand (e.g., after changing their job). Also, we could not quantify the amount of knowledge being transferred by job change. Although results indicate little knowledge transfer within the defense industry due to lower labor mobility, the concrete amount of knowledge may only be measured when taking the type of job changes (from one business area to another or within the same area of activity) into consideration. Thereby, it would be possible to retrieve users' job titles that have mainly stayed in their area of expertise as an indicator of a higher level of knowledge transfer. This may be due to employees changing their areas of activities to undergo a learning process and having fewer options to apply knowledge, at least when it comes to explicit, specific knowledge.

Additionally, one may consider the time span over which a job position was held to approach the amount of transferred knowledge. Approaching knowledge transfers from a temporal perspective requires the assessment of job titles and project changes. However, the privacy of the social network users needs to be protected, and even with anonymized datasets declaration of job titles, the combination of job changes or skills might lead to public identification of employees and their biographies (Hoser & Nitschke, 2010).

8.5   Comparison of the Approaches

This paper aims to answer the question *"What are the spillover effects that can be measured using career-network analysis?"* The empirical results of the churn rates between defense and civilian job positions in LinkedIn of 513 persons showed that the fewer people changed the industry, the less they changed job positions. This finding supports the hypothesis (H1) that spillovers are less likely between defense and civilian sectors and even indicates that churn rates in the defense sector are much lower than in the civilian sector. In the sample, we had a high rate of people only working in the defense sector (50%, Group D, see Figure 8.2), while the other half of the sample had a higher percentage of positions in defense companies (group DC, equal and more than 50% of their positions) and the other had a lower percentage (group C, less 50% of their positions).

Comparing our results of reluctant flow of defense innovation into the civilian sector to the patent study of Acosta, Coronado and Marín (Acosta et al., 2017), the results are similar: Germany has the second-highest rate of military registered patents (22% of all patents) worldwide. At the same time, the civilian use of these patents is rather low, with 16.8% of citations by other patents in civilian classifications (Acosta et al., 2011). The most cited kind of patents were dual-use patents. Therefore, in future research, SMA of companies that produce dual-use technologies may provide useful insights with respect to potentially critical knowledge spillovers.

The approach focuses on the embodiment of knowledge through human professionals that change their positions and share their knowledge within their teams. While this allows for an approximation of knowledge flows, it does not guarantee growth-inducing spillover. The evaluation of formal knowledge transfers by examining patent references (Acosta et al., 2011, 2017; Hur, 2017) necessarily excludes those that are informal and taking place through other institutional channels. With respect to the theoretical background of knowledge economies or industrial districts (Carbonara, 2018; Tappi, 2001), which are characterized by interactional relationships among actors, this work stands out in relation to patent analysis due to its empirical source of the social network LinkedIn. As a reliable representation of relevant industrial actors, envisaging the case as a network seems less constructed than rather abstract patent networks. It needs to be considered that sometimes, a patent citation is motivated by reasons other than relying on the formerly formulated knowledge. Further, there is always the option of secret patents, prohibiting insight into knowledge transfers between both civilian and defense industries, especially in defense research with national security interests (German Patent and Trade Mark Office, 2017). Compared to patent network analysis, an investigation of individuals' job movements does not exclude tacit knowledge a priori (Robertson & Jacobson, 2011). Detailed project descriptions on respective profiles reassured the knowledge-based character of jobs. Further, our study allows for an economically-interested analysis of civilian and defense enterprises. Usually, in patent analysis, the type of industry (civilian vs. defense) is operationalized according to the patent family, categorizing an invention as a weapon or as a technology for civilian use. In contrast, our approach includes not only the type of technology, considering a company's share of arms sales or main business activities. It also considers that knowledge transfer does not mainly takes place from one patented invention to the other, but that companies are the places where knowledge is created intra-organizationally and passed on to other socioeconomically embedded actors. With the assumption of working forces embodying both tacit and explicit knowledge, there is a legitimate focus on labor mobility with respect to spillover-inducing knowledge transfers.

8.6   Conclusion

In this work, it has been shown how spillover effects between defense and civilian sectors can be measured using social career-networks, such as LinkedIn. Our approach did not only confirm the assumption on churn behavior, but also provides insight into the networks of the professionals. Thus, social media analytics can be used for further network analysis, such as a skill-oriented approaches (Ramanath et al., 2018), the investigation of centrality of actors in networks (Mutschke, 2008), or users' contacts, among which (tacit) knowledge transfers may take place, e.g., during conversation or visits of same events (Leistner, 2012). Yet, Social Network Analysis of immediate relationships (Leistner, 2012), in contrast to connections via employing companies, yields research ethical controversies due to the analysis of data which might be taken out of the context of consent the users agreed to or even violate the privacy of the users (Hoser & Nitschke, 2010). In this regard, patent analysis proves to pose fewer challenges of ethical research as databases offering public access are well-known, and there is less focus on individual inventors, who are usually aware of the publication of their involvement (Bradbury, 2011). Thus, one may analyze patent information, including its content, to gain a deeper insight into the features of knowledge being transferred without potentially identifying individuals by analyzing their characteristic skills or biographies. Being aware of ethical issues regarding anonymity or informed consent is crucial conducting social media research (Quan-Haase & McCay-Peet, 2016); the latter offering new ways of approaching spillover dynamics based on knowledge transfer via social and job networks.

Dual-Use and Trustworthy? A Mixed Methods Analysis of AI Diffusion between Civilian and Defense R&D

9.1 Introduction

General consensus among ethics researchers underscores that as technologies based on Artificial Intelligence (AI) shape many aspects of our daily lives, necessary steps to be taken in technology development should include the assessment of risks and the implementation of safeguarding principles (Floridi et al., 2018; Taebi et al., 2019). AI is a general-purpose technology with manifold applications (Agrawal et al., 2018), and is considered a driver in emerging security-relevant technologies (Favaro, 2021). Further, China and the USA have joined the "global AI arms race" (Pecotic, 2019), indicating that they are ready to use AI for their military advantage. The prospect of proliferating autonomous weapon systems has not only convinced China and the USA but has also led other states to reevaluate their military advantage (Riebe, Schmid, & Reuter, 2020). These innovations are often developed in the private sector, increasingly permeate social spheres, and have a high dual-use potential (Meunier & Bellais, 2019).

ORIGINAL PUBLICATION Schmid, S., Riebe, T., & Reuter, C. (2022). Dual-Use and Trustworthy? A Mixed Methods Analysis of AI Diffusion Between Civilian and Defense R&D. *Science and Engineering Ethics, 28*(2), 1–23. https://doi.org/0.1007/s11948-022-00364-7

Supplementary Information The online version contains supplementary material available at https://doi.org/10.1007/978-3-658-41667-6_9.

Accurately assessing risks of a dual-use emerging technology is challenging. The technology might develop in unprecedented ways, it might be used by hostile actors or accidentally cause harm. Therefore, understanding the diffusion of innovations is a decisive factor in the development of tailored risk assessment, governance measures, and opportunities of intervention regarding unintended and unexpected outcomes of emerging technologies (Tucker, 2012; Winfield & Jirotka, 2018). Regarding AI, civilian actors appear to be more engaged in Research and Development (R&D) for commercial end-use than actors in the defense sector. This suggests that directions and centralities of technology diffusion may have changed towards a stronger use of commercial innovation by defense firms (Acosta et al., 2019). Approaching the diffusion of AI in European civilian and defense industries and its implications for responsible R&D, we pose the following question: *To what extent does AI diffusion occur in the EU and which patterns does it follow?*

We approach AI as a dual-use technology empirically and capture indications of envisaged trustworthiness in recent R&D as well. We investigate not only the extent of AI diffusion, which may already imply (ir)responsible R&D, but also norms that are diffused across civilian and military fields as well as normative patterns of AI R&D which may be indicated by values specific to the field of application (e.g., robustness for military applications vs. explainability for civilian applications).

Diffusion between military and civilian spheres implies that ethical guides such as the EU's *Trustworthy AI* should consider the values of both military and civilian AI. The number of weaponry patents building on AI (G06N) patents is a measure of diffusion between spheres, as well as knowledge transfers between companies. Responsible R&D is characterized by awareness of technological development, and identification and regulation of unintended developments. Our mixed-methods approach draws on a combination of patent citation network analysis and qualitative content analysis. The quantitative analysis of AI diffusion is based on patents from EU member countries, which as such are commonly studied to approach innovations and knowledge transfers (Lupu et al., 2011). The qualitative content analysis, capturing specific values that are translated into military and civilian AI applications, focuses on projects of a German research institute dedicated to dual-use research (Fraunhofer IOSB, 2020). After presenting related work, as well as our methodological approach, we proceed to outline our findings. These are subsequently discussed regarding dual-use assessment and with reference to *Trustworthy AI*, which represents an approach of responsible R&D of AI, followed by a conclusion.

9.2   Related Work and Theoretical Background

9.2.1   Responsible R&D of Dual-Use Technologies

Commercial dual-use technologies have been discussed as a security matter and issue of risk assessment (Harris, 2016; Tucker, 2012). Research has examined the impact of defense innovations on civilian and commercial end-use, such as the invention of the internet (Mowery & Simcoe, 2002). By highlighting high-risk scenarios that do not impact military but rather civilian actors, the conception of dual-use technology has recently shifted towards being framed based on their socially "beneficial" or "harmful" (Brundage et al., 2018; Olteanu et al., 2015) or "good" and "malicious" purposes (Floridi et al., 2018). Recent understandings mainly focus on such purposes and (non-state vs. state) actors. Accordingly and focused on the character of the item only, Forge (2010) distinguishes between artefacts that are either purpose-built or improvised weapons. These considerations have prompted normatively oriented debates about dual-use and how to assess risks of emerging technologies while researchers and developers lack knowledge on future use and deployment of technologies (Grunwald, 2000). Our approach to capture AI R&D considers these various understandings and aims to set the foundation for a responsible assessment of dual-use research of concern (Evans, 2014; Riebe & Reuter, 2019).

The European patent network of AI inventions mainly considers whether such an invention belongs to the patent classification of weaponry (F41, F42). As this classification does not, however, take the context in which such inventions might be developed into consideration, we specifically take actors' economic activity in the defense industry into account to determine either civilian or military use. We also follow this broader view on dual-use technology as applied both for defense and civilian reasons (by respective actors) when conducting the qualitative analysis of a research institute's knowledge production. Thereby, we look for values of *Trustworthy AI* which may or may not be apparent in military and civilian applications and thus synthesize the assessment of dual-use technology with more recent, general ethical requirements. Determining the technology-specific characteristics of dual-use early in the process of R&D is part of the iterative process of technology assessment (TA) to further establish measures and to balance "risks and benefits" (Tucker, 2012).

9.2.2   EU Trustworthy AI Principles

Trust and trustworthiness have previously been discussed focusing on interactions among both autonomous and human agents (Taddeo, 2010; Wagner & Arkin, 2011). Trustworthiness is understood as "the guarantee required by the trustor that the trustee will act as it is expected to do without any supervision" (Taddeo, 2010). Further, trust is defined as in the following:

> "If the trustor chooses to achieve its goal by the action performed by the trustee, and if the trustor considers the trustee a trustworthy agent, then the relation has the property of being advantageous for the trustor. Such a property [...] is called trust" (Taddeo, 2010).

Concerning AI's potential to secure systems from cyberattacks, Taddeo et al. (2019) argue that trust is unwarranted due to vulnerabilities, while reliance on AI indicates "some form of control over the execution of a given task". Tavani (2018) stresses that relational approaches, which are more interested in technology's appearance to humans than its properties, may consider the diverse and diffuse relationships defining trust. People may forget that they are dealing with artificial agents (Taddeo, 2017), which is only remembered "when something goes (badly) wrong". In this regard, the question has been raised whether artificial agents, including military drones, should imitate human characteristics like empathy or the feeling of guilt (Arkin, Ulam, & Wagner, 2012). The research towards mimicking humans and human behavior has been criticized by Grodzinsky et al. (2011) as accurate identification of agents may determine trust. They further stress that self-modification of artificial agents poses high risks for public safety. Therefore, the loss of human control in interaction with artificial agents which mimic well-known human behavior may carry more risks than advantages for the trustor.

Public trust can be achieved through the establishment of ethical codes, responsible practices, and procedures that ensure ethically aligned governance of technology (Winfield & Jirotka, 2018). Nissenbaum (2001) has argued that trustworthiness is crucial for the acceptance of technology by referring to N. Luhmann (1979) understanding of trust as a "mechanism for reducing complexity". As such Nissenbaum (2001) argues that trust allows for "creative, political, unusual, [...] possibly profane, [...] risky modes and activities" to flourish in a loosely secured cyberspace. Thereby, she emphasizes trust's productive nature which allows for the adoption of AI in various fields of application (ibid.). While trust may facilitate procedures, substantial guides such as *Trustworthy AI* which formulate requirements do not simplify human engagement. Instead, they may indicate regulation (and securitization) efforts which allow for the establishment of trust in the first place.

While *Trustworthy AI* is one of the most important documents by the EU in this regard, overviews of institutional guidelines echo common vocabulary and the direction of recent guidelines. Roberts et al. (2021) investigate the 2017 "New generation artificial intelligence development plan" and highlight socio-political conditions which may have shaped China's AI strategy. Although an important actor, China had at first only seldomly engaged in ethical debates regarding AI but is now propagating shared values of AI R&D, such as human well-being, fairness, and transparency (Roberts et al., 2021). Similar to other relevant actors in AI innovation, it has started to raise ethical questions about AI R&D. Thiebes et al. (2020) have compared current approaches of trustworthy AI, highlighting requirements like robustness, lawfulness, as well as various principles (e.g., beneficence), which summarize the core values of different ethical frameworks on AI (Hagendorff, 2020; Thiebes et al., 2020). Our work adopts this perspective on diffusion of AI by contextualizing it as a dual-use technology which is supposed to meet normative, albeit differently defined, criteria of trustworthiness.

The "Ethics Guidelines for *Trustworthy AI*" (European Commission, 2019) were published in 2019 and comprise legal, ethical, and technical pillars. While the expert group highlights the importance of the three pillars, the guideline itself heavily focuses on the second and third dimensions (European Commission, 2019).[1] may be reflected at the institutional and technological level (European Commission, 2019). Representing norms, the document also provides a set of criteria for TA by developers and end-users (European Commission, 2019). In our study, we include the most relevant values and summarize some of them thematically. For the analysis, we follow the Value-Sensitive Design (VSD) approach, which is interested in deriving values from human-technology interaction[2] (Cummings, 2006). The EU guideline deviates from a traditional understanding of dual-use and stresses the differentiation between beneficial and malicious use (European Commission, 2019),

---

[1] The associated values can be viewed in Appendix 16.1 in the electronic supplementary material.

[2] For exemplifying works building on VSD in their analysis of military AI, see Umbrello (Umbrello, 2019b; Umbrello & De Bellis, 2018) or (Verdiesen, 2017a).

referring to a publication by Brundage et al. (2018). This corresponds to the recent R&D policy of the EU, aiming for synergies between civilian and military knowledge production and application (Edler & James, 2015; European Commission, 2015; Uttley, 2019).

9.2.3 Knowledge Diffusion of AI

To capture AI development, political actors have conducted analyses relying on different measurements. This includes a focus on citations and keywords of patents and scientific literature as well as analysis of open source software. Insights into processes as well as spatial and temporal frames of R&D have become crucial for governments which are engaged in funding AI innovation (Baruffaldi et al., 2020). Patent data serves as an indicator for applied knowledge or technological innovation (Lupu et al., 2011; Meunier & Bellais, 2019), as patents demonstrate intellectual property of inventions while citation networks indicate diffusion of purposeful, codified knowledge (W. Liu et al., 2019; Pereira & Quoniam, 2017). It should also be noted that AI is a contentious term contouring different techniques (Cady, 2017; Goodfellow et al., 2016; Klinger et al., 2018).

Interested in the diffusion of AI in both the EU's civilian and defense spheres, our work is inspired by the extensive body of patent analyses and thereby adopts a relatively classic approach of innovation research as a first step. Zambetti et al. (2018) conducted a patent network analysis focusing on machine learning (ML) and AI-related techniques to examine relevant industrial players. They show how ML-related technologies are mostly driven by software companies but also spread to other sectors. This has led to the 4th industrial revolution, as companies can invest in capitalizing their data and analytic capabilities (Zambetti et al., 2018). However, these contributions do not distinguish between defense and civilian industries, and either omit or do not entirely consider the ethical questions of AI diffusion.

Other patent analyses interested in defense economics or arms control have specifically concentrated on warfare technologies, such as drones, ammunition, or radar technology, and looked at the extent of diffusion or tested explanatory hypotheses on the impact of defense R&D funding (Acosta et al., 2011, 2013, 2017, 2019; Meunier & Bellais, 2019; S. Schmid et al., 2022). Our study on AI diffusion ties in with existing works on dual-use technology and comprises patent analysis. However, as other arenas of knowledge transfer need to be considered as well, we accompany this approach with a qualitative analysis of knowledge diffusion, referring to the EU guide *Trustworthy AI*.

9.3   Research Design

9.3.1   Patent Analysis: The Case of AI

AI may be part of computer-implemented inventions (Okakita, 2019) and thereby fall under a patentable subject matter, which can be distinguished from discoveries, scientific theories, mathematical methods and "mental processes" by its "technical character". This implies a "'further technical effect', which goes beyond the 'normal' 'physical' interactions between the program (software) and the computer (hardware)" (European Patent Office, 2021b; Okakita, 2019). This understanding is prevalent across patent offices, such as within the European Patent Organization (EPO), and the US Patent and Trademark Office (USTPO) (Okakita, 2019). Further, inventions must be novel and applicable to a specific industrial area (WIPO, 2019). This includes, e.g., "the use of a neural network in a heart-monitoring apparatus for the purpose of identifying irregular heartbeats" or new classification systems (Okakita, 2019). The standards for patent eligibility might also change due to the rise of AI and the need for patent regulation to adopt to them. In 2018, the EPO published a new guideline on ML and AI, which was criticized as it did not acknowledge AI and ML the same way as other highly abstract areas, such as encryption (European Patent Office, 2021a; Korenberg & Hamer, 2018). In the context of military applications, due to their confidential nature, innovations may not always be published as patents, while economic disadvantages may prevail as well (J. Schmid, 2017; Urquhart & Sullivan, 2020).

In our research design, we follow existing studies which have focused AI's patentability and its inventiveness (Okakita, 2019). We therefore focus on the CPC class G06N[3] of "systems based on special computational models", with sub-classes like "artificial life" or "computer systems based on biological models" (CPC, 2019) and build on previous work which has focused more broadly on G06 patents in their investigation of innovation spillovers regarding unmanned aerial vehicles (UAVs) (Kim et al., 2016). Here, patent information, comprising publication date, country, back and forward citations, applicants, and thematic classifications, provide the foundation for quantitative investigation of cross-country knowledge diffusion. The patent analysis also includes an exploration of company networks. It focuses on German patents, with Germany being an important market for both AI and weaponry, reflected by a large German share of the European sample. We thus focus on the

---

[3] For example, an invention by Amazon Technologies, Inc. falls under the category G06N. Callari et al. (2021) present techniques for managing a group of autonomous vehicles (AVs) to perform delivery tasks and thereby also rely on other G06N patents.

most populated and economically strongest country in the EU. While the EU constitutes an important norm-setting actor, Germany plays an important role in the EU as a civilian power (Cath, 2018; Koenig, 2020).

9.3.2   Research Bodies: Arenas of Knowledge Diffusion

Since the focus of our quantitative analysis lies on company networks in Germany and German patents, and considering that diffusion may also take place without patenting inventions, our qualitative analysis focuses on the normative patterns of AI diffusion on research projects of the German research institute Fraunhofer Institute of Optronics, System Technologies and Image Exploitation IOSB. The institute belongs to a prestigious group of Fraunhofer institutes and is one of the main scientific actors regarding research on military applications in Germany (Fraunhofer IOSB, 2020; German Federal Ministry of Defense, 2017). Fraunhofer IOSB encompasses both civilian and military business units (Fraunhofer IOSB, 2020), in which relevant knowledge for AI applications is produced. The text documents selected for this analysis imply inter-organizational knowledge transfers between the Fraunhofer IOSB, the German Ministry of Defense, and Armed Forces. They reflect knowledge of specific military AI applications, produced in close cooperation with military actors and sometimes transferred intra-organizationally (Fraunhofer IOSB, 2018). This allows a comparison of projects regarding both civilian and military applications of AI.

9.3.3   Data Collection

To conduct the statistical part of the analysis, we retrieved data from the EU patent database Espacenet. Interested in the recent developments of diffusion, we limited our search to patents from January 1, 2008, to June 1, 2018. We collected data based on all country codes of EU member states and the patent classifications of AI (G06N) as well as ammunition and weaponry (F41, F42). This resulted in a data set compromising 5,365 patents, with weaponry-related patents representing military and AI patents constituting civilian inventions. The sample was then reduced to patents that cited other patents, reducing the sample to 724 patents with a total of 2,438 patent citations (see Figure 9.1). The second step of the analysis focused on the specific type of AI diffusion and allowed insights into the R&D of AI applications. We selected 13 documents, all of which were freely accessible online via the Fraunhofer IOSB homepage. The corpus of different types of documents reflects both military and civilian applications, as well as different conceptual and techno-logical levels of detail, ranging from web pages with project descriptions, flyers to scientific publications of all business areas.[4] They allow a deeper and balanced, yet not representative insight into R&D of AI applications.

9.3.4   Data Analysis

For the data analysis, we chose a mixed-methods approach (see Figure 9.1). This two-step analysis can shed light on the various fractions of how diffusion of AI has taken place, including the patterns it follows. We conducted descriptive statistics in Microsoft Excel. Further, we constructed two networks in RStudio, both based on our data set, one focusing on links between patent classifications and the other among German patent applicants. Our work follows the logic of patent network analysis, where relevant entities form nodes connected by patent citations. For the qualitative analysis, we performed a content analysis   (Flick, 2014; Gray et al., 2007). The code categories and (sub-)codes were developed abductively, inspired by the EU's formulation of *Trustworthy AI* and related scholarly works as well as based on the empirical material of Fraunhofer IOSB. Frequencies of words were examined through text mining. While this qualitative part of our work does not

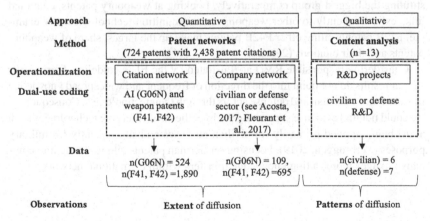

Figure 9.1 Mixed-methods research design, data and observations

---

[4] The corpus of documents can be viewed in Appendix 16.1 in the electronic supplementary material.

constitute a representative study and only specifically refers to a few documents, we used all selected documents for the quantification of results.

9.4   Analysis

9.4.1   Quantitative Analysis: Patent Citation Networks

Our study of patent information comprises the analysis of a patent citation network based on the patent groups of weaponry and AI and a subsequent focus on German patents and relationships between involved companies.

European Network Based on Patent Classes
We assumed CPC classes[5] to constitute nodes, while edges were determined by patent citations. Our data set contains 2,438 patent citations, including 24 of unknown origin. While 524 patents are cited by AI patents, 1,890 patents are cited by weaponry patents. Most of the patents referred to patents of the same CPC class.[6] Since we are particularly interested in linkages representing knowledge transfers across the fields of weapons and ammunition (F41, F42) and special computational systems (G06N), we note that there is no such transfer-representative patent citation. Among AI patents, however, 14.6% of the patents cited other G06N patents, constituting the biggest group comparatively. Looking at weaponry patents, citational links exist frequently to other weapons and ammunition technologies. For example, F42B patents citing other F42B patents make up the largest share of weaponry patents and their citations (23.6%).

Considering responsible R&D as illustrated by the EU's guideline *Trustworthy AI*, our results do not point into the direction of frequent and widespread knowledge transfer among civilian and defense actors through their technologies. Consequently, we could not find evidence supporting the hypothesis of emerging technologies such as AI being applied primarily for civilian purposes and subsequently for military purposes (Verbruggen, 2019). Focusing on German patents allows diving into company linkages representing knowledge transfers within the national network.

---

[5] Groups of patents were defined according to the Cooperative Patent Classification (CPC) system https://www.cooperativepatentclassification.org/index.
[6] The associated data can be viewed in Appendix 16.1 in the electronic supplementary material.

The German Company Network

Taking a closer look at German patents, knowledge transfers between defense and civilian industries can be approached apart from solely relying on the CPC system. We assume companies as applicants of patents to be the driving actors for inventions. Therefore, we reconfigured a network based on companies as nodes, while one company is linked to another company by citing at least one patent of the respective applicant. In the interests of precision, we concentrated on German patents and their cited patents from companies occurring more than once in the sample.

An operationalization approach guided less by classifications assumes that certain companies might remain very active in the defense industry, despite not formally considering filing a patent application. Following the Stockholm International Peace Research Institute's (SIPRI) Top 100 list of companies in arms sales, these companies can be categorized as part of the defense industrial sector (Acosta et al., 2017; Fleurant et al., 2017). Even though many of the companies are mainly active in other industrial sectors such as aviation and aerospace, producing revenue of more than $840m. per year in the defense sector allows these companies to specialize in R&D of defense technology and consequently compete with other actors in this regard (Riebe, Schmid, & Reuter, 2021). Other companies are labeled as a military company if their share of arms sales represents more than 50% of total sales. In case no figures are available and qualitative analysis is applied to determine whether most of the produced[7] goods' business areas are part of the defense industry. This allows to re-illustrate German companies' relationships in form of a network.[8]

The analysis of the patent citation shows almost no diffusion between civilian and military companies. Most AI patents are based on interactions between civilian entities, with only one citation pair among defense companies (Airbus citing Lockheed Martin). Additionally, there are three patent pairs with civilian actors that cite patents from defense companies. Another 72 pairs of citing and cited weaponry patents are from companies that usually produce for civilian markets The prevalence

---

[7] Following Riebe, Schmid, and Reuter (2021), a company's website and respective insight into its business areas, range of products, or alliance of cooperation partners proves helpful. If a company is not included in the SIRPI Top 100 arms selling companies list and most of its sales lies within the civilian industries, it is defined as "civilian". An ideal type of a dual-use company is defined by equal (50:50) share of civilian and defense sales. While suppliers for military infrastructure like telecommunication may also have industrial contracts with national governments, we focused on companies that are involved in the production of weapon systems.

[8] The associated data can be viewed in Appendix 16.1 in the electronic supplementary material.

of defense actors is evident in the large number of weaponry patents. The most active applicants rely on actors of the same type or mostly on themselves. For example, Rheinmetall has cited 231 of its own patents. The concept of *Trustworthy AI* generally highlights the importance of corporate ethical requirements and potentially unintended consequences (European Commission, 2019). However, it disregards the relevance of industrial civilian-defense sector ties or the dual-use activities of companies. Further, we shed light on research projects that entail the diffusion of AI across civilian and defense spheres. In contrast to the quantitative approach, the qualitative approach allows us to gain a more concrete picture of how AI diffusion takes place, illustrating which values of trustworthiness are incorporated into the technology and are revealed in human interactions with AI.

9.4.2   Qualitative Analysis

Trustworthiness of Military AI Applications
Robustness, accuracy, and information quality seem to be apparent values which support *Trustworthy AI,* when considering military purposes. This does not mean that these norms are entirely absent when it comes to civilian AI applications. Instead, our analysis indicates that they are relatively more prevalent in the military context Thus, as a value, *robustness* is comparatively more significant in the context of military (D11) applications, including resilience as an important standard (D10). Further, *accuracy* is particularly important in the context of military applications, including transparency on problems of inaccuracy:

> "Although the RMS [root mean square; author's note] errors for building reconstruction
> [...] indicate that our method provides reasonable geometrical *accuracies* (height error
> is the same as for single points if the parallax accuracy is about one image pixel), the
> results in building detection are *less precise*." (D12.; own emp.)

Similarly, the EU guideline stresses the importance of the technical values of robustness and accuracy. These relate to both safety and security, which are crucial in warfare scenarios. Military AI applications may support standards of *Trustworthy AI,* paying special attention to robustness and accuracy (European Commission, 2019) in more critical contexts. This reflects the potential to ensure security as proposed by the EU guideline (European Commission, 2019), while also indicating the technology's possible normative ambiguity regarding general human and environmental well-being. *Information quality* has also been relatively more important for military (D1) applications. Given the high stake of a military operation, errors due to low information quality may have a greater impact on people, e.g., by mistaking civilian infrastructure for military bases or by falsely engaging civilians as combatants.

Trustworthiness of Civilian AI Applications
At the same time, there is a comparatively stronger interest in civilian projects in *awareness*, indicating the importance of capturing the environment in all its complexity. For example, SPARC, a project on autonomous driving in urban traffic, relies heavily on orientation in the context of moving and directing surrounding objects, opting for a "holistic representation" (D3), while at the same time training data is focused on "eventful [...] and [...] unique situations" (D13). Whether in terms of space, time, or speed, there is a strong reference to environmental information. This is surprising, as situational awareness is not only stressed by the EU (European Commission, 2019) but is mostly apparent in military contexts.

Overall, civilian applications emphasize the relevance of *explainability*, which is referred to as "retaining many of the advantages of variational trajectory optimization methods, in particular *expressiveness*" (D11; own emphasis). Others underline that "[t]he ability for humans to understand the reasoning process is essential to the presented case study" (D13). This highlights the ambivalence of explainability as a normative concept. While it may be defined as the ability to explain, interpretability, namely the ability to provide (grounds for) an interpretation, is often associated with the concept of explainability, as it is also the case in the *Trustworthy AI* guide (European Commission, 2019). This requirement for civilian applications may be plausible, should special attention be paid to a broader and more diverse group of end-users. This becomes particularly apparent considering that the project on autonomous driving in cities (D11) stresses explainability (or expressiveness) the most.

It should be noted that both *security and safety* were also qualitatively deduced regarding military applications, indicating human-centric approaches albeit in different terms. Human dignity, implying human-centric approaches, represents one of the core values of *Trustworthy AI* (European Commission, 2019). Such statements are more common in the context of civilian applications; as they apply AI applications that put focus on human reasoning, hand gestures, or the human body Military applications accordingly reflect less interest in a precise analysis of the social or intimate environment. Yet, a strong focus on people's movements or behavior does not necessarily imply the implementation of a human-centric AI in terms of human dignity or personal rights.

Diffused Values across Civilian and Military Applications
Regardless of the field of application, the authors of scientific publications were *transparent* about procedural problems. In contrast, AI was depicted relatively flawless in online presentations of projects or product flyers. This may be due to the nature of scholarly debates, supporting values such as transparency (of problems). Problematic issues were not made transparent in shorter, more easily accessible online contributions, while such documents contained more direct references to economic merits. The European expert group's guide would suggest presenting complex, inconvenient facts to a broader audience and allow for understandability independent from personal background (European Commission, 2019). Furthermore, the figurative alignment of AI and animal behavior became visible. AI projects were oriented towards phenomena in nature, for example in the development of "swarms" of UAVs or processing as in an "ant colony" (D10). AI was also designed to imitate the human essence. This is reflected in notions about the AI's self and its abilities *Trustworthy AI* refers to approaches such as values-by-design, implying a certain degree of technological agency   (European Commission, 2019). However, Fraunhofer projects do not reflect the awareness of such interactional approaches or non-human agency. While projects indicate anthropomorphization of AI as well as bionic models, they do not guarantee trustworthiness based on environmental awareness.

9.5   Discussion

9.5.1   Implications for Dual-use Assessment

The patent citation network analyses did not indicate direct diffusion of AI into patents for weapons and ammunition (F41, F42). This contradicts hypotheses stating that AI diffuses relatively easily from civilian to military industries due to its innovative and intangible nature (Acosta et al., 2019; Gill, 2019; Reppy, 2006; Shields, 2018). While inventions of weaponry mainly rely on other patents of the same field, they have also benefited from patents of civilian categories in the past. However, most of citations and cross references are found within the same patent category.

As pointed out in an interview with the Patent and Brands Center Rhein-Main, there is always the option of classified patenting (2019, personal communication). Looking at the patent networks, AI diffusion across defense and civilian fields is low and could only be observed within individual organizations. Drawing from this, TA, which aims at prospective knowledge for responsible R&D, should focus on other spaces of knowledge transfer among businesses and research bodies instead of patent regimes. In general, regulation through the publication of patents may generate trust. While we do not share the dichotomous perspective of unregulated trust relationships vs. highly regulated ones (Nissenbaum, 2001), we follow the idea of trust allowing for "risky" modes of behavior. To create relationships based on trust, regulatory efforts such as TA that focus on the diffusion of foundational knowledge of research may be necessary in the first place. In this context, the case of Europe is very interesting as the EU tries to incentivize synergies between defense and civilian industries to increase competitiveness of the defense and security sector (Edler & James, 2015; European Commission, 2013; Uttley, 2019). At the same time, the EU has fostered research to monitor the diffusion of dual-use innovations, to understand the networks and technological developments.[9] Dual-use research of concern has provided approaches of risk assessment for individual researchers and organizations (Evans, 2014; Tucker, 2012), such as raising awareness, defining norms and supporting public discourse on technology related risks and possible future developments of socio-technical systems (Grunwald, 2020). Coeckelbergh (2020) has developed the discussion of distributed responsibility further by discussing a relational framework, making AI experts responsible for risk communication. Winfield and Jirotka (2018) showed a framework for ethical governance of AI and robotics companies, in which a network of regulatory bodies, regulations, and verification work together to build public trust. However, the discourse on effective yet flexible regulations and norms is still ongoing. In the following, we consider implications for *Trustworthy AI* regarding dual-use research.

9.5.2 Implications for Trustworthy AI

The parallel increase in scientific publications on AI (WIPO, 2019) allows to highlight an additional focus on innovation diffusion by knowledge transfers in applied research. In this regard, the patterns of values reflecting responsible R&D, i.e., *Trustworthy AI* may be identified depending on the specific field of application or diffused across technologies. While differentiating between beneficial and malicious usage of AI may prove valuable in assessing the societal impact of an application (Brundage et al., 2018), a stronger focus on AI as a dual-use technology applicable for both

---

[9] As part of their strategy to monitor emerging technology in security critical and dual-use areas, the EU has supported the development of the TIM Dual-use data mining tool, which uses scientific texts, like abstracts, patents, and EU project description to map the network of dual-use relevant innovation hubs (https://knowledge4policy.ec.europa.eu/text-mining/tim-dual-use_en).

civilian and defense purposes allows considering applications that have a decisive impact on human life. Such applications include the automated surveillance and analysis of people to gain intelligence information as well as automated functions in armed systems to engage selected targets.

Design approaches referred to in the EU guide and other studies ((European Commission, 2019; Umbrello & De Bellis, 2018) offer possibilities for appropriate implementation. As an umbrella organization of research institutes, Fraunhofer has incorporated interdisciplinary work (Marzi et al., 2018). However, concerning the studied research groups, the documents did not suggest room for a diverse discourse in favor of a *Trustworthy AI*, which would promote further deliberations (European Commission, 2019) on trust, the anthropomorphization of AI (Ryan, 2020), and general acceptance of AI technologies (Winfield & Jirotka, 2018). A transparency report, as suggested by Winfield and Jirotka (2018), could include a statement on results that may be difficult to interpret, as well as a reflection on institutional contexts and diverse societal effects of implementation. Additionally, the different approaches towards trust and moral decision-making by artificial agents (Arkin, Ulam, & Wagner, 2012) may become an increasingly important issue for TA. *Trustworthy AI* might benefit from encouraging discussions about concrete procedures for fruitful interdisciplinary work and clarification of contextual conditions, such as economic competitiveness in the application of ethics. Interpreting the different values of civilian and military AI applications suggests that *Trustworthy AI* is more consistent when the diversity of contexts is included. As *Trustworthy AI* is considered a "horizontal foundation to facilitate the development of trustworthy innovation, the EU suggested to add "sectorial" perspectives to adjust to the context-specificity of AI systems (European Commission, 2019). To assess the diffusion of innovation the context needs to be considered, while expanding the focus on related sectors. Prioritization of values differs regarding the context of application. This influences the diffusion of innovation as adjustments to other requirements have to be made but more significantly, as values are inscribed in the technology. While we illustrate how the prevalence of values may differ across fields of application, we do not propose that they are exclusive to specific sectors. Instead, our study proposes a vantage point for future research on norm emergence such as dual-use focused TA, potentially including stakeholder analysis.

Finally, our study indicates that some of the values are closely associated, such as explainability and interpretability or well-being, safety, and security. Thiebes et al. (2020) propose five principles of trustworthy AI, offering a synthesis of relevant values or requirements of ethical frameworks, such as in the EU guide (European Commission, 2019). While there is indeed common ground regarding relevant values that influence relationships of trust, our analysis emphasizes the importance of finding a common language and clarifying the existence of divergent understandings that may prevail across different national frameworks, albeit references to the same labels (Roberts et al., 2021).

9.5.3 Limitations

As we focus specifically on AI patents, we did not include patents for advanced robotics of the class B64G 2001 (USPTO, 2019) or other commercial areas (e.g., aviation and aerospace), and therefore limited the sample to G06N patents. In addition, our sample only includes patents that cited at least one other patent, which is further limited by a focus on German patents for reasons of clarity. Even though the EU is one of the most active regions with regard to filing patents, especially in the AI field, many more patents are filed in Japan, the US, and China (Baruffaldi et al., 2020), thereby limiting the scope of this study and its implications to the EU with a focus on German R&D. Furthermore, certain innovations may be protected by secret patents and others may be subject to trade secrets or copyrights, or refrain from patent registration due to complicated analysis of territorial eligibility (Tiedrich et al., 2020). Companies may remain competitive, using Machine Learning as a service instead of developing their own applications (Guthrie, 2019).

9.6 Conclusion

AI is seen as a general-purpose technology, and the study of the patterns of diffusion of innovation between civilian and defense applications is relevant not only for TA but also regarding normative concepts that influence the R&D of AI, such as *Trustworthy AI*. As a mixed method approach, we conducted a patent citation network analysis in the first step. Considering member states of the EU as well as defense and civilian contexts of application, this work studied innovation transfers between AI and weaponry patents and took company relations into account. While the patent citation network did not show any diffusion between weaponry patents and AI, the close-up on the German company network revealed that a few defense companies publish both AI and weaponry patents, which might also be due to their dual-use products. As the second part, the qualitative analysis of technology descriptions of both civilian and defense R&D projects of the Fraunhofer IOSB, allows reevaluating established measurements and playgrounds of technological diffusion. The diffusion of trustworthy AI norms between defense and civilian R&D projects revealed the hierarchical context-specific application of certain *Trustworthy*

AI norms, such as robustness and accuracy for defense projects and explainability for civilian projects. While attention is paid to R&D of AI, both economically and politically, it is relevant to gain insight into this development and to establish methods for its tailored dual-use and risk assessment and awareness measures to prevent unintended outcomes (Tucker, 2012; Winfield & Jirotka, 2018). Advanced and further work may address the political context of *Trustworthy AI* and accompany EU strategies of fostering the development of dual-use technologies, with a focus on economic synergies (Edler & James, 2015).

Meaningful Human Control of LAWS: The CCW-Debate and its Implications for Value-Sensitive Design

10

10.1 Introduction

The debate on the development and deployment of lethal autonomous weapon systems (LAWS) as an emerging technology is of increasing importance, with discussions stalling and technological development progressing. Monitoring the progress of increasingly autonomous weapons systems in civilian and military use (Riebe, Schmid, & Reuter, 2020), as well as regulating possible autonomous systems early on, is demanded by civil society actors, like the Campaign to Stop Killer Robots and the International Red Cross, while nation states follow a variety of interests and strategies, showing little room for consensus on central terms and questions (Ekelhof, 2017; Rosert & Sauer, 2020). This article therefore sheds light on the work of the Group of Governmental Experts (GGE) of the UN Convention of Certain Conventional Weapons (CCW). The CCW, offering an arena for international cooperation, has dedicated itself to the purpose of finding a common ground with respect to an understanding of LAWS as well as the necessary degree of human control. From an ethical perspective, the concept of Meaningful Human Control (MHC) supports a

ORIGINAL PUBLICATION Riebe, T., Schmid, S., & Reuter, C. (2020). Meaningful Human Control of Lethal Autonomous Weapon System: The CCW Debate and its Implications for Value-Sensitive Design. *IEEE Technology and Society Magazine, 39*(4), 36–51. https://doi.org/10.1109/MTS.2020.3031846

Supplementary Information The online version contains supplementary material available at https://doi.org/10.1007/978-3-658-41667-6_10.

human-centric approach. Several IEEE projects, series and publications (Adamson et al., 2019) are dedicated to this prioritization, especially regarding civilian use. As autonomous technology is increasingly at the center of contemporary military innovations, questions of (human) agency and responsibility in warfare have become even more pressing (Hellström, 2013). As stressed by the United Nations Institute for Disarmament Research (UNIDIR), the concept of MHC may prove useful in the context of development and use of (semi-) autonomous weaponry (UNIDIR, 2014).

Acknowledging the need for a multidisciplinary approach (Boulanin, 2016), we present our analysis of the respective CCW discourse as a first step towards answering the question of how to ensure MHC in the interaction with LAWS. Asking for factors supporting the implementation of MHC, we look for values and underlying, more abstract discourses which may converge with the idea of MHC. The identification of such values and dominant discursive narratives may contribute to a better understanding of the political, ethical, legal and technological requirements for MHC, a concept which has been introduced in both political and legal debates to allow for improved regulation of the use of force in armed conflicts (Meier, 2016). The regulation of certain conventional weapons which are considered especially injurious or indiscriminative, such as landmines and blinding lasers, is part of the protocols of the UN CCW. However, in the past, the effectiveness of the CCW has been called into question in light of Cold War politics (Carvin, 2017), consensual decision-making, or difficulties in advancing arms control in the context of humanitarian and military arguments (Cottrell, 2009). Beside these difficulties, the CCW has helped set relevant norms of arms control in the past and may so with regards to the regulation of LAWS (Bode & Huelss, 2018).

First, we give an overview of related work and identified research gaps. In the following, we elaborate our theoretical perspective, inspired by Value-Sensitive Design (VSD). Further, we offer insights into the research design, i.e., our sample of 43 CCW documents and discourse analysis as the method used. Subsequently, the results of the analysis are presented. Our focus lies on the CCW's prevalent understanding of autonomy and LAWS as well as on control, particularly concerning MHC in human-computer interaction. These conceptual clarifications are necessary foundational work for retaining human control of LAWS. Then, we give an overview of identified values with respect to the interaction with LAWS technology, putting them into relation with MHC as well as with each other. To gain a deeper understanding of the crucial values, we illustrate correlations between respective values and dominant discourses, which may not always support an implementation of MHC. The work is concluded by a formulation of implications, a discussion of results, and an outlook.

10.2 Related Work

Scholars of various disciplines are dedicated to LAWS and the question of human control. Most works focus on autonomous weapons from a legal perspective with regard to international humanitarian law (IHL). Crootof (2016), focusing on the applicability of international humanitarian law and accountability, reflects on the inherent imprecision of the concept of MHC, while stressing the need to interpret the evolving norm as convergent with existing international law. Anderson (K. Anderson, 2016; K. Anderson & Waxman, 2013; K. Anderson et al., 2014) elaborates on the applicability of the law of armed conflict on emerging technologies and explicitly argues against a ban of LAWS. Walker-Smith (2016), concentrating on MHC, criticizes a human-biased view by pointing out that autonomous weapon systems can potentially limit lethal human behavior. Walsh (2015) notices a concomitant shift of accountability with the development of LAWS, increasingly including designers and programmers. Yet, these legal debates are often characterized by repetitive arguments, echoing difficulties regarding legal accountability while stressing the merit of existing international humanitarian law principles.

Ethical contributions stress that the technological advances towards more autonomous functions and systems, which are increasingly interacting with humans, need to be designed with more attention towards responsibility (Umbrello, 2019a; Umbrello, 2019a), control (de Sio & van den Hoven, 2018), and effects on human dignity (A. Sharkey, 2019), thus arguing to limit the possible consequences on the lives of affected people (Datenethikkommission, 2019; Zweig, 2019). Scholars of ethics agree that LAWS run counter the principle of human dignity as only humans can be moral agents that can take live-affecting decisions and be held accountable (Amoroso & Tamburrini, 2019; A. Sharkey, 2019). Sharkey (2016) introduces a classification system of human supervisory control, which is adapted by Amoroso and Tamburrini (2019), putting it into relation with the concept of MHC, as well as by Weber and Suchman (2016), who focus on autonomy of human-machine configurations. Ekelhof (2019, 2018) asks for the feasibility of operational implementation of MHC, suggesting other ideas like "distributed control" to be more practical. It can be identified that the discourse has moved towards discussing autonomous functions, especially regarding the target selection and target engaging process (Amoroso & Tamburrini, 2019; Riebe, Schmid, & Reuter, 2020).

Scholars of international relations and strategic security (Altmann & Sauer, 2017; Haas & Fischer, 2017; Sauer, 2016; Schörnig, 2019) have discussed the strategic consequences of autonomy. On the one side, the autonomous systems are a central part of the network-centric warfare (NCW) doctrine, which plans for autonomous weapon systems to increasingly assist humans as human-machine teaming (Dillon, 2002; Vice Admiral Cebrowski & Garstka, 1998). However, the autonomy of armed systems is increasing the pressure or even the likelihood of a first strike due to reduced conflict threshold, which might destabilize nuclear deterrence. However, others like Cummings (2019) refer to the advantages of automated systems over humans to carry out attacks due to the likelihood of human error under the stressful conditions of combat.

To further the progress of work towards a limitation of harm, it is important to take a closer look at computer science and engineering, especially robotics. Linked publications are frequently interested in the development of semi-autonomous drones (Albers et al., 2010; Chao et al., 2010), machine learning techniques (Schramowski et al., 2020), and human-computer interaction. Often focusing on civilian environments, some scholars pay special attention to disruptive situations (Adams & Friedland, 2011) or warfare technology (Hocraffer & Nam, 2017). Still, many engineering studies are interested in optimizing automatic or autonomous processes and robotics, disregarding ethical questions or highlighting the potential of LAWS (Arkin, 2010; Arkin, Lyons, et al., 2012; Scharre, 2018).

From the perspective of machine ethics, Canellas et al. (2016) investigate the "mismatch between authority and responsibility in an exemplar military scenario [which] can still plague the human-AWS interactions". The interaction of the autonomous system with its complex environment during mission-related tasks. Thus Hägele and Söffker (2017) introduce a real-time environmental situation risk assessment approach to improve the safe situational behavior of the autonomous system. Beside the question of safety, Chmielewski (2018) tries to incorporate non-Western values and stresses the need for an ethical evaluation of the use of LAWS, referring to IEEE's "Ethical Considerations in Artificial Intelligence and Autonomous Systems" (IEEE, 2016). Others focus on norm change initiated by countries of the Global South (Bode, 2019) or gendered perspectives on autonomous weapon systems (Csernatoni, 2019; Santos de Carvalho, 2018). The cognitive engineering approach (Feigh & Pritchett, 2013) by Canellas and Haga (2016) is one of the few works, which has analyzed different understandings of MHC and concrete options, realized in human-computer interaction. The authors highlight implications for function allocation to autonomous systems vis á vis human operators, derived from definitions of MHC (Canellas & Haga, 2016). Yet, interested in establishing MHC in warfare human-machine interaction, they disregard important questions regarding software and interface design and take a less critical stance by assuming definitions to be exogeneous.

Value-Sensitive Design (VSD) as a "theoretically grounded approach to the design of technology" serves to investigate the discourse on LAWS thus helps to fill these gaps Friedman et al. (2013). Friedman et al. (2006) defined values as "what a person or group of people consider important in life". Usually, a VSD design process consists of three types of investigations: conceptual, empirical and technical. For this paper, only the conceptual investigation is of relevance. Such an investigation aims at understanding the interests and conflicts across the stakeholders' debates within their cultural and strategic contexts (Friedman et al., 2006). Moreover, it proposes approaches to mitigate conflicts and prioritize values in trade-off situations. Within the scope of this study, VSD is thus used to understand the stakeholders' interests and values towards the control of autonomous weapon systems. VSD in the context of autonomous weapons systems has also been used by Asaro (2009), taking important work on autonomy by Cummings (2004); Cummings (2006) into account, referring to her concept of automation bias and the VSD-study of the cruise missile Tactical Tomahawk (Cummings, 2006). Thornton et al. (2018), de Sio and van den Hoven (2018), as well as Umbrello (2019a) use the VSD method on autonomous vehicles and AI, arguing for human-centered approaches like MHC in civilian innovation as well. Our analogous approach tries to grasp challenges of today's discussion of LAWS.

This work is a contribution to the field of IT peace research (Reuter, 2020), as well as natural science/technical peace research (Altmann, 2019; Reuter, 2020) and sheds light on technology's normative and social effects in crisis and conflict. While Boulanin and Verbruggen (2017) have dedicated several papers to autonomous weapon systems, following a more reflective and open research path Boulanin and Verbruggen, (2017), this work contributes by incorporating VSD. So far, only one contribution focusing on LAWS and VSD exists: Verdiesen asks for moral values which are important to military personnel and the public, disregarding the merit for a more critical, deconstructivist stance (Verdiesen, 2017b; Verdiesen, 2019; Verdiesen et al., 2018). Finally, this work aims at offering interdisciplinary approaches of social scientific, like Pugliese's (2015), and technical, like Arkin, Lyons, et al. (2012), perspectives towards challenges for international security.

10.3 Theoretical Background

We chose to analyze MHC with regard to LAWS from a perspective of the Value-Sensitive Design (VSD) approach. Shedding light on LAWS' inscribed attributes, we follow the VSD approach by Friedman et al. (2013). VSD yields theoretical and methodological implications by assuming more or less abstract values to be reflected in interfaces or software and thus indicate the need of interpretative work (Friedman & Nissenbaum, 1996). Thereby, we understand values in affirmation of the definition of Friedman et al. (2013) as norms or standards assessed by a collective while neglecting values as norms by individuals. These values, also supporting a common understanding by VSD scholars, do not necessarily have to be explicitly moral values (Friedman et al., 2013). Following this approach, we consider the design process to be especially relevant with respect to the interaction between human operators and LAWS, an assumption which is already prevalent in debates about the regulation of autonomous weaponry (Canellas & Haga, 2016; Cummings, 2006; de Sio & van den Hoven, 2018).

In this work, we focus on the first and fundamental step of the three-pronged iterative approach, i.e. conceptual investigations of LAWS (Cummings, 2006). Here, we search for values incorporated into LAWS, which may be competing against each other due to different stakeholder positions across the CCW arena (Friedman et al., 2013). Thus, we pose the question: *"What values can be derived for MHC from the stakeholders' discourse in the 2018 Group of Governmental Experts on Lethal Autonomous Weapons Systems?"*

Hence, we are interested in approaching MHC in relation to its empirical context, constituted by various perspectives in the CCW debate, which reflect different values, and broader discursive narratives. Understanding the expert's groups debate as well as the diverse notions of MHC also allows to formulate value implications or priorities in technology development, as well as for the regulation and control of increasingly autonomous weapon systems. Answering this question, we investigate the CCW GGE's divergent conceptual understandings of MHC of LAWS (first gap). The divergent understandings of human-LAWS interaction can be deconstructed by choosing the theoretical perspective of VSD (second gap) as well as a thorough the investigation of CCW-relevant socio-technological values and their interrelatedness (third gap). Our analysis of influential discourses and values leads to the formulation of implications for the design of LAWS (fourth gap).

10.4   Research Design

As we are interested in the question of how to retain MHC of LAWS, we focused on the Group of Governmental Experts on LAWS, which meet in the forum of the Convention on Certain Conventional Weapons (CCW). These experts constitute the most relevant international body dedicated to understanding respective human-machine interaction in a military context, and it is the main organizational forum for the conceptual debate regarding autonomy and control with respect to lethal weaponry. To answer the question of how MHC may be achieved within this forum, we choose a discourse analytical approach, grasping mindsets and conceptualizations of the stakeholders. Our sample and method of analysis are presented in the following.

10.4.1 Data Collection

We concentrated on documents of the *2018 Group of Governmental Experts on Lethal Autonomous Weapons Systems* (LAWS) (GGE on LAWS), thus restricting our sample to working papers and statements by states as well as non-governmental actors, which were formulated in the course of the first meeting, taking place from 9 to 13 April 2018, and the second meeting, held from 27 to 31 August 2018 (UNOG, 2018). In sum, we analyzed 43 documents[1]. The number of member country statements needed to be reduced, not at least due to repetitiveness of content and to reflect actors' relative dominance in the discussion. Thus, we included strong positions of US and European countries such as the UK. As Western countries' statements were more frequently represented and accessible, our selection of country statements tried to reflect a certain unequal distribution of participation. China's and Russia's positions were reflected in the working papers they submitted. Special attention was given to the US due to their prevalence in the development of LAWS and network-centric warfare. To reflect transnational work done in the arena of the GGE on LAWS, we included statements by debate-steering non-governmental actors, again mirroring the diversity of positions as well as dominance in the discourse. We also regarded positions of military-relevant industry partners and marginalized critique by whistleblowers. This was useful to gain more insight into discursive narratives and actors' positions, serving as points of references for participants of the CCW expert group. While the number of documents by non-state actors may seem high in comparison to GGE documents, the latter were considerably longer and offered more in-depth content. All sources are accessible online.

10.4.2 Data Analysis

For the analysis of data, we used the open-source software of R, in particular RQDA (R. Huang, 2016), allowing for a qualitative analysis of text files. Following our theoretical assumptions of discursivity, we conducted a discourse analysis, inspired by Fairclough's Critical Discourse Analysis of communicative events (Jørgensen & Phillips, 2012). Textual documents, like the working papers and state-

---

[1] The associated data can be viewed in Appendix 16.2 in the electronic supplementary material.

ments by states on autonomous weapons systems, may contribute "to the construction of systems of knowledge and meaning" (Jørgensen & Phillips, 2012). For the qualitative analysis of text files codes were developed abductively. The codes are derived from the documents as well as taking into consideration the existing literature regarding network-centric warfare. Network-centric warfare conceptualizes an technology-oriented strategy of warfare being particularly time- and space-oriented, forming a decentralized network of synchronizing entities and man-machine teaming (Dillon, 2002; Vice Admiral Cebrowski & Garstka, 1998). Codes that regard the relationship between humans and LAWS are created by the per-

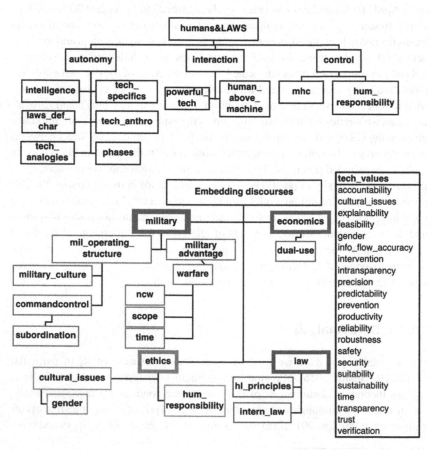

Figure 10.1 Code categories "humans&LAWS", "Embedding discourses" and "tech_values"

ception of technology as an entity with clear boundaries (Tatnall & Gilding, 1999). Codes were also grouped by the three code categories humans and LAWS interaction, socio-technological values and embedding discourses, the latter comprising military discourse as an important sub-category of LAWS-embedding discourses. However, it was singled-out due to its hypothesized importance. Hierarchical relationships were noted in the respective memos and are visualized in this work (see Figure 10.1). Because the derivation of inter-code relationships proved costly, we chose to rely on the R text mining package tm (Feinerer & Hornik, 2018) as well as related packages to grasp relationships of proximity of word stems. To look for associations of word stems, the text corpus was split into 230 files. Punctuation and numbers were removed, and a rather simple algorithm reduced words by cutting of suffixes.

10.5 Results

10.5.1 Autonomy and LAWS

To gain a deeper insight of the dominant conceptual and empirical understanding of autonomy and LAWS, we created "autonomy" as a code for covering all instances in the CCW discourse in which the respective signifier was named and its meaning temporarily fixed. We also coded phrases describing defining characteristics of LAWS with "laws_def_char". To approach not only what is conceptually envisaged with respect to autonomy and LAWS but also how these concepts may materialize, we created the codes "tech_specifics" and "tech_analogies". These four codes all fall under the code category humans and LAWS interaction.

We retrieved 168 codings for "autonomy", and while these were often made with references to humans not being in the loop anymore or the general problem of defining and differentiating between autonomy and its various degrees, one can notice a recurrent focus on autonomy as a function. The following references were found: "using a weapon with autonomous functions" (WP4-US), "[s]ystems with advanced artificial intelligence and enhanced autonomous functions" (GenEx-AU), that "its understanding changes with shifts in the technology frontier, and different functions of a weapons system could have different degrees of autonomy" (SummaryReport), that "[a]utonomy is in and of itself a function" (WP5-BR), that "some semi-autonomous machines can have highly autonomous critical functions while highly autonomous machines can have no or limited autonomy in critical functions" (SummaryReport).

Thus, within the CCW debate, it becomes a clear objective to focus on auton-omy of such critical functions. As critical functions, "different parts of the targeting cycle" (SummaryReport) are to be taken into consideration. Especially, functions of selecting and attacking targets are looked at critically. Out of 168 codings regard-ing "autonomy", 56 were specifically referring to selecting and targeting as critical functions. This is illustrated in documents by various actors, pointing out that "[t]he ICRC has correctly noted that the main and perhaps what states should be concerned about characteristic of AWS is that they have autonomy in the critical functions of selecting targets and attacking without human intervention" (SARCIL). The United Kingdom also stressed that "many participants [had] call[ed] for human control of 'critical functions', often specifically referring to 'select and engage', but it was unclear precisely what these terms mean" (WP1-UK). Looking at empirical refer-ences to technological specifics, it is referred to "[p]attern matching algorithms [...] used for target selection (WP2-ES/F) or "weapons with advanced sensors such as millimetric wave radar [that] can operate beyond visual range (for example, the AIM 120 Advanced Medium-Range Air-to-Air Missile (AMRAAM)) or engage multi-ple targets from a single platform (such as Hellfire or Brimstone guided missiles)" (WP1-UK; own emp.).

In general, sensors are often named as crucial features of LAWS: "Computers can enable machines to respond to inputs from sensors through an application of the algorithms or other processes with which they have been programmed" (WP4-US); "[e]ach munition is equipped with heat and radar sensors which can scan a 200m diameter area. If a target is detected, the warhead is activated; otherwise it self-destructs" (SummaryReport). These statements, as well as others such as – "[t]he projectile has sensors that allow it to identify the target that the human operator intends to hit, and computers and guidance systems that allow it to select and engage that target" (WP4-US) – yield two implications. On the one hand, the CCW discourse treats the detection or identification of a target as part of selecting it, constituting them as one process of selection. Within the CCW discussion, the International Committee of the Red Cross (ICRC) noted that a "weapon system with autonomy in its critical functions" is one "that can select (i.e. search for or detect, identify, track, select) and attack (i.e. use force against, neutralize, damage or destroy) targets without human intervention" (WP5-BR, ICRC). Thus, detection or identification is seen as a synonym or subcategory, respectively, for selecting. This already implies the significance of an autonomous identification of a target with respect to its actual, fixating selection. On the other hand, it becomes clear that the identification or detection of targets is another critical function which is to be distinguished from the ultimate selection of a target. The interpretation of the statements indicates that detection is a critical function belonging to the targeting cycle, preceding the actual selection and subsequent attack of a target. Numerous statements point to the detection and identification of a target, while most times they do not offer explanatory details: "Both primary sensors (laser scanners, millimeter-wave radars, hyperspectral imaging, etc.) and signal processing Algorithms" (WP2-ES/FI); "the Lightweight Counter Mortar Radar can identify indirect fire threats by automatically detecting and tracking shells and backtracking to the position of the weapon that fired the shell" (WP4.2-US).

Besides these functions belonging to the targeting cycle, CCW participants also pointed to other tasks which may be categorized as autonomous. These are supportive tasks like "cyberattack warning, supply chain logistics" (DARPA_2) or automatization of (US) Department of Defense "business processes, such as security clearance vetting or accrediting software systems for operational deployment" (DARPA_2), for accident prevention, i.e. ground collision (WP4-US), or logistical calculations (WP1-UK). In general, references that were made with respect to autonomy of certain critical functions stressed repetitively that a weapon system might consist of autonomous as well as non-autonomous parts and functions, e.g., "weapon systems that have been deployed still require human remote authorization to launch an attack (even though they may identify targets autonomously)" (ICRC/WP5-BR). At the same time, CCW participants did not omit referring to autonomy's different degrees. Often, autonomy of a system meant automatization of processes, but references to artificial intelligence and machine learning, indicating self-learning capabilities and independence, were also prevalent (WP2-ES/FI). No references regarding specific types of deep learning algorithms or the like were made.

10.5.2 Human-Computer Interaction

To understand the dominant and respective marginal counter-discourses on human-LAWS interaction across the CCW debate, we created and organized the codes in a continuum with technological anthropomorphization and MHC at its extremes (see Figure 10.2). The first stage defines human-LAWS interaction to be dependent on technology's "behavior", treating technology as an essential being with human-like features (e.g., intelligence or decision-making authority). In contrast, MHC, at the other end of the continuum, implicitly assumes a hierarchical relationship between humans and technology, with humans having legitimate authority over technology as an instrument. We only marked phrases specifically referring to MHC with the respective code, while all other statements regarding control (without further conceptualization as meaningful) where marked accordingly (i.e., "control").

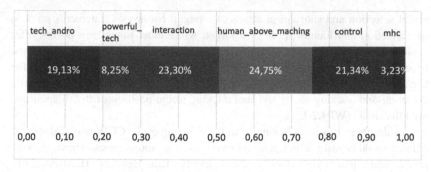

Figure 10.2 Continuum of human-LAWS relationship (100% = 1,176 codings)

The code "powerful_tech" was used to grasp statements which indicated to perceive technology (and technological development) as a driving force while not anthropomorphizing it. In cases where perceptions of "both sides" (technology vs. human) were used, they weighted each other out to "interaction", reflecting a rather equal relationship. This code was naturally also used when actors explicitly referred to interaction as a relationship. The code "human_above_machine" refers to a hierarchical relationship of humans, yet not necessarily being always in control. It is important to note that this process heavily focused on linguistic formulations, assuming that language shapes actors' perceptions of human-LAWS interaction Ekelhof, (2017). Speaking in relative terms, statements indicating hierarchical relationships of humans and subordinated technology were found almost twice as much as statements supporting the autonomy of technology (49% vs. 27%). At the same time, "interaction", as a rather neutral or non-hierarchical position, made out roughly a quarter (27%) of the respective human-LAWS interaction statements. This indicates that perceiving humans to be superior to technology is the dominant view within the CCW GGE forum. These relative frequencies yield several implications: First, it becomes clear that explicit MHC-related statements are very rare (in absolute as well as relative terms). This reflects that despite its initial trendiness as an ethical-legal buzzword (Roff & Moyes, 2016; UNIDIR, 2014), CCW GGE participants are rather uninterested in its highlighting. In cases of referring to MHC, it is either done by a non-governmental participant like the Campaign to Stop Killer Robots (GGE_CTSKR) or the ICRC, elaborating the concept in a more detailed manner (WP5.2-ICRC). When used by states, MHC is framed to be important merely by (potential target) states which are dedicated to a ban of LAWS, like Pakistan or Brazil. In such cases, stronger normative terms were used: "The task for the GGE now should be to ascertain the scope and extent of human control necessary to address the various concerns associated with LAWS to ensure that it is meaningful" (6b-PAK); "[t]he proposal that humans retain 'meaningful control' over LAWS seems to us the most promising avenue to explore" (6b-BR). Other nation-states' representatives do not seem similarly interested in the MHC concept, disregarding the concept considering its level of abstraction and necessity: "[I]t becomes difficult to provide a technical statement of meaningful human control. [...] To be meaningful, human control does not necessarily have to be exercised contemporaneously with the delivery of force. [...]" (WP2-ES/FI).

The US also relativizes the conceptual impact of MHC, as "an operator might be able to exercise meaningful control over every aspect of a weapon system, but if the operator is only reflexively pressing a button to approve strikes recommended by the weapon system [...]" (WP4-US). Pointing out its lack of value because of its conceptual unclarity functions as a devaluation mechanism of the MHC concept across the CCW discourse: "'Control' and 'judgment' are, however, flexible terms, even when qualified by adjectives such as 'meaningful' [...], [...] used [...] to signify different things" (6b-Estonia). Most decisively stated, MHC "or a similar notion" is not considered "to reflect a new or emerging norm of international law" (6b-Estonia), while one participant seems to regret "exploring the scope of meaningful human control in the delegation of decisions to intelligent machines *instead* of what we must regulate on LAWS" (GenEx-KO, own emp.).

Nevertheless, the widespread references to human control stress the respective participants' underlying interest in a hierarchical relationship, with human operators controlling LAWS to varying degrees. As laid out in the following Section 10.5.3, such control may be associated with various values, with the latter being regarded as defining characteristics of the concept of MHC. Thus, even though actors show little support of the concept, they widely refer to technological requirements defining the concept of interest (Roff & Moyes, 2016).

Third, while dominantly retaining human-focused arguments within the CCW debate, there is still a considerable amount of statements carrying a supportive notion of technology, i.e., perceptions of technology as a societal driving force or as essentially *being*. Phrases which were coded as "tech_anthro" or "powerful_tech", respectively, show such instances: "The development of artificial intelligence (AI) should be seen as a logical process in computing science", while demanding that "the discussions on LAWS must reflect the undeniable direction of technological development" (WP2-ES/FI). Interest in the support of LAWS and related AI technology is further formulated, declaring "the system would be capable of defining and thereby deciding the ultimate goals of its functioning, very much like humans do" (WP2-ES/FI), peaking in the following explicit statement for implementation: "The level of abstraction of computing keeps getting higher and higher, leading towards increasing possibilities for various levels of machine autonomy. Past experience has shown that once new technology proves to work, society quickly adopts it, and later its use becomes the accepted norm" (WP2-ES/FI). While remarks which were coded by "interaction" may also imply *characterizations* of technology, they also suggest a more reflective awareness of interactional relationships between humans and LAWS as well as related effects: "[T]he way humans use machines and interact with them is changing […] [because] [i]n complex systems the human role will have various postures in relation to the machine" (WP2-ES/FI).

10.5.3 Socio-Technological Values of LAWS

The NGO Article 36 has issued a briefing within the CCW forum (Roff & Moyes, 2016), in which it points to the question of value-sensitive design while identifying certain "key elements" for MHC: (1) predictability, reliability, and transparency of technology; (2), information accuracy regarding planned outcome, operation, function of technology, and context of use; (3) "timely human action and a potential for timely intervention", and (4) "accountability to a certain standard" (Roff & Moyes, 2016). We assume such elements of MHC to be implementable into technology. Our analysis reveals more important values and looks for mutually tense and supportive relationships, respectively, to put them into context. Thus, we identified 23 values and looked for frequencies and locations of occurrences (see Figure 10.3).

The codes "accountability", "cultural_issues", "gender", "scope", "time", and "verification" were not always used for the explicit description of technology, but also with respect to general procedural issues. Yet, such phrases implied that participants found the respective characteristic very important. Therefore, they are included as relevant socio-technological values that are reflected in the conceptualization of LAWS and interaction. The other value-grasping codes were linked directly to technological requirements.

Most crucial are the codes "time", "predictability", and "reliability" (77, 74, and 70 codings). Additionally, references coded as statements regarding "productivity" (n=64), "accountability" (n=58), "explainability" (n=53), or "safety" (n=50) could be made out at a relatively high frequency, while CCW documents surprisingly referred to issues of (human) "intervention" (n=21) or an accurate flow of information (n=14) only at a relatively moderate rate. Yet, not every technological requirement considered necessarily has a supportive impact with respect to the establishment of MHC. Thus, we screened arguments pointing out MHC or human control.

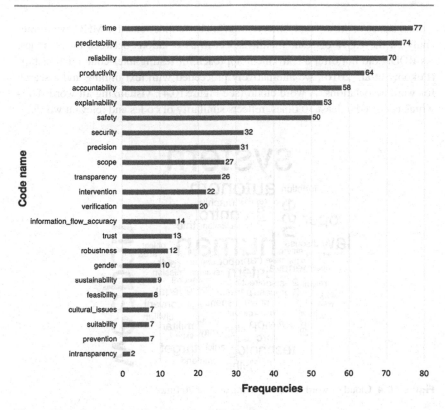

Figure 10.3 Occurrences of socio-technological values

For example, a statement formulated by Brazil stresses that "meaningful human control can only be achieved if the role of the human [...] is such as to ensure [...] *the capacity to intervene and override machine functions when operationally possible*" (6b-BR, own emp.). Furthermore, the non-governmental actor ICRAC defines "*sufficient* time for deliberation on the nature of targets [...] [as one of the] necessary conditions for meaningful human control of weapons" (ICRAC-WP3, own emp.).

Besides having the possibility to intervene – also with respect to the issue of time – France, perhaps taking a less critical stance on LAWS compared to ICRAC, points out with regards to "[d]eveloping autonomy and human-machine interaction" that [t]he human command must be aware of and be able to assess system reliability and predictability" (WP3-FR, own emp.). Assuming reliability and predictability as well as issues of "time" and "intervention" to be foundational for MHC, we further analyzed the CCW discourse with respect to associations between these values. As RQDA did not offer a convenient approach for testing inter-code relationships (Pokorny et al., 2016), we alternatively proceeded with text mining and a search for word associations. A word cloud (see Figure 10.4), visualizing all word stems which occurred at least 70 times, reflects similarity of codes and relevant words.

Figure 10.4 Cloud of word stems occurring at least 70 times

Consequently, we screened the CCW corpus for associations occurring at least by 30% with respect to predictability. This revealed that (1) "predict" is not rarely associated with aspects relating to the question of MHC. For example, "agency" (56% of all occurrences of "predict"), "dignity" (46%), "human control" (43%), "moral" (34%), or "ethical" (30%) are associated with predictability. Second, testing for associations also showed that predictability is often (78%) associated with reliability. Similarly, reliability is often associated across CCW documents with control ("software control", "human control") or agency (42%), "trustworthy" (70%) as well as "knowledge" (43%) or "consequence" (38%). At the same time, "intervention" may be associated by at least 30% with "overriding" (46%), "capacity" (38%), "conscious" (37%) and "constrain" (38%).

As the preceding coding process revealed, "time" was not only coded referring to statements directed at values, but also with respect to elaborations on warfare (as well as less substantially-laden phrases like "in the meantime, at the same time"). Thus, there are a lot of words associated with "time", among which some like "faster"

(36%), "able" (31%), or "deliberately" (30%) indicate the issue of time pressure and necessity of time to intervene or decide, respectively. Yet, besides pointing to enough time as a requirement for human control of LAWS, associations of "time" also already reflected the signifier's relevance of the current military discourse (see 5.4).

Another group of values named across CCW documents did not seem to support the actual implementation of MHC. Among these was precision, which is associated by 53% with efficiency, military terms like "troop" (52%), "military" (33%) and "Afghanistan" (48%), "Syria" (33%), "Iraq" (30%), "Libya" (48%). At the same time, precision was comparatively often used along empirical examples of LAWS like "torpedo" (38%) and negatively-laden words like "cruel" (48%) or "deteriorat-ing" (33%). Similarly, efficiency was not rarely associated with the same words as well as "easier" (47%), "cost" (34%), or "kill" (34%). Screening for associations also suggests efficiency-related phrases not to be formulated alongside issues of control, ethics, and international humanitarian law. The third group of codes within the category of values seemed to be neutral towards MHC, as the coding process suggested. Values like "feasibility", "suitability" and "sustainability" were present across documents, yet the respective substantial understanding of these features did not become clear straightforwardly. Looking at other word occurrences along fea-sibility raised the possibility of it constituting an empty signifier (Giesen & Seyfert, 2016), rather reproducing cost-effective ratio instead of proactively supporting MHC (cf., 34% "rule", 31% "advantageous", 32% "commercial", 40% "applicable", 31% "certified").

10.5.4 Influencing Discourses

As our work carries discourse theoretical assumptions, i.e., of discourses reproduc-ing mindsets and practices, we checked for codes referring to overarching societal topics or thematic areas. Figure 10.5 reveals dominant trains of thought functioning as points of reference throughout argumentative structures.

"Ethics" as a structuring discourse of MHC was coded almost 400 times across CCW documents. The frequency shows how ethical vocabulary is serving as a dominant frame for discussion. The relevance of ethics as a guiding discourse is also illustrated considering respective sub-codes "hum_responsibility" (n=121) or "HL_principles" (n=205), with the latter clarifying the close link between ethics and law ("intern_law" n=349). While Pakistan states that "its [LAWS'] use should be considered unethical and unlawful" 6b-PAK), paralleling law and ethics, other remarks stress the normativity of law due to its causal links to ethics by respective as well as actively demanding vocabulary: "All weapons systems must comply with International Law in general and, in particular, with *International Humanitarian Law* and with International Human Rights Law" (WP5-BR, own emp.) and "[w]e *believe* that any legal discussion about LAWS should centre on compliance with International *Humanitarian* Law, including *the obligation for all States to ensure the lawfulness of their weapons, means and methods of warfare. These should be our constant reference points*" (GenEx-CA, own emp.).

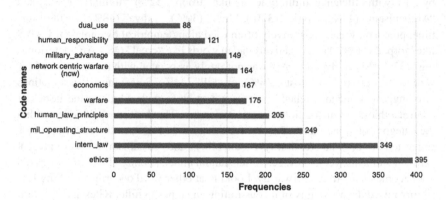

Figure 10.5 Reflections of relevant discourses

Besides ethics and law, we identified "economics" (n=167) and the military discourse consisting of military signifiers ("mil_operating_structure" n=249, "warfare" n=175) and indicating military logic ("military_advantage" n=149) to function as structuring forces. While "dual_use" (n=88) constitutes a sub-code of the economic discourse due to its recurring references to R&D in the civilian sector, the code "NCW" (n=164) is grasping all phrases related to the so-called network-centric warfare. However, the code "NCW" is formed the military discourse, it is also influenced by economics (Dillon, 2002; Vice Admiral Cebrowski & Garstka, 1998).

Thus, we categorized thematic reference points by four subjects, forming two interrelated pairs: law and ethics as well as military discourse and economics. These pairs are not only illustrated in the text documents[2], but also inspired by NCW-literature (Dillon, 2002).

When looking at the word stem associations of "law", we did not find any immediate reference to ethics. Yet, there are associations with "humanitarian" (50%),

_____
[2] The terms which represent the major discourses can be found in the Appendix 16.2 in the electronic supplementary material.

"principle" (45%), "mean" (31%), and "remind" (34%), indicating the cognitive work of ethics. When testing for word associations of "ethics", it is revealed that "ethic" is very often used along "predictability" (50%) and "unexpect" (32%), thereby indicating that ethical arguments are associated with the value of predictability or vice versa. Furthermore, "ethical" is associated across the CCW corpus with "disobey" (50%), "nonacceptable" (50%), and "question" (32%), all reflecting on the option of intervention regarding decision-making (37% "decision"). At the same time, "ethics" is also associated with the value of sufficient time (32% "acute").

Associations of "military" did not point to any of the dominantly stated values. Yet, besides references to weaponry ("laser-guided", "microcomputer", "bomb", "radar") or military vocabulary ("battlefield", "submarine"), it is mostly associated with "civilian" (44%), "harm" (35%), "accuracy" (34%), and "collateral" (33%). These word stems point to the humanitarian principle of distinction as well as the technological value of "precision" (or "accuracy"). Both associations of "command" and "advantage" neither refer to values like "predictability", "reliability", "time" or "intervention". Rather, they are also associated with military vocabulary as well as with relatively diffuse values like "appropriate" (35%, "suitability"), "initially defined" (41%), "feasibility" (31% with "advantage"), and again with precision (i.e., "accuracy" 51%). Associations of "efficiency" neither revealed any reflections of values related to MHC. Instead, paragraphs deal with "cost" (34%), "war" (58%), "military" (67%), but also with "precision" (53%) and "quick" (30%), reflecting current NCW-ratio.

10.6   Discussion and Conclusion

Our analysis revealed a variety of new findings, some of which reside on a higher level of abstraction while others are more closely tied to existing practices and materiality. Independent from their theoretical-practical position, our results yield various implications with regards to the question of conflicts of interests regarding the implementation of MHC. Additionally, it is useful to consider not only this paper's value but also existing limitations. This allows for an outlook as well.

10.6.1   Implications

Analysis of recurrent understandings of both autonomy and LAWS across CCW GGE discussions revealed disagreement among the parties as well as a focus on the targeting cycle and its "critical functions" (see Section 10.5.1). To retain MHC, it seems helpful to reach a consensus on working definitions by concentrating on critical functions of engaging and the different steps of selecting and targeting. Second, looking at autonomy and LAWS understandings, parties may need to find some common ground with respect to empirical examples of LAWS while at the same time being aware of risks of transparency.

Approaching underlying perceptions of human-machine interactions again revealed the necessity to be conscious about *automation bias* and blinded views on technology (see V.B). Even though the establishment of MHC relies on human-centric arguments, our analysis offered the added-value of reflective positions on interacting networks. To still be able to hold humans responsible, a special focus on human machine "touchpoints" is needed. The research by Braun et al. (2019) and Verdiesen's work (2017b) allows a first glance at the CCW GGE debate in this respect. In contrast to Verdiesen's work (2017b), our chosen VSD-perspective poses a first approach to the CCW GGE parties' understanding of MHC-relevant technological features.

Even though the stakeholders might not agree on Meaningful Human Control as a concept, the issue of control is at the heart of the debate (de Sio & van den Hoven, 2018; A. Sharkey, 2019). Regarding human control, a sufficient amount of time to intervene was found to be one of the most important technological requirements (see 10.5.2). To incorporate this feature of human-controlled LAWS, such weapon systems need to be designed accordingly. It is therefore critical to avoid automatization of firing when identification is seen as successfully completed. Options of multi-channel communication between operator and system are already under research (Hocraffer & Nam, 2017). Yet, with respect to assuring MHC, it is (a) important to ensure the option of intervention, while (b) active confirmation or denial of an attack might reduce the risk of technology-biased behavior. Thus, designing an interface offering (obligatory) yes/no-options with regards to an attack may ensure human authority. At the same time, values like reliability, predictability, information accuracy, or explainability might be carried by a usable interface, offering transparent listing of target detection processes. Situational awareness by commanders, consisting of some of the named requirements, is crucial for the meaningful human control of autonomous weapon systems (Australia, 2019; IRAC, 2019).

The expert group's debate mainly focused on the fifth phase of the targeting process, in which the mission is planned and executed, entailing the F2T2EA cycle of "find, fix, track, target, engage, and assess" Ekelhof, (2018). As "[i]t is during this phase that the selected lethal or nonlethal means will be used[,] [...] this is the phase [the debate is] focused on the most" Ekelhof, (2018). With respect to the detection of a target, training of deep learning algorithms should ensure both reliability and predictability by systematically recording and evaluating single steps.

Regarding machine learning, it may also be necessary to discuss implications of diverse degrees of depth, i.e., representation and abstraction of layers. A focus on testing indicates, as do our findings referring to the importance of verification and validation of soft- and hardware, that procedures apart from the planning and execution phase, on which the debate has mainly concentrated, are critical to ensure predictable and reliable execution of the targeting process. As our work on the debate's surrounding and influencing discourses shows, international humanitarian law principles are still a dominant reference point for evaluation (see Section 10.5.4). With respect to the principles of distinction and proportionality, several procedural measures may prove helpful. Software developers, certainly aware that surveillance, detection, or identification are crucial parts of the targeting process, need to intensify sensitivity towards biases. Still ongoing is the discussion whether it is possible to design autonomous weapon systems that can adhere to the principles of international humanitarian law, e.g., to protect civilians and to ensure the use of appropriate and necessary force only (A. Sharkey, 2019; USA, 2019). Cummings (2019) has argued with regards to the strategic target selection by commanders that in case the precision of the system performs better than the human operators, autonomous target selection follows the IHL. Cummings (2019) suggests that autonomous systems are potentially better in performing and preventing unnecessary suffering due to the stress-bias commanders face in a combat situation. Thus, a research culture which fosters open communication about systemic errors (e.g., in imagery analysis) as well as responsibility in R&D need to be initiated urgently (van den Hoven, 2013). This culture may be enhanced by recording design processes (Aldewereld et al., 2015).

To summarize, control of autonomous systems matters, however with divergent implications on how, what (regarding the function and situation), and in which circumstances. As we asked for supporting conditions of MHC within the respective CCW forum, tense associations between predictability and reliability, on the one hand, and precision and efficiency on the other hand, become visible. While precision may prove crucial for reliability and predictability, it is neither sufficient to aim solely for precision. Additionally, as reflected by the value of efficiency as well as various references to time as an important factor, developers need to weigh options for timely interventions against rapidity of actions. This supports prioritizing situational awareness of the human operator within the design process (Weber & Suchman, 2016). Lastly, and with respect to our finding of economic and military discourses not necessarily supporting MHC, restrictions of software development may neither be grounded in economic interests nor in a military advantage ratio. Paying special attention to human-LAWS perception among CCW participants, it is revealed that MHC heavily relies on a human-centric hierarchy. This may contradict a decentralized network-centric warfare. Yet, as commercial industries as well as the military are relevant (if not the most relevant) actors, deliberation among involved actors is necessary.

10.6.2 Limitations and Outlook

Reacting to the legal (Crootof, 2016) and technical (Kindervater, 2017) debates of LAWS and human control, we tried to put them into relation. Our work offers a first conduct on the question of MHC within the CCW GGE discourse. Naturally, this study yields several limitations. Parallel coding by several researchers and mea-surement of inter-rater reliability may improve the robustness of the findings. We presented a list of LAWS-incorporated values and sketched tendencies of MHC-supportive values and rather competitive relationships. Future works may focus on other relationships or ambivalences of values like "precision" or "time". At the same time, we tried to grasp discursive patterns, norms, and practices forming par-ticipants' perceptions of LAWS features by using VSD as a theoretical starting point. Crediting the initiative, one may consider that while the sample tried to represent existing power relations, it does not pay, in contrast to other works, special attention to racism or sexism (Bode, 2019; Santos de Carvalho, 2018). Future studies may contribute by investigating these issues, in particular with regards to stakeholders' positions on MHC. Because of purposive inclusion of indirectly involved actors, the quantitative results of coding frequencies and word stem occurrences should not be taken to be absolute but rather be seen as an indication of relationships. To complement the focus on discourse, future analysis may shed light on material capabilities, long-term national interests as well as innovation and defense politics. Our study may be accompanied by analyses comprising the entire body of the CCW expert group's documents to increase representativeness and validity of our findings, including statements of all actors and of more recent meetings. At the same time, focusing specifically on the different understandings of socio-technological values like accountability may prove valuable insights. Further, it may prove valuable to dig deeper into technological specifics, which CCW participants did not communicate in a very detailed way.

U.S. Security Policy: The Dual-Use Regulation of Cryptography and its Effects on Surveillance

11

11.1 Introduction

Today, there are numerous cryptographic algorithms ensuring the availability, confidentiality, and integrity of our data. They are ubiquitous in today's information and communication technology (ICT) devices and services, most of the time being used in the background, e.g., the TLS protocol (Krawczyk et al., 2013), which is used to provide confidential web browsing. Cryptography is one of the central aspects of information security as it prevents unauthorized access to information, thus keeping it confidential, and supports the integrity of information (AbuTaha et al., 2011). The strength of a cryptographic algorithm is measured by its used security key's length[1]. It is based on the fact, that cryptographic algorithms are secure by design, i.e., the only weak link is the cryptographic key, which needs to be brute-forced in

---

[1]Since symmetric cryptographic algorithms usually offer the same security strength as their key length, the strength of other cryptographic families (like asymmetric encryption or elliptic curve cryptography) is given as their symmetric counterparts, e.g., the strength of 3072-bit RSA is equivalent to its 128-bit symmetric counterpart. Current cryptographic systems consider a symmetric key-strength of 128bit and more to be secure (Barker & Roginsky, 2019)

ORIGINAL PUBLICATION Riebe, T., Kühn, P., Imperatori, P., & Reuter, C. (2022). U.S. Security Policy: The Dual-Use Regulation of Cryptography and its Effects on Surveillance. *European Journal for Security Research*, 1–27. https://doi.org/10.1007/s41125-022-00080-0

Supplementary Information The online version contains supplementary material available at https://doi.org/10.1007/978-3-658-41667-6_11.

---

order to maliciously access the encrypted information[2]. While this might offer great security at one point of time, it might be weakened by advances computing capacity which makes breaking encryption faster[3]. The access to cryptographic algorithms exceeding a certain key length (in the following paper bundled under the term cryptography) has been regulated and restricted, while intelligence and law enforcement agencies have worked to break or circumvent encryption to access data.

The trade of cryptography is regulated internationally as a dual-use good and is subject to export and import restrictions (Vella, 2017; Wassenaar Arrangement Secretariat, 2021). As cryptography has become omnipresent in communication technology, it is to this day regulated as a dual-use good like nuclear technology components, biotechnological instruments, and certain chemical tools. However, unlike the aforementioned dual-use goods, cryptographic innovations and products are not likely to be part of a weapon system or an improvised weapon (Forge, 2010). Nor does it seem to be dual use in the sense that the technology can be used in beneficial and harmful ways (Evans, 2014, p. 277). Then why is cryptography considered dual use? The answer lies in the security policies which assess the risks of unsecured IT against the risk of "going dark" (Comey, 2014). Restricting the access to cryptographic innovation seems to be limited at guaranteeing access to encrypted information and the possibility of "global commercial and state-led mass surveillance" (Monsees, 2020).

Since the United States (U.S.) industry was a global leader in developing computers and communication technologies early on (Southard, 1997) and dominates the application-based IT market with companies like Apple, Alphabet, and Amazon today (Andriole, 2018), it has access to diverse information about customers all around the world worthy of protection (Giles, 2018). Likewise, U.S.-based companies have significant dominance in the global cyber security software market: in 2015, their market share was near 61% (Australian Cyber Security Growth Network, 2018). However, this economic strength is accompanied by a restrictive security policy. Cryptographic tools were even regulated as a weapon in the U.S. for several decades until 1994 and were prohibited to be exported due to strong regulations (Black, 2002) The National Security Agency's (NSA) global surveillance and

---

[2] This assumption has been shown to be false for some encryption algorithms and has always been tested by security experts by searching for security flaws in the algorithms design. But there are, of course, other ways to access encrypted information, e.g., by blackmailing, threatening, or compromising a computer system.

[3] One example is the DES algorithm with 40bit key length, which offered a reasonable security in 1975, but was easily crackable in 1998. Another aspect is technological advancement like quantum computers, which might make a whole family of cryptographic algorithms insecure (Electronic Frontier Foundation, 1998).

espionage programs, revealed by the publication of classified documents by former NSA agent Edward Snowden beginning in 2013, casts an unprecedented perspective on U.S. security policy. Moreover, it was mostly U.S. products with worldwide distribution that were infiltrated in these programs (Castro, 2020). In the following years, new immense and expensive surveillance programs were built to overcome encryption on a global scale. At least at this point, both, export regulations and the work of the NSA, were and are essential instruments of the U.S. policy on encryption. However, it is unclear in what way and to what extent cryptography is restricted and how this still influences recent calls for the complete ban of "warrant-proof" encryption (Castro, 2020). Subsequently, to analyze the regulation of cryptography as a dual-use good and the practices of the national security organizations in the U.S. from the 1990s to today, we ask: Why was the regulation of cryptography liberalized for mass communication services from 2000, while the surveillance politics focused on similar services?

To compare the historical policy development and the dual-use regulation and surveillance policy, this paper first illustrates the related work (Section 11.2). In the following, the method of research, data collection, and policy analysis are described (Section 11.3). The results (Section 11.4) compare the dual-use and surveillance policies during three time periods in the 1990s (11.4.1), the 2000s (11.4.2) and the 2010s (11.4.3), providing the historical and technological context of the periods. This is followed by a discussion of the results and the research question (Section 11.5) and a conclusion (Section 11.6).

11.2   Related Work

The security policies regarding cryptography are part of many scientific discourses and disciplines. The discourse on surveillance and securitization of cryptography are discussed in Section 11.2.1, while the related work concerning the regulation of cryptography as a dual-use good is discussed in Section 11.2.2, followed by the research gap 11.2.3.

11.2.1   Surveillance Studies Perspective on Security Practices

The increased access to information technology for private users as well as for security organizations has led to the increased use of "surveillance-oriented security technologies" (SOSTs). SOSTs are technologies that are designed to monitor terrorists and criminal groups but are also capable of and have been used to monitor the public on a large scale (Degli Esposti & Santiago Gómez, 2015; Pauli et al., 2016, p. 437). The acquisition of SOSTs has been legitimized as prevention of criminal and terrorist attacks; however, it has also led to critical discussion of surveillance measures (Ball et al., 2013; Bauman et al., 2014; Bigo, 2006; Lyon, 2006). Kaufmann (2016) illustrates how the technologization of security leading to "the rhizomatic" spread of surveillance, not only top down, but fragmented and without a single sovereign power, as described by Haggerty and Ericson (2000)as an assemblage. Kaufmann (2016, p. 93) argues that this assemblage is characterizing the security governance, as it "occurs in parallel, sometimes in complementary and sometimes in conflicting forms: security practices are undertaken in the mode of military and disciplinary access, in the mode of legally oriented police work, and in the mode of preventing and pre-empting political risks."

The contradictions of security governance have also been discussed by Poscher (2016) who argues that in criminal civil law there is a "heightened sense of vulnerability" which drives the changes of law towards, among others, the internationalization of security threats (which we can also observe regarding the use of cryptography), the blending of prevention and repression, as well as the blending of police and secret services. The effective governance of the secret services seems to pose problems, as their programs and practices are usually not debated within the public sphere. This leads to "a conundrum", as the same organizations which are obliged to protect the democracies are undermining the same (Poscher, 2016, p. 69). The public discourse on the capabilities of secret services is also discussed by Murphy (2020), who stresses the need for a democratic debate that moves away from the scandal-driven narrative of a binary choice between user privacy and "unfettered state access to communication". In his analysis, Murphy (2020) compares four types of legal instruments to gain access to communication by the Five Eyes states (USA, UK, Australia, Canada, and New Zealand). He concludes that there is already a broad range of legal means, which lack public awareness and oversight. This is even more difficult, due to the "cross-territorial nature of the internet". However, among other measures, encryption is driving up the cost of surveillance. Cayford and Pieters (2018) have analyzed the effectiveness of surveillance technology, as it is legitimized and perceived by U.S. and U.K. intelligence officials through their public statements. They found that effectiveness feeds into what is seen as proportionate, as well as on the legal framework regarding privacy and the overall costs of the operations. In addition to the evolution of the use of cryptography, Kessler (2020) trace the debate regarding legal issues, particularly in relation to privacy. Like Murphy (2020), they conclude that the installation of backdoors or vulnerabilities is not desirable due to the security ramifications.

In contrast to the U.S, the EU Commission opposed key escrow plans already in 1997 ("EU Commission Rejects U.S. Plan on Encryption", 1997). In 2016, the European Union Agency for Cybersecurity (ENISA) repeated this statement and justified its stance by stating that backdoors are not effective in combating criminal activity and instead undermine the security of the digital society. The negative effects of such an approach could thus in turn be observed in the U.S. Instead, ENISA advocates strong encryption as a safeguard for the individual's right to privacy (ENISA, 2016).

11.2.2 Governance of Cryptography as a Security Relevant Dual-use Good

To control goods that can be used as parts of weapon systems or for military applications, trade regulations serve as a tool of security policy to control the proliferation of technologies. Internationally, the Wassenaar Arrangement is a multi-lateral export-control regime, which has 42 member states. These states agree on lists and definitions for relevant technologies, which are regularly updated. However, the arrangement is non-binding (Wassenaar Arrangement Secretariat, 2022). Therefore, especially in the case of cryptography, as well as regarding the origin of many ICT services and companies, the U.S. regulation is internationally relevant to users and customers of U.S. ICT products. The current trade regulation of cryptography is presented and summarized based on U.S. laws in the comparative study by Vella (2017). She describes in detail the legal categorization of cryptography assets and the distribution of enforcement roles among authorities, and briefly considers the historical development of the legislation internationally. She concludes that in contrast to the EU, the U.S. has aligned their concept of dual use from national security interests legitimized by the war on terror, while the EU has integrated human security as an important argument to support the proliferation of encryption technologies. Like the U.S., the EU follows a broad definition of the scope of encryption controls and incorporates activation codes. However, the EU has always included "mass-market" components. Moreover, unlike the U.S., the EU clearly defines what falls under control and what does not. However, there is no uniformity of export regulations among the member states. While countries are united in their dedication to liberal encryption regulation and export control laws are subject to European law, the implementation of these laws is up to the member states. In some cases, they may interpret the regulation differently or have additional national laws. Furthermore, military goods, for example, are regulated solely by national export regulations (Vella, 2017).

Similarly, Saper (2013) compares the regulation of encryption technology internationally and outlines the export policy and its implications and provides practical recommendations for exporters on how to manage them. The U.S. does not restrict the use or import of cryptography, however, has strict restrictions about the export of the same. When exporting cryptography, which is not designed to be part of medical end-use, or to protect intellectual property functions, the primary factor is the key length. Encryption products that provide keys above a certain threshold face export restrictions (Saper, 2013, p. 680). However, "mass-market products", like e-mail encryption products, are excluded. However, the domestic use of cryptography has been scrutinized as well. (Landau, 2015) points out, how the NSA influenced the recommended encryption standard by the National Institute of Standards and Technology (NIST) which was not considered secure and would have allowed easy decryption by outsiders. In her article, she draws various parallels between the historical and current actions of the NSA, specifically referring to the controversy surrounding a possible backdoor of the 1970s Data Encryption Standard (DES) with the attempts regarding the standard Dual Elliptic Curve Deterministic Random Bit Generator (Dual EC_DRBG). Schulze (2017) makes a similar comparison between the Clipper Chip program and the Snowden revelations, while he restricts the study to NSA activities and mostly excludes the regulating policy. He highlights the similarities in the arguments of officials who claim that encryption impedes effective law enforcement, seeking to establish "the norm of government control over cryptography vs. the right of every user to communicate privately" (Schulze, 2017). The increasing use of encryption is much more a reaction to the previous, inconsiderate, and in part unlawful actions of states. After this, Rubinstein & van Hoboken (2014) focus on the organizational and technical responses to the disclosure of transnational surveillance by the NSA in a historical context. Using the cloud service industry as an example, they show that providers mostly responded by implementing even stronger privacy protections and advanced cryptographic protocols, which in turn raises the question of how the U.S. government may deal with this increased resistance to surveillance. Deconstructing the security discourse, Monsees (2019, p. 81) shows how encryption has been turned into a question of security policy, as not only a matter of "the state" vs. "the public", but rather "various forms of publicness emerge, or their emergence is complicated by the prevailing security narratives".

These narratives have been evolving ever since. After Edward Snowden revealed the programs and extent to which the NSA deployed surveillance technologies until 2013, the U.S. has passed two new laws, the EARN IT Act and the Lawful Access to Encrypted Data Act (LEADA) in 2020, which regulate the access of security agencies to user data (Figas, 2020; Pfefferkorn, 2020). While the EARN IT Act enforces the implementation of commissions within tech companies to formulate best practices dealing with content on social media platforms for example, LEADA has been criticized to force companies to provide back-doors for law enforcement agencies while making end-to-end encryption unlawful. This shows how the laws regarding encryption, legal decryption, as well as import and export restrictions for dual-use goods, influence the access to cryptography for U.S. and non-U.S. citizens.

11.2.3 Research Gap

Considering the recent approaches to prevent "going dark" (Pfefferkorn, 2020), it seems contradictory that the regulation of cryptographic technologies for mass communication technologies has been liberalized from the year 2000, even before most of the mass communication and social media companies have been founded and became internationally successful. And although the key length is still one of the most important characteristics to measure the security of encryption, it has become less important for the regulation of the same. As the literature on SOSTs and cryptography politics has acknowledged the effects of dual-use regulation on the effectiveness of surveillance technology use, the historical development of both policies and its interactive effects have not been compared in detail. Further, the role of intermediaries as proliferators of encryption and surveillance infrastructure has gained little attention (Kaufmann, 2016; Rozenheim, 2018). Therefore, this paper contributes to this discourse in comparing the security policies regarding dual-use regulation and surveillance programs.

11.3   Method

The paper aims to examine encryption policy measures in terms of evaluating encryption as a dual-use technology. Therefore, a comparative literature analysis will be conducted, considering regulative foundations, scientific publications as well as journalistic works. In the following, we will describe the specifics of our research method.

11.3.1 Data Collection

For the data collection, primarily the databases Google Scholar and Springer Link were used to select scientific publications that focus on regulations. For ease of comparison, current regulations and historical intelligence activities are additionally examined so that a comparative analysis is possible. Table 11.3 shows the regulative foundations for dual-use goods. The summary of the NSA's activities is based on the paper "The U.S. Surveillance Programs and Their Impact on EU Citizens' Fundamental Rights" published by the European Parliament (Bowden, 2013). The revelations and programs of the NSA are summarized in Table 11.2. For analyzing the NSA programs solely journalistic works using at least three of the four keywords "Snowden", "Encryption", "BULLRUN" and "NSA" are considered (Table 11.1).

Table 11.1 Overview: Regulative foundations

Type	Dual-use Goods	Military goods
Law on control	Export Administration Act (EAA)	Arms Export Control Act (ACEA)
Authorized authority	U.S. Commerce Department's Bureau of Export Administration (BXA)	U.S. Department of State
Definition of regulations	Export Administration Regulations (EAR)	International Traffic in Arms Regulations (ITAR)
Control list	Commerce Control List (CCL)	U.S. Munitions List (USML)
Maximum waiting time for a decision on exports	120 days (Dam & Lin, 1996)	Unlimited (Dam & Lin, 1996)

11.3.2 Data Collection

Based on the selected documents, our analysis aims to highlight regulatory attempts of the U.S. cooperation with the NSA. Therefore, we use policy analysis in general and the approach of policy process. To do so, we selected a small number of cases where cryptography has been used to outline different cryptography practices conducted by (1) the U.S. government, and (2) by the NSA. Table 11.3 and 11.2 give an overview of the two further types of selected documents: (1) regulatory foundations for the practices of the U.S. government, and (2) the different NSA programs following up on the U.S. regulatory attempts. Generally, the policy process approach puts its focal point onto political processes and the involved stakeholders while the scope is on the broader meso-scale. In this context, it aims at determining what processes, means, and policy instruments, e.g., regulation, legislation, or subsidy, are used. Within this policy process, the role and influence of stakeholders needs to

Table 11.2 Overview of NSA Programs

NSA Program	Specialization
PRISM	Surveillance program with access to servers operated by large (groups of) companies (Google, Microsoft, Apple, Yahoo, YouTube, Facebook, AOL, and Paltalk) (Greenwald, 2013a)
Upstream collection	Data collected by intercepting transoceanic cables and surveillance of communication data of numerous providers (Timberg, 2013; Timberg & Nakashima, 2013)
XKeyscore	Far-reaching surveillance program that was used to monitor the individual internet activity (visited websites, chats, emails, transmitted documents, metadata) of people all over the world in real time. Because of the amount of data, it was only stored for a limited number of days (Greenwald et al., 2013)
BULLRUN	Decryption program in which various encryption technologies were compromised, loopholes were installed into existing systems, and global cryptography standards were manipulated (Ball et al., 2013)

be discussed (Hult, 2015). In our analysis, the relevant stakeholders identified are the above mentioned (U.S. Government and NSA) but also the (4) civil society and (5) economy. Against the background of our selected policy field, the stakeholders have been chosen based on an examination of the dual-use export politics and their related practices as well as the policies of the security agencies.

Following the typology of Gerring & Cojocaru (2016), we conduct a two-case causal analysis and compare our selected cases longitudinally in three different time periods. Since we want to identify the causes of our outcomes, namely the surveillance policies/practices and dual-use policies/regulation, the case study can be described as exploratory: The outcome (Y) is specified and framed as a research question – in our study, "Why does Y occur?". Thus, the purpose of our study is to identify X, which is considered a possible cause of Y (Gerring & Cojocaru, 2016). To compare the two outcomes, it is necessary to develop comparison categories. As described, means and policy instruments as well as relevant stakeholders are the focal point of our analysis. Furthermore, the public perception and the usage of cryptography seem to be relevant factors for the policy implementation. Based on these considerations, we identified several guiding questions to develop our comparison categories. Accordingly, the categories derived for the comparison are (1) **targeted actors**, (2) **implementing organizations**, (3) **methods and regulations**, and context factors such as (4) **developments in cryptography and usage** (see Table 11.4, Table 11.5).

We conduct a longitudinal case study by referring to three different time periods (see Figure 11.3). We chose these periods as they are all characterized by specific events and attitudes and are thus distinct from each other. The first period is defined by Key Escrow as the main strategy of the U.S. government, expressed in the attempted implementation of the Clipper Chip (T1: 1990–2001, see Section 11.4.1). However, with September 11 and the resulting Patriot Act, a new period of U.S. surveillance policy began in 2001, characterized by mass surveillance by the NSA. At the same time, major tech companies, such as Twitter and Facebook, emerge (T2: 2001–2013, see Section 11.4.2). This period ends with the revelations of Edward Snowden, during which the BULLRUN program became public. Our third chosen period can therefore be considered the post-Edward Snowden era (T3: 2013–2021, see Section 11.4.3). End-to-end encryption is increasingly becoming the standard, and users' content is no longer accessed by companies as intermediaries between private industry and politics. In this context, the "going dark" debate is gaining momentum, resulting in the LEADA Act. In addition, the research into exploits and the so-called Vulnerability Equity Process are increasingly coming into focus.

11.4   Results

11.4.1 The 1990s: Cryptography and the Internet become Accessible

The 1990s were marked by significant innovative breakthroughs in technological development – not least manifested in the development and commercialization of the World Wide Web (WWW). As the internet emerged as a network of networks, which were connected to exchange information and businesses, the question of encryption also became a discourse that would significantly shape the next years of technological development. Due to the commercialization of the internet, cryptography became more important for the needs of companies and end-users, which challenged the monopoly of the government over the technology (Sircar, 2018, p. 29).[4] While in 1992 nine types of encryption were excluded from regulations[5] (Grimmett,

---

[4] The historic development is outlined in the electronic supplementary material in Appendix 16.3 showing how the level of security and the categorization of cryptography changed.

[5] These 9 types of encryption include: (1) decryption of copy-protected software; (2) use in machines for banking or money transactions; (3) cryptographic processing using analog functions in certain broadcast and fax equipment; (4) personalized smart cards; (5) access control, such as in ATMs; (6) data authentication; (7) fixed data compression or coding techniques; (8) reception of limited- audience radio or television programs (decryption must

2001, pp. 5–6), and only a few goods with a weak 56-bit symmetrical encryption were tolerated, "Key Escrow" was becoming the method of choice since it met both the interest of economy and prosecution (Dean, 1999, p. 11).

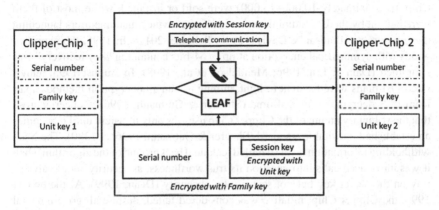

Figure 11.1 Representation of the communication of two Clipper Chips (own illustration)

To bring the industrial and government sectors under one umbrella, as early as April 16, 1993, the White House planned a voluntary program to improve communications security and privacy, considering prosecution authorities' requirements (The White House, 1993). First, this was put into practice using a hardware module called Clipper Chip (The White House, 1993), based on NSA competencies (R. J. Anderson, 1996, p. 79). It was developed to decrypt conversations and was built into appropriate devices such as telephones (Dam & Lin, 1996). A symmetrical encryption algorithm called "Skipjack" with an 80-bit key length incorporating a key escrow technology that was developed by the NSA (Hodkowski, 1997) is illustrated in Figure 11.1. While the used symmetric encryption was 224 times more secure, it was backdoored using the key escrow functionalities, enabling law enforcement agencies to decrypt the Law Enforcement Access Field (LEAF) which was part of each transmission and hence knew the involved chips' serial numbers. However, authorities needed court orders to request device keys matching the serial numbers. This allowed them to get the session keys that were included in the LEAF and to decrypt communications (Dam & Lin, 1996).

---

be limited to video, audio or management functions; and (9) anti-virus software (Grimmett, 2001)

Ten months later, this method became Federal Information Processing Standard (FIPS) under the name "Escrowed Encryption Standard" (EES, see Figure 11.2) (Black, 2002; U.S. Department of Commerce & National Institute of Standards and Technology, 1994). However, only a few goods including the Clipper Chip, (approximately 10,000–15,000) were sold or installed, while most of them were bought by the U.S. administrative itself to convince manufacturers launching these programs (Banisar & Davies, 1998; Schulze, 2017). In 1995, the export of goods with symmetrical encryption at up to 64-bits containing "key recovery" was simplified (Dam & Lin, 1996; Mendelson et al., 1998). In August 1995, authorized FBI plans were brought to light, aiming to ban all encryption methods apart from EES decryptable in real-time (Shearer & Gutmann, 1996). Concerns arose that the voluntary nature of the Clipper Chip use was only transient until it becomes an established, inevitable standard (Shearer & Gutmann, 1996, p. 1380). The NSA withholding information on the detailed technical background of the algorithm when it was introduced calls into question its trustworthiness, as security should always rely on the secret key but not security-by-obscurity (Dean, 1999). At the end of 1995, the Clipper Chip initiative was considered failed, despite all governmental efforts. The main objection to Clipper Chip was the proposed key collection sys-

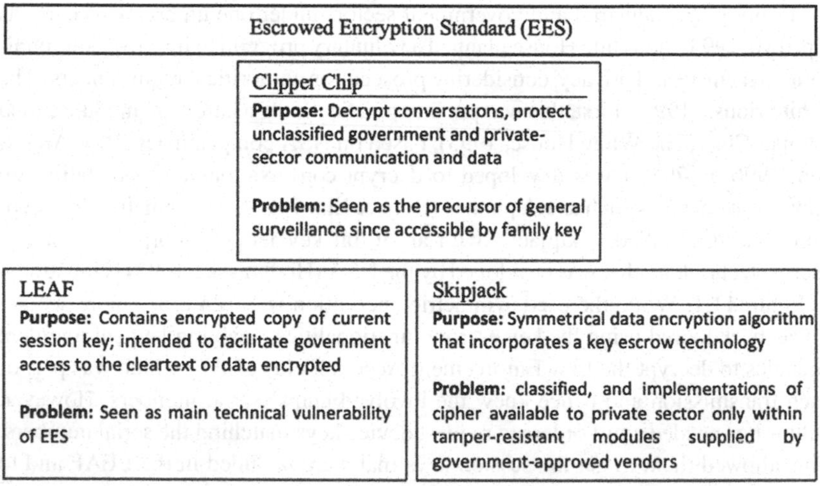

Figure 11.2 Outline of the main encryption practice before 2013 (own illustration). The shown encryption standards and methods have been developed by the NSA to ensure access to information

tem that was seen as a precursor to general surveillance. Anyone who wanted real security would either use other programs or use the Clipper Chip to add a second layer of non-government-approved encryption (Shearer & Gutmann, 1996, p. 130). Leading backdoors for symmetrical encryption at 40-bits bits (or RSA at 212-bits), calculations indicated that the NSA's budget was sufficient to break this kind of encryption and information accessing was easier for authorities (Ames, 1996).

There were two main developments in 1996: On the one hand, President Clinton transitioned encryption software from USML to the CCL and altered regulation from the Department of State to the Department of Commerce through Executive Order 13026. In general, the Clinton Administration enacted new measures to reform the encryption export regulations by permitting more powerful encryption technology and enabling mass-marketing of higher strength encryption products (Eichler, 2018, p. 13). On the other hand, since 1996, cryptography has been assessed as a dual-use technology if it exceeds the security level limit which is the maximum non-regulated symmetrical key length. Due to the exponential increase in computing powers (Moore, 1965), cryptography needed to keep up with this progress, due to the abilities of stronger attacks on encryption. Figure 11.3 shows the requirements for the key length (in bits) of cryptographic procedures because of technological developments, as well as the respective legally allowed key length. A distinction is made between short-term and long-term security of 20 years. The axiom of the recommended key length is that cryptography is secure if decryption would take an intelligence service with a 300 million funding several months. These assessments trace back to the report of (Blaze et al., 1996). Furthermore, since 1998, the NSA was using malware to tap data before computers encrypt it (Gallagher & Greenwald, 2014), while not detectable and remotely controllable (Boon et al., 2013). Further, it was planned to automatize these efforts on a large scale to infiltrate millions of computers (Gallagher & Greenwald, 2014). In terms of dual-use, a liberalization of U.S. export policies started in 1998, when the Clinton administration announced a new policy to reform the previously strict export regime.

Generally, it can be observed that due to increased digitalization cryptography became important for companies and for civilian purposes. Especially for global actors, the problem of the necessity to export encryption arose, which was prohibited by U.S. regulations. However, not least due to the increasing societal relevance and commercialization of the internet, there is a growing public discourse on the role of encryption that goes beyond a solely organizational debate. While in the 1990s communication encryption has been used by a few, there were critical voices from the security community demanding stronger encryption policies (Sircar, 2018).

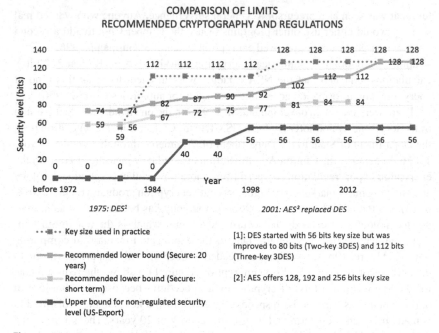

COMPARISON OF LIMITS
RECOMMENDED CRYPTOGRAPHY AND REGULATIONS

Figure 11.3 Recommended security levels compared with their regulations (own illustration, data sources: Abdalla et al., 2018; Babbage et al., 2012; Blaze et al., 1996; ENISA, 2014)

11.4.2 The 2000s: The War on Terror and the Spread of Social Media

The historic context changed with the attacks on the world trade center on 9/11, which led to the war on terror and to legislation increasing the abilities of law enforcement agencies, such as the Patriot Act. On the technological side, from the early 2000s on, social media companies emerged and expanded their user group from the U.S. to Europe and across the world. LinkedIn was founded in 2002, Facebook was founded in 2004, Twitter in 2006, and with the emergence of social media, the publicly available data as well as communication increased, leading to research on big data for surveillance. These globally active companies did not only sell the data of their customers for business-reasons but also became relevant as surveillance intermediaries for law enforcement agencies (Rozenheim, 2018). Due to their access to millions of consumers' data and the lack of regulation, concerns on privacy arrived and led to the first users of open-source end-to-end encryption software, OpenPGP (OpenPGP, 2020).

In the year 2000, key length was no longer the only important factor for export licenses, as exporting mass-market cryptography of all key lengths became possible. However, this applied to license exception for mass-market encryption at up to 64-bits. In March 2010, there was a remarkable change to the export regulations: Barack Obama announced a reform of the export controls of cryptography to facilitate trade and innovations (Fergusson & Kerr, 2018). Prior to this reform, most exporting manufacturers had to pass a 30-day long technical examination (Fergusson & Kerr, 2018). From now on, exporters only needed to register the exports to the Commerce Department and the NSA in a mail and send a report of export sales to the Commerce Department at the end of the year (U.S. Department of Commerce, 2010). This was not a free ticket to export for companies as this was only the framework of legislation for sensitive mass-market goods.

In 2013, secret programs by the NSA were revealed by NSA agent Edward Snowden. The information shed public attention on espionage activities of the NSA and were essential for the further evaluation of U.S. cryptography policy, stimulated a societal debate on privacy and data security, and brought the debate on cryptography policy into focus. In this context, the Guardian exposed an NSA program confirming their practices of continuously registering the metadata of millions of phone calls in the network of a large telecom operator (Greenwald, 2013b). Especially the NSA program BULLRUN was focused on the work with cryptography (Cayford et al., 2014, p. 646). Starting in 2000, the NSA had spent several billion U.S. dollars on the confidential project BULLRUN to be able to survey communication in the future (Larson, 2013) and to bypass or break some encryption algorithms protecting global trades, banking systems, business secrets, medical data, emails, web searches, internet chats, and phone calls as the leaked documents show (Perlroth & Goel, 2013). This was achieved by influencing international cryptography standards, using immense computing capacities of supercomputers as well as by cooperating with technology companies and internet providers (Ball et al., 2013).

A leaked guide for NSA employees revealed that BULLRUN was used to survey VPN, VoIP, and SSL (Ball et al., 2013). Apart from that, the NSA was able to decrypt the stream cipher A5/1 (Timberg, 2013), allowing them to easily access billions of phone calls and SMS messages (Timberg, 2013). In its SIGINT Enabling Project, the NSA worked with technology companies and an annual budget of 250 million dollars aiming to pursue manufacturers to purposely add weaknesses to commercial encryption systems (Timberg, 2013). The computer and network security company RSA was given 10 million dollars by the NSA for including a backdoor ("key escrow") to their encryption software (Menn, 2013). By allowing the NSA to surpass encryption, Microsoft could have given access to Outlook.com (Greenwald, 2013a), although stating that this had happened unintentionally (Greenwald, 2013a).

In some cases, the NSA pressured companies into providing keys or installing backdoors by taking legal action against them (Larson, 2013). Some stated that numerous keys were in the hands of the NSA because of their efforts to hack corporate networks (Perlroth & Goel, 2013). The NSA kept an internal database of keys for specific commercial goods (Perlroth & Goel, 2013). An internal report explicitly explained how the NSA has regularly received routers, servers, and other computer network devices of U.S. manufacturers, functioning as an intermediate stop on the distribution journey, installing a backdoor technology for surveillance and then repacking the goods with a factory seal and exporting them (Greenwald, 2013a). Moreover, the NSA built a backdoor into the algorithm Dual EC_DRBG which NIST treated as encryption standard, later followed by the "International Organization for Standardization" and its 163 member states (Landau, 2015; Perlroth & Goel, 2013). Additionally, the NSA worked on a quantum computer to break virtually all types of asymmetric encryption (Rich & Gellman, 2014).

Worldwide, the NSA infected 50,000 computer networks with malware to access sensitive information and to control various functionalities (Boon et al., 2013), including microphones, webcams, and histories together with login details (Gallagher & Greenwald, 2014). These attacks were executed by a special department called Office of Tailored Access Operations (TAO), now Computer Network Operations, which consisted of more than a thousand hackers (Boon et al., 2013; Gallagher & Greenwald, 2014). Following a Washington Post report which appeared in 2013, all 16 U.S. intelligence agencies had an annual budget of 50 billion dollars (Gellman & Miller, 2013). The following Figure 11.4 shows the crosshairs made of the NSA's fundamental methods to avoid cryptography.

Summarized, the exposure of NSA surveillance programs contrasts with the historically lengthy process toward liberalized cryptographic regulation. The outlined practices show, (1) how the U.S. government's attempts at regulation in cooperation with the NSA have not led to sufficient results and (2) how intelligence agencies have sought unofficial avenues. In the years between 2001 and 2013, the increasing use of end-to-end encryption in commercial communication goods led to a liberalization of the export of dual-use goods. Nevertheless, there were still restrictions of certain stronger encryption products, especially outside of mass-communication goods, e.g., for cryptography within military goods (Eichler, 2018). However, after the end of the Clipper Chip initiative, the strategy of law enforcement agencies started to shift towards the use of vulnerabilities and the cooperation with ICT companies as surveillance intermediaries (Greenberg, 2019). The same companies, however, profited from the liberalization of dual-use export regulations.

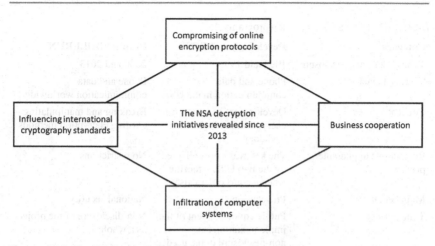

Figure 11.4 The NSA's decryption initiatives (own illustration)

11.4.3 The 2010s: From the Snowden Revelations to Today

Due to the increasing computing power, new challenges for encryption technologies arise today. The excessive use of internet-enabled devices such as smartphones also formulates new requirements on encryption. This is a time when big data analytics has become mainstream (Stieglitz, Mirbabaie, Fromm, & Melzer, 2018). As previously elaborated, adopted U.S. regulations have consistently fallen short of recommendations for short- and long-term security, and the U.S. government's policy assessment of cryptography based on key length can be judged restrictive rather than liberal. This discrepancy is illustrated by the fact that any encryption using the minimum required key length would be classified as a dual-use item, and that the limit on items that may be exported and not classified as dual-use items was last raised in 1998 to 56-bit. This value is maintained, even though NIST recommends the use of keys with a minimum strength of 112-bits of security to protect data until 2030, and 128-bits of security thereafter (ENISA, 2014) – more than double the value and consequently implying a 2(128-56) = 272 times larger range of keys. Thus, it can be argued that the "too slow" and too restrictive regulation of cryptography on the part of the U.S. government has not been able to keep up with the rapid pace of technical progress, leaving room for unofficial ways of intelligence agencies.

   Notably, there was not only a lack of anticipation of technical development, but also a lack of public discourse. Only after project BULLRUN produced an interna-

Table 11.3 The NSA's decryption programs

Category	Development of EES	Project "BULLRUN"
Time of start and disclosure	1993 and 1993	2000 and 2013
Surveyed Data	Phone and data communication in the USA	Phone and data communication worldwide
Concept	Development of a state-run encryption method with a backdoor	Breaking and manipulating existing encryption methods
Restrictions to guarantee privacy	The key was only delivered by the two U.S. authorities when a court order existed	No restrictions
Main beneficiary	Prosecution	National security
Transparency	Public announcement of the implementation but non-disclosure of the used method	Non-disclosure of the project as a whole
Success	Execution failed	Effective for decrypting communication surveyed by other NSA projects

tional backlash and increased the urge to use end-to-end encryption in messenger services such as Facebook and WhatsApp (Isaac, 2019), has a more active social discourse emerged – not only in the U.S., but worldwide, which is why Monsees speaks of a social sensibilization (Monsees, 2020). The intelligence and law enforcement officials have since taken the public perception of surveillance technology into account (Cayford and Pieters, 2018).

This led to the discussion of two new bills, making access to user data legally available by the support of the ICT companies. In March 2020, the U.S. Congress proposed the EARN IT Act, aiming to combat child abuse material online (Figas, 2020). This is based on Section 230, which states that online platforms cannot be held liable for the content of users on their platforms. According to the EARN IT Act, providers need to earn this immunity by complying with a set of guidelines developed by a commission of experts within the company to create effective guidelines (Pfefferkorn, 2020). These guidelines will probably affect end-to-end encryption (Pfefferkorn, 2020) since law enforcement officials have the option to search the data stored on servers to find criminal material online. By weakening end-to-end encryption, the data of all internet users will be less secure (Jordan & Polk, 2020). The second initiative is the "Lawful Access to Encrypted Data Act of

2020" (LAEDA), a bill to ban providers from offering any encryption that cannot be decrypted or by law enforcement (Pfefferkorn, 2020). This bill covers providers who recorded one million or more users annually in any year since 2016, if data is stored. When the data is in motion like in communication, providers with more than a million monthly active users in any month since January 2016 are affected by the ban. To access encrypted material, law enforcement needs a warrant based on a probable cause (LeClair, 2020). With law enforcement able to decrypt data stored on servers, companies cannot offer end-to-end encryption to their users anymore. Either they have the option to build backdoors into their encryption or not to use encryption at all Olmstead and Polk (2020). The massive roll-out of end-to-end encryption after Edward Snowden's revelation of the BULLRUN program primarily increased the costs for the NSA to collect and decrypt communication. Both legal initiatives are still in discussion, however, they show how security agencies face increasing financial and legal pressure (Savage, 2020).

The export of cryptography with a key length of 128 bits or more is considered as dual-use, which simplifies the export of strong encryption methods such as AES. Generally, most of the omnipresent cryptography technologies are currently still classified as dual-use and regulated by the Commerce Control List (Maurer et al., 2014; Schwechter, 2016). Goods with strong encryption require an export license unless they are distributed to Canada (Schwechter, 2016). Contrary to this, weak cryptography is not subject to strict regulations; as a license, it is only required for trades to terror-supporting or embargoed states (Schwechter, 2016). Presently, the CCL controls goods exceeding the 56-bits threshold for symmetrical cryptography and the 512-bits threshold for asymmetrical cryptography (Vella, 2017). In today's age, encryption with this key length is considered weak (Saper, 2013). However, as the U.S. Commerce Department Bureau of Industry and Security (BIS) elaborated: a broad range of license exceptions differentiating between various types of products, end-users, core benefits, and export destinations are included in the law (U.S. Department of Commerce, 2020). Moreover, for defense companies, the rules have been relaxed (Eichler, 2018, p. 27), so that sensitive electronic data is not considered to be classified as an "export good" if the data is end-to-end encrypted. There would be only a few forms of cryptography, including stronger ones, that could not be exported because of these license expectations (Eichler 2018, p. 27). For example, cryptography positioned as a mass-market good only requires an inquiry for categorization or a self-disclosure to the U.S. Commerce Department when it is at 64-bits for symmetrical encryption and 768-bits for asymmetrical encryption (U.S. Department of Commerce, 2016, p. 2). Furthermore, open-source cryptography is not affected by the export controls if the BIS is informed via email (U.S. Department of Commerce, 2020). This also simplifies the export of strong encryption methods such as AES. Only certain goods are still controlled: those of military nature, quantum key distribution, or cryptography for ultra-wideband systems (U.S. Department of Commerce, 2020).

11.5   Discussion

To answer the research question: **Why was the regulation of cryptography liberalized for mass communication services from 2000, while the surveillance politics focused on similar services?**, we compared the historical development of surveillance and dual-use policies in the U.S. in three time periods (1990–2021). Analyzing the development of **dual-use regulations** and the surveillance policies, we found it puzzling how mass communication services have been excluded from 2000 on. In the 1990s, the dual-use regulations were adapted to the increasing access to cryptography as part of the commercial internet (see Table 11.4). This was acknowledged, by changing the legislation from the United States Munition List (USML) to the Commerce Control List (CCL), while also enforcing the implementation of key escrow for symmetrical encryption. However, with the rising use of encryption, the exceptions and key lengths accelerated until 2000. In the 2000s, the use of end-to-end encryption increased, which made the key escrow approach impractical. The products for mass-marked communication have been excluded from the dual-use export restrictions, which were still in place for other exports with market encryption at up to 64-bits following a technical examination. However, the bureaucracy was further removed, requiring only self-reports and many exceptions, or even supporting the use of end-to-end encryption for military goods and information since 2016 (Eichler, 2018). Today, the export of cryptography with key length of 128 bits or more is considered dual-use. Within the U.S., the import, or domestic sales of cryptography, however, were never restricted.

The surveillance policy in the 1990s (see Table 11.5), in alignment with the dual-use policy, was developed to ensure a key escrow mechanism with the Clipper Chip initiative. In the 2000s, mass communication services became popular, as well as the first possibilities to implement end-to-end encryption for end-users. To retrieve data, security agencies made a bilateral agreement between the ICT companies and exploited weak encryption standards or software vulnerabilities. This way, intelligence organizations, like the NSA, profited from the export restrictions in two ways: First, the increased and global use of social media platforms and other commercial services for mass communication which did not use strong encryption. And second, as these companies would provide data to law enforcement agencies.

Edward Snowdon's revelations have drawn public awareness to the debate on cryptography. Consequently, U.S. companies had to rebuild their reputation and image: Apple and Alphabet reacted by establishing automatic encryption that makes it near to impossible to provide data even after a court order (Craig Timberg, 2014). They also cooperate in a coalition called Reform Government Surveillance with companies such as Amazon, Dropbox, and Microsoft (Reform Government Surveillance (RSG), 2020). They publicly stand up for privacy and the limitation of surveillance. Numerous companies expanded their security measures with investments running into the millions and started a digital arms race against the NSA (Perlroth & Goel, 2013). The U.S. has developed legal instruments that improve the possibility to access data by enforcing the cooperation of ICT companies (Murphy, 2020). ICT companies have faced pressure from both sides: from the government to implement different forms of key escrow, as well as from the customers, and have become surveillance intermediaries (Rozenheim, 2018). Murphy (2020, p. 260) states that the "increase in use of encryption is an example of escalation – a response to reckless (and unlawful) behavior by states in the past" and describes the "back door" as dual-use, as it is not only for the "good guys". However, surveillance technologies proliferate in a fragmented way driven by a diversity of factors and different sectors (Haggerty & Ericson, 2000; Kaufmann, 2016). The proliferation is influenced by the costs for decryption and effectiveness of surveillance as well as the public discourse. These factors influence what is perceived as proportionate (Cayford and Pieters, 2018) to legitimize the use or surveillance technologies.

Looking at current innovations in cryptography, such as better performance in asymmetric encryption technologies with Elliptic Curve Crypto (ECC) or the research in the field of quantum computing, key length, with respect to the symmetric counterparts (see Section 11.1), will still be an important measurement to determine, whether a cipher can be considered secure. Moreover, it enables researchers to discuss the strength of cryptographic algorithms (Paterson, 2015). Innovations in cryptography usually impact the computational capabilities of machines, which required longer key lengths or a new family of cryptographic algorithms. Such impacts are currently discussed with the development of quantum computers, which, if they become available, can solve currently known mathematical problems. This would break currently popular asymmetric cryptographic algorithms and thus, require new standards. Moreover, quantum computers also impact symmetric cryptographic algorithms due to their properties, which would require twice the key length for the same security (Bennett et al., 1997). Besides the key length, other factors also impact the security of cryptographic algorithms (Paterson, 2015). One such factor is the actual implementation of the cryptographic algorithm. It might be implemented with vulnerabilities compromising the otherwise mathematically proven to

Table 11.4 Overview of Dual-use Regulation

Dual-use Regulation	1990s	2010s	2020s
Targeted Actors	(1) Exporting companies (2) Non-U.S. citizens	(1) Exporting companies (with exceptions regarding the sector and key length) (2) Non-U.S. citizens (until 2010)	(1) Exporting companies (with exceptions regarding the sector and key length)
Implementing Organizations	• USML → CCL	• CCL • BXA → BIS, Department of Commerce	• CCL • BIS, Department of Commerce
Measures and Regulations	• Prohibition • Classification as weapon/dual-use item • Liberalization since 1998 for mass communication products	• Unilateral controls • Export license for goods with strong encryption • Trade-deregulation since 2010	• Dual-use: key length of 128-bits or more • Simplification of strong encryption exports • liberalization to support encryption of military information and goods (2016)
Changes in Cryptography	• Symmetric keys • Problematic export	• Public-key-encryption (end-to-end) became more used	• E2EE • Distributed reimplementation of social media platforms

be a secure algorithm. Another factor is the system itself, which is used for cryptographic operations since it might be compromised. These organizational factors of security however can be created or unknowingly taken advantage of by companies which are forced to implement access to their data by the government to prevent users to "go dark" (Murphy, 2020). Many states, e.g., in the EU have evoked ideas of legal state hacking, however, without paying enough attention to the safeguards towards these methods (B.-J. Koops & Kosta, 2018). In addition, there is a growing industry which offers "surveillance as a service", in which law enforcement agencies and secret services outsource the technological hacking capacities or to exploit software vulnerabilities when needed, instead of building the capacity them-

Table 11.5 Overview of NSA Surveillance Practices

Surveillance Practices	1990s	2010s	2020s
Targeted Actors	(1) Manufacturing companies	(1) Companies as intermediaries (2) U.S. and non-U.S. citizens	(1) Companies as intermediaries (2) U.S. and non-U.S. citizens
Implementing Organizations	• Law enforcement agencies, • Secret Services	• Law enforcement agencies, • Secret Services	• Law enforcement agencies, • Secret Services
Measures, Programs and Regulations	• Key Escrow • Clipper Chip • Skipjack • LEAF	• BULLRUN • SIGINT Enabling Project	• EARN IT • LEADA
Innovations in Cryptography	• Proven insecurity of old standards	• Facilitation of trade/innovations • Reduced bureaucracy • Bypass/break of encryption exports	• Formation of privacy-focused tech-companies • Surveillance as a service (NSO)

selves (Kirchgaessner et al., 2021). This makes the use of the service more flexible for organizations. However, the proliferation and use of such services is difficult to safeguard, as the U.S. has put the NSO Group on a trade blacklist, because it has conducted "transnational repression [..] targeting dissidents, journalists, and activists" (Clayton, 2021).

Our research has limitations: First, the information that we have about current surveillance programs is very limited. To our knowledge, there is no information if and how the surveillance programs by the NSA are continued. Only little is known from fact-finding committees, like in Germany, which only focused on the cooperation between the BND and the NSA (Gopalakrishnan, 2016). The surveillance by the NSA of non-U.S. and non-EU citizens needs to be further studied, focusing on the quality and quantity of surveillance technologies, as well as the question of global coverage while there is a lack of political representation in the discourse on proportionality. Regarding the assessment of metadata surveillance, a comparison to the discourse on data preservation programs by internet providers can be drawn (Riebe, Haunschild, et al., 2020). Second, the ambivalent role of ICT companies as surveillance intermediaries needs further investigation. In addition, the case of the surveillance software Pegasus has shown how intelligence organizations partly outsource surveillance technologies (Kirchgaessner et al., 2021). This reduces the already difficult process of attributing accountability for surveillance practices.

11.6   Conclusion

Encryption of information is ubiquitous and serves to secure most of today's ICT infrastructure. This paper has illustrated how the regulation of cryptography as a dual-use good as well as the practices of the US intelligence and law enforcement agencies to break or weaken encryption have developed since the 1990s. While the regulation of dual-use goods has been liberalized, ICT companies have become both allies of and antagonists to the secret services. Strategies to break encryption or work around encryption using key escrow approaches, like the Clipper Chip, have been unsuccessful, due to public backlash and security vulnerabilities of the system and thus moved to bilateral agreements and cooperation with individual companies. Further approaches to regulate and break encryption, as well as public discourse to outlaw strong encryption, have shown how the security narratives are still used up to this day. As the restrictions of the export of cryptography have been liberalized to some extent, they help to reinforce the surveillance through the exceptions for surveillance intermediaries. The authors conclude that as surveillance technologies are increasingly proliferating, the role of ICT as surveillance intermediaries needs to be further discussed. Recent attempts to ban law enforcement-proof encryption should be used to foster a discourse on the transparent process of balancing the conflicting security interests and the means of intelligence and law enforcement organizations.

Values and Value Conflicts in the Context of OSINT Technologies for Cybersecurity Incident Response

12

12.1 Introduction

Research on Computer Supported Cooperative Work (CSCW) has driven the field of crisis informatics, which has been described as a multidisciplinary field "concerned with the ways in which information systems are entangled with socio-behavioral phenomena connected to disasters" (Soden & Palen, 2018, p. 2). To respond to crises, gathering and analysing social media data for emergency services has been studied. Especially its use for emergency operators in collaboration with informal response communities (Purohit et al., 2014), the mitigation of information overload (Kaufhold et al., 2021), and social media users' expectations towards crisis communication (Petersen et al., 2017; Reuter et al., 2017) has been explored. Similar to existing emergency services for natural disasters, Computer Emergency Response Teams (CERTs), which are also known as Computer Security Incident Response Teams (CSIRTs) serve as a central point of contact, advice, and coordination for government institutions and private actors in the event of cybersecurity incidents and threats (Kossakowski 2001; Riebe, Kaufhold, & Reuter, 2021).

ORIGINAL PUBLICATION Riebe, T., Bäumler, J., Kaufhold, M.-A., & Reuter, C. (2023). Values and Value Conflicts in the Context of OSINT Technologies for Cybersecurity Incident Response: A Value Sensitive Design Perspective. *JCSCW*. https://doi.org/10.1007/s10606-022-09453-4

Supplementary Information The online version contains supplementary material available at https://doi.org/10.1007/978-3-658-41667-6_12.

CERTs do not only respond to incidents, which are reported to them, they also monitor various media sources for new vulnerabilities and other threats, verify different pieces of information, analyse threats, communicate with other CERTs, and are expected to support "stakeholder[s] with specific recommendations, to provide (daily) reports for selected stakeholders (e.g., a daily vulnerability report for ministries), or to issue a general warning for multiple stakeholders (in case larger- scaled ICT infrastructures are threatened)" (Riebe, Kaufhold and Reuter, 2021, p. 11). The main challenge CERTs face when executing their tasks, lies in ensuring adequate cyber situational awareness when evaluating information from numerous public and closed sources (Franke & Brynielsson, 2014; Riebe, Kaufhold and Reuter, 2021). Relevant public sources such as social media, blogs, websites, and feeds can be included in this process, as part of an open-source intelligence (OSINT) approach (Glassman & Kang, 2012). Considering the risk of information overload when evaluating public sources, especially in the case of serious security incidents with many potential civilian casualties, the use of technical systems utilising machine learning (ML) algorithms for information filtering and analysis has become common (Kaufhold et al., 2020). In such decision support systems, artificial intelligence (AI) agents are becoming increasingly relevant as assistants for decision-making (Chouldechova et al., 2018). CERT members have stated that they are in need of (semi-)automated assistance for data gathering, (pre-)processing, analysis, and communication of cyber threats based on ML (Riebe, Kaufhold, & Reuter 2021; Van der Kleij et al., 2017). Thus, there is the increasing use of OSINT systems within CERTs (Kassim et al., 2022). As OSINT mostly relies on private data from users of online media to be an effective tool for cybersecurity operators, the acceptance of such a system is decisive. Value conflicts may arise as a consequence of different groups in society being directly or indirectly affected in different ways, depending on the application of OSINT technologies. Therefore, it is imperative that not only OSINT systems be further researched and investigated, but also arising value conflicts. Research that focuses primarily on the values and value conflicts relevant to the development of OSINT systems for cybersecurity incident response has not yet been conducted extensively. This paper is guided by the collaborative Value Sensitive Design (VSD) method (Friedman, 1996) and will contribute to answering the following research question: **Which values and value conflicts emerge due to the application and development of ML-based open-source intelligence technologies in the context of cybersecurity incident response?**

Our study is part of the CYWARN research project developing OSINT artefacts for CERTs (M.-A. Kaufhold et al., 2021), and contributes to the CSCW-discourse with (1) a systematic literature review about technical research on OSINT technologies for the application in the domain of cybersecurity, (2) an empirically grounded elaboration of relevant stakeholder values and value conflicts in connection to the application and development of OSINT technologies for cybersecurity incident response, and (3) an outline of implications for the research on and the design of ML-based OSINT technologies for collaborative cybersecurity incident response.

This paper is structured as follows: In Section 12.2, related work on OSINT and VSD is presented and the research gap is outlined. Afterwards, Section 12.3 introduces the research design. We employ a triangulation of methods that combines an empirical case study consisting of a focus group (N=7) and semi-structured expert interviews (N=9) with a systematic literature review of technical research on OSINT technologies in the context of cybersecurity (N=73). The results of both the literature review and the empirical case study are presented in Section 12.4. In Section 12.5, insights obtained are synthesised by elaborating research and design implications and it is discussed how value sensitivity can facilitate collaboration. Finally, the limitations of the study are indicated, possible starting points for further research are outlined, and in Section 12.6 a brief summary of the work is provided.

12.2 Background and Related Work

As the design and application of novel information and communication technology (ICT) artefacts interferes with existing social practices, it is necessary to engage with the practices and problems of professionals, institutional arrangements, and technical infrastructures of the respective application environment (Wulf et al., 2011). Approaches for participatory design, which aim to address this issue, have been part of the CSCW discourse (Randall et al., 2007), as they follow the objective of facilitating cooperation (Kensing & Blomberg, 1998). Extensive research has focused on the design for collaboration in crisis response to better understand the collaborative practices and, thus, design systems which support response teams (Büscher et al., 2016; Cobb et al., 2014; Liegl et al., 2016; Reuter et al., 2014). Here, collaboration can be described as the development of a set of common practices which could be adopted by newcomers without previous participation and explanation (Heath & Luff, 1992). With regard to CERTs, this includes monitoring of and responding to cyber threats and incidents, as well as evaluating and sharing relevant information with outside parties. OSINT systems can help collaborating distributed teams to gain a shared situational awareness due to their support of context awareness, thus facilitating the establishment of a meta-perspective (R. Jones et al., 2021).

This section will first provide an overview on how OSINT systems as AI agents assist CERTs (Subsection 12.2.1), second introduce VSD as our participatory design approach and situate the paper in context of previous research (Subsection 12.2.2) and third, outline the research gap (Subsection 12.2.3).

12.2.1 OSINT Systems as AI-based Decision Support in Cybersecurity Incident Response

Central to OSINT is the idea that various pieces of publicly available information can be combined in unforeseen ways to gain innovative insights about the subject of interest (Glassman & Kang, 2012). OSINT can accordingly be defined as an activity that "involves the collection, analysis, and use of data from open sources for intelligence purposes" (B. -J. Koops et al., 2013, p. 677). Approaches for cybersecurity incident response predominantly use social media as their main source (Riebe, Wirth, et al., 2021), thereby taking advantage of crowdsourcing. Crowdsourcing for emergency response, however, depends on the quality and the trustworthiness of the information (Tapia & Moore, 2014).

ML algorithms are increasingly used for the automation of data gathering, preprocessing, and analysis (Williams & Blum, 2018). With the adoption of ML, challenges of explainability arise, as non-expert users are often unable to comprehend how an algorithm produces a certain output (Burrell, 2016). This is problematic as explainability is crucial to establishing users' trust in a system (Dzindolet et al., 2003). Therefore, recent research focuses on possibilities of explainable artificial intelligence (XAI) (Longo et al., 2020; Wang et al., 2019).

As part of decision support systems, AI has gained importance in assisting teams with particular types of expertise (Bansal et al., 2019). In their study on Human-AI interaction, Q. Zhang et al. (2022, p. 1) study "how people trust and rely on an AI assistant that performs with different levels of expertise relative to the person, ranging from completely overlapping expertise to perfectly complementary expertise". In their experiments, they found that the "ideal partnership between humans and AI has been based on the premise of their complementary expertise" (Q. Zhang et al., 2022, p. 20). In addition, they found that trust in AI was lowest when there was a complete overlap in the expertise of AI and human operators. Thus, trust in an AI agent is associated with the perceived usefulness of the AI and its complementary expertise. For the trust of the human operator, the style of communication of the AI agents has also been shown to be relevant (Q. Zhang et al., 2022). As shown in an study by Feng & Boyd-Graber (2019) using human-computer teams to perform play a trivia knowledge game, the skill level of human operators is crucial for the interpretation of the expertise of AI. This is supported by Schaffer et al. (2019), who found in their study (N=529), that an AI agent was only effective at lower levels of self-assessed knowledge, whereas self-confident users often rejected the agent's suggestions. In summary, for an effective Human-AI-Teaming in decision-making processes, the expertise of the users, the capabilities of the AI systems, e.g. managing large amounts of data in real-time and identifying similarities, as well as the communication style of the AI agents towards the users are relevant.

For cybersecurity incident response, OSINT technologies leveraging ML are primarily used in three areas. First, they are used for investigative purposes, e.g., to support digital forensics (Quick & Choo, 2018), or cyberattack attribution (Layton, 2016). Second, they are utilised for gathering cyber threat intelligence (CTI), which can be understood as "threat-related information which allows cyber security experts to investigate on a certain threat, e.g. the name of a malware, adversary or vulnerability" (Tundis et al., 2020, p. 454). Third, they are also used for risk assessment and mitigation purposes, e.g. to assess the attack surface of organisations (D. R. Hayes & Cappa, 2018), or to expose social engineering attack opportunities (Edwards et al., 2017).

In a study comprising an online survey and semi-structured interviews with staff of 13 national CERTs from Asia, Europe, the Caribbean, and North America, Kassim et al. (2022) found that the use of OSINT tools in cybersecurity incident response is on the rise. In accordance to Riebe, Kaufhold and Reuter (2021), they found that CERTs lack the resources to manage the increasing amount of public available data, which requires further verification and risk analysis. In their study on the collaborative practices of German CERTs, Riebe, Kaufhold and Reuter (2021) found that the (semi-)automation of threat detection and analysis, as well as reporting interfaces were found to be useful improvements.

12.2.2 VSD Research on OSINT

VSD, as a theoretically grounded method, is particularly well suited to anticipate value conflicts that arise through technology use, and proactively addresses them during design (Friedman et al., 2013). As a central theoretical assumption, VSD takes an interactional position on the relationship between technology design and social context; design features support or undermine certain values, but ultimately only their interplay with users and the context of use determines how a technology influences society (Davis & Nathan, 2015). A value can be defined as "what a person or group of people consider important in life" (Friedman et al., 2013, p. 57). VSD strives to consider direct and indirect stakeholders and their values during design (Friedman et al., 2013). As often differing values are considered important, value conflicts may arise. A value conflict exists, if competing values suggest incompatible choices as the best for the design of technical artefacts and no single value trumps all others (van de Poel & Royakkers, 2011).

In order to ensure that values are taken into account, VSD proposes a methodology that is composed of three interdependent and iteratively applied types of investigation (Friedman et al., 2013). In conceptual investigations, stakeholder groups affected by the envisaged technical artefacts are identified, and values expected to be important to them are elaborated as well as conceptualised (Friedman et al., 2013). In empirical investigations, social science methods are used to revise these findings with a focus on the opinions of stakeholders, as well as anticipated usage contexts (Manders-Huits, 2011). During both types of investigations, potential value conflicts may be identified (Friedman et al., 2013). Finally, in technical investigations, design choices that support identified and prioritised values are derived (Manders-Huits, 2011). Concerning value discovery, Le Dantec et al., (2009) argue that values should be identified during direct stakeholder engagement. In agreement with this, we utilise empirical investigations for value discovery in this work.

Several studies have specifically explored values and value conflicts in the cybersecurity domain. Among others, potential conflicts have been identified between the values security and privacy, the values security and fairness (Christen et al., 2017; Domingo-Ferrer & Blanco-Justicia, 2020; van de Poel, 2020), as well as the values security and autonomy (Christen et al., 2017; Domingo-Ferrer & Blanco-Justicia, 2020). Further, privacy was found to be potentially conflicting with both fairness and accountability (van de Poel, 2020). However, the identified conflicts mostly involve either security or privacy and altogether the works remained on a conceptual level, without reference to specific technical artefacts. Other publications referred to specific OSINT artefacts for other security purposes, but they were narrowly focused on safeguarding the value privacy through regulatory Privacy by Design approaches (Casanovas, 2014; Casanovas, 2017; Casanovas et al., 2014; Cuijpers, 2013; B. -J. Koops et al., 2013; Rajamäki, 2019; Rajamäki & Simola, 2019).

12.2.3 Research Gap

While values and value conflicts relevant to cybersecurity have been investigated conceptually (Christen et al., 2017; Domingo-Ferrer & Blanco-Justicia, 2020; van de Poel, 2020), to the best of the authors' knowledge, there are no publications that primarily focus on the values relevant to ML-based OSINT technologies for cybersecurity incident response, despite their increasing significance. Moreover, the consideration of Privacy by Design principles (Casanovas, 2014; Casanovas, 2017; Casanovas et al., 2014; Cuijpers, 2013; B. -J. Koops et al., 2013; Rajamäki, 2019;

Rajamäki & Simola, 2019) has only been studied in connection to OSINT artefacts for other security related scenarios. Riebe, Wirth, et al., (2021) have further shown that Privacy by Design principles are hardly taken into consideration in technical research on the development of OSINT artefacts for cybersecurity event detection. Accordingly, a research gap can be found with regard to the empirical investigation of relevant stakeholder values related to potential value conflicts resulting from the application and development of such technologies as ML-based decision support systems. The derived implications for design and research may be essential for the future development of OSINT systems for cybersecurity incident response in order to ensure their societal acceptance and stakeholder cooperation.

12.3 Methods

To elaborate which values and value conflicts emerge due to the application and development of ML-based OSINT technologies in the context of cybersecurity incident response, the research design uses a triangulation of methods (see Figure 12.1). While the empirical investigation of relevant values and value conflicts is performed on the basis of a case study in which the results of a focus group (N=7) and of semi-structured expert interviews (N=9) are content-analysed, along with a preceding conceptual investigation of direct and indirect stakeholder groups, a systematic literature study (N=73) reviews technical research on OSINT technologies for the domain of cybersecurity. A combination of these approaches is reasonable,

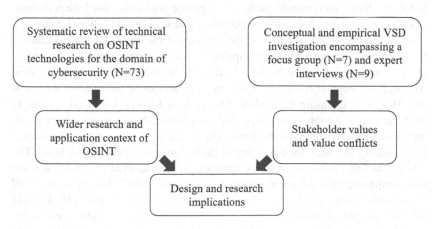

Figure 12.1 Illustration of the research design

particularly taking into account the elaboration of the values and value conflicts can be based on an adequate empirical basis, and that it is possible to complement the gained insights with perspectives from other OSINT artefacts and application scenarios. While the methodological procedure of the literature review is described in Subsection 12.3.1, the details regarding the case study are presented in Subsection 12.3.2.

12.3.1 Systematic Literature Review: OSINT in the Domain of Cybersecurity

To situate the findings of the empirical case study within the broader context of technical research on OSINT-technologies for application in the field of cybersecurity, the literature review section seeks to answer the **following questions**:

1. For which deployment scenarios in the cybersecurity domain are OSINT technologies being developed?
2. What technical features, techniques, and data sources are used?
3. Are ethical, legal, and social implications taken into consideration?

As this review follows an explicit and reproducible method to identify and evaluate the publications, it can be considered a systematic literature review (vom Brocke et al., 2015). Specifically, a sequential review approach is used in which literature search, analysis, and the writing of the review follow a step-by-step process (Levy & J. Ellis, 2006). As research conducted by private actors and state bodies in many cases is not accessible, only research published in academic publications is taken into account. For the review, a search in the literature databases ACM Digital Library, IEEE-Xplore, Science Direct, and Springer Link was conducted. As the review focuses on technical research, the selection of the databases was based on their coverage of computer science literature and the number of publications they contain. Moreover, to ensure the quality of the reviewed works, it seemed sensible to limit the search to publications in peer-reviewed journals and conference proceedings. Finally, only work published from the beginning of the databases' coverage to the end of May 2021, the beginning of the literature research, was included. The full-text and metadata search in the databases was conducted with the following search expression using Boolean operators: *("cyber security" OR cybersecurity OR "information security" OR cybercrime) AND (OSINT OR SOCMINT OR WEBINT OR "open-source intelligence" OR "social media intelligence" OR "web intelligence").* The procedure of publication search and selection is illustrated in Table 12.1.

Table 12.1 Procedure of the publication selection for the systematic literature review, differentiated by database

Database	Initial results	Journals & Proceedings	Relevant publications
IEEE-Xplore	409	356	44
ACM Digital Library	155	147	8
Springer Link	569	313	16
Science Direct	286	136	5
Total	1,419	945	73

The search resulted in 1,419 preliminary results, of which 945 were papers published in journals and conference proceedings. In a next step, the articles' abstracts were screened to identify irrelevant publications to the goal of the review. First, publications not focused on the development of OSINT artefacts for the cybersecurity domain, including those related to cybercrime in a broader sense, were excluded. Second, publications in which the processing of publicly available data is only a secondary aspect of an artefact were excluded. Third, research published in languages other than English was excluded. Finally, inaccessible papers and duplications were excluded. This resulted in the exclusion of 872 publications. The remaining 73 were quantitatively analysed with Excel.[1] The categories were compiled in response to the three guiding questions of the review. A structured examination of the usage scenarios, features, technical approaches, and data sources of available OSINT approaches, as well as their attention to ethical, legal, and social implications (ELSI), is crucial to derive design and research implications that extend beyond the individual case studied in depth in this paper. The subcategories were initially generated by screening review papers and chapters on OSINT (Pastor-Galindo et al., 2020; Simran et al., 2020; Tundis et al., 2020). They were then revised in light of a preliminary engagement with the selected publications before the final analysis was performed.

12.3.2 Conceptual and Empirical VSD Case Study

Conceptual Stakeholder Analysis
A conceptual investigation helped to identify the stakeholders directly and indirectly affected (Friedman et al., 2017). For this purpose, a structured workshop was conducted within the research project team, in which, building on potential use cases, it

---

[1] The categories and subcategories of analysis can be found in the electronic supplementary material Appendix 16.5.

was asked which groups interact with or are affected by OSINT artefacts. The results are presented in Subsection 12.4.2. In a next step, the authors identified potential harms and benefits for stakeholders as well as potentially implicated values and established working definitions based on relevant literature (Friedman et al., 2013).

Data Collection: Focus Group and Semi-structured Interviews
In order to identify relevant values and value conflicts, we conducted a focus group within the team of developers and researchers and nine semi-structured interviews with key stakeholder groups. In designing the procedure for data collection, we adapted the approach of Mueller and Heger, 2018. Table 12.2 summarises the interviews and the focus group conducted.

Table 12.2 Overview of the interviews and the focus group with the involved stakeholder groups and the respective types of organisations

No.	Type	Stakeholder	Organisation
I1	Interview	Direct Users	State CERT
I2	Interview	Direct Users	State CERT
I3	Interview	Direct Users	State CERT
I4	Interview	Direct Users	State CERT
I5	Interview	Direct Users	University CERT
I6	Interview	Potential Users	State company
I7	Interview	Potential Users	Humanitarian organisation
I8	Interview	Potential Users	Civil protection VOST
I9	Interview	Affected by Data Collection	Civil society
F1	Focus Group	Developers & Researchers	Public university, software development company, state CERT

The focus group (F1) involved seven participants from the fields of computer science, media and cognitive sciences, and software development, who were all part of the CYWARN research project, including one staff member of a German state level CERT. The sample consisted of six male participants and one female participant. The design of the focus group followed the recommendations by Krueger and Casey, (2015). The discussion was held digitally and was semi-structured by a moderation guideline. After an input about VSD and a hypothetical usage scenario of the OSINT artefacts in development as a stimulus to facilitate a discussion, we asked the participants to brainstorm and write down ethical, legal, and social implications on a digital board. Afterwards, we went through the issues collected and asked the participants to discuss them with a focus on potentially implicated stakeholder values and value conflicts.

The semi-structured expert interviews (Gläser & Laudel, 2010; Kallio et al., 2016) were designed to gather empirical insights on the values important to key stakeholder groups. To collect the data, we followed a convenience sampling approach and sent interview requests to relevant organisations and individuals. When selecting the participants, we drew on the insights of the stakeholder analysis (see Subsection 12.4.2) and took care to involve both stakeholders directly and indirectly affected by technology development; however, since indirect effects may be experienced by a wide array of actors, we restricted the scope to stakeholders that might be most significantly affected (Friedman et al., 2017). Overall, we interviewed nine individuals from three stakeholder groups: (1) Five interviews were conducted with CERT employees, as they belong to the prospective user group of the developed artefacts. (2) Three interviews were conducted with further potential users as it is intended to transfer the artefacts to other application domains as well (I6, I7, I8). Specifically, we interviewed information security officers of a state company (I6) and a humanitarian organisation active in disaster relief (I7), as well as the head of a virtual operations support team (VOST) (I8). (3) Finally, to consider the perspective of individuals potentially affected by OSINT gathering, we interviewed one individual who is regularly disseminating cybersecurity information on social media and is active in cybersecurity related civil society organisations (I9). After obtaining the interviewees' informed consent, several blocks of questions were asked based on an interview guideline, which was slightly adapted to suit the particularities of the different stakeholder groups. The interview sessions were conducted online, were recorded and lasted on average 74 minutes.

Data Analysis: Qualitative Content Analysis
After the focus group and the interviews were transcribed, a software-assisted and category-based structuring qualitative content analysis following Kuckartz (2016) was conducted. We worked with thematic categories that were developed deductively on the basis of existing literature on values, as well as inductively during the analysis of the empirical material. In this study, the main category *Value* with ten subcategories, as well as the main category *Value Conflict* were used. The categories were defined in a codebook and supplemented with coding rules and examples.[2] The

---

[2] A shortened version of the codebook can be found in Appendix 16.5 in the electronic supplementary material.

transcripts were coded with the qualitative content analysis software MAXQDA. First, all the material was revised to select coding examples for each category. Then, the focus group and two interviews were coded to verify the intercoder agreement with MAXQDA. This resulted in a kappa coefficient after Brennan & Prediger (1981) of 0.69, what can be interpreted as a good result (Rädiker & Kuckartz, 2019). Furthermore, the codebook was later revised in order to further increase intercoder agreement. The text segments assigned to each category were then assembled and analysed together.

12.4   Results

In the following, the results of the literature study are presented in Subsection 12.4.1. Afterwards, Subsection 12.4.2 introduces the stakeholder groups identified and outlines the results of the content analysis of the empirical material.

12.4.1 OSINT-Technologies in the Domain of Cybersecurity

Of the 73 publications evaluated in the review, 10% named investigative purposes as the intended **scenario of use** for the systems. In 74% of the publications, systems were developed for primary use in the context of gathering CTI, in 12% for use in the area of risk assessment and mitigation, and in 4% for both investigative and CTI purposes. The temporal distribution of publications per year is shown in Figure 12.2.

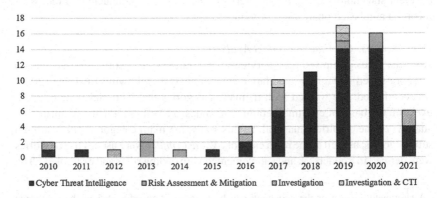

Figure 12.2 Number of publications per year, differentiated by intended scenarios of use

The publications were also examined concerning respective **features** of the systems. In 44 publications, data gathering methods were either an integrated part of the artefacts, or new data sets were specifically created in the context of research. In 36 publications, approaches for the detection of cybersecurity events have been developed. This included models for the detection of emerging cybersecurity topics (Al-Ramahi et al., 2020; Dalton et al., 2017; Kawaguchi et al., 2017; Schäfer et al., 2019), the aggregation of individual pieces of information into security events (Alves et al., 2019; Alves et al., 2021; Azevedo et al., 2019; Vacas et al., 2018), the detection of distinct types of information (Behzadan et al., 2018; Gonzalez-Granadillo et al., 2019; Gonzalez-Granadillo et al., 2021; Liao et al., 2016; Syed, 2020), and the detection of threats related to specific infrastructures (Dionisio et al., 2019) or products (Kannavara et al., 2019; Neil et al., 2018; Nunes et al., 2018). Approaches to the classification or filtering of relevant information are presented in 26 publications, and 15 systems comprise data visualisation functions, including Social Network Analysis to explore relationships in hacker forums and marketplaces (S.-Y. Huang & Ban, 2019; S.-Y. Huang et al., 2019; Schäfer et al., 2019).

While twelve systems have the capacity to generate reports or structured pieces of information, e.g. Indicators of Compromise (IoCs), eleven systems aim to identify specific users or communities. This is related to the assessment of organisational attack surfaces or penetration testing (Chitkara et al., 2020; Edwards et al., 2017; Urban et al., 2020), the identification of individuals with insider threat potential (Kandias, Mitrou, et al., 2013; Kandias, Stavrou, Bozovic, Mitrou, & Gritzalis, 2013; Kandias, Stavrou, Bozovic, Mitrou, & Gritzalis, 2013; Kandias et al., 2017), and the investigation of hacker forums and marketplaces (Fallmann et al., 2010; S.-Y. Huang et al., 2019; S.-Y. Huang & Ban, 2019; Schäfer et al., 2019). Finally, five papers demonstrate techniques to analyse the quality or credibility of CTI (Ghazi et al., 2018; Gong et al., 2018; Jo et al., 2021; N. Khurana et al., 2019; R. Liu et al., 2017), and three propose methods to assess the quality or credibility of CTI sources (Gong et al., 2018; R. Liu et al., 2017; Tundis et al., 2020).

Additionally, the publications were analysed for the use of selected **algorithmic approaches** (see Figure 12.3).

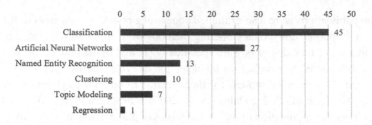

Figure 12.3 Algorithmic approaches implemented in the artefacts developed

Most frequently, in 45 cases, algorithms for classification were implemented. Clustering, on the other hand, was only used ten times and regression only once. In addition, 13 papers used named-entity recognition, i.e. the classification of named entities in unstructured text into predefined categories for the purpose of information extraction, and seven papers used latent Dirichlet allocation for topic modelling, i.e., the discovery of previously undefined topics in a document corpus. Artificial neural networks were used in 27 systems. Concerning the use of ML, 46 systems used supervised ML, 28 unsupervised ML, one semi-supervised ML and 19 none. In line with the features of the examined OSINT systems, the research is focused on ML algorithms that assist operators in managing the high volume, variety, and velocity of big data by using trained classifiers, self-learning neural networks, named entity recognition, clustering, topic modeling, and regression to identify cybersecurity events, threats, and threat actors, as well as to assess the relevance, quality, or credibility of CTI and respective sources.

A variety of different **sources of information** were used with the systems.

Twitter was used 20 times, followed by cybersecurity blogs, forums, or websites that were utilised eleven times. Information from hacker forums, as well as from CTI feeds and platforms was accessed ten times each. Information from other social networks, e.g. Reddit, Facebook, and YouTube, was processed in nine instances, while seven systems made use of data gathered from dark web forums and marketplaces. Less common data sources can be found in Figure 12.4.

Finally, it was examined whether **ELSI** of the respective systems were discussed. Of the 73 papers, only eleven considered such issues. While some authors argued that using only publicly available data circumvents ethical issues (Pournouri & Akhgar, 2015; Pournouri et al., 2019), Edwards et al., 2017 justified their decision not to list individuals in reports on organisations' social engineering attack surface with the concern that this could cause disciplinary action. In addition, to increase algorithmic comprehensibility, they decided to use decision tree classifiers to iden-

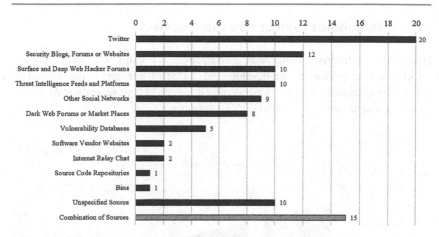

Figure 12.4 Publicly available information sources used for data gathering with the artefacts developed

tify employee profiles. In a similar study, Urban et al., (2020) emphasised strict compliance with data protection requirements and the avoidance of any legally or ethically questionable strategies for data acquisition. With regard to the investigation of dark web marketplaces, Lawrence et al., (2017) mitigate the risk of legal ramifications by restricting web scraping to cybercrime related sections, textual data, and non-personal information. Ranade et al., (2018) motivated their development of a deep learning model for CTI translation partly on the premise that analysts are often not allowed to use third party services due to privacy, security, and confidentiality policies. Beyond that, a trade-off between data protection and demands of forensic investigators to have access to proactively collected data is discussed by Nisioti et al., (2021). The most extensive discussion of ELSI is found in the context of research on the identification of employees with insider threat potential. Negative effects on personal and human rights of those affected, as well as dangers concerning algorithmic profiling are discussed, and the recommendation that such screenings should be subject to strict preconditions is provided (Kandias, Mitrou, et al., 2013; Kandias, Stavrou, Bozovic, Mitrou, & Gritzalis, 2013; Kandias, Stavrou, Bozovic, Mitrou, & Gritzalis 2013; Kandias et al., 2017).

12.4.2 Stakeholder Values and Value Conflicts

During the preliminary conceptual investigation, six main stakeholder groups affected by the application and development of OSINT artefacts in the domain of cybersecurity incident response were identified. Figure 12.5 presents the stakeholder groups and their interaction with OSINT artefacts.

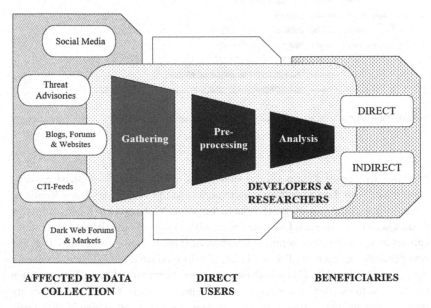

Figure 12.5 Main stakeholder groups of the prospective OSINT framework and their interaction with OSINT artefacts

The first stakeholder group consists of the individuals that interact directly with OSINT systems. In the context of this case study, these are the employees of CERTs who are expected to use a demonstrator with OSINT components. The second stakeholder group comprises actors that are indirectly affected by the collection of publicly available data with OSINT systems. In this case study, these include, in particular, actors that disseminate information on threats on social media. While the third stakeholder group, the direct beneficiaries, is directly advised and supported by the direct users of OSINT artefacts – in the case of CERTs primarily public authorities, critical infrastructure operators, and enterprises – the fourth group, the indirect beneficiaries, only receives unidirectional communication about threats and best practices – in the case of CERTs, among others, citizens and other cybersecurity organisations. The fifth stakeholder group, the potential users, comprises actors that have an interest in using OSINT systems. In our case study, there may be both potential users in the field of cybersecurity and in other domains, e.g., law enforcement, civil protection, and emergency services. Finally, the developers and researchers concerned with OSINT artefacts comprise the sixth stakeholder group. In our case, this encompasses individuals from both academic research and private software engineering.

Stakeholder Values
During the content analysis, ten values were identified. Table 12.3 shows which values were discussed in the individual interviews and the focus group, and how often they were coded in total.

Table 12.3 Overview of the identified values and the number of coded sections. X signifies that a value is present in an interview or the focus group

Value	I1	I2	I3	I4	I5	I6	I7	I8	I9	F1	$\sum$
Accuracy	X	X	X	X	X	X	X	X	X	X	69
Security	X	X	X	X	X	X	X	X	X	X	68
Efficiency	X	X	X	X	X	X	X	X	X	X	67
Accountability & Responsibility	–	X	X	X	X	X	X	X	X	X	27
Autonomy	X	–	–	X	X	–	X	X	–	X	27
Transparency	X	–	–	X	X	–	–	X	X	X	27
Privacy	X	–	–	X	X	X	X	X	X	X	25
Ownership & Property	–	X	–	X	X	X	–	–	X	X	22
Freedom from Bias	X	–	X	X	–	–	X	–	X	X	21
Trust	X	–	–	–	X	X	X	X	X	X	19

Accuracy can be defined as the correspondence or closeness of a statement or piece of information to the truth, the reality, or a differently defined standard (P. Hayes et al., 2020). Accuracy is particularly relevant in connection to ML algorithms and the quality of data. CERT staff, potential users, and developers emphasised the importance of the accuracy and quality of different types of data. The accuracy of data collected was considered very important (I1, I3, I4, I5, I7, I8, F1). Gathered information should not only be correct, but also structured consistently and have minimal redundancy to enable effective analysis (I1, I4). Since this requires repetitive and time-consuming activities, interviewees suggested drawing on the expertise of ML algorithms to harmonise information from heterogeneously structured texts and aggregate multiple pieces of information related to the same topic (I1, I4). Furthermore, the issue of disinformation was highlighted: "You also have to be cautious not to be fooled by people who try to make themselves important and publish something that is not true" (I1). The output data of algorithms needs to be relevant for OSINT analysis (I1, I4, I6, I8, F1), as well as for the information requirements of clients (I1, I2, I4, I5, I6, I7, I8, F1). For these reasons, specifically the accuracy of algorithmic decisions and the quality of training data for ML algorithms were highlighted (I5). Yet, it was argued that the application of ML should be limited to very specific tasks, as human expertise is crucial for creative or unstructured activities:

> "ML-supported systems …are built for pattern recognition and the patterns are trained. And you just have to get out of the pattern thinking, which is really thinking inside a box" (I5).

The interviewee potentially affected by data collection pleaded for a reduction of biases in algorithms (I9). This was also emphasised by the developers with a view on algorithms for prioritisation and credibility assessment of CTI (F1).

At a high level of abstraction, **security** can be conceptualised as "the state of being free from danger or threat" (van de Poel, 2020, p. 50). CERT employees and potential users highlighted the importance of security in relation to the IT infrastructure of organisations in their area of responsibility and the data processed by clients (I1, I2, I3, I4, I5, I6, I7). To ensure security, OSINT is used to leverage the expertise of numerous cybersecurity experts (I1, I3, I5, I6, I7, I9). Their expertise lies in detailed and up-to-date knowledge of specific cyber threats (I1, I9), threat actors and their strategies (I1, I9), vulnerabilities (I1, I6, I7, I9), and protection and mitigation measures (I6, I7). The civil society representative called for OSINT tools to be operated in a secure environment (I9). Finally, the developers also addressed the security of the ML algorithms against poisoning attacks, especially if information about training data and algorithmic models used is publicly accessible:

> "If a hacker notices something like this, that in some form [data] is merged and recommendations are derived from it, …he can carry out a targeted attack based on it" (F1).

Efficiency describes the ability to accomplish specific tasks or outputs with minimal expenditure of resources (Cousins et al., 2019). In the interviews with CERT staff and potential users, efficiency considerations were cited as a key rationale for the intention to use OSINT tools (I1, I2, I3, I4, I5, I6, I7, I8). Furthermore, the efficiency gain may also improve the quality of certain services:

> "If the data collection process is simplified, then it will be intensified on the other side. Because if I am relieved of the data collection, then the evaluation will probably be more intensive. Then I might take a much closer look at the reports, which I might have published before with the watering can principle" (I6).

Specifically, possible efficiency gains were identified through technical support in the acquisition and evaluation of security advisories (I6, I7, I8), the evaluation of cybersecurity websites and blogs (I1, I3, I6, I7), the search of Twitter and other social networks for cybersecurity-relevant information (I6, I7), and supporting communication by providing target-specific cybersecurity reports or alerts (I1, I2, I3, I4, I6). Particularly for the extraction of information from unstructured texts, the use of ML algorithms has been suggested (I1, I8, I9). Here, the expertise of ML-based information extraction techniques, is to discover specific pieces of information in unstructured texts or to create summaries (I1, I9). The developers saw an interest in efficiency gains through OSINT tools also among the direct beneficiaries of CERT activities, who could receive faster support in case of incidents (F1). Finally, with a view on development, it was also suggested to keep in mind that it should be as easy as possible to adapt the artefacts to changing legal requirements (F1).

Accountability can be seen as "the (moral) obligation to account for what you did or what happened (and your role in it happening)" (van de Poel, 2011, p. 39). In contrast, **responsibility** is directed towards current actions and their prospective consequences, as it refers to the obligation to evaluate one's own role and duties in relation to a situation or a context of action (van de Poel & Royakkers, 2011). CERT staff members pointed out that alerts and reports must be approved by superiors for reasons of political accountability. (I2, I3, I4). In particular, a fixed approval process for alerts hinders automation: "There are too many sensitivities or responsibilities involved to automate something like this" (I2). With regard to disaster management, the importance of documenting verification steps and analysts involved was also pointed out in order to render the evaluation of information comprehensible for decision-makers (I8). Referring to CERTs' use of OSINT tools, the interviewee from civil society pleads for a responsible protection of the data infrastructures used (I9). It was also pointed out that when processing certain data, the design of OSINT tools should consider the obligations for CERTs to comply with reporting chains and guidelines (F1). In this context, the question was raised to what extent clear responsibilities for the consequences of incorrect predictions of ML algorithms can be ensured:

> "So if security vulnerabilities are perhaps not taken seriously, even though they are announced on social media, because this relevance algorithm has perhaps decided that it is irrelevant for various reasons, there would also be the question of whether CERTs would perhaps even be legally liable in some way, because they should actually have acted" (F1).

With regard to ICT, **autonomy** can be understood as users' ability to control the technical systems in a context appropriate manner, and to enable decisions deemed suitable for them to achieve their objectives (Friedman & Kahn, 2002). The consideration of the autonomy of stakeholders was brought forward by direct users, potential users, and developers. One interviewee in particular places the value at the centre of human-computer interaction:

> "So really the point is that you don't have to replace anyone in that sense, but you can support everyone. So I see the point with all technology that it should still be supportive, it should be a tool for people. But it should not determine people" (I5).

The complete automation of analytical OSINT processes with the help of ML is seen particularly critical, as "artificial intelligence logic always trims someone down to blinkered thinking and an increasingly narrow focus" (I5), thus restricting the analysts' evaluative capabilities. Furthermore, ensuring the autonomy of users was also discussed in the context of the adaptability of the selection of sources (I1) and the relevance assessment of information (I4, I5). For the latter, an evaluation by experienced analysts was considered crucial (I4, I5). Potential users also advocated for a prioritisation of information that could be individually adapted to the respective infrastructure (I7, I8).

Transparency can be best understood in relation to a situation in which it is beneficial for actors to make knowledge and information about a certain topic extensively available, accessible and comprehensible, without obscuring any information (Turilli & Floridi, 2009). A CERT employee advocated for the disclosure of contextual information on algorithmic decisions of OSINT artefacts to analysts (I5). Similarly, a potential user reported that the degree of transparency of algorithmic decisions should always depend on the expertise and task of the respective user group, as too much information can also be counterproductive, especially in time-sensitive situations (I8). The developers discussed the promises and pitfalls of open sourcing the code of the OSINT artefacts to be developed (F1), while our interviewee from civil society requested transparency on the part of the developers and, ideally, an involvement of the cybersecurity community in the development of OSINT artefacts:

"So of course I would be happy if the whole system is open source as far as possible, subject to this evaluation and the risks, and is also open development. So it's not just open source, here's the software. But open development" (I9).

For this work, **privacy** can be defined as "the claim of individuals, groups, or institutions to determine for themselves when, how, and to what extent information about them is communicated to others" (Westin 1967, p. 7). The importance of privacy was raised by CERT employees in conjunction with compliance with the legal requirements of data protection legislation (I1, I4, I5). In particular, the automated analysis of personal data is legally problematic and sometimes only granted with special permission (I1). Thus, "in the ideal case, the data …is completely without personal reference" (I1). In the interviews with potential users it became clear that organisations are subject to very different regulations regarding privacy and data protection (I7, I8). The respondent from the group of those potentially affected by data collection considered the protection of private data a central principle: "Well, I would generally have a stomach-ache with it, if it was private data. So not publicly available data" (I9). The developers discussed privacy aspects of the development of the OSINT artefacts with a focus on the principles of data minimisation, the necessity of a justification for storing data, requirements on data deletion and anonymisation, as well as the adaptability of artefacts to changing legal requirements (F1).

According to Friedman and Kahn (2002), the value **ownership and property** is related to the rights of individuals or groups to possess, use, manage, derive profit from, or bequeath objects or pieces of information. For CERT employees and the developers, questions of ownership and property are important when it comes to legal requirements regarding the extent of data collection and the type of data to be collected (I1, I4). One CERT employee describes that the e-government law of the respective state strongly affects the processing of personal data, which should also be taken into account in the design of OSINT artefacts (I1). One potential user expressed the view that organisational policies on data processing may need to be changed before OSINT tools can be applied (I6). In addition, a part of the focus group discussion focused on the question of who should have the right to use the artefacts:

"Perhaps it would be conceivable for a government to somehow offer the tool ...to make it available as open source and that even the public can somehow co-develop it or use it" (F1).

The value **freedom from bias** is associated with the absence of systematic unfairness against individuals or groups (Friedman & Kahn, 2002). Both the CERT staff and other organisations' employees stressed the importance of addressee-oriented communication that is free from any systematic bias (I3, I4, I7). Pre-formulated templates for alerts were mentioned as a possible solution to this issue, because "if you have different stakeholders with technical skill levels, you can relatively easily find the right tone" (I4). Furthermore, when distributing warnings for a broad target group, appropriate communication channels should be chosen (I7). Specifically with regard to the use of ML in OSINT systems, our interview partner from civil society warned against the tendency to systematically replicate a pre-existing bias in training data:

"The problem such systems always have is that, whatever framing or bias exists in the data and structures, machine learning ...will simply consider it as a relevant parameter" (I9).

During the focus group it was raised that the algorithmic credibility assessment of information sources may have detrimental consequences, if the labelling of an actor as an untrustworthy source became public or lead to permanent non-inclusion in future analyses (F1).

For the purpose of this paper, **trust** may be understood as "expectations, assumptions or beliefs about the likelihood that another's future actions will be beneficial, favorable or at least not detrimental to ones' interests" (Robinson, 1996, p. 576). For direct stakeholders, trust in respective providers of information plays a major role in the verification of information from public sources (I1, I5). The developers, however, discussed trust in context of the societal acceptance of the use of OSINT technologies (F1). The trust of citizens in those using such systems may be influenced by the transparency towards the public:

"But perhaps trust in general also depends very much on who operates the tool in the end, whether the whole thing is transparent, i.e. how much is communicated about the artificial intelligence to the outside world, what data is collected" (F1).

Value Conflicts

While engaging with the stakeholders, eight value conflicts arised. These are illus-trated in Figure 12.6 together with the associated design issues.

Privacy conflicts first emerge between the privacy of actors affected by data collection and the value of ownership and property in terms of the requirements for CERT staff to be allowed to use non-anonymised data with reference to individuals (F1, I1, I4). While respect for the privacy of data subjects requires refraining from collecting personal data, it may be of interest for CERTs to collect such information. "So we're pretty restricted there, and I think if you develop us a tool that we use in the CERT, it's subject to those same regulations" (I1), stated a CERT employee. Thus, besides the ethical weighing of both values, the consideration of privacy and data protection requirements is central, e.g. when determining what data is col-lected or whether personal data is minimised, anonymised, or deleted (F1, I1, I4). Demands of safeguarding privacy and compliance with data protection regulations also partially conflict with the value of efficiency on the part of the CERT staff (I1). Semi-automated aggregation and analysis of public information is a key require-ment of CERTs that would come with time savings, yet it was pointed out that data protection requirements might prohibit such functionalities: "This automated evaluation of public sources is not permitted to all CERTs, some of them are not allowed to do this for legal reasons" (I1).

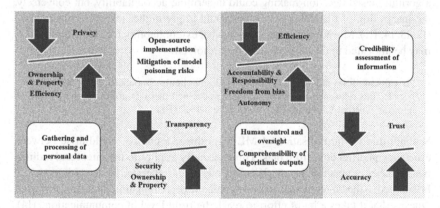

Figure 12.6 Value conflicts and associated design issues identified in the empirical material

Transparency conflicts arise, as the interviewee potentially affected by data collection, in particular, demands transparency about the specifications of the technical artefacts, training data, and ML algorithms used in, as well as the scope of data collected with OSINT tools (I9). Developers suggested that such transparency-motivated decisions could be counterproductive to the value of security, in terms of ensuring the reliable functioning of the ML models:

> "If it is known from which sources learning has taken place, one has of course again…you obviously provide an attacker the opportunity to poison the models. To do this model poisoning" (F1).

In connection to a prospective open-source implementation, a possible conflict with the value of ownership and property on the part of the developers of OSINT tools was brought forward: "You might not want to disclose the training data or explain the algorithms in detail so that you can still earn money commercially with it" (F1).

The interviews and the discussion revealed three different **efficiency conflicts**. First, due to the use of ML to accelerate OSINT processes, a conflict with the values of accountability and responsibility might arise. Considering the stakeholders whose data is processed, and the actors who receive information from CERTs, it is imperative for information to be correct, guidelines to be adhered to during processing, and misconduct to be clearly attributed to responsible actors (I2, I3, I4). ML algorithm based decision-making could undermine accountability, but conversely, the integration of manual control steps could imply higher resource consumption (I2, I3, I4, F1). Moreover, the question to what extent liability for algorithmic errors may be allocated to CERT personnel is unresolved:

> "If vulnerabilities are not taken seriously, despite being announced on social media, because this relevance algorithm has perhaps decided that it is irrelevant, there is the question whether CERTs might somehow be liable" (F1).

Second, due to the utilisation of ML algorithms, a conflict could arise between efficiency and freedom from bias. This especially applies to the direct and indirect beneficiaries of generated alerts. Warning messages generated by algorithms should be adapted to the target group to avoid systematic discrimination (I4). This, however, "means that it takes a lot of effort to reach the right level of communication" (I4), thus coinciding with a higher consumption of resources during development and application. Since CERT members expressed concerns that the present state-of-the-art is not sufficient to automatically generate target group-specific alerts (I2, I4), it seems appropriate to split the communication step into two individual tasks, thereby leveraging the expertise of both ML-based natural language processing (NLP) techniques as well as CERT analysts. In a first step, efficiency in communication could be enhanced by using NLP models to generate text segments based on a set of threat scenario- and target group-related parameters (I2, I4). In a second step, the expertise of analysts is employed to adapt the text to ensure that it actually reflects the status, requirements, and expertise of the target audience (I2, I4, I5, I9). Thereby, it is ensured that bias in communication is limited.

Third, a conflict between efficiency and users' autonomy emerges. It is particularly important for users of OSINT artefacts to remain in control over technical processes (I1, F1). However, it was highlighted that "many of the points that are aimed at, for example, additional manual control would significantly increase the time it takes for decisions to be made and solutions to be developed" (F1), thus resulting in a lower efficiency. Conversely, an exclusive focus on resource-saving optimisation may diminish operators' autonomy. Trade-offs arise especially at the stages of the design process when it is determined which decisions should be handed over to ML algorithms and to what extent users should be able to supervise these decisions. An adequate balance between both values is particularly important for OSINT tasks, where the expertise of ML algorithms and CERT analysts complement each other and can thus yield advantages over exclusively manual or automated solutions. In our context, this is especially the case with the relevance and credibility assessment of CTI. While the strength of ML in relevance assessment lies in a rapid evaluation of large amounts of information using predefined relevance criteria (I1, I6, I7), analysts can draw on this to select actually relevant information using their contextual knowledge about serviced infrastructures, e.g. deployed software (I1, I4, I5, I6, I7). During credibility assessment, three types of expertise may interact. While the expertise of ML algorithms is to compute a credibility rating using features of information previously evaluated as credible or non-credible (I5, I8), analysts, taking into account the rating and underlying contextual information, supplementary research and personal experience, as well as, if necessary, the opinions of external experts, can ultimately verify a piece of information (I1, I3, I5, I7, I8, I9). Whereas for these two tasks the trade-off between autonomy and efficiency can be mitigated by a two-step procedure, interviewees advocated for a non-automated criticality evaluation of vulnerabilities, hence prioritising autonomy (I1, I4, I6). Here, analysts resort to the expertise of external experts, which lies in their ability to determine the general criticality on basis of detailed knowledge about affected hardware, software, or corresponding exploits (I1, I4, I5). This evaluation, which can be reflected in a rating according to the Common Vulnerability Scoring System, enables analysts to decide, on basis of knowledge of the serviced infrastructure, whether there is a necessity to prioritise the vulnerability (I1, I4, I5, I6).

An **accuracy conflict** involving the value trust became apparent in the context of the credibility assessment of CTI. Both interviewed CERT staff and potential users emphasised the importance of trust in the respective providers for the selection and verification of information (I1, I5, I7, I8). In this context, trustworthiness is determined based on respective sources' past reliability (I1, I5). However, it was pointed out that trustworthy sources "But that is indeed a problem, that only the trustworthy position of a communication partner does not of course ensure that he does not publish nonsense anyway" (I1). Thus, in the development of ML algorithms for credibility assessment, an exclusive consideration of characteristics of trustworthy sources could compromise the accuracy of the output data.

12.5   Discussion and Implications

To answer the research question: **Which values and value conflicts emerge due to the application and development of ML-based open-source intelligence technologies in the context of cybersecurity incident response?** this paper has investigated the state of technical research on OSINT technologies for cybersecurity, as well as stakeholders, values, and value conflicts relevant for their application in the field of cybersecurity incident response. In this section, implications for the design of OSINT systems for this domain and for research are elaborated (Subsection 12.5.1). This is followed by a discussion on how sensitivity to the uncovered values and value conflicts can facilitate collaboration (Subsection 12.5.2), as well as an outline of the study's limitations and opportunities for future work (Subsection 12.5.3).

12.5.1 Research and Design Implications

The use of OSINT increases in many domains (Pastor-Galindo et al., 2020). In the area of emergency management, OSINT is used for the purpose of crisis response and shared situational awareness and collaboration (Akhgar et al., 2013; Backfried et al., 2012; R. Bernard et al., 2018), data sharing (Mtsweni et al., 2016; Skopik et al., 2016), and collective sense-making (Büscher et al., 2018). This has led to an increased discussion of participatory design and technology assessment methods which account for the specific organisational and legal characteristics and technology use of emergency management organisations (Büscher et al., 2018; Liegl et al., 2016). OSINT is not a single technology, but a framework in which individual steps can be performed with various technical approaches. In all three steps envisioned in Figure 12.7, ML algorithms can be used. While they can support the extraction, deduplication, and harmonisation of cybersecurity information during data gathering and pre-processing, they can also contribute to the relevance and credibility assessment of CTI in the following analysis phase. Finally, in terms of communication, they can be used to pre-formulate warning messages as a foundation for their customization by CERT staff to fit the respective target groups. In the described steps, human and ML-expertise can be complementary and in interaction increase the effectiveness of CERTs. However, this study also identified values and value conflicts that need to be considered when designing OSINT technologies for cybersecurity incident response. In the following, implications for the individual OSINT steps will be discussed, while taking the findings of the literature survey and the identified value conflicts into account.

The systematic literature review revealed that **information gathering (1)** is mostly conducted using publicly available data from social media platforms. As personal information is shared on such platforms, surveyed stakeholders have indicated that challenges arise in connection to privacy protection and compliance with data protection regulations. Therefore, Privacy Impact Assessments specifically for OSINT in the context of cybersecurity are needed (Liegl et al., 2016; Wright & Friedewald, 2013). The extent to which privacy infringement can be prevented by exclusively using sources specialised on the distribution of cybersecurity related information should be further analysed (Riebe, Wirth, et al., 2021). In an evaluation of the Cyber Threat Observatory dashboard with CERT-employees, Kaufhold et al. (2022) found that the modular and customisable integration of different data sources

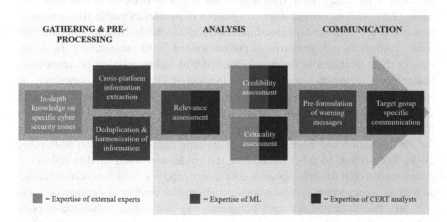

Figure 12.7 Human and ML expertise in the cybersecurity OSINT process

and feeds has been identified as a crucial feature. With regard to information extraction from long unstructured texts, ML approaches offer clear advantages over the performance of human analysts. Specifically, their expertise lies in topic discovery and information summarisation. Since interviewees emphasised that the use of such ML techniques would increase efficiency and consequently enable the gathering of a larger amount of data for subsequent steps, their use can be recommended. For a summary of the observations and the derived implications see Table 12.4.

Table 12.4 Observations and design implications for information gathering

Key Observation	Design and Research Implications
(1) Sources not specialised on cybersecurity such as social media are utilised more frequently than cybersecurity specific sources	(1) Examine legal requirements relevant to data gathering
(2) Privacy vs. Efficiency: Interest in collecting data collides with requirements of proportionality and event-relatedness	(2.1) Utilise cybersecurity specific sources (2.2) Implement data minimisation and data deletion intervals
(3) ML outperforms human analysts in extracting information from long unstructured texts	(3) Use ML-based information extraction techniques for topic discovery and information summarisation

The **preprocessing (2)** of gathered information is a sensitive part of the system, as biases in the data used to train algorithms might be detected in this stage (see Table 12.5). Serious consequences may occur if an artefact's objective is to infer human characteristics and relationships or to profile individuals, as was the case with some of the artefacts described in the publications of the literature review. However, none of these publications discussed issues of bias and potential countermeasures. Stakeholders' demands to minimise bias in training datasets for ML algorithms as part of OSINT systems should therefore be addressed in research through studies on the creation and evaluation of appropriate datasets, the development of guidelines for the inclusive annotation of training data, and the establishment of guidelines for the evaluation and documentation of training datasets (Friedman & Hendry, 2019). With regard to cyber threat data, the guidelines would need to reflect the cybersecurity context, the respective data source, and potential bias related human as well as other characteristics. Another challenge, according to our interviewees, is to structure collected data in a consistent way and reduce redundancies prior to further analysis. Since associated tasks are repetitive and time-consuming, they suggested drawing on the expertise of ML algorithms, which lies in harmonising information from heterogeneously structured texts (e.g. named entity recognition) and in grouping multiple pieces of information on the same topic together (e.g. clustering), thus reducing the amount of redundant information.

Table 12.5 Observations and design implications for preprocessing

Key Observations	Design and Research Implications
(1) No discussion of bias in training data in the reviewed publications	(1) Develop guidelines to understand and limit bias in datasets
(2) Structuring gathered data in a coherent way and reducing redundancies is time-consuming	(2) Use ML techniques for information harmonisation (e.g. named entity recognition) and redundancy reduction (e.g. clustering)

Implications for the development of ML algorithms arise in connection to the **analysis (3)** of OSINT information (see Table 12.6). While the literature review showed that algorithms are used for a variety of tasks, algorithm selection was rarely reflected from an ethical or social point of view, with exception of a publication that justifies the selection of a decision tree classifier by improving the comprehensibility of algorithmic decisions (Edwards et al., 2017). The empirical investigation showed that value conflicts can occur when algorithm selection disregards operators' needs regarding the comprehensibility, traceability, and influenceability of algorithmic decisions. With respect to the selection and development of algorithms that meet end-users' requirements, there is a need for further research on exploring the applicability of XAI and white-boxing approaches for OSINT and the evaluation of different algorithmic solutions with end-users, e.g. by considering the recommendations for XAI by (Wang et al., 2019), which include support reasoning and hypothesis-generation, as well as access to source and situational data. During the interviews, it became apparent that ML can support analysts primarily in relevance and credibility assessment. As shown by Q. Zhang et al. (2022), ML algorithms with complementary expertise are most useful to human operators. However, since in ML-assisted relevance and credibility assessment the human and algorithmic expertise overlap on a specific task, it is particularly important to ensure that human and algorithmic steps are clearly delineated by design so that advantages and limitations of both can surface. This can be achieved by implementing a two-step procedure in which the analyst always makes the final decision on the basis of an algorithmic pre-assessment, under disclosure of relevant decision parameters. In addition, as indicated by research on human-AI interaction experiments, understanding the parameters of algorithmic decisions will be crucial to establish system operators' trust (Feng & Boyd-Graber, 2019; Schaffer et al., 2019).

Table 12.6 Observations and design implications for analysis

Key Observation	Design and Research Implications
(1) Efficiency vs. Autonomy: Safeguarding human control and oversight may restrict scope and efficiency of data analysis	(1.1) Examine applicability of algorithmic white-boxing solutions to models for cybersecurity purposes (1.2) Give operators possibility to adapt algorithmic decision-making
(2) CERT analyst and ML expertise overlap during relevance and credibility assessment	(2) Implement two-step procedure that enables analysts to definitively assess relevance and credibility based on algorithmic pre-assessments
(3) Accuracy vs. Trust: Relying exclusively on characteristics of trustworthy sources may impair the accuracy of algorithmic credibility assessment	(3.1) Include features of pieces of information in credibility assessment (3.2) Disclose criteria used for credibility assessment to system operators

In the literature review, we found that NLP techniques are used in many systems, but with regard to the **generation of alerts and text (4)**, this is limited to the creation of pre-structured texts such as IoCs (see Table 12.7). It seems worth investigating whether NLP approaches can also be used for the generation of target group specific alerts and notifications. Advances in fundamental NLP research, especially in conjunction with the development of large pre-trained language models, might be leveraged for the development and training of models for these specific cases. However, the use of such models must be seen in light of the tension between the values efficiency and freedom from bias. In order to streamline communication while ensuring that warnings and notifications do not disadvantage relevant target groups, it is advisable to implement a two-step process. In a first step, large pre-trained language models can swiftly generate text segments based on a few parameters. In a second step, analysts can draw on their knowledge and experience of the needs and proficiency of target groups to adapt the texts accordingly. This mitigates the tension and leverages the complementary expertise of NLP models and CERT analysts, potentially increasing confidence in the system (Q. Zhang et al., 2022).

Table 12.7 Observations and design implications for communication

Key Observation	Design and Research Implications
(1) Applications of NLP for text generation are limited to the creation of pre-structured texts	(1) Harness advancements in NLP research for the generation of target specific cybersecurity alerts
(2) Efficiency vs. Freedom from bias: Algorithmic generation of warnings and notifications may reduce target group specificity	(2) Manually adapt NLP generated text segments to ensure target group specificity of warnings and notifications

With regard to OSINT systems' **implementation into the context of cybersecurity incident response (5)** (see Table 12.8), some of the reviewed studies raised questions of accountability and responsibility in connection with consequences of processing illegal material (Lawrence et al., 2017), or compliance with organisational secrecy and security regulations (Ranade et al., 2018). However, the challenge that state actors are often subject to enhanced requirements in terms of safeguarding accountability and compliance with different standards and responsibilities, which were also emphasised by consulted stakeholders, remained unaddressed. Since considering such requirements results in a higher resource consumption and may prevent the utilisation of particular ML algorithms, a trade-off with the value efficiency occurs. Thus, the challenge lies in developing OSINT systems that support the documentation of the operators' decisions without disproportionately impairing efficiency and usability. It is advisable to conduct case studies on the specific requirements of respective governmental user groups with regard to ensuring accountability, clear responsibilities, and reporting chains, and based on this derive concrete guidelines for the legitimate application of OSINT systems as well as requirements for their design. Finally, in the empirical investigation, stakeholders voiced a demand for transparency on training data used for ML algorithms and on OSINT system specifications, which, in turn, may increase opportunities for model poisoning and, thus, conflict with safeguarding the security of ML models. While first studies have proposed solutions to mitigate this threat (N. Khurana et al., 2019; Longo et al., 2020), there is a need for continued research on the magnitude of the problem and technical countermeasures. With regard to the reconciliation of transparency and security, the involvement of stakeholders in a scrutiny committee that reviews algorithm design could be a reasonable solution.

12.5.2 Value Sensitivity as a Facilitator of Collaboration

Understanding value conflicts is not an end in itself, but offers venture points for value-sensitive technology design and detailed evaluations of conflicts in complex socio-political systems. From a CSCW perspective, three implications for supporting multi-actor collaboration emerge from the findings of this research paper: First, as the work of CERTs strongly relies on collaboration with other CERTs, authorities, and organisations (Riebe, Kaufhold and Reuter, 2021), a tool for shared situational awareness needs to be trustworthy and support the operators reasoning and sense-making (Ley et al., 2014; Lukosch et al., 2015). Trust can be achieved by supporting the operators alignment with legal provisions and social norms. As OSINT systems work with different ML algorithms, research on the explainability of the systems and on solutions to maintain the autonomy of the operators are crucial in all application domains. Second, with regard to the communication of cyber threats, CERTs need to collaborate with different stakeholders to improve their situational awareness and provide risk mitigation strategies. It became apparent that bias-free and addressee-specific communication is pivotal to fulfilling these objectives, a factor also to be taken into account in the design of systems with communication functionalities. Additionally, the spread of social media, in particular, has opened up opportunities for CERTs to leverage novel resources. However, this paper also highlights the challenges and concerns of how this information is used and processed in such a demanding and time-sensitive collaborative environment. Therefore, the results of

Table 12.8 Observations and design implications for the implementation of the OSINT system into the CERT context

Key Observation	Design and Research Implications
(1) Transparency vs. Security: Demands for transparency on system capabilities may increase security risks (e.g. model poisoning)	(1) Examine model poisoning risks and possible mitigation measures
(2) Efficiency vs. Accountability & Responsibility: Prerequisites of governmental organisations to link the processing and analysis of OSINT data to human decision-making in order to ensure accountability could impair system speed and efficiency	(2.1) Involve stakeholders in scrutiny committee that reviews algorithms (2.2) Conduct case study research on specific accountability requirements and reporting chains of governmental user groups (2.3) Develop guidelines for a legally compliant use of OSINT systems

this study can be of use for the field of control room research, e.g. in the context of traffic management (R. Jones et al., 2021) or other emergency services (Normark & Randall, 2005). Third, OSINT, especially when using social media as sources, is dependent on information provided by the respective medium's users. Therefore, it involves the use of crowdsourcing, which is collaborative (S. B. Liu, 2014). Social media users need to trust OSINT operators using their data (Tapia & Moore, 2014), which can be achieved by ensuring transparency and accountability, e.g. by organisational oversight infrastructures, as well as data minimisation by Privacy by Design approaches.

12.5.3 Limitations and Future Work

The findings of this work must be considered in the light of some limitations, which at the same time, however, offer impulses for future research. First, the empirical investigations in this study were limited to selected stakeholder groups. In addition, only one individual potentially affected by data collection was interviewed. Thus, to consolidate the findings, further qualitative interviews and focus groups are necessary. For enquiries about citizens' attitudes, however, quantitative surveys appear to be more suitable. Our future research will therefore also include a representative survey on the attitudes of the German population towards the use of OSINT technologies. Second, the generalisability of the results is limited due to the case study design of the VSD-approach. However, similar cases of ML-based OSINT systems for cybersecurity can utilize the design implications. Within this limitation, this work pursued the goal of elaborating values and value conflicts as abstractly as possible. Nevertheless, as the interviews and the discussion were strongly focused on the design of OSINT systems for aggregating CTI for the CERT context, the results are primarily relevant with regard to artefacts for this application field. Accordingly, studies focusing on systems for investigation and risk assessment and mitigation purposes represent promising avenues for further research. Third, this work only includes conceptual and empirical VSD investigations. In the further course of our project, it is therefore intended to conduct technical VSD investigations to derive concrete design requirements and find technical solutions through which value conflicts are minimised and preferred stakeholder values are supported as adequately as possible.

12.6   Conclusion

In this paper, we employed a triangulation of methods to investigate which values and value conflicts are relevant to the application and development of ML-based OSINT technologies in the context of cybersecurity incident response. In order to situate our empirical findings in the broader research and application context, we first systematically reviewed the technical research literature on the development of OSINT artefacts for the cybersecurity domain (N=73). Then, an empirical VSD case study, comprising semi-structured interviews (N=9) and a focus group (N=7) for data collection, including a subsequent qualitative content analysis of the gathered material, was undertaken to identify values of key stakeholders and to systematise potential value conflicts. The results of the literature review underlined the identified research gap, as despite research activities on OSINT for cybersecurity have increased, stakeholder values and other ethical, legal, and social issues have only been addressed in a minority of publications. In the empirical investigation, we identified ten values and eight value conflicts, particularly involving privacy, transparency, efficiency, and accuracy, that are relevant to the application and development of OSINT artefacts for cybersecurity incident response. Drawing on our findings, we derived implications for the design of and research on ML-based OSINT technologies for this application domain and discussed how sensitivity to the uncovered value conflicts and the division of tasks between human operators and ML algorithms can facilitate collaboration. Though certain limitations remain, this paper offers a systematic review of the technical research literature on the development of OSINT technologies for cybersecurity (C1), an empirically grounded elaboration of values and value conflicts related to the development and application of OSINT technologies for cybersecurity incident response (C2), and an elaboration of research and design implications for ML-based OSINT technologies for collaborative cybersecurity incident response (C3).

Computer Emergency Response Teams and the German Cyber Defense: An Analysis of CERTs on Federal and State Level

13

13.1 Introduction

Research into computer-supported cooperative work (CSCW) has driven the field of crisis informatics (Palen & Anderson, 2016), which is a multidisciplinary field "concerned with the ways in which information systems are entangled with socio-behavioral phenomena connected to disasters" (Soden & Palen, 2018). Despite acknowledging the impact of human induced emergencies, most research so far has focused on collective and individual behavior in natural disasters (Olteanu et al., 2015; Reuter & Kaufhold, 2018) and the use of social media in the context of crisis response (Vieweg et al., 2010; Zade et al., 2018). However, driven by the increasing digitalization and interconnectedness of society, cyberattacks pose an increasing threat to both the virtual and physical realm. Looking at the 2015 Ukraine power grid cyberattack, the 2017 WannaCry ransomware attack, or the 2020 University Hospital of Düsseldorf hack, the vulnerability of critical infrastructures and society to cyberattacks becomes apparent (Al-rimy et al., 2018; Davis et al., 2017; Ehrenfeld, 2017). As a consequence, securing information technology and cyber incident response for citizens, public services, and critical infrastructures have become part of national security agendas (Azmi et al., 2016; Kolini & Janczewski, 2017;

ORIGINAL PUBLICATION Riebe, T., Kaufhold, M.-A., & Reuter, C. (2021). The impact of organizational structure and technology use on collaborative practices in computer emergency response teams: An empirical study. *Proceedings of the ACM on Human-Computer Interaction*, 5(CSCW2), 1–30. https://doi.org/10.1145/3479865

Supplementary Information The online version contains supplementary material available at https://doi.org/10.1007/978-3-658-41667-6_13.

T. Riebe, *Technology Assessment of Dual-Use ICTs*,
https://doi.org/10.1007/978-3-658-41667-6_13

Skopik et al., 2018). Related strategies do not only focus on the security of governmental organization and communication but also emphasize the importance of public-private partnerships (PPP) and multi-organizational collaboration for incident communication and response (Papastergiou et al., 2019; Pardo et al. 2004; Pardo et al., 2006; Skopik et al., 2018).

The need for incident response and management led to the deployment of Computer Emergency Response Teams (CERTs), sometimes also called Computer Security Incident Response Teams (CSIRTs), in the public and private sector across the world. CERTs are monitoring, analyzing, and communicating threats and incidents (ENISA, 2020), offering reactive services and preventive measures for authorities, citizens, and enterprises (Kossakowski 2001). However, managing these tasks while processing the increasing amount of available data across different channels, such as blogs, feeds, social media, and websites has become a complex challenge (Franke & Brynielsson, 2014; Reuter et al., 2017; Stieglitz, Mirbabaie, Fromm, & Melzer, 2018). Besides information overload, the quality and speed of incident response is threatened by false or inaccurate information (Kaufhold, Rupp, et al., 2020). In order to provide effective incident management and response, CERTs are not only required to conduct ad hoc analysis to enhance their cyber situational awareness (Franke & Brynielsson, 2014), but also to collaborate with other teams or third parties, sometimes with less advanced skill levels (Van der Kleij et al., 2017). As security incidents become more widespread in interconnected infrastructures both in the public and the private sector, their services and collaboration by sharing threat information and specialized skills is becoming increasingly important (Ioannou et al., 2019; La Fleur et al., 2021; Settanni et al., 2016).

The collaboration of CERTs, to the best of our knowledge, has not been studied from the CSCW perspective yet. The study of CERTs in Germany offers an interesting case to address this gap. As a federal country with 16 states, Germany has installed 13 CERTs (from which the CERT Nord is responsible for four states) as well as a CERT for the federal administration (CERT-Bund). Since 2001 they have become "a focal point for preventive and reactive measures in security-related incidents in computer systems" (BSI, 2019) in Germany. The states have implemented individual plans, resulting in a network of differently structured and resourced CERTs. In the light of resulting deviations in expertise, organizational structures, and used technologies, effective collaboration is of utmost importance to increase cyber situational awareness, the analysis and response to cyber incidents, and thus the cyber security of the public sector, society, and industrial production. However, there is a lack of empirical studies examining the collaborative practices of CERTs (Van der Kleij et al., 2017). We investigate German CERTs that work in and for the public administration to answer the following research question:

- How do organizational structure, technology use, and cross-organizational collaboration contribute to cyber incident response of German state-level CERTs?

To answer our research question, we conducted semi-structured expert interviews with 15 participants and analyzed 25 secondary documents. Through a qualitative content analysis of the captured data, we:

- Offer insights into the organizational structure and work processes of German state-level CERTs.
- Describe the technologies and practices used for cyber incident awareness, collaboration, and incident response.
- Analyze the collaboration and its constraints among German state-level CERTs and external stakeholders.
- Provide key insights, challenges, and design and policy implications for successful organizational structure, technology use and cross-organizational collaboration in German state-level CERTs.

Our study contributes to the CSCW discourse by describing "a work environment/setting where collaboration is important" (Wallace et al., 2017), connecting cyber security, crisis informatics and CSCW, and building foundations for design and evaluation studies to support the collaboration of CERTs. The paper is structured as follows: First, we present related work on the organization, technology use, and collaboration for cyber incident response to highlight our research gap (Section 13.2). Second, we outline the methodology in terms of case selection, mode of content analysis, conducted interviews, and analyzed documents (Section 13.3). Based on this, we present the results of our qualitative content analysis (Section 13.4). The paper concludes with a discussion of findings, implications for design and policy, limitations, and future work (Section 13.5).

13.2   Related Work

The collaboration of spatially and temporally distributed emergency response teams in general and specifically in the public sector is a central research field within CSCW (Cobb et al., 2014; Mendonça et al., 2001; Mendonça et al., 2007; Reuter et al., 2014). There has been extensive research on how the design and use of technology influences and supports response teams, their workflows, and collaborative work (Cobb et al., 2014; S. B. Liu, 2014; Reuter et al., 2014; Schafer et al., 2007). In this sense, collaboration can be described as the development of a set of common practices to monitor individual behavior and enable task coordination as well as flexible division of labor. In this context, technology provides a set of tools through which certain activities within the present setting become visible or publicly accessible. To allow the effective management of crises, the practices are designed to be independent of personnel, so that they can also be adopted by newcomers without previous collaboration and without much explanation (Heath & Luff, 1992).

13.2.1 Organization of Governmental CERTs

Incident response in situations of uncertainty and high pressure has been studied in CSCW with regard to natural and man-made disasters, focusing on the collaboration among different emergency services, as well as with citizens (Olteanu et al., 2015; Reuter, Ludwig, & Pipek, 2018; Reuter et al., 2014; Schafer et al., 2007; Soden & Palen, 2018). In terms of cyber incident response, state-level CERTs have become important organizations to protect citizens, public administration, and critical infrastructures against cyberattacks and their potential real-world impact (Kossakowski 2001). CERTs exist in public and private organizations and offer a variety of proactive and reactive services (Wiik et al., 2006) to achieve their goal "to be a focal point for preventing, receiving and responding to computer security incidents" (Killcrece et al., 2003). Existing studies have been emphasizing the necessity of collaboration between the different CERTs (Pethia & van Wyk, 1990; Slayton & Clarke, 2020) as well as other security experts and volunteers (Fathi et al., 2020; Werlinger et al., 2010). In a comparison of national security strategies, Boeke (2018) has highlighted that due to the state size, Estonian cyber security is largely dependent on the help of state-directed civilian volunteers and international cooperation. In the United Kingdom, studies have found that cyber security is the task of private companies with less importance of state interference as a consequence of privatizing communication infrastructure (Collier, 2017).

With specific regard to Germany, research has focused on the federal structure and its consequences for cyber security (Stiftung Neue Verantwortung, 2019). Legal experts have suggested to update federal security architectures in line with the increasing challenges of cyber security, including the effective integration of local and state level response into the national security strategy (Duvillard & Friedli, 2018). In accordance, studies have shown that a decentralized approach to security can also provide benefits in crisis response (Scavo et al., 2007) . Distributed management as well as the sharing of information and experiences has shown to positively impact effectiveness of cyber security (Duvillard & Friedli, 2018; Weatherseed, 2018). Van der Kleij (2017) identified additional factors influencing the performance of CERTs, such as "coordination and sharing information with outside parties", "collaborative problem-solving capacity and shared incident awareness", and "organizational and incident learning". This is supported by Ahmad et al. (2012), who suggests double-loops for learning, which means that the learning should not only include individual incidents but also systematic response structures, as well as taking part in cyber security defense competitions for simulation training (La Fleur et al., 2021). To create educational simulations for the training of municipal security experts for effective defense, Gedris et al. derived design implications for cyber security scenarios which highlight the complex socio-technical context of public infrastructure (Gedris et al., 2021).

13.2.2 Technology and Collaboration of CERTs

To fulfil their tasks, CERTs use a variety of different technologies, especially Cyber Threat Intelligence (CTI) platforms, to enhance cyber incident response. Furthermore, they maintain cross-organizational collaboration with other CERTs and external stakeholders to facilitate collective crisis management (Kühn et al., 2020). Incident monitoring has shown to be complex due to increasing digitalization and services that CERTs have to provide. Often, incident reporting and procedures in connection with incidents are not standardized, and sometimes there are legal and psychological restraints in reporting due to data protection and company policies (Badsha et al., 2019). Therefore, receiving and analyzing threat incident information made additional security infrastructure and access for CERTs necessary, such as information on network traffic (Valladares et al., 2017), deep packet inspection (Pimenta Rodrigues et al., 2017), and the use of machine learning to support incident detection (Krstic et al., 2019). Parayachee and Worku (2017) have pointed out the advantage of collaboration among CERTs as they are more easily alerted to large-scale cyber security incidents and better capable to manage them adequately than alone. While many private and governmental organizations manage cyber security incidents individually, the protection of interconnected networks against internationally operating criminal groups can be better addressed with a shift towards cross-organizational information exchange (Skopik et al., 2016). Khurana et al. (2009) propose the prototype "Palantir" to enable effective multi-site cyber incident response including a collaborative workspace for discussions and data sharing. The authors highlight the crucial role of trust between organizations for sharing incident data.

Despite the identified need for cross-organizational collaboration and information sharing between cyber security organizations such as CERTs (Settanni et al., 2016; Van der Kleij et al., 2017; Werlinger et al., 2010), mainly the cooperation between law enforcement agencies has been examined (Croasdell, 2019; M. Ioannou et al., 2019). With view to the collaboration of German CERTs, the communication between the federal- and the state-level, CERTs as well as the private CERTs is considered as crucial to gain the situational awareness on the scope and severity of an incident and decide on the response (Hellwig, 2015; Huber, 2015; Skopik et al., 2018). When CERTs were first established in Germany, Kossakowski (2001); Kossakowski and Neufert (2012) observed that in addition to a lack of time resources, also insufficient mutual trust also resulted in low levels of cooperation. Thus, the work of security experts consists of "heterogenous bundles of practices" for the shared commitment towards cyber security (Kocksch et al., 2018). Therefore, our study takes the organizational structure and the technology use into account.

13.2.3 Adapting Crisis Informatics Research to the Cyber Security Domain

Since the 2001 September 11 attacks, a considerable body of knowledge has been established in the research domain of crisis informatics, including empirical investigations of social media use and role patterns in crises (Starbird & Palen, 2011; Vieweg et al., 2010; Villodre & Criado, 2020) collection, processing, and refinement of social media data (Alam et al., 2020; Castillo, 2016; Kaufhold 2021), system design and evaluation (Aupetit & Imran, 2017; M.-A. Kaufhold, Rupp, et al., 2021; Onorati et al., 2018), as well as cumulative and longitudinal research (Imran et al., 2015; Olteanu et al., 2015; Reuter et al., 2018). Although it is common to distinguish anthropogenic (e.g., building collapse, shootings) and natural disasters (e.g., earthquakes, epidemics, hurricanes, floods, wildfires) in crisis informatics (Olteanu et al., 2015), only little domain-specific research considers the anthropogenic risks of cyberattacks (Gedris et al., 2021). However, like regular emergency services, such as fire or police departments, CERTs provide preventive and reactive capabilities and started to use social media (tools) to enhance their situational awareness but in response to cyber threats (Hiltz et al., 2020; M.-A. Kaufhold, 2021). Since CERTs are confronted with similar issues when analyzing open and social data, including information quality and information overload (Plotnick & Hiltz, 2018), it seems sensible to examine the adoptability of findings from crisis informatics to the domain of cyber security.

Besides researching formal crisis response organizations, crisis informatics has examined the emergence of digital volunteers, which are citizens that assist crisis response using the virtual realm and sometimes organize as Virtual and Technical Communities (V&TCs) (Reuter et al., 2013; Starbird & Palen, 2011; van Gorp, 2014). Grasping the potentials of organized digital volunteers, so-called Virtual Operations Support Teams (VOST), comprising of trusted volunteers, were deployed during the 2011 Shadow Lake fire in the USA to monitor social media activities related to the emergency (St. Denis et al., 2012). In the following years, VOSTs were deployed across the globe to assist emergency services by crowdsourcing emergency-related tasks, among them the VOST of the German Federal Agency for Technical Relief (VOST-THW) (Fathi et al., 2020). This concept is also becoming more interesting for the domain of cyber security: for instance, to overcome the resource limitations of federal and state-level CERTs in Germany, a recent initiative seeks to utilize the capabilities of organized digital volunteers by establishing a formalized Cyber Relief Agency (Arbeitsgruppe Kritische Infrastrukturen, 2020).

13.2.4 Research Gap

Our literature review revealed a body of research on the organization of CERTs, including structure (Hellwig, 2015; Kossakowski, 2001; Kossakowski & Neufert, 2012; Slayton & Clarke, 2020; Sundaramurthy et al., 2014), national comparisons (Boeke, 2018; Collier, 2017), governmental frameworks (Cichonski et al., 2012; Deutscher Bundestag, 2009; IT-Planungsrat, 2013, 2016; NIS Directive, 2016), management (Hove et al., 2014; Mitropoulos et al., 2006), and their effectiveness (Ahmad et al., 2012; Buchler et al., 2018; La Fleur et al., 2021; Van der Kleij et al., 2017). Further studies investigated situational awareness, including the access (Badsha et al., 2019; Pimenta Rodrigues et al., 2017) and analysis (Grispos et al., 2019; Krstic et al., 2019; Valladares et al., 2017) of data, and the dissemination of warnings (Ioannou et al., 2019; Papastergiou et al., 2019). While plenty of research has been conducted on data collection and data visualization, in their systematic literature review, Franke and Brynielsson (Franke & Brynielsson, 2014) noted a lack of empirical research on information exchange between relevant actors. Especially the collaboration between IT security teams, not only from the perspective of IT security, but also focusing on socio-technical systems has been highlighted as a field for further research (Kocksch et al., 2018; Van der Kleij et al., 2017). At the same time, the lack of exchange has been named as an obstacle in responding to large-scale cyberattacks (Skopik et al., 2016). To the best of our knowledge, no empirical studies on the collaboration of state CERTs in the federal system of Germany have been published yet, calling for an analysis through the lens of CSCW. However, the lack of exchange has been named as obstacle in responding to large-scale cyberattacks (Skopik et al., 2016).

An exercise that aimed to test the defense skills of 900 participants from EU member states showed that public-private cooperation is central for guaranteeing cyber security, but also stressed the importance of strengthening cooperation on a national level by establishing more structured operating processes (ENISA, 2018). In a survey with CERT members, Ioannou et al. (M. Ioannou et al., 2019) identified important challenges in communication and coordination that weakened cyber security culture. Van der Kleij et al. (Van der Kleij et al., 2017) conducted semi-structured interviews with Dutch CERT members, highlighting the need across CERTs for collaborative sensemaking, including collaborative problem-solving capacity and shared incident awareness However, as it was a study from the field of psychology and the focus was on team effectiveness, it did not address the aspect of technologies used or required for collaboration and situational awareness. By analyzing empirical data from documents and interviews, our paper contributes findings on the implications for cross-organizational collaboration and technology design for German state-level CERTs.

13.3   Methodology: Empirical Study with German CERTs

The German federal administration provides an interesting case as it facilitates the collaboration between independent cyber security organizations for the 16 states and the federal government. The states are represented by 13 CERTs within the public administrations or in state companies, whereas the federal CERT-Bund is integrated in the German Federal Office for Information Security (BSI). The individual CERTs are part of the Administrative CERT Network (Verwaltungs-CERT-Verbund, VCV) which provides an information exchange platform for public administration, thus offering an institutionalization of CERTs' partnerships (Deutscher CERT-Verbund, 2021). The structure, size, and the skill set of these CERTs depend on financial resources and the requirements of the target groups. They usually have a strategic head, the chief information security officer (CISO), and an operational head of team, who leads a small number of incident managers and cyber security specialists. In some cases, CERTs provide a public safety answering point (PSAP) for citizens and enterprises. The basic skill sets of CERT employees comprise IT security knowledge to detect threats and estimate their severity as well as communication skills to enable a proper response to incidents (Donegan & Sullivan, 2022). In 2019, the BSI reported 770,000 emails containing malware in German governance networks, 114 million new versions of malware, and 252 reported incidents by critical infrastructure operators (BSI, 2020). While the skills and level of organization of criminals increase, one CERT employee (I14) assumed that the number of incidents at least doubles once per year, making the collaboration between CERTs even more important. The objective of our empirical study, which comprises semi-structured interviews and document analyses, is to examine the organizational structure, technology use and cross-sector collaboration in German state CERTs.

13.3.1 Data Collection: Interviews and Document Research

The semi-structured interviews were designed to provide insights into the organizational structure, technology use, and collaborative practices within and between CERTs. To acquire the necessary data, we sent requests for semi-structured expert interviews (Gläser & Laudel, 2010; Kallio et al., 2016) in two rounds. We approached all 14 CERTs on federal and state level, but only six CERTs responded and agreed to participate the interviews. After receiving their acceptance and informed consent, each interview session lasted around 50 minutes. In the first round of interviews (n=8, I1–I8), we put a strong emphasis on organizational factors and collaborative practices. Our interview guide[2] comprised nine open-ended questions structured in three parts: (1) an introduction of the interviewee and his/her organizational role, (2) the deployment, organization, and work processes of the CERT, and (3) the communication and cooperation between CERTs.

As we wanted to gain further insights into technology use by CERTs, we conducted a second round of interviews with those CERTs that were interested in further research collaboration (n=7, I9–I15). In this second round, we also included the perspective of some non-CERT organizations (I09, I10, I15). For instance, we approached a civil protection VOST (I09) and a voluntary humanitarian organization (I15) to gain insights into cyber security practices and technology use in the domain of crisis management and civil protection. Furthermore, we interviewed an information security officer (I11) of a state company who previously worked in a CERT organization to utilize his prior experience and get insights into how his work has changed as an information security officer. The interview guidelines comprised technology-focused questions on the (1) interviewees' role and organization, (2) reporting of cyber incidents, (3) monitoring of cyber incident data (e.g., indicators of compromise), (4) analysis, prioritization, and verification of gathered evidence, as well as (5) communication of recommendations and warnings.

To include and gain insight into the remaining eight state-level CERTs of Germany which were not available for interviews, we conducted document analyses using public CERT websites, protocols of parliamentary debates, and administra-

---

[2] The interview guide is available in the electronic supplementary material Appendix 16.4.

tive documents $(N=25)^3$. While these official documents are publicly available and allow the identification of the related CERT, we at least had to ensure the anonymity of the interviewed CERTs. Table 13.1 summarizes the analyzed documents and conducted interviews

Table 13.1 Overview of the interviewed organizations, theirs types, as well as corresponding documents and interviews, only one interviewee participated in both rounds (I3, I10). Abbreviations: Head of Team (HT), Incident Manager (IM), Information Security Officer (IS), Public safety Answering Point (PSAP)

Organization Type	Documents	Interviews (First Round)	Interviews (Second Round)
Ministry CERT	–	I04 (IM), I05 (IM)	–
Service CERT	D01–D03	–	–
Ministry CERT	–	I08 (HT)	–
Service CERT	D04–D06	–	–
Service CERT	D07–D10	–	–
Ministry CERT	–	I1 (IM), I02 (HT)	I12 (HT), I13 (PSAP), I14 (IM)
Ministry CERT	D11–D13	–	–
Service CERT	D14, D15	–	–
Service CERT	D16–D19	–	–
Service CERT	–	I03 (HT)	I10 (HT)
Ministry CERT	–	I07 (IM)	–
Ministry CERT	D20–D23	–	–
Service CERT	D24, D25	–	.
Civil Protection	–	–	I09 (HT)
State Company	–	–	I12 (IS)
Civil Protection	–	–	I15 (IS)

13.3.2 Data Analysis: Codebook Development and Structured Content Analysis

We conducted a qualitative content analysis following the step model of deductive category application (Mayring, 2000). This requires defining analytical categories and developing a codebook, which comprises analytical categories, defini-

---

^{3} The detailed list can be fount in the electronic supplementary material in the Appendix 16.4.

tions, examples, and coding rules to be applied to our interview transcripts and collected documents. We preferred this deductive approach over an inductive, bottom up, or open coding to allow a structured comparison of the capabilities and services of CERTs. The codebook design was deductively informed by relevant literature and especially by the work of Skopik et al. (2018), who assume that CERTs serve as interface organizations which monitor and collect data on threats, assess risks for their customers, communicate and handle incidents, as well as interact, cooperate, and collaborate with other organizations. The latter includes expert networks, such as the VCV, where CERTs exchange knowledge and services. Based on the literature, the first two authors identified ten analytical categories summarized under the domains of organization (CERT association membership, defined protocols for cross-organizational collaboration, distinct target group definition for incident reporting), technology (use of exchange platforms, alerting and reporting service, advisory service), and collaboration (information access, coordination competence, public-private partnerships, information interface to emergency services). For each category they developed definitions and coding rules, which are specified in the detailed codebook.[4]

For the analysis and interpretation of the collected documents (D1–D25) and conducted interviews (I1–I15), we followed the approach of Kaiser (Kaiser, 2014), which comprises the steps of transcription, coding of text, identification of core statements, extension of the data corpus, as well as theoretical analysis and interpretation. First, we created full transcripts of the interview data. Since we had to delete the audio material after transcription to ensure anonymity, we refrained from paraphrasing to preserve the richness of the data. Then, we analyzed the collected documents and created interview transcripts carefully to apply codes of the developed codebook to fitting passages. Four coders were involved in the process: while three coders conducted the initial round of coding, the main author checked and—if required—amended codes in a second round to ensure consistent coding across all interviews and documents. Also, core statements were added as examples to the codebook. Although our work was guided by the codebook, we also inductively considered categories that emerged from data in our qualitative analysis.

Besides the qualitative analysis of documents and interviews, one aim of our study was to understand the ways in which differences in the hierarchical establishment influence the capabilities and services provided by CERTs. The information whether a CERT is embedded into a ministry or into a separate state company was extracted from the individual CERT websites. To facilitate a comparison of both ministry and service CERTs, we used the categories of the codebook to quantify

---

[4] The codebook can be found in the Appendix 16.4 in the electronic supplementary material.

Table 13.2 Anonymized CERT scores in terms of organization, technology, and collaboration. Note that the character "–" is used when no information was available based on our interview and document analyses; however, it is treated as 0 when calculating sums

Domain	Category	Service CERTs							Sum		Ministry CERTs							Sum	
		#1	#2	#3	#4	#5	#6	#7	Σ	%	#8	#9	#10	#11	#12	#13	#14	Σ	%
Organization	CERT association member (VCV)	1	1	1	1	1	1	1	7	100%	1	1	1	1	1	1	1	7	100%
	Defined protocols for cross-organizational communication	1	–	0.5	1	1	1	1	5.5	79%	1	1	1	0.5	1	1	0.5	6	86%
	Distinct target group definition for incident reporting	1	1	1	1	1	1	1	7	100%	1	1	1	0.5	1	1	1	6.5	93%
Technology	Use of exchange platforms	1	1	1	0.5	1	1	1	6.5	93%	1	1	0.5	1	1	1	1	6.5	93%
	Alerting and reporting service	1	1	0.5	0.5	1	1	1	6	86%	1	1	1	1	1	1	1	7	100%
	Advisory service	0.5	0.5	0.5	0.5	1	0.5	0.5	4	57%	1	1	0	1	0	1	1	5	71%
Collaboration	Information access	–	1	–	0.5	–	1	1	3.5	50%	1	–	0	1	0	1	1	4	57%
	Coordination competence	–	–	1	0	–	1	1	3	43%	1	0	1	0.5	1	1	1	5.5	79%
	Public-private partnerships	1	–	0.5	0.5	0.5	0.5	0.5	3.5	50%	0.5	0.5	0	0	1	0.5	1	3.5	50%
	Information interface ES	–	–	1	1	0.5	0	1	3.5	50%	1	1	0.5	0	1	0	1	4.5	64%

their organizational, technological, and collaborative capabilities and services. We used the interview data of the six interviewed CERTs plus the analyzed documents of the eight non-interviewed CERTs to determine the scores. Since each category of the codebook represents a specific capability or service, we used a 3-point scale to evaluate whether a CERT meets the definition of the category to full extent (1 point), only partially (0.5 points), or not at all (0 points). For each category, a different coding rule is used to determine its score. The coding was conducted by two researchers initially and then checked and amended by the leading author. The individual but anonymized CERT scores are presented in Table 13.2. Besides the descriptive and summative lines and columns, each line represents a category (e.g., capability or service) and each column either a service CERT (n=7) or ministry CERT (n=7). In the following Tables 13.5, 13.4, and 13.3, we summarize the scores per category for both ministry and service CERTs and display the percentage-based results. For instance, service CERTs achieve a 79% score for the "defined protocols for cross-organizational communication" category, which means that they acquired 5.5 of 7 possible points.

13.4   Results

In this section, we present our findings categorized by the themes of organization structure, practices and technologies for cyber incident response, as well as collaboration among CERTs and other stakeholders.

13.4.1   Organizational Structure, Interorganizational Exchange and Target Groups

The organizational establishment of state-level CERTs in Germany was driven by a directive of the IT Planning Council (I3), which is an institution that coordinates the collaboration between the federal government and states in Germany: "States are obliged to follow and implement the resolutions of the IT Planning Council" (I1). Aside from this legally binding dimension, there are various ways to associate CERTs either within a state ministry or an IT service provider. The latter can be so-called state companies which are legally dependent, but organizationally outsourced parts of the state administration (I10). In accordance with the different forms of hierarchical establishment, it became evident that there is a "administrative-focused perspective" in ministry CERTs, which work more closely with other ministerial security organizations, in contrast to a "technology-focused perspective" in service

CERTs, which work closer to the operators of IT infrastructures. Due to different hierarchical establishments, internal administrative regulation, external regulations of superordinate authorities, but also a lack of necessary regulations, challenges in daily work and collaboration become apparent:

> "The legal basis for this is not yet available in the level of detail that would actually be necessary, so that colleagues from [another CERT, anonymized] can work with us at all, and it is not yet clear how a common file storage system can be created. It is probably not even possible" (I1).

When examining the *interorganizational exchange* between CERTs, the interviewees indicated that the VCV network is used for bilateral cooperation and multilateral exchange: "And there is a general interest to work hand in hand because without such a network you are nothing" (I5). Besides state CERTs, the federal CERT-Bund (as part of the BSI) is present in the VCV but operates at federal-level and thus works under different framework conditions (I3). Still, the cooperation with state CERTs is defined by agreements, guidelines, and technology:

> "The cooperation on a state and federal level is organized by a cooperation agreement, a guideline of the IT Security Council and a formal, political decision. This decision provides the contents, complemented by a regulation for reports, and is supported with a wiki page and a shared chat software by the CERT-Bund" (I5).

Facilitated by the role of the BSI (I3), cooperation among CERTs is planned to be shifted towards service level agreements:

> "There need to be respective contact persons, there needs to be appropriate conversation, and the BSI needs to appropriately support the states. This is why the BSI has built a centre for liaison in the past months. Therefore, various cooperation agreements exist that are planned to become service level agreements" (I5).

There are different protocols and standards that regulate the work, information management, and communication of CERT teams (Table 3). These include, amongst others, the standard on how to report cyber threats, for instance, via phone call or online form and the information sharing traffic light protocol (TLP), which is used to determine the confidentiality of information in intra- and interorganizational communication by classifying documents or information as red, amber, green, or white (with decreasing confidentiality). Almost all CERTs mentioned those two procedures either in the interviews or in public documents. All CERTs primarily support the public administration as their main target group. Still, some of them also

Table 13.3 Categories (representing capabilities or services) and anonymized CERT scores (percentage-based, cf. Table 13.2) in terms of organization and work

Categories	Sevice CERTs	Ministry CERTs	Observations and identified challenges	Design or policy implications
CERT association member (VCV)	100%	100%	All CERTs are in regular and institutionalized exchange in the VCV	Inclusion of open access sources, like social media expert communities, into automated system, which gathers incident relevant information
Defined protocols for cross-organizational communication	79%	86%	Almost uniform standardization regarding the structure of information is observed (TLP)	Although the TLP is the most common protocol, support for different information classification protocols is required
Distinct target group definition for incident reporting	100%	93%	Service CERTs seem to have a more precise definition of target groups, while ministry CERTs address a broader range of groups (such as citizens and SMEs)	Service CERTs seem to have a more precise definition of target groups, while ministry CERTs address a broader range of groups (such as citizens and SMEs)

include citizens, small and medium-sized enterprises (SMEs), or critical infrastructure providers as their target group (I12). Due to their variations in employee expertise and quantity, hierarchical integration, and specified target groups, all CERTs offer a different portfolio of services: "Therefore, the teams are relatively difficult to compare because they all have a little bit different focus" (ID3). Within the ministry, CERTs have IT-security appointees as a point of contact. The coded documents and the interviews showed no difference regarding this target group. In summary, the values in Table 13.3 confirm that interorganizational exchange is well developed both regarding ministry and service CERTs due to the establishment of the VCV. Still, protocols and work processes could be improved in at least four CERTs.

13.4.2 Technologies and Practices for Cyber Incident Response

When analyzing responses of the second-round interviews (I10–14), we identified differences and similarities in their use of ICT. An attempt to generalize ICT use of German state CERTs is depicted in Figure 13.1. The process can be roughly divided into the steps of acquisition, analysis, and response. First, incidents are either reported by customers (via mail or telephone) or detected by software (such as intrusion detection). After initial information about the incident is gathered, CERTs use a ticketing and reporting system to collect their evidence for incident response. Second, this evidence is collected and analyzed using awareness-focused (e.g., manufacturer websites, security advisory feeds, and social media channels) and collaboration-oriented (e.g., malware information sharing platforms, the VCV collaborative chat) channels. Third, the collected evidence is then used to inform a certain stakeholder with specific recommendations, to provide (daily) reports for selected stakeholders (e.g., a daily vulnerability report for ministries), or to issue a general warning for multiple stakeholders (in case larger-scaled ICT infrastructures are threatened).

The acquisition of information about incidents differs among CERTs. For instance, while one of the CERTs relies only on the reporting of incidents, another uses an intrusion detection software (IDS) to monitor their state administration network (I10, I11). In order to structure incident reporting, two CERTs defined a list of required information for further processing and damage assessment, of which the latter one is based on the RFC2350 specification. However, to reduce entry barriers, in the first contact usually only the most important information is discussed:

> "We try to set a relatively low inhibition threshold so that people report at all. You can't ask for all when there is a security incident and people are nervous. Then it is actually enough for us if they pick up the phone and inform us" (I10).

In terms of awareness-based evidence, the backbone of CERT activities lies in analyzing manufacturer websites and security advisories to identify Indicators of Compromise (IOCs). While manufacturer websites report incidents on their specific hardware or software (e.g., Apple, Cisco Systems, Google, IBM), security advisories are often curated feeds of security organizations (e.g., BSI, DFN-CERT, US-CERT) that integrate incident information across different sources. However, there are multiple issues with collecting open source information. First, they are provided in different and regularly changing formats, which makes it hard to maintain software for structured acquisition. Second, as a consequence, CERTs have to manually check manufacturer websites and security advisories on a daily basis for

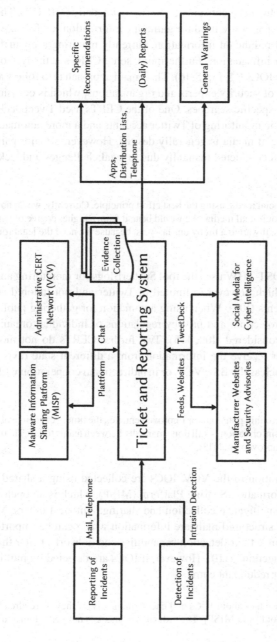

Figure 13.1 Example of a state-level CERT information and communication technology infrastructure

their reporting, which can consume up to two hours daily (I10, I12). Third, as multiple security advisories are used for gathering information, CERTs are confronted with the issue of redundant information, currently requiring a manual deduplication of entries or information. Furthermore, some CERTs actively monitor social media to identify IOCs (I1, I3, I5, I6). Their main approach is to follow and monitor Twitter accounts of security experts and organizations, which is occasionally combined with topic-specific searches. One of the CERTs used TweetDeck to support the semi-automatic monitoring of Twitter accounts and a more automated monitoring of further social media is generally desired. However, a major part of Twitter monitoring is still conducted manually due to legal challenges and lack of tailored technology:

> "We monitor social media using the best effort principle. Currently, we do not have the capacities to monitor all media. We would benefit from a higher degree of automation, however, we are thwarted a bit by our lawyers, because we need the legal foundations before" (I1).

Furthermore, VOST-THW uses the tool ScatterBlogs for monitoring and analyzing social media, which however is limited to Twitter and not tailored according to CERT requirements (I09). When using automation for gathering public data, data minimization, protection, and privacy regulations of individual organizations and states must be considered (I09, I15). Two further CERTs do not monitor social media, but either receive the information from a different state division or other organizations, such as the BSI, VCV, or in bidirectional cooperation with a different CERT:

> "But there is certainly potential for improvement, i.e., the timely exchange of technical safety-relevant information is still done manually between teams today. There is a clear potential for improvement" (I3).

Besides collaboration in the VCV, IOCs are collected using a shared instance of the Malware Information Sharing Platform (MISP), which is an open source platform for threat intelligence collection and sharing. Amongst others, MISP allows the provision of structured malware information which can be imported into IDS software to enhance their detection capabilities and it "works better than solutions using pattern detection" (I10). However, if IOCs are detected by multiple CERTs, there is a risk for redundant entries:

> "In the VCV, we talk about IOCs and check [manually] if they were already entered twice or threefold [into MISP]. The redundancy check is not yet automated" (I6).

In this way, technological shortcomings are compensated by the collaborative practices among CERTs. Still, interviewees considered the redundancy of security advisories as "an unsolved problem in the CERT community" (I10), which could be relieved by automated redundancy handling algorithms (I10, I14). Based on these infrastructures, CERTs are able to offer their alerting, reporting, and advisory services (Table 13.4). In terms of alerting, CERTs provide recommendations for action to allow their target groups to respond to cyber incidents. If a security vulnerability could potentially affect multiple organizations or target groups, a warning with preventative information is sent via e-mail distribution lists. Besides individual incident handling, CERTs create daily vulnerability reports to sharpen the security awareness of their target groups. In summary, alerting contact points in the administration or the target groups is at the core task of all CERTs. Other communicative practices of CERTs are advisory services and education of stakeholders, such as citizens, ministries, municipalities, or small and medium-sized enterprises. However, some CERTs are highly specialized and have a more specialized division of labor, than others. They focus on incident management, while outsourcing communication aspects such as awareness and education raising to other departments. In contrast to the organizational structure, Table 13.4 indicates that technologies and services for cyber incident response are less, but still well established across different CERTs (avg. 79%–88%). However, an aspect that is not covered by our initial coding scheme is the lack of supportive technology for gathering open source intelligence (OSINT) from manufacturer websites, security advisories, and social media. This issue implicates a lot of manual intraorganizational work, which can only be partly alleviated by interorganizational collaborative practices due to different requirements and technologies used across state administrations, SMEs, or other clients (I10, I12). In ministry CERTs, their advisory and alerting functions appear to be somewhat more strongly developed due to the focus on the overall situational awareness reports.

Both organizational structure and technology shape the collaboration among CERTs. Our interview participants especially valued the mutual exchange in the VCV network. The regular meetings of the VCV are an essential part of the communication (I4) and CERTs are highly intrinsically motivated to participate in the meetings that normally take place twice a year (I1) and are used to guide upcoming collaboration (I3). The CERTs can benefit from synergies within the VCV, for example, by sharing forms that follow the incident report standard (I3). The meetings of the VCV help to build relationships and networks on a personal level (I3):

> "Over the years, we have established something like a web of trust which comprises trustworthy people and, for instance, helps to verify information gathered online" (I10).

Table 13.4 Categories (representing capabilities or services) and anonymized CERT scores (percentage-based, cf. Table 13.2) in terms of technology

Categories	Sevice CERTs	Ministry CERTs	Observations and identified challenges	Design or policy implications
Use of exchange platforms	93%	93%	• All CERTs participate in the exchange platforms by the VCV, in a Wiki and a Chat, but there is a lack of tools for gathering OSINT	• Design of tools to increase automation and reduce redundancies when gathering OSINT for incident and threat processing and sharing
Alerting and reporting service	86%	86%	• All CERTs inform their target groups on vulnerabilities, however some CERTs (mostly in ministries) produce regular additional vulnerability reports	• An alerting and reporting tool should be able to generate vulnerability reports, design should also consider possibilities for automatization of generation of alerts, threat and incident data analysis and reporting
Advisory service	57%	71%	• As ministry CERTs address more target groups, their advisory services seem to focus on a broader spectrum of groups	• Further investigation on the possibilities of automation of standard cases Improve the pooling and sharing of expertise for complex incidents

Furthermore, the VCV allows employees of CERTs to visit other institutions (I5) so that knowledge is shared and they can "immerse into the daily operations on-site and learn how they live, how the information appears. This form of communication is very versatile, a whole range of possibilities to learn from each other and the CERT-Bund" (I5). However, due to varying organizational guidelines among CERTs, such as slight variations of the TLP confidentiality levels, the acting individuals have a great responsibility to assess the confidentiality of exchanged information and prevent their unintended disclosure (I3). Furthermore, the VCV provides the possibility to request resources from other CERTs but only in a non-binding manner:

"But it is not binding, when [another state] says they have a new Sand Box solution, they cannot say 'please send all our malicious software to them' [...]. It is an offer, we can accept it or decline it, but we will not reach a binding decision in the VCV except for standards for reporting and other such things" (I2).

The network is also used to establish bilateral cooperation to facilitate knowledge sharing or service exchange. For instance, due to limited financial resources, smaller CERTs may not be able to deliver all required services (I4). To address this problem of lacking resources, in one case tasks were delegated to a different state CERT:

"Yes, we are not a complete CERT but cooperate with (anonymized state). This also means that tasks that should be carried out by us are covered by the CERT of (anonymized state)" (I4).

This cooperation shows that also smaller states with less resources can enhance their capabilities in the context of cyber security and can therefore contribute to the security measures against cyberattacks (I2, I4). In this specific case, the cooperation affects tasks such as the creation and distribution of warning reports, tickets, and guidelines as well as the checking of suspicious e-mails (I4). In terms of information access, some CERTs state that are not oriented towards the CERT-Bund with its unique position at federal level but rather focus on mutual observation and learning of other state CERTs as they take on similar tasks that need to be adjusted to local peculiarities (I5). However, as a challenge, bilateral cooperation can be subject to asymmetrical information flows:

"The (anonymized CERT) is sufficiently different from us, we have nothing to do with them technically, we do not really know who they are associated with, they simply get our information, but the return flow is low" (I3).

The nature of collaboration is further influenced by the different types of public ministerial and service CERTs. This has an impact on the specific expertise of the recruited personnel: "This makes a difference, the CERTs of an IT service provider are organized in a technical way, they are usually technicians. There often are people who are less technically experienced in the ministries" (I2). Especially different profiles of expertise, regular exchange, and generation of trust are crucial for networking:

"The personal contact, knowing who you are dealing with, developing bonds of trust beat all formalities, beat all regulations, because if there is a will, there is a way. And with this model of personally getting to know each other this will is built, a network of personally known actors. When you need help or have limited resources, as a first step, you rely on those who you have a good relationship with" (I5).

The collaboration among CERTs can also be viewed from the perspective of *public-private partnerships*. In contrast to their ministry-embedded counterparts, service provider CERTs of some states are based in economic state companies. In this case, the activities and coordination of the BSI and VCV facilitate intensified and formalized cooperation between ministry and service CERTs:

> "The cooperation between states is encouraged by the BSI, because they want to reduce their effort of consulting. Therefore, we try to coordinate ourselves in the VCV before requesting help from the BSI. But the support of all sides and also from the BSI is excellent. We usually get an answer on the same working day if it is particularly important and urgent" (I1).

However, regardless of their organizational embedding, state CERTs compete with CERTs in the private sector, which are part of bigger enterprises:

> "The labor market offers almost no personnel, the teams cannibalize each other, which is admittedly not constructive. [In] the state CERTs, fluctuation, and lots of migration between the CERTs take place. This is not good" (I3).

There are huge differences in employer attractiveness of either public or private CERTs. While state CERTs are bound to the tariff agreements for the civil service of the states, the salary of employees in the private sector tends to be higher, thus attracting higher numbers of applicants (I3).

As highlighted in Table 13.5, collaborative features of state CERTs are less developed than organizational and communicative features, achieving rather mediocre scores (avg. 54%–70%). Both ministry and service CERTs indicate that information dissemination is very well or at least moderately developed. It can also be seen that their access to information scores considerably lower, which however could be due to the fact that some tasks are outsourced to other organizational units. Only about half of the CERTs mentioned that they maintain public-private partnerships. However, there are regular and important exchanges and partnerships between ministry and service CERTs in at least two cases, incidents are collaborated on to improve their effectiveness. Coordination competences and information interfaces to emergency services are higher in ministry CERTs, probably due to easier access and exchange with other authoritative units, such as emergency management or police.

Table 13.5 Categories (representing capabilities or services) and anonymized CERT scores (percentage-based, cf. Table 13.2) in terms of collaboration

Categories	Sevice CERTs	Ministry CERTs	Observations and identified challenges	Design or policy implications
Information access	50%	57%	• Information access depends on the organizational structure: beside the incident notification, CERTs collect information from various sources. Access to more open sources can be considered	• Inclusion of open access sources, like social media expert communities, into automated system, which gathers incident relevant information
Coordination competence	43%	79%	• Ministry CERTs seem to be more capable of coordinating tasks between CERTs and other organizations. The allocation of resources between CERTs seems to be unequal	• The unequal distribution of resources can be addressed by (semi)automation of standard tasks, as well as by pooling expertise and resources
Public-private partnerships	50%	50%	• Due to protection of sensitive data, the collaboration with private CERTs is equally limited	• Tools supporting collaboration between public sector and private sector CERTs need to consider legal restrictions regarding privacy and sensitive information
Information Interface Emergency Services	50%	64%	• The contact to other authorities seems to be stronger for ministry CERTs	• The design should support the information exchange with emergency services for cross-organizational incidents response

13.5   Discussion and Conclusion

In this paper, we investigated the organizational structures, technology use, and cross-organizational collaboration of German federal and state CERTs. Existing literature on the topic highlighted a lack of empirical research on collaboration among CERTs (Van der Kleij et al., 2017). Our multi-method empirical study, which comprises semi-structured interviews (N=15) and supplementary document analyses (N=25), provides findings to answer our research question: How do the organizational structure, technology use, and cross-organizational collaboration contribute to cyber incident response of German state-level CERTs? In the following, we discuss our findings, implications for design and policy, as well as limitations and opportunities for future work.

13.5.1 Discussion and Findings

First, in terms of organization, German state CERTs have been established either as part of state ministries or in external service companies. In both cases, their aim is to provide preventative and reactive security measures securing the ICT infrastructures of their respective target groups, such as public administrations, small and medium-sized enterprises, or citizens (Kossakowski 2001; Kossakowski & Neufert, 2012; Slayton & Clarke, 2020; Sundaramurthy et al., 2014). Due to the digitalization of the administration (e.g., establishment of e-governments), critical infrastructures and enterprises (e.g., deployment of IoT), and society (e.g., use of mobile devices), their tasks of monitoring, analyzing, communicating, and responding to cyber threats and security incidents are becoming more complex (Mitropoulos et al., 2006). However, in some state CERTs, a lack of personnel and resources impair a functional division of labor and successful delivery of their services (La Fleur et al., 2021). One issue lies in the competition between state CERTs, which are bound to collective wage agreements, and private sector CERTs that can provide higher wages. This is partly alleviated by an increasing cross-organizational collaboration, involving a multitude of actors, such as other CERTs and IT security appointees in other authorities and organizations. Especially the collaboration among state CERTs, which was established in the VCV network, has been highlighted as the most important aspect of effective incident management.

Second, we saw that CERTs use a variety of technologies to support the acquisition, analysis, and reporting of information related to cyber security incidents (Figure 13.1). As a starting point, incidents are either reported by customers or detected by software. Subsequently, some CERTs use a ticketing and reporting system to collect and analyze evidence for incident response. On the one hand, this evidence is gathered from publicly available data, such as manufacturer websites, security advisories, or social media. On the other hand, further evidence is gathered by collaboration using shared platforms, such as MISP or the VCV. For example, a chat and wiki are used in the VCV to facilitate collaboration between federal and state CERTs. However, the divergent allocation of resources negatively influences the participation of some CERTs within the chat. Trusting relationships between individuals needs to be supported by a reliable system based on common understandings and practices (Hellwig, 2015; H. Khurana et al., 2009; Slayton & Clarke, 2020), such as the common use of protocols for confidentially (e.g., traffic light protocol, TLP) of security-relevant information and for documenting cyber threats. Similar to our study, Van der Kleij et al. (2017) have found that the communication of threats and "in-depth technical communication" needs more support by formalization and communication tools, which should be supported by threat intelligence standards, such as STIX and MEAC. This is also important because monitoring and diagnosing security threats otherwise often relies on the tacit knowledge of practitioners, which is difficult to share (Werlinger et al., 2010). Such a formalization would support the development of explicit expert knowledge, which in turn would benefit the efficiency of communication between CERTs and external actors (Buchler et al., 2018; Sundaramurthy et al., 2014). Still, once enough evidence is collected via awareness-focused and collaboration-oriented channels, a report is generated that either provides specific recommendations for a certain stakeholder or general warnings for multiple stakeholders.

Third, the interviews showed that there is strong bilateral collaboration between CERTs, especially between ministry and service CERTs, as their different access to IT services and communication infrastructures can lead to useful exchange of expertise, knowledge, and services. We observed that there are specialized skills in every CERT that are shared within the CERT community using the VCV as a platform. Generally, cooperation between CERTs is organized within the VCV, which is considered essential as it combines the perspectives of ministry and service CERTs, offering added value for all actors and serving as a web of trust. One value that was frequently highlighted is the mutual learning within the VCV; this is in accordance with the suggestion of Ahmad et al. (2012) to implement "double-loop learning", which is not only focusing on learning from the individual incidents but also reflecting on systematic corrective actions. This is achieved through mutual support and exchange between state CERTs in the areas of awareness raising, response strategies, and technology, such as anti-phishing campaigns to raise awareness and shared

sand boxes to analyze malware. Regular VCV meetings also have a social component, which later forms a basis for collaboration and the use of shared technology for
information and service exchange. In the case of ad hoc incident responses, it was
pointed out that individual trust and informal contacts, based on formal contacts, are
key to a fast and effective response. The federal level, represented by the BSI, has
more extensive tasks and competences, including the provision of security-relevant
information to state CERTs. In comparison, the BSI's technical and organizational
infrastructure is significantly more advanced due to division of labor into separate
departments for situational awareness and response capabilities. This feature is used
for a distribution of tasks between the federal and the state level that supports the
regular monitoring and exchange of threat information. However, the sharing of
information between CERTs and non-CERT actors is sometimes limited due to privacy and confidentiality restrictions [46] and different legal frameworks for ministry
and service CERTs.

13.5.2 Implications for Design, Policy, and Research

Based on our key observations and identified challenges, we propose design and
policy implications (Table 13.6) to support the cross-organizational collaboration
of German state CERTs and to increase cyber situational awareness (Hevner, 2007).
First, we saw that the organization, structure, and work processes of CERTs are
based on legal regulations and organizational embedding, which shaped different
perspectives and service portfolios across CERTs. Thus, when developing ICT, an
interoperable and modular architecture to address the different focuses and services
of CERTs should be provided, while still maintaining the extended need for collaboration. From a policy perspective, a shift from loose cooperation towards service
level agreements should facilitate the organizational and technological development
of work since a lack of liabilities and regulations for daily work in interorganizational
exchange was observed.

Second, a variety of different technologies and practices for communication
among CERTs was observed. While regular meetings were perceived as working measures for collaboration, knowledge sharing, and relationship building, a
lack of technology support for analysis and communication became apparent. In
order to address these issues, ICT should facilitate a mainly automated but privacy-
preserving (Imran et al., 2018) cross-platform monitoring and analysis of incident
data, including blogs, databases, social media, or websites. Moreover, deduplication
techniques and standardized threat exchange formats would help to prevent redundant IOCs and to increase efficiency of operations in shared threat intelligence plat-

forms. Third, in terms of collaboration, we identified strong bilateral collaborations and delegations of tasks among CERTs but also multilateral coordination in conjunctions with the BSI, CERT-Bund, and VCV. Still, a lack of financial, human, and time resources was identified as a barrier for extensive collaboration and operation. By utilizing the benefits of (semi-)automation of monitoring and reporting processes, functional and useable ICT could help to further alleviate such resource constraints. Furthermore, an asymmetry of information, power, and size across CERTs was identified as a challenge for collaboration. Here, transparent reporting and tool structures could help to enhance awareness and trust among CERTs.

In the past, crisis informatics research has focused on the use of prominent social media, such as Facebook or Twitter. Soden & Palen (2018) suggested to broaden the scope of crisis informatics and look "beyond social media", including domains such as participatory mapping. In light of the increasing interconnectedness of real and virtual realms, first, we suggest crisis informatics research to also tackle the issues of cyberattacks, which threaten critical infrastructures and society. Our study highlights the need for intense collaboration between relevant stakeholders to monitor and respond to cyberattacks. Second, it became apparent that besides social media, other open source information based on expert blogs, security advisory feeds, or manufacturer websites are important sources of insight for cyber incident response. In our study, the co-creation of knowledge was implemented in an interplay of establishing cyber situational awareness (e.g., monitoring of available open and social information) and cross-organizational collaboration (e.g., exchange of expertise, provision of shared services, and verification of information). In terms of situational awareness, crisis informatics leveraged the advent of social media analytics tools designed according to the needs of emergency services (M.-A. Kaufhold, Rupp, et al., 2020; Onorati et al., 2018; Thom et al., 2016). While they are certainly not tailored to the requirements of CERTs and do not account for significance of other OSINT sources, the knowledge created and shared around these tools can be used—in combination with empirical studies such as ours—to inform the design of specific CERT technologies. Our interview participants expressed a positive attitude towards the established cross-organizational collaboration between CERTs. Still, since the above-mentioned technology seems promising to reduce the time strain of daily routine (monitoring) tasks, this would open up further opportunities to conduct other (collaborative) tasks with higher standards of quality. Moreover, tools facilitating the creation and dissemination of reports and warnings could help to improve the collaboration among CERTs and interaction with customers.

Table 13.6 Summary of observed behaviors, identified challenges, and design or policy implications

	Key observations	Identified Challenges	Design or policy implications
Organization	• Organizational structure is driven by federal characteristics, directives, and laws	• Lack of standards and regulations for the daily work, which are required to remain sustainable	• Interoperable and modular architecture for different CERT focuses and services
	• Embeddings shape different ministry- and technology-focused perspectives	• Lack of liabilities in interorganizational exchange	• Shift from loose cooperation towards service level agreements
Technology	• Use of a variety of different tools for communication among CERTs	• Lack of automatization in the monitoring of open, public, or social data	• Reduction of resource costs by (semi-)automation of monitoring and reporting processes
	• Embeddings shape different ministry- and technology-focused perspectives	• Lack of liabilities in interorganizational exchange	• Shift from loose cooperation towards service level agreements
		• Communication and reporting redundancies of IOCs	
Collaboration	• Bilateral collaboration and delegation of tasks among CERTs	• Lack of financial, personnel, and time resources	• Privacy-preserving cross-platform monitoring and analysis of incident data
	• Coordination of collaborative actions by the BSI and VCV	• Asymmetry of information, power, and size	• Use of deduplication techniques and standardized threat exchange formatsements
		• Competition between public and private sectors	

13.5.3 Limitations and Future Work

The analysis of the interviews showed that the form and the type of association of CERTs can substantially influence their work. In contrast to the content analysis of official documents, the interviews allowed a different kind of insight into the informal practices of CERTs. The former did not provide information on the networks between the CERTs but only on formal aspects, such as the organizational structure, target group definition, task portfolio, and reporting templates for cyber security incidents. Hence, the part of the analysis that focuses on technology and collaboration strongly relies on information extracted from the interviews. Furthermore, more ministry CERT employees agreed to be interviewed than those from service CERTs. This might have influenced the imbalance between the coding based on the interviews and the documents, causing the higher scores of the ministry CERTs as presented in Tables 13.5, 13.3 and 13.4. As every CERT has differences regarding its service portfolio and tasks, the comparison might be biased towards the interviewed CERTs as well as towards CERTs with a broader spectrum of tasks and less division of labor. If some tasks, such as the communication of cyber threats, are not realized in CERTs but in a different state organization, this is not reflected in the study design. However, the more resources organizations allocate to incident response, the more likely they are to change the organization of the division of labor of monitoring, response, and communication. Still, most of the CERTs studied (12 of 14) combined the tasks within the CERT.

When discussing the generalizability of results, several aspects need to be considered. On the one hand, our data is based on an empirical study with German CERTs, which is why we cannot provide a grounded assessment on the situation in other nations. Differences in national capabilities and legislations likely influence the activity, permissions, and privacy-preserving behavior of CERTs (Boeke, 2018; Collier, 2017). Further in-depth research would be required to compare different analytical technologies (e.g., the degrees of automation and modularity) and collaborative practices (e.g., cooperations or service level agreements) across nations on a fine-grained level. On the other hand, cyber emergency response is a global problem requiring extensive collaboration across CERTs on both national and international level (Pethia & van Wyk, 1990; Slayton & Clarke, 2020). On average, more than ten CERTs are established per European nation (ENISA, 2020), highlighting the necessity for standardized threat intelligence exchange, transparency, and trust among teams. This is further emphasized in international collaboration, which is required in large-scale cyberattacks, such as the 2017 WannaCry ransomware attack that infected over 200,000 victims across 150 countries (Zade et al., 2018). Furthermore, the 2021 Microsoft Exchange vulnerabilities have been exploited by a variety of professional criminal groups, and which led to the BSI reaching out directly to 9,000 possibly affected enterprises in Germany (BSI, 2021). To respond to the professionalization of cyber criminals, CERTs increase their capacities and their interorganizational collaboration. Thus, we assume that our design and policy implications are viable requirements across international CERTs that require different implementations based on national capabilities and legislation. However, in the next step of our national research project, we intend to use the framework of design case studies (Wulf et al., 2011) in order to complement our empirical findings with other stakeholders views and translate them into more fine-grained requirements to iteratively design and evaluate a ICT demonstrator facilitating the data analysis and collaboration practices among state-level CERTs in Germany.

Privacy Concerns and Acceptance Factors of OSINT for Cybersecurity: A Representative Survey

14

14.1 Introduction

Open Source Intelligence (OSINT) is considered to be one of the most promising approaches to fight crime and corruption. It is a framework that consists of using publicly available data that is collected, processed, and correlated to provide timely information, e.g. for cyber situational awareness (Pournouri & Akhgar, 2015), or for investigative research and journalist teams, like Bellingcat. OSINT has also been used and has been specialized to detect cyber crime and cyber threats worldwide, using a semi-automated process (Pastor-Galindo et al., 2020). When social media data is used exclusively, OSINT is referred to as Social Media Intelligence (SOCMINT).

The monitoring and crisis management by emergency services has been studied in the field of crisis informatics (Reuter, Hughes, & Kaufhold, 2018; Reuter & Kaufhold, 2018). The approach aims to use public data to gain situational awareness and provide effective incident prevention and response to improve public security in crisis situations. In the case of cybersecurity, (governmental) Computer Emergency Response Teams (CERTs), also known as Computer Security Incidents Response Teams (CSIRTs), have been adapting this approach from other emergency services

ORIGINAL PUBLICATION Riebe, T., Biselli, T., Kaufhold, M.-A., & Reuter, C. (2023). Privacy Concerns and Acceptance Factors of OSINT for Cybersecurity: A Representative Survey. *Proceedings on Privacy Enhancing Technologies (PoPETs)*. https://doi.org/10.56553/popets-2023-0028

Supplementary Information The online version contains supplementary material available at https://doi.org/10.1007/978-3-658-41667-6_14.

and government agencies (Riebe, Kaufhold and Reuter, 2021). CERT members collect information on potential cyber threats from different public sources like Twitter, vulnerability databases and software vendor websites to gain situational awareness. This process is increasingly (semi)automated (Kassim et al., 2022).

With growing numbers of cyber threats, OSINT has become an increasingly important approach, as more data is available, which can be used for early risk prevention. As OSINT approaches to detect cyber threats mostly use social media data (Pastor-Galindo et al., 2020; Riebe, Wirth, et al., 2021), many ethical and social questions arise at the complex intersection of privacy and security. In a systematic study of OSINT systems for cybersecurity, Riebe, Bäumler, et al. (2023) have found that in 73 OSINT systems, only 11 discussed ethical and social implications, such as privacy impact. Therefore, the principles of "privacy by design," such as data minimization, must first be applied when using such tools to collect and analyze any individual's data.

Such OSINT systems can be used to detect novel threats or to identify and profile individuals or groups. Profiling in the case of targeted advertising can have dramatically different consequences than profiling conducted by governments, law enforcement or emergency services. Studies have shown, that citizens express the want or need for government agencies to perform democratically legitimized forms of "surveillance-oriented security technologies" (SOSTs) to ensure protection from harm (Dinev et al., 2008). The kind of and the extent to which online surveillance is considered appropriate has been studied with regard to culture (Dinev et al., 2005), trust in the government (Kininmonth et al., 2018; Trüdinger & Steckermeier, 2017), and fear of terrorism and crime (Furnham & Swami, 2019; Wester & Giesecke, 2019), as well as in relation to specific technologies, such as private communication, financial data, and camera use in public spaces (Wells & Wills, 2009; S. Zhang et al., 2021). However, the acceptance of SOSTs is not static and can change due to technological or contextual events.

The effects of surveillance on people are described by Lyon's work on the surveillance society (Lyon, 2001) and by Haggerty and Ericson (2000) as the creation of data doubles that can be monitored. With more and more areas being represented digitally, the rhizomatic spread of surveillance into all spheres of daily life has shifted security and privacy norms (Kaufmann, 2016). On the one hand, people are aware of their privacy and advocate for privacy enhancement; on the other hand, they view surveillance as a necessary method to prevent harm, manage human-made or natural disasters or respond to incidents affecting public infrastructure. Due to this ambiguity in privacy concerns, the study of ethical, legal, and social implications (ELSI) has become increasingly relevant.

While this study focuses on the case of OSINT for cybersecurity for German governmental CERTs in particular, the ethical implications transcend this case and can therefore be used for other OSINT systems which are used for the public security. Focusing on these implications supports the development of technologies that anticipate the complex and non-binary nature of privacy and security regarding surveillance technologies (Wester & Giesecke, 2019). Therefore, participatory approaches, such as ELSI-co design (Liegl et al., 2016) and value-sensitive design (VSD) (Friedman et al., 2013), offer research frameworks that include indirect and direct stakeholder perspectives in the design and development of technologies. Thus, this study aims at understanding the factors associated with the acceptance of OSINT systems for cybersecurity contexts to inform the design of these systems.

Therefore, this study's leading research question asks: **How do people evaluate the use of OSINT for cybersecurity by governmental organizations and which factors are associated with the acceptance of OSINT?**

Our results indicate that cyber threat perception and the perceived need for OSINT are positively correlated to acceptance, while privacy concerns show a negative correlation. The awareness of OSINT as an interactive factor only affects the association between privacy concerns and OSINT acceptance. Privacy behavior shows no correlation with OSINT acceptance, which shows that additional research needs to be done on contextual factors for privacy-decision making and data disclosure.

This paper is structured as follows: Section 14.2 discusses related studies on surveillance technologies, factors for their acceptance and privacy-preserving technologies and behavior. In Section 14.3, the design and methodology of the representative survey of the German population as well as the construction of the concepts are explained. Afterwards, Section 14.4 presents the results of the descriptive and statistical analysis. Section 14.5 discusses the results regarding the state of research and Section 14.6 provides a comprehensive conclusion.

14.2   Related Work

The related work section introduces the discourse on the acceptance of surveillance technologies (14.2.1) as well as on privacy concerns and behaviors regarding the use of OSINT for cybersecurity (14.2.2). The subsections introduce the concepts used in the study to answer the research question, on which basis, the hypotheses are developed (14.2.3).

14.2.1 Acceptance of Surveillance Technologies

Surveillance technologies, such as OSINT, have been researched in the context of public security to monitor terrorists and criminal groups. Their capability to monitor the public on a large scale, as well as existing cases thereof have also been researched (Esposti & Santiago-Gomez, 2015; Pauli et al., 2016). Surveillance can be defined as the systematic monitoring of individuals or groups for a given purpose (Lyon, 2001; Trüdinger & Steckermeier, 2017). In the case of OSINT for cybersecurity, there are two kinds of systems: Cyber Threat Intelligence (CTI), which focuses on the detection and analysis of cyber threats, and risk mitigation systems, which work towards identifying actors and groups (Riebe, Bäumler, et al., 2023).

The legitimacy of SOSTs depends on the acceptance and the public approval (Trüdinger & Steckermeier, 2017). Many scholars agree that the perception of threats is associated with the acceptance of the use of surveillance technologies (Furnham & Swami, 2019; Trüdinger & Steckermeier, 2017). In this context, threat perception is conceptualized as the fear of crime or terror. For example, In their representative telephone survey with 2.176 participants, Trüdinger and Steckermeier (2017) investigated how information is associated with trust in different institutions (legislative, executive, and judicature) and how this might affect the acceptance of surveillance technologies. They concluded that among other factors, threat perception and the perception of surveillance measures' effectiveness correlate with the acceptance of the same category. On the other side, the protection against these threats is also used to legitimize the application of surveillance technologies (Brown & Korff, 2009).

The study by Furnham and Swami (2019) shows that that attitudes towards the government and public authorities are associated with the acceptance of surveillance measures. They developed a scale of 25 items to test attitudes towards surveillance based on personality traits and punitive attitudes, such as the threat perception and the attitude towards authorities. They have further shown that "demographic and personality factors were weakly related to attitudes to surveillance while general attitudes to authority were the strongest predictor" (Furnham & Swami, 2019).

The prerequisites for the acceptance of surveillance measures can also be linked to various threats, which the COVID-19 pandemic has shown. For example, A. Ioannou and Tussyadiah (2021) studied the acceptance of surveillance and privacy protection behaviors during the global health crisis in the US. In accordance with Trüdinger and Steckermeier (2017), they found that trust in the government and the need for proactive surveillance are positively associated with acceptance.

Threat perception and attitudes towards the government and authorities are also associated with the perceived need for surveillance measures. People with a higher threat perception are more likely to support government surveillance technologies

(A. Ioannou & Tussyadiah, 2021; Trüdinger & Steckermeier, 2017). Trust in authorities is positively correlated to the increased acceptance of surveillance measures (Furnham & Swami, 2019; Trüdinger & Steckermeier, 2017). Therefore, people who perceive the need for surveillance technologies and trust their government are more inclined to accept and support measures on this issue (Dinev et al., 2008). As norms and threat perceptions change, Wilton (2017) argues, that there is a sift of the threat perception from a focus on predominantly commercial threats "to a recognition that government activities, in the sphere of intelligence and national security, also give rise to significant privacy risk". Thus, people might perceive threats different with regard to their culture or experiences (Dinev et al., 2005; Dinev et al., 2008; Wilton, 2017). As a result, people might not perceive OSINT as the best approach to deter crime or monitor cyber threats. Therefore, we developed a construct consisting of items that measure both aspects of threat perception, namely, acceptance and perceived need.

Like Furnham and Swami (2019), many scholars agree that the perception of threats is associated with the acceptance of the use of surveillance technologies (Furnham & Swami, 2019; A. Ioannou & Tussyadiah, 2021; Trüdinger & Steckermeier, 2017). People with a higher threat perception are more likely to support government surveillance technologies. Therefore, people who perceive the need for surveillance technologies are also more inclined to accept them (Dinev et al., 2008). However, this does not imply that people are willing to share any kind of information in any situation. The context of a threat (like terrorism or a natural disaster) is associated with the information people are willing to provide to an organization (Aldehoff et al., 2019): "The more intimate the type of information, the lower the approval of the subjects. Telephone numbers, addresses and location information belong to the data that is not considered critically intimate and would be communicated by a large portion of subjects." Therefore, as the public data and the use cases of OSINT in emergency response and monitoring increases, studies are needed that focus on the context factors for acceptance of OSINT regarding specific data and information, as well as the machine learning-driven algorithms for analysis.

14.2.2 Privacy Impact of OSINT

Privacy considerations are relevant to the development of OSINT systems, as they gather publicly available data, mostly from social media platforms. Privacy is a well-researched term, which has been explored by psychologists, sociologists as well as information systems and management research (Dinev et al., 2005; Dinev et al., 2008; Kokolakis, 2017; Smith et al., 1996). Privacy has been defined by Westin

(1967) as the right to control, edit, manage, and delete information about one-self and to decide when, how, and to what extent information is communicated to others.

Due to the rise of digital communication, privacy research has gained more interest and has been operationalized as privacy concerns, meaning "the anticipation of future possible loss of privacy" (Dinev et al., 2005). As research on privacy concerns has been conducted focusing on a variety of contexts, like online shopping, online social networks and IoT, our approach focuses on the context of online social media, in which people deliberately share personal and other information. Social theory and behavioral research have studied reasons why people take part in social media, such as benefits of participation, profiling and social connection (Debatin et al., 2009). Debatin et al. (2009) found the reasons for self-disclosure to be "(a) the need for diversion and entertainment, (b) the need for social relationships, and (c) the need for identity construction".

Privacy concerns and their explanations have been studied mostly regarding commercial contexts (Buchanan et al., 2007; Smith et al., 1996)[1], and only a small number of studies have addressed governmental surveillance and monitoring (Dinev et al., 2008; A. Ioannou & Tussyadiah, 2021; Kininmonth et al., 2018; Trüdinger & Steckermeier, 2017). In their study on privacy concerns and their effects on the acceptance of surveillance in Australia, Kininmonth et al. (2018) tested several factors associated with the acceptance of surveillance technologies. In particular, they examined the privacy concerns and practices, the concerns regarding secondary use of data, the perceived need for surveillance, the trust in the government, as well as the trust in data management and protection. They found that privacy concerns have a significant influence on the acceptance of surveillance technologies.

The relation between privacy concerns and the need for surveillance was studied by Dinev et al. (2008). They found that people who have privacy concerns would not perceive surveillance as necessary, and are less likely to disclose personal information. However, they also noted that "surveillance technology is being adopted and used faster than public awareness of it and is outpacing the public debate" while people are willing to give information to fight terrorism. Further, they added that this is also a result of "the nature of the search for a balance between security and privacy within the context of the continuous flow of information technology advancements and their implementation in private and public institutions." The pace of technological and political change on surveillance measures makes longitudinal studies necessary.

---

[1] For a systematic overview on privacy behaviors and concerns see the meta study by Kokolakis (2017).

Such a longitudinal study has been conducted by byWester and Giesecke (2019). They investigated the attitudes towards privacy and surveillance and their change over time. In this context, they found that the risk perception of surveillance has decreased while the call for transparency has increased "dramatically" between 2009 and 2017, concluding that "this suggests that citizens not only make distinctions between different technologies, but also what actor is collecting and analyzing the data. Discussions about trust, transparency and accountability should then be held in relation to the different owners—and perhaps the relation between them." This again strengthens the need for context-focused research, which also takes data-gathering institutions into account.

As privacy concerns are the anticipation of possible future privacy violations and/or the loss thereof, the risk perception of certain technologies helps to better understand user behavior. In their study, Gerber et al. (2019) conducted an online survey with 942 participants on the risk perception of social networks, smart home and smart health devices. They found that participants perceived abstract risks to be more likely but moderately severe, while specific risks were perceived as moderately likely and more severe. Additionally, people did not seem to be aware of specific privacy risks in abstract scenarios, illustrated by standard disclaimers like "your data are collected and analyzed". As a result, the authors call for measures that raise people's awareness about what is collected and analyzed and how information can be used or even abused.

Actual privacy behaviors in contrast to privacy concerns have been the subject matter of many studies, leading to the discourse on the privacy paradox (Barnes, 2006; Kokolakis, 2017), which assumes a disconnect between desired privacy and potentially contradicting behavior. However, other studies have questioned the privacy paradox and its resulting claims. This means, that observed behavior does not necessarily contradict privacy claims. For example, the privacy calculus suggest that all behaviors protecting one's privacy follow a rational choice in which giving up privacy can be rewarded (Dienlin & Metzger, 2016). Another branch of research has focused on privacy socialisation and the effects of groups and activism, especially as social media platforms have become relevant to political activists (Monsees, 2020). Therefore, people actively avoid surveillance as an expression of shifting privacy norms and question the legitimacy of government surveillance or individual measures (Joh, 2013).

In their study on the development of measures for privacy concerns and behavior during online shopping, Buchanan et al. (2007) have found two separate factors that build the foundation to behavior aimed at protecting privacy. For the two factors, the general caution and common sense needs to be distinct from the "sophisticated use of hardware and software", which requires a more specialized knowledge and technical training for the actual protection.

Looking at the OSINT systems which were developed for cybersecurity purposes in a systematic study, Riebe, Bäumler, et al. (2023) identified 73 systems, from which 11 discussed ELSI implications. Especially when systems aim at focusing on particular actors, this could include the profiling of individuals (Edwards et al., 2017). Thus, privacy and legal implications must be assessed for systems which aim at profiling as well as detecting insider threats. However, systems which focus less on individuals and more on cyber threat intelligence (CTI) to detect and analyze threat early, can also impact privacy. First, the use of online social networks (Riebe, Wirth, et al., 2021) and second the processing and analysis of data are relevant for privacy implications (Ranade et al., 2018). In this context, the trade-off between data protection requirements and the demand for forensic investigators are discussed by Nisioti et al. (2021).

14.2.3 Research Gap and Hypotheses Development

The research on surveillance has focused on different application areas, such as camera surveillance in public spaces (Wells & Wills, 2009), and online surveillance (Kininmonth et al., 2018), as well as causes of legitimization, such as fighting crime, terrorism but also public health monitoring (A. Ioannou & Tussyadiah, 2021; Ishmaev et al., 2021). Thus, surveillance has been studied regarding its factors associated with acceptance as well as concerning different scenarios. The importance of the scenario, the surveillance actors and their use of information has been identified (Aldehoff et al., 2019; Kininmonth et al., 2018; Trüdinger & Steckermeier, 2017; Wester & Giesecke, 2019). Thus, for the use of OSINT in cybersecurity, these factors and scenarios need to be researched.

While OSINT systems can also be useful in the early detection and monitoring of cyber threats and incident communication, they, like other SOSTs, can create uncertainty (Lyon, 2001). Therefore, to understand the attitudes towards OSINT in the case of cybersecurity, we conducted a representative survey among the German population asking about the aforementioned constructs and how they relate to the acceptance of OSINT (see Table 14.1).

In the following, the research question is further operationalized in hypotheses. Furnham and Swami (2019), A. Ioannou and Tussyadiah (2021), and Trüdinger and Steckermeier (2017) have shown, that the level of threat perception is associated with the level of acceptance of surveillance measures. Threat perception is defined as the participant's fear of crime, terrorism, and of being harmed (see Table 14.1).

As OSINT is a group of surveillance technologies, we derive the first hypothesis based on their research:

H1:   People with a higher cyber threat perception are inclined to be more accepting of OSINT.

However, the perception of a threat might not necessarily mean that people would perceive the use of surveillance technology as the preferred approach to detect and to deter criminals and terrorist, or as the preferred measure of ones protection against these threats (Dinev et al., 2008; Kininmonth et al., 2018). Therefore, we asked participants for their perceived need of OSINT separately. This concept has been studied by Kininmonth et al. (2018) and Dinev et al. (2008). Following their work, we defined the perceived need for OSINT as the perception that government surveillance is necessary to protect citizens (see Table 14.1). The concept is also used by A. Ioannou and Tussyadiah (2021) in the case of surveillance during the COVID-19 pandemic. Thus, the second hypothesis assumes a positive association between both concepts:

H2:   People who think there is an overall need for OSINT are inclined to be more accepting of OSINT.

Privacy concerns, defined as the anticipation of a future possible loss of privacy (see Table 14.1, Dinev et al., 2005), have also been negatively associated with the acceptance of surveillance in related studies, such as by Kininmonth et al. (2018) and Dinev et al. (2008). They have shown, that people with higher privacy concerns are less likely to accept surveillance. Thus, regarding the use of OSINT for cybersecurity, we expect a negative correlation between privacy concerns and the acceptance of OSINT:

H3:   People with greater privacy concerns are inclined to be less accepting of OSINT.

Privacy research has intensively studied how privacy concerns are related to privacy behavior (Barnes, 2006; Dienlin & Metzger, 2016), and has found their association to be complex, with potentially divergent behavior (Kokolakis, 2017). Therefore, we separately investigate privacy behavior as the protective behavior to protect one's privacy (see Table 14.1). Because stronger privacy behavior can, to a certain degree, be viewed as a manifestation of higher privacy concerns, we assume that it is negatively correlated with OSINT acceptance:

H4:   People with stronger privacy behavior are inclined to be less accepting of OSINT.

In their study on the acceptance of surveillance policy, Trüdinger and Steckermeier (2017) research the effect of awareness of surveillance policies on the trust and acceptance of these policies. They use the concept of awareness, as an individual's knowledge on the existence and use of surveillance (see Table 14.1) is as an interactive factor. This is especially interesting for OSINT, as the gathering and analysis of public data online are not observable for the individual and the effects are rather abstract for people, which might affect their evaluation of the policies and measures (Gerber et al., 2019). However, in their study on the effects of the Snowden revelation on the public's opinion, Valentino et al. (2020) show that awareness is not associated with the rejection of SOSTs. Thus, following Trüdinger and Steckermeier (2017), we formulated a more exploratory hypothesis using awareness of OSINT as an interactive factor:

H5:   The level of awareness of OSINT changes the associations between cyber threat perceptions, privacy concerns, privacy behavior, as well as perceived need for OSINT and OSINT acceptance.

Table 14.1 Constructs used in the survey

Construct	Definition	Source
OSINT Acceptance	Acceptance of a range of surveillance activities	(A. Ioannou & Tussyadiah, 2021; Kininmonth et al., 2018; Trüdinger & Steckermeier, 2017)
Threat Perception	Fear of crime, terrorism, and of being harmed	(Dinev et al., 2008; Kininmonth et al., 2018; Trüdinger & Steckermeier, 2017)
Perceived Need for OSINT	Perception that government surveillance is necessary for the protection of citizens	(Dinev et al., 2008; A. Ioannou & Tussyadiah, 2021; Kininmonth et al., 2018)
Privacy Concerns	Anticipation of future possible privacy violation and/or the loss thereof	(Dinev et al., 2008; A. Ioannou & Tussyadiah, 2021; Kininmonth et al., 2018)
Privacy Behavior	Protective behaviors enacted to preserve online privacy	(Buchanan et al., 2007; Kininmonth et al., 2018; Kokolakis, 2017)
OSINT Awareness	Knowledge on the existence and use of OSINT	(Gerber et al., 2019; Trüdinger & Steckermeier, 2017; Valentino et al., 2020)

14.3   Research Design

In this section, the research design is presented, including the design of the survey as a representative study (14.3.1). This section further introduces the questions posed in the questionnaire (14.3.2), as well as the data collected and the criteria for the representative survey (14.3.3). In section (14.3.4), the methodology for the data analysis is described and section (14.3.5) presents the ethical consideration of the survey design.

14.3.1 Survey Design

The survey was designed within the scope of a three-year research project, which aims to develop novel strategies and technologies for CERTs to analyze and communicate the security situation in cyberspace. To design and refine the questionnaire, the process included a review of published cybersecurity surveys and two workshops with four cybersecurity practitioners from German state CERTs (team leader, incident manager, information security officer and public safety answering point employee) and four interdisciplinary researchers (digital humanities, human-computer interaction, IT security and political sciences). The first workshop comprised these phases. First, we held a presentation (15 minutes) to introduce the overall topic, the procedure for conducting a representative survey, and the aim of this workshop to generate a questionnaire. Examples of closed and open-ended questions were also introduced. Second, we conducted a reflection phase (15 minutes) where, participants were instructed to note their ideas or questions on a digital board. Third, the workshop ended with a presentation phase (30 minutes) during which participants presented their ideas, which we subsequently arranged thematically on the digital board. Based on this input, we created a preliminary version of the questionnaire.

In the second workshop, we presented and discussed the preliminary questionnaire by reviewing all questions individually. Participants discussed and refined existing questions, generated new ones, and reflected upon their thematic grouping or relevance for the research project. Based on the workshops input, we created a second draft of the questionnaire and distributed it via email to the workshop participants for a final round of feedback and revision. The final version of the questionnaire is summarized within the next subsection.

14.3.2 Questionnaire

In its final version, the questionnaire comprised 20 closed questions. First, we obtained consent for participation (Q1) and then asked about demographic variables of age (Q2), gender (Q3), education (Q4), region (Q5), and monthly income (Q6).

Second, we wanted to gain insights into how citizens assess the current and future threat situation and possible protective measures in cyberspace. Thus, the participants were asked about their usage of internet devices (Q7), their general perception of cyber threats (Q8), how familiar they were with institutions that contribute to cybersecurity in Germany (Q9), how often they had been victims of specific cyberattacks in the past five years (Q10), whom they would ask for help in the event of a cyberattack (Q11), how they estimate the risk of becoming a victim of a cyberattack in the next five years (Q12) and how continuously they use security tools or measures on personal devices (Q13).

Third, we intended to gain insights into what disadvantages and advantages citizens see in the analysis of public data (OSINT) by authorities, government, and companies. Accordingly, participants were asked to evaluate statements regarding the prevalence, use, and impact of OSINT (Q14), as well as OSINT activities by security agencies (Q15). Finally, in a second part of the survey we posed questions concerning citizens' communication and information needs and behaviors (Q18-20), which were not analyzed in this study and had no halo-effect on the previous questions.[2]

Most questions were designed as five-point verbal rating scales (VRS), with the exception of Q1 (binary consent), Q2 to Q6 (demographic variables), Q7 (four-point VRS), Q10 and Q12 (six-point VRS), and Q18 (multiple choice with up to three items). However, due to the broader scope of the research project, not all questions were incorporated within the analysis of this specific study. The use of a neutral midpoint option on a five-point rating scale is a debated issue. On the one hand, a neutral midpoint enables the accurate response for those with a truly neutral opinion, while the omission could lead to a potentially arbitrary, forced choice. On the other hand, the neutral option may be interpreted differently by individuals and potentially misused as a simple and quick response option (see (Chyung et al., 2017; Nadler et al., 2015) for discussions on the use of a midpoint option). We included a midpoint mainly to provide an option for those with truly neutral opinions and thus reduce arbitrary choices.

---

[2] The questionnaire and the items can be found in the electronic supplementary material Appendix 16.6.

14.3.3 Data Collection

We transmitted the questionnaire to GapFish who programmed and hosted the online survey. After final quality checks and mutual agreement, they invited participants from their panel to conduct the survey in September 2021. The sample of N=1,093 participants was selected to represent the German population in terms of age, gender, education, income, and state (represented by ISO 3166-2 codes).

- **Age**: 18-24 (8.9%), 25-34 (14.6%), 35-44 (15.0%), 45-54 (16.7%), 55-64 (18.2%), 65+ (26.5%)
- **Gender**: Female (50.2%), male (49.6%), diverse (0.1%), not stated (0.1%)
- **Education**: Lower secondary education (28.5%), middle or high school (55.3%), academic degree (16.3%)
- **Monthly Income**: <1,500€ (24.5%), 1,500€-2,600€ (30.8%), 2,600€-4,500€ (28.9%), >4,500€ (15.7%)
- **State**: DE-BB (2.6%), DE-BE (4.5%), DE-BW (13.4%), DE-BY (15.9%), DE-HB (0.8%), DE-HE (7.6%), DE-HH (2.3%), DE-MV (1.6%), DE-NI (9.7%), DE-NW (21.7%), DE-RP (4.9%), DE-SH (3.6%), DE-SL (1.2%), DE-SN (4.9%), DE-ST (2.7%), DE-TH (2.6%)

These criteria ensure that we can infer the German usage patterns with minimal biases, avoiding selection biases inherent in surveys, as a predominant bias includes favoring specific groups based on specific criteria, e.g., based on occupation and/or availability.

14.3.4 Statistical Analysis

The analysis was conducted using the software tools Microsoft Excel and RStudio Version 4.0.5. Answers with the rating of "no response" were excluded as missing values from the subsequent analysis. The sample was reduced by two participants because they did not answer quality check questions correctly, such as requests to mark a specific answering box. Initially, a descriptive analysis with response distributions for separate items related to the acceptance of OSINT was conducted. For the statistical analysis, items were combined with regard to their corresponding superordinate construct. Since summed values of the Likert-Scores were used in this course, the corresponding scales were treated as interval-scaled for the subsequent statistical analysis. The reliability of the corresponding scales was established based on the internal consistency with Cronbach's Alpha and also Omega (as a measure of congeneric reliability, see Raykov, 2001).

To analyze the hypothesized associations between cyber threat perception, OSINT need, privacy concerns, privacy behavior, and OSINT acceptance, a multiple linear regression was applied. In this course, the former were used as predictors while the latter (OSINT acceptance) represented the dependent variable in an ordinary least squares (OLS) regression model. Several assumptions for running multiple linear regression (linearity of associations, multicollinearity, normality of residuals, homogeneity of residuals) were checked and did not reveal any severe issues. The regression was conducted twice. Whereas the first model represented independent effects, the second, more exploratory model, represented interaction effects with the factor OSINT awareness.

14.3.5 Ethics

The study was conducted in accordance with the requirements of the local ethics committee at our university. These requirements include, but are not limited to, avoiding unnecessary stress, excluding risk and harm, and anonymizing participants. In the study, the demographic variables of age (Q2), gender (G3), education (Q4), region (Q5), and monthly income (Q6) were collected. Particularly sensitive data (e.g. ethnicity, religion, health data) was not collected. Participants were not misled, but were transparently informed about the study's procedure and goals, and subsequently gave their informed consent to participate. GapFish (Berlin), as the selected panel provider, is ISO-certified and ensures panel quality, data quality, security, and survey quality through various (segmentation) measurements for each survey within their panel of 500,000 active participants.

14.4   Results

In this section, the descriptive results focusing on the awareness and acceptance of OSINT for cybersecurity are be presented in the first (Subsection 14.4.1). In the second (Subsection 14.4.2), the factors associated with the acceptance of OSINT are analyzed.

14.4.1 Descriptive Results

To understand the general and case-specific **OSINT acceptance**, we asked participants about their agreement regarding seven abstract and specific use cases for OSINT in cybersecurity. Scenarios asked for the acceptance of the use cases and the use of artificial intelligence algorithms for the analysis of data. Here, the analysis of publicly available data by the police to pursue criminal activities has the highest acceptance. However, the acceptance is lower when participants were asked if they would agree that artificial intelligence should be used to analyze publicly available data. Notably, they expressed greater dissent to having information shared without their knowledge, i.e., without their consent. However, the neutral positions are among the largest groups among the participants (see Figure 14.1). This could mean, that many participants had not yet formed an opinion due to the lack of public discourse on this topic. Overall, the combination of the six items shows a high internal consistency for the construct with an alpha of 0.85 and omega of 0.89.[3]

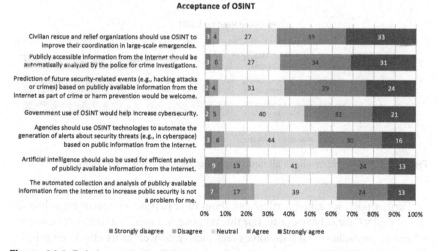

Figure 14.1 Relative results in all items regarding the acceptance of OSINT

To understand participants' cyber **threat perception**, we asked them to assess the likelihood of them, or society, or the information infrastructure becoming a victim

---

[3] The values for all constructs can be found in the Appendix 16.6 in the electronic supplementary material.

to a range twelve cyber threats within the next five years Regarding infrastructure threats, malicious software was considered to be the most likely threat in the next five years, while the threat by distributed denial of service-attacks and advanced persistent threat were perceived to be less likely, both with high numbers of neutral participants. Regarding the individual threat perception, participants perceived the following risks to be most likely: Spam messages, spyware phishing and unauthorized access to personal social media channels. Identity theft and social engineering to obtain personal information were perceived as the least likely risks . All 17 items show high internal consistency (alpha = 0.97, omega = 0.98).

We used three items to ask participants to evaluate the **need for OSINT** for cybersecurity. There was a higher perceived need and level of acceptance to use OSINT to prevent terrorism and crimes, than for authorities to have more OSINT powers in general see Figure 14.2). Participants responded similarly, when asked if the use of OSINT would support preventing crime. However, it is also interesting that all items show high rates of neutral positions. The consistency of the items as part of the construct is high with an alpha of 0.84 and omega of 0.85.

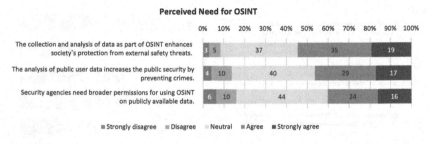

Figure 14.2 Relative results in all items regarding the perceived need of OSINT

Furthermore, we asked participants about their **privacy concerns** regarding the use of OSINT for cybersecurity. For this purpose, we used four items covering the effects of surveillance on individuals and society, as well as its effects on privacy. Overall, 48% strongly disagreed or disagreed with the feeling of being constantly watched and monitored. Interestingly, many participants (49%) showed neutral positions towards the use of OSINT by government agencies and the majority did not view OSINT as a violation of their privacy online (see Figure 14.3). All items show a high internal consistency (alpha = 0.83, omega = 0.84).

Concerning **privacy behavior**, participants answered seven items on how often they used certain measures to protect their privacy. With 38-52%, the percentage of

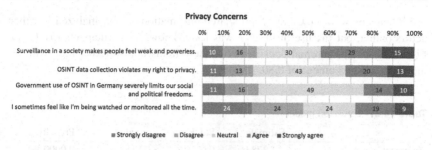

Figure 14.3 Relative results in all items regarding the privacy concerns

people who had never used any of the protective measures was high for all requested items. However, a few differences in privacy behavior can be observed. Among the different behaviors, measures such as covering the camera lens of laptops and smartphones as well as the use of encrypted messengers were much more common than the other measures listed. These are followed by different forms of encryption, e.g., for emails and files, as well as the use of VPN connections which help to encrypt online traffic. The least used methods are the use of anonymization services, e.g., proxy services, and meta search engines that protect user data (see Figure 14.4). Again, the items show a high internal consistency (alpha = 0.84, omega = 0.87).

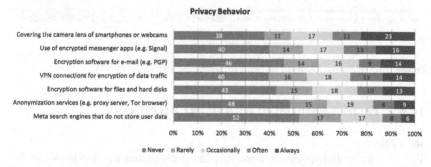

Figure 14.4 Relative results in all items regarding the privacy behavior

To research the **OSINT awareness**, participants were asked to what extent they were aware of OSINT activities using public and social media data. The three items asked participants for their awareness of publicity, the gathering of such public data as well as for actors conducting the OSINT activities. Seventy-two percent of participants were aware that their shared information can be analyzed by other actors online, but the use of OSINT was lesser-known to participants (51%, see Figure 14.5). The internal consistency of these items is also rather high with an alpha of 0.77 and omega of 0.80.

Table 14.2 Regression model

	Estimate	Std. Error	t value	Pr(> |t|)
Intercept	1.3783	0.0759	18.16	0.0000
Privacy Concerns	−0.0624	0.0156	−4.00	0.0001
Privacy Behavior	0.0205	0.0141	1.46	0.1445
Threat Perception	0.0497	0.0111	4.46	0.0000
OSINT Need	0.6323	0.0156	40.46	0.0000

Residual standard error: 0.4464 on 1086 degrees of freedom
Multiple R-squared: 0.6268, Adjusted R-squared: 0.6254
F-statistic: 456 on 4 and 1086 DF, p-value: < 2.2e-16

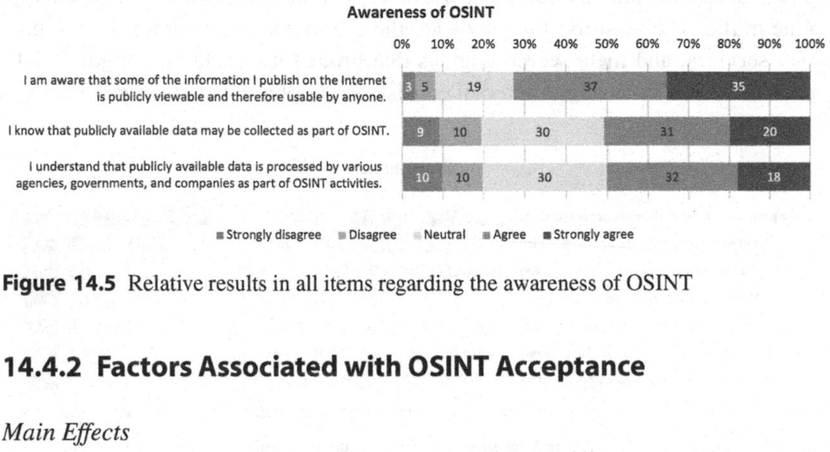

Figure 14.5 Relative results in all items regarding the awareness of OSINT

14.4.2 Factors Associated with OSINT Acceptance

Main Effects
To assess the main hypotheses, a multiple linear regression was applied to predict OSINT acceptance based on (H1) cyber threat perception, (H2) need for OSINT, (H3) privacy concerns, and (H4) privacy behavior. The overall regression equation was found to be significant ($F(4,1086) = 456$, $p < .001$) with an R-squared of .63. Thus, the regression model contained significant predictors and the overall model explains around 63% of the variance observed in the dependent variable OSINT acceptance (see Table 14.2 for an overview of the regression results).

Of the hypothesized factors, privacy concerns ($\beta = -.06$, p < .001), threat perception ($\beta = .02$, p < .001) and OSINT need ($\beta = .63$, p < .001) significantly predicted OSINT acceptance, whereas privacy behavior did not ($\beta = .02$, p < .145). Hence, the parameter estimates indicated a positive relationship for all predictors except for privacy concerns, which is in line with the hypotheses. Among the latter, an increase in privacy concerns was associated with a decrease in OSINT acceptance.

When comparing the relative size of the parameter estimates, the strongest increase in OSINT acceptance was observed based on perceived OSINT need. For an increase in self-reported OSINT need, OSINT acceptance increased by .63 points, which is at least 10 times higher than the change in OSINT acceptance based on the other predictors (see Fig. 14.6 for a graphical representation of the relative size of the parameter estimates). This is theoretically plausible, since OSINT need is more closely linked to potential OSINT acceptance than to the other predictors.

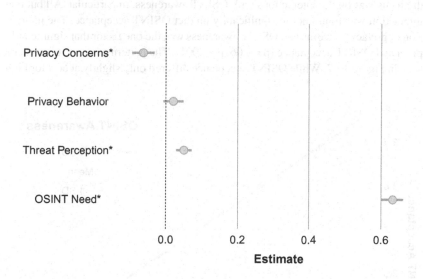

Figure 14.6 Coefficient estimates from multiple linear regression (Significant predictors for OSINT acceptance are marked with a *). The horizontal lines indicate the 95 % Confidence Interval of the point estimates

Effect of OSINT Awareness

A second, more exploratory regression model was created to examine the extent (H5) to which the awareness of OSINT technologies might affect the associations between the previously analyzed factors. In this course, the same model was established, except for one addition: OSINT awareness was added as an interaction term for (H1) cyber threat perception, (H2) need for OSINT, (H3) privacy concerns, and (H4) privacy behavior. The objective was to evaluate whether significant interactions exist that might provide additional information on the dynamics of OSINT acceptance.

The resulting overall regression equation was found to be significant ($F(9,1081) = 224.4$, $p < .001$) with an R-squared of .65. The complete regression results can be found in Table 14.3. Through the novel interaction term OSINT awareness, slight changes in the original model became apparent. For example, the previously significant predictor threat perception did not represent a significant predictor anymore ($\beta = .01$, $p = .89$). Moreover, the interaction model did not represent a superior explanatory model compared to the initial model. The 2% increase in explained variance by the interaction model can be considered rather negligible. Furthermore, the interaction model was actually more exploratory from a theoretical point of view. Here, the focus was on the interactions with OSINT awareness, in particular. All but one interaction was found not to significantly predict OSINT acceptance. The interaction of privacy concerns and OSINT awareness was the one factor that significantly predicted OSINT acceptance ($\beta = -.06$, $p < .001$). The pattern of interaction can be seen in Figure 14.7. While OSINT acceptance differed only slightly at best for high

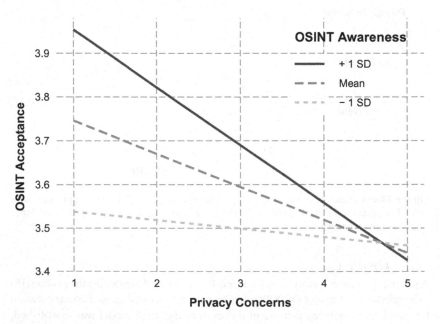

Figure 14.7 Interaction of Privacy Concerns and OSINT Awareness

Table 14.3 Regression Model with Interaction

	Estimate	Std. Error	t value	Pr(>|t|)
(Intercept)	0.5775	0.2265	2.55	0.0109
Privacy Concerns	0.1406	0.0530	2.65	0.0081
Privacy Behavior	−0.0246	0.0531	−0.46	0.6431
Threat Perception	0.0061	0.0436	0.14	0.8881
OSINT Need	0.6525	0.0499	13.06	0.0000
OSINT Awareness	0.2799	0.0603	4.64	0.0000
Privacy Concerns: OSINT Awareness	−0.0602	0.0133	−4.52	0.0000
Privacy Behavior: OSINT Awareness	0.0103	0.0139	0.74	0.4600
Threat Perception: OSINT Awareness	0.0091	0.0114	0.79	0.4275
OSINT Need: OSINT Awareness	−0.0138	0.0129	−1.07	0.2851

Residual standard error: 0.4324 on 1081 degrees of freedom
Multiple R-squared: 0.6513, Adjusted R-squared: 0.6484
F-statistic: 224.4 on 9 and 1081 DF, p-value: < 2.2e-16

levels of privacy concerns, OSINT acceptance was dependent on OSINT awareness for lower levels of privacy concern. Higher OSINT awareness was associated with higher OSINT acceptance, whereas lower OSINT awareness was associated with lower OSINT acceptance. Thus, minor privacy concerns and low OSINT awareness were associated with low OSINT acceptance, while minor privacy concerns and high OSINT awareness accompanied higher OSINT acceptance.

14.5 Discussion

In this section, empirical results are discussed in relation to related work in (Subsection 14.5.1). Afterwards, implications for the design and organizational factors for the use of OSINT in the context of cybersecurity are presented in (subsection 14.5.2). Finally, the implications and venture points for future work are discussed in (Subsection 14.5.2).

14.5.1 Factors Associated with the Acceptance of OSINT for Cybersecurity

This study aims to answer the following research question: which factors are associated with the acceptance of OSINT in the context of cybersecurity? Surveillance of public data is increasingly being applied in many areas, from public health policy (Boersma et al., 2022), to the protection against crime and terrorism (Furnham & Swami, 2019; Kininmonth et al., 2018; Trüdinger & Steckermeier, 2017).

The factors positively associated with the acceptance of OSINT are cyber threat perception and the perceived need for OSINT. As the threat perception has been studied, this finding is in accordance with the literature (Furnham & Swami, 2019; Kininmonth et al., 2018; Trüdinger & Steckermeier, 2017). However, most studies have focused on the unspecific fears of crime and terrorism associated with higher trust in authorities and the state (Furnham & Swami, 2019). We examined the specific fear of cyber threats against the individual as well as infrastructure. Similar to other areas of application in cybersecurity, one might assume that the effective use of surveillance to prevent crime can help to gain trust in authorities, should people be aware of this measure (Trüdinger & Steckermeier, 2017).

However, people who had already trusted authorities were more inclined to accept surveillance measures (Furnham & Swami, 2019). This might be also the reason why some people believe in the need for surveillance as a measure and are thus more inclined to accept surveillance technologies. In our study, the perception that OSINT is needed has been the strongest effect regarding the acceptance of surveillance, which is not surprising.

The correlation between acceptance and privacy concerns is negative, meaning that people with higher concerns tend to be less accepting of surveillance (see Table 14.2). This hypothesis is supported by related work (Dinev et al., 2008; Joh, 2013) and can be explained by the fact that OSINT may pose risks to people's privacy. In contrast to other SOSTs, gathering public data on social media platforms is invisible and poses abstract risks. Gerber et al. (2019) have shown that people estimate more abstract risks as less severe than specific ones.

Interestingly, our hypothesis on the effect of privacy behavior was not supported by the analysis. This could be explained by the so-called privacy paradox (Barnes, 2006). The privacy paradox has been contested by research on the privacy calculus, which assumes a rational choice in which people weigh the benefits against their privacy concerns (Dienlin & Metzger, 2016). As our model has shown, privacy behavior is not associated with the acceptance of OSINT, in contrast to the effect of privacy concerns. Whether participants suffer from the paradox or follow rational choice might also depend on their awareness of actual surveillance. Kokolakis

(2017) has discussed the literature on divergent privacy concerns and behavior, and identified five different explanations for divergent concerns and behavior in the literature: a) privacy calculus theory, (b) social theory, (c) cognitive biases and heuristics in decision-making, (d) decision-making under bounded rationality and information asymmetry conditions, and (e) quantum theory homomorphism. Most of the approaches offer explanations for decision-making which take context factors into account. However, among others, particular trade-offs, social settings, as well as heuristics in decision-making and information asymmetries within the process, have yet to be researched in detail in our field of application.

According to social theory, which explains self-disclosure, Taddicken (2014) has shown that privacy concerns hardly impact self-disclosure behavior. Nevertheless, there are factors which seem to moderate the relation. As the majority of users disclose personal information, the author found that there might be different degrees of self-disclosure "with clearly defined communities where users feel safe from privacy invasion". Therefore, as users might have divergent privacy concerns regarding more or less public communities, the author concluded that it would be helpful for users to know their audience.

Therefore, in the final and exploratory hypothesis, we tested awareness as an interactive factor. Our results show that awareness only changes the dynamic of association between privacy concerns and OSINT acceptance. Here, awareness showed the effect that lower awareness and few privacy concerns were associated with lower rates of acceptance, while higher awareness and fewer privacy concerns were associated with higher acceptance. Thus, the results highlight the importance of transparency and information about OSINT for its acceptance by participants. This has been suggested by Wester and Giesecke (2019), who in a longitudinal study showed that the risk perception of privacy loss decreased between 2009 and 2017, while calls for transparency had increased "dramatically". They further suggest "that citizens not only make distinctions between different technologies, but also what actor is collecting and analyzing the data. Discussions about trust, transparency, and accountability should then be held in relation to the different owners—and perhaps the relation between them." Thus, Wester and Giesecke (2019) are indicating the role of contextual factors, such as the actors and technologies being used. Research on privacy behavior and its motivations has shown how the role of context influences sharing decisions (Kokolakis, 2017) as well as how context can be conceptualized for the technological design as "privacy in context" (Nissenbaum, 2018; Nissenbaum, 2004). Nissenbaum has identified two norms for contextual integrity to be followed: the norm of appropriateness and the norm of flow or distribution (Nissenbaum, 2004). Hence, a privacy violation would be when informational norms are breached. For this, the parameters are information type, the actors and transmission principles. On the other side, Nissenbaum's concept enables to the secondary use of data as long as the social context of the self-disclosure is respected (Nissenbaum, 2018).

14.5.2 Implications for Design and Organization

As OSINT in cybersecurity draws insights from the fields of crisis informatics (Boersma et al., 2022; Reuter, Hughes, & Kaufhold, 2018) as well as surveillance studies (Pauli et al., 2016), the research from similar cases can be used to derive implications for the design of OSINT systems and their evaluation regarding the factors which are associated with the acceptance of such systems. The discourse on privacy and relevant context factors (Nissenbaum, 2018; Nissenbaum, 2004) has shown that the following aspects need further consideration: the kind of data which is collected (1), the actors or organization gathering the data (2) and the transmission principles and platforms which allow for the data gathering (3).

The introduction of the General Data Protection Regulation (GDPR) in the European Union has resulted in a shift in data gathering and analysis by increasing users' power over data processing, retention periods, and use (Linden et al., 2020). The GDRP has greatly influenced the coverage of privacy topics in data protection, such as safeguarding user data "with the options to access and rectify their information" (Linden et al., 2020). In contrast to other organizations, authorities can only collect data for a legitimate and legally approved reason and have to comply with retention periods (Riebe, Haunschild, et al., 2020).

OSINT uses a variety of machine learning and deep learning approaches for threat detection and analysis (Pastor-Galindo et al., 2020). Thus, machine learning research with greater attention to privacy is a promising area, which helps to include privacy preserving requirements. In particular, machine learning as a service raises privacy concerns, while privacy-preserving computation techniques still demonstrare a lack of "standard tools and programming interfaces, or lack of integration with [deep learning] frameworks commonly used by the data science community" (Cabrero-Holgueras & Pastrana, 2021).

Regarding the organizations using OSINT beyond the context of cybersecurity, investigative journalistic organisations like Bellingcat and OCCRP follow different interests than, e.g, organisations from crisis management and law enforcement. Emergency services are not allowed to collect personal data without a reasonable suspicion. However, in crisis management, social media data can become a useful tool for situational assessment. In this case, however, the aim is not to collect personal data, but to complete the situational assessment. Research in crisis informatics has shown (Aldehoff et al., 2019) that the tendency to share more personal data with emergency services changes in crisis situations. Thus, OSINT systems can be used for event detection and analysis, while profiling and analyzing personal data have higher legal barriers. However, this discourse will continue, as questions of accountability and transparency have to be discussed (Eijkman & Weggemans, 2012).

As many OSINT systems rely on social media platforms, they face the challenge that social media platforms not only provide information about individuals, but sometimes support the sharing of information of third parties. This touches upon issues of interdependent privacy (Humbert et al., 2019; Pu & Grossklags, 2016), in which a person shares information about another individual.

Therefore, particularly in the context of sensitive cybersecurity information, approaches that help to assess and manage risks from privacy conflicts in collaborative data sharing need to be taken into account for further research (Hu et al., 2011). As Riebe, Bäumler, et al. (2023) have shown, most OSINT systems for cyber security focus on detecting new cyber threats, and might offer additional analysis for incident managers. Concepts of contextual privacy could support this approach, for example, as part of limited data gathering approaches.

Thus, when designing OSINT systems which work on the basis of CTI, the following **implications** should be considered:

- OSINT systems should consider the types of data which is gathered and how it can follow data minimization approaches. In changing threat situations, the gathering strategy could be adopted, and thus could react to changed threat perceptions which are associated with higher OSINT acceptance.
- The system should stay within the social context, which could be achieved by using professional sources (vendors, vulnerability and cybersecurity experts, ...), and could react to larger threats by expanded beyond the context when the need changes.
- Platforms should update their safeguards against disproportionate data collection and support data minimization.
- Individuals' awareness could be raised by using participatory design and maintenance methods .

The results of our study indicate that the awareness of OSINT in combination with lower privacy concerns is a relevant factor associated with the acceptance of OSINT in cybersecurity. This supports findings by Trüdinger and Steckermeier (2017). Therefore, authorities and organizations planning to implement such OSINT systems need to develop strategies to inform affected indirect stakeholders, as well as to include them in the development and implementation process (Friedman et al., 2013; Liegl et al., 2016). Research on risk assessment has shown that people assess the severity and likelihood based on specific scenarios (Gerber et al., 2019).

Discourses on social media analysis and emergency management provide venture points for ethical impact assessment. Scholars have argued not to follow a simple logic of "privacy v.s. security", but to consider a wider field of arguments from digital ethics (Boersma et al., 2022; Floridi et al., 2019). Participatory approaches, such as ELSI co-design and Value Sensitive Design (VDS), can make use of the identification of factors which are associated with the acceptance of OSINT systems in the context of cybersecurity. Further, such approaches include civil society in the design and implementation of security-oriented technologies (Liegl et al., 2016). Participatory approaches could also aim to increase the knowledge of non-experts regarding OSINT systems. This would help to raise awareness on these systems.

14.5.3 Limitations and Future Work

Limitations to our study are presented in the following: As the sample is representative for the German population only, the results are not directly transferable to other countries. Studies have shown that factors like privacy concerns are associated with cultural socialization (Dinev et al., 2005). Therefore, the effect of the factors we have identified, especially regarding cyber threat perception and privacy concerns, may differ in other cultural contexts. Individualistic cultures, like the United States, might be an interesting and relevant case for further studies on the acceptance of OSINT for cybersecurity. A direct comparison of different cultures would be especially promising in this context. Further, studies have shown, that people have varying understandings of what they perceive as personal, private or even intimate information (Taddicken, 2014), which was not part of the questionnaire and should be investigated further. Similar, contextual factors (Nissenbaum, 2018) and interdependent concepts of privacy (Humbert et al., 2019) need to be studied in greater detail.

Another limitation arrives due to the random sample of the representative study. Many items scored high for "neutral" positions among the participants. While this is to be expected for normally distributed response patterns, this pattern was also evident for asymmetric items. This might have been due to participants' lack of technology-specific expertise, as the development of OSINT systems has not been part of a broader public debate yet, and the use of different technological approaches might not be known to many participants. This also makes specific questions regarding single technological approaches difficult and not feasible in the study design. Thus, further studies need to take expert perspectives into account, as well. We also did not control for affiliation and familiarity with cyber security topics, which could have provided an additional opportunity for analyzing differences between individuals with more and less expertise. However, this was not one of our study's primary goals—an occasional presence of a higher level of expertise, as would be expected in a random sample, was sufficient for our purpose.

With regard to the items, the issue of neutral responses could also have been avoided by not offering a neutral option at all. The usefulness and pitfalls of using such a category have already been discussed in relevant, related literature (see (Chyung et al., 2017; Nadler et al., 2015) for an overview). One the one hand, we could have potentially gained more insights by not providing such a neutral option. On the other hand – particularly in light of the non-expert sample and potentially actual neutral opinions – this would have introduced more noise into the data by forcing arbitrary choices. Nonetheless, the issue of providing a neutral midpoint should be considered in future studies. Regarding the specific items assessing OSINT needs, it should be noted that some of them were not ideally worded and represented compound questions, which may have increased noise in the data. Lastly, the study uses the data based on self-reported behavior. Thus, the actual privacy behavior might differ from the data in this study.

14.6 Conclusion

The use of OSINT for cybersecurity is a growing research topic, and the number of systems for cyber threat detection and analysis using public online data is increasing (Pastor-Galindo et al., 2020; Riebe, Wirth, et al., 2021). In areas of emergency and crisis management, the surveillance of public data has increased, not only since the COVID-19 pandemic (Boersma et al., 2022; A. Ioannou & Tussyadiah, 2021). Research on factors associated with the acceptance of such systems has studied the use of surveillance technology to fight crime and terror, as well as to support people during human-made and natural disasters. Particularly in cybersecurity, new information on cyber threats appears early on online social networks (Behzadan et al., 2018). This is increasingly being used by security operators and government authorities to detect cyber threats early on.

As research on other areas of application has shown, the acceptance of surveillance and of specific measures depends on the context of application, the measures themselves, the information about the measures, and the implementing institutions. The acceptance of OSINT for cybersecurity as a particular case of security-oriented surveillance is an important piece in the puzzle. Thus, a representative study with 1,093 participants in Germany was conducted to understand how people evaluate OSINT in the context of cybersecurity and which factors are associated with the acceptance thereof. The results indicate that:

- Cyber threat perception and the perceived need for OSINT are positively corre-lated to acceptance, while privacy concerns show a negative correlation.
- The awareness of OSINT, however, has only affected the association between privacy concerns and OSINT acceptance.
- Specifically, high OSINT awareness and minor privacy concerns were associ-ated with higher OSINT acceptance, whereas low OSINT awareness and minor privacy concerns were associated with lower OSINT acceptance.

Implications for further research and the use of OSINT systems for cybersecurity by authorities include conducting research on the implementation of data mini-mization as a design principle, as well as the association of contextual factors for acceptance, such as the data types and scenarios for situational adaption of gath-ering strategies. Such approaches should additionally make use of improvements in privacy-preserving computation and machine learning innovations. In terms of OSINT use, we support approaches that provide transparency to people regarding the use of the systems and the data they gather, analyse and retention periods.

CySecAlert: An Alert Generation System for Cyber Security Events Using Open Source Intelligence Data

15

15.1 Introduction

Social Media has become a viable source for cyber security incident prevention and response, helping to gain situational awareness for Computer Emergency Response Teams (CERTs). Therefore, the trend towards processing Social Media data in real-time to support emergency management (Reuter & Kaufhold, 2018) continues to grow. Husák et al. Husák et al. (2020) show how Cyber Situational Awareness (CSA) is an adaptation of situational awareness to the cyber domain and supports operators to make strategic decisions. To perform such informed, situational decision-making, CERTs have to gain CSA by gathering and processing threat data from different closed and open sources (Yang & Lam, 2020). These include Open Source Intelligence (OSINT), which uses any publicly available open source to accumulate relevant intelligence (Mittal et al., 2016). Especially the micro-blogging service Twitter has proven itself as a valuable source of OSINT due to its popularity among the cyber security community (Behzadan et al., 2018), as well as its available content and metadata for analysis (Tundis et al., 2020). Alves et al. (2020) have shown that there is a small but impactful subset of vulnerabilities being discussed on Twitter

ORIGINAL PUBLICATION Riebe, T., Wirth, T., Bayer, M., Kühn, P., Kaufhold, M.-A., Knauthe, V., Guthe, S., & Reuter, C. (2021). CySecAlert: An Alert Generation System for Cyber Security Events Using Open Source Intelligence Data. International Conference on Information and Communications Security, 429–446. https://doi.org/10.1007/978-3-030-86890-1_24

Supplementary Information The online version contains supplementary material available at https://doi.org/10.1007/978-3-658-41667-6_15.

© The Author(s), under exclusive license to Springer Fachmedien Wiesbaden GmbH, part of Springer Nature 2023
T. Riebe, *Technology Assessment of Dual-Use ICTs*,
https://doi.org/10.1007/978-3-658-41667-6_15

before they are included into a vulnerability database. Increasingly big amounts of data make the use of more complex models possible. While concentrating on volume might be the best variable for some use cases, focusing on near real-time and data minimizing (B. -J. Koops et al., 2013) approaches have been neglected in the recent state of research. Therefore, this paper seeks to answer the following main research question: **(RQ) How can relevant cyber security related events be detected automatically in near real-time based on Twitter data?**

By answering this research question the proposed paper aims to make the following contributions **(C)**: The first contribution **(C1)** deducts the concept and presents the implementation of an automated near real-time alert generation system for cyber security events based on Twitter data (Section 15.2). The second contribution **(C2)** covers the evaluation of the *CySecAlert* system that assists CERTs with the detection of cyber security events in order to improve CSA by automatically generating alerts on the basis of Twitter data (Section 15.3). The near real-time capability is achieved by labelling and clustering the Twitter stream within the required 15-minutes time frame (Sabottke et al., 2015). The third contribution **(C3)** provides a comparison of existing tools based on the systematic of Atafeh and Khreich Atefeh & Khreich (2015) that are suitable to detect relevant cyber security related events based on Twitter data (Section 15.4). Lastly, the results are summed up (Section 15.5). To enable further improvement of our work, we will make the source code and the labelled Twitter dataset available.[1]

15.2   Concept

This section presents the concept of *CySecAlert*, including the data source and architecture (15.2.1), data preprocessing (Subsection 15.2.2), and training of the relevance classifier (15.2.3) which serve as input to detect novel cyber security events (15.2.4). It concludes with a concise description of the concept's implementation (15.2.5).

15.2.1 Data Source and Architecture

Twitter offers a multitude of advantages over other Social Media platforms. Firstly, Twitter is frequently used for the early discussion and disclosure of software vulnerabilities (Alves et al., 2020). Secondly, Twitter accommodates a broad variety of participants, that are involved in the discourse evolving around cyber security top-

---

[1] https://github.com/PEASEC/CySecAlert

ics. Since most important cyber security news feeds (e.g., NVD, ExploitDB, CVE) are present on the platform, Twitter serves as a cyber security news feed aggregate (Alves et al., 2021) and is used by both individuals and organisations (Trabelsi et al., 2015). In addition, tweets can be processed fast and easily (Alves et al., 2021), due to their limited length.

Hasan et al. (2018) propose a general framework for *Event Detection* systems. We added a relevance classifier to the architecture that filters out irrelevant tweets. By classifying relevance per tweet, the individual relevance of each tweet was determined before the clustering process, reducing the number of tweets at an early stage. This extension was necessary because our tweet retrieval method is account-based, leveraging preexisting lists of cyber security experts' Twitter accounts.[2]

15.2.2 Preprocessing and Representation

In a preprocessing step, we standardized the tweet representation by converting their content to a lower case and removing any textual part that is unlikely to contain relevant information, i.e., stop words, URLs, and Social Media specific terms and constructs (e.g. "tweet", "retweet", user name mentions) as well as non-alphanumerical characters. Then the text was tokenized and stemmed.

We applied a clustering-based approach to *Event Detection*. Therefore, a representation of individual tweets was necessary. To address this issue we adopted the setting of Kaufhold, Bayer, and Reuter (2020), where a *Bag-of-Words* approach was applied. Clustering and classification were performed online. Therefore, the Inverse Document Frequency (IDF) regularization term would have had to be updated after every iteration, undermining the benefits of online techniques. In the context of crisis informatics, it has been suggested that the regularization via IDF does not necessarily yield a relevant benefit on classification performance (M.-A. Kaufhold, Bayer, & Reuter, 2020). Therefore, we omitted IDF regularization and represented tweets by Term Frequency (TF) vectorization only.

15.2.3 Relevance Classifier

To filter relevant tweets, we used an active learning approach (Habdank et al., 2017), which has been found to reduce the amount of labelled data that is required to reach

---

[2] The list of experts can be found in the Appendix 16.7 in the electronic supplementary material.

a certain accuracy level (Imran et al., 2016; Settles, 2010). We employed *uncertainty sampling* in order to obtain beneficial tweet samples for labeling. Therefore, we examined the suggestion of Kaufhold, Bayer, and Reuter (2020) regarding rapid relevance classification. Lewis and Catlett (Lewis & Catlett, 1994) point out that it is reasonable to label the post which the current classifier instance is least confident about. Thus, the *Relevance Classification* is performed by application of *pool-based sampling* with the *least confidence* metric. *Pool-based sampling* refers to an algorithm class that picks an optimal data point out of the set of non-labelled data points utilizing a metric that refers to the data's information content (Settles, 2010). We applied the *least confidence* metric that regarded a data point as the most optimal labeling sample if the classifier was least confident about its classification (Settles, 2010). Therefore, the datum with a prediction confidentiality closest to the decision boundary was selected.

Uncertainty sampling requires retraining of the classifier after every labeling process (Lewis & Catlett, 1994), which is not done in online learning. M.-A. Kaufhold, Bayer, and Reuter (2020) have shown, that this improvement in training time comes at the price of classifier accuracy, which can be addressed by using a fast online learning algorithm for the selection of data to be labelled, while batchwise creating a more sophisticated offline classifier with the same labelled data in parallel (Lewis & Catlett, 1994). The combination of an incremental k Nearest Neighbor (kNN) classifier for *uncertainty sampling* and Random Forest (RF) is suggested to perform well on datasets in crisis informatics (M.-A. Kaufhold, Bayer, & Reuter, 2020). The Evaluation shows that this is true for the domain of cyber security as well (Section 15.3.2). Despite the increase of deep learning algorithms in this field, the utilization of classical machine learning algorithms suits best for this use case as the retraining can be performed automatically without the need for long training phases and specific training optimizations for every batch.

15.2.4 Detecting Events and Generating Alerts

Clustering based event detection approaches utilize vectorized representations of Social Media posts. In this scenario, every cluster represented a candidate event. We applied a simple greedy clustering algorithm that utilizes similarity metrics of new Social Media posts to old ones by considering them part of a new cluster if they exceeded a certain similarity threshold and otherwise adding them to the most similar preexisting cluster (Allan et al., 2000). We performed the clustering based on nearest-neighbor search and used cosine similarity to the nearest cluster's centroids.

Alves et al. (2021) propose a more sophisticated method that applies regular offline k-means clustering to improve the cluster quality. However, we chose not to do so as we put a special emphasis on near real-time applicability on our system. Furthermore, we justify the choice of relatively simple event detection techniques by the fact that the active learning approach for relevance classification in the cyber security *event detection* domain constitutes the core novelty of our contribution.

To *obtain significant events*, candidate events are filtered by their significance. Depending on the costs of alert processing and underlying costs regarding false alerts, it is reasonable to allow a system operator to configure the system's alert generation sensibility. *CySecAlert* supports the prediction of candidate events based on (1) overall post count associated with the event, (2) count of experts covering the event, and (3) the number of retweets.

The significance of candidate events based on the system operator's configuration was evaluated when a new tweet was added to the respective cluster. If the cluster met the significance criteria and no alert had been issued based on the candidate event before, an alert was issued to the system operator. In order to assure the application's near-real-time capabilities tweets older than a certain time threshold (14 days by default) were removed from their respective cluster.

To *summarize events*, research suggests that textual clusters can be represented by display of their respective centroid (Concone et al., 2017; Ritter et al., 2015). We chose this event representation because it is cost-efficient and maintains the feeling of handling original Twitter data. We additionally allowed the display of the entirety of posts associated with an event to allow a system operator to further examine the event.

15.2.5 Implementation

CySecAlert was implemented in Java 11 and utilized a MongoDB database because of its high performance in handling textual documents. Figure 15.1 serves as an overview of the implementation's architecture.

The Crawler module requested the most recent tweets of a list of trusted Twitter users in a regular manner. For this purpose, it used the Connector module. This functionality was implemented using Twitter4J[3]. To train a relevance classifier, it is necessary to manually label a set of tweets. The proposed application offers the use of active learners to reduce labeling effort. We evaluated an active batch RF, an active

---

[3] Twitter4J Version 4.0.7 (twitter4j.org/en/index.html on 14.08.2020)

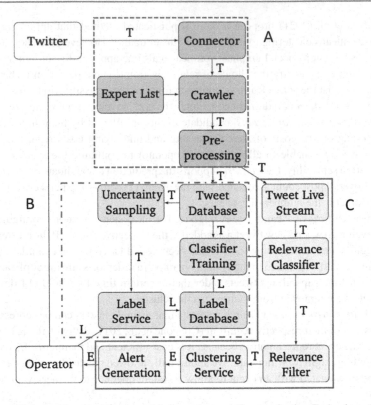

Figure 15.1 Architecture of proposed Information and Communication Technology (ICT) illustrating the information flow for [T]weets, [L]abels and [E]vents. The ICT is divided into Tweet Retrieval (A), Relevance Classifier Training (B) and Real-Time Event Detection (C)

Naive Bayes, and an active kNN classifier. We used the classifier implementation of Weka[4]. A Relevance Classifier was trained based on the labelled data. The tweets to be labelled depended on the chosen sampling method. We chose an RF because its performance is well-proven in the context of Twitter Analysis, which was verified by qualitative evaluation. Our implementation utilized the Weka implementation of an RF in its default configuration. The Relevance Classifier was used to filter out irrelevant tweets.

---

[4] Weka v3.8.4 (https://www.cs.waikato.ac.nz/ml/weka/ on 14.08.2020)

Then relevant tweets that covered the same topics were clustered to candidate events. This allowed an estimation of how much coverage a topic has on Twitter and helped to avoid alerts being used twice for the same topic. Therefore, we employed a greedy streaming clustering algorithm, which assigned each new tweet to the cluster with the most similar centroid according to the cosine similarity. If this similarity was smaller than a certain operator-defined threshold (*Similarity Threshold*) the tweet was designed to a new cluster.

A pre-evaluation has shown that the TF-IDF representation yielded performance benefits compared to the TF representation for the clustering task. Due to the sparsity of these vectors, we modeled them as *HashMap*s. Since classical IDF had to be updated after every added tweet, we stored the tweets in TF vectorized form and a centralized instance of IDF vector. The IDF regularization was applied on-demand if calculations required a vectorized representation. After every tweet insertion, the altered cluster was examined regarding its qualifications for an alert. Such a cluster was eligible for an alert if no alert had yet been issued for it and the count of unique tweets it contained exceeds a predefined threshold (*Alert Tweet Count Threshold*). The cosine similarity threshold and the tweet count threshold for the issuing of alerts were passed during program initialization.

15.3 Evaluation

This section presents the dataset (15.3.1). The dataset is used to evaluate the active learning (15.3.2), relevance classification (15.3.2), alert generation (15.3.3), system performance (15.3.4), and near real-time capability (15.3.5) of *CySecAlert*.

15.3.1 Dataset

We gathered 350,061 English tweets (151,861 tweets excl. retweets) published by 170 Twitter accounts of leading cyber security experts in the time period between 1st January 2019 and 31st July 2020. The list of accounts was derived based on a set of blog entries that provide lists of leading cyber security experts on Twitter[5].

In Relevance Classification, it is common to apply a binary classification into *relevant* and *irrelevant* tweets (Alves et al., 2021; Bose et al., 2019; Dionisio et al.,

---

[5] The list of expert can be found in the Appendix 16.7 in the electronic supplementary material.

2019). The class definitions of *relevant* and *not relevant* we applied are illustrated in a codebook[6] after Mayring (2004).

Table 15.1 Class Distribution over Tweets of Ground Truth Datasets

	S1	S2
From	01/12/2019	01/05/2020
To	31/12/2019	14/05/2020
Irrelevant	5,801 (88.9%)	5,780 (85.25%)
Relevant	724 (11.10%)	1000 (14.25%)
Total	6,525	6,780
κ	0.9318	0,9377

Based on the dataset and the proposed annotation scheme, we created an annotated ground truth dataset consisting of two subsets (S1, S2) covering different time frames. The Datasets S1 and S2 were annotated by an additional researcher to estimate the inter-rater reliability of the coding scheme as shown in the codebook. Our ground truth shows a high level of inter-rater reliability (κ > 0.90) measured by Cohen's kappa (κ). We used S2 for evaluation purposes. The class distributions of these datasets are illustrated in Table 15.1.

15.3.2   Relevance Classification

Sampling Method
We evaluated the influence of active learning and the selection of a sampling method and sampling classifier on the performance of a relevance classifier in order to choose a high-performing classifier. Therefore, we used the preprocessed and stemmed ground truth datasets S1 and S2. In this evaluation, a scenario was simulated where no labelled data is available initially. A virtual expert incrementally labelled tweets that were chosen by different sampling methods. The labels were taken from the respective ground-truth dataset. We examined a Naive Bayes classifier, a kNN classifier with k = 50 and an RF classifier. As *uncertainty sampling* technique we applied *least confidence* measure in a *pool-based sampling* scenario were examined.

While Naive Bayes and kNN can be implemented in an incremental manner and thus allow to add single tweets without retraining, the RF classifier did not

---

[6] The detailed codebook can be found in the Appendix 16.7 in the electronic supplementary material.

offer this property. For this reason, kNN and Naive Bayes were updated after every new labelled tweet and the next uncertainty sampling step was performed on the updated classifier. In contrast, the RF classifier sampled a set of most uncertain tweets (rather than one) which were labelled as batches before being added to the training set. Thereafter, the classifier was retrained on the updated dataset.

An evaluation of the experiment[7] showed, that the active version of the Naive Bayes classifier performed worst, representing nearly random classification behaviour. However, the kNN classifier was able to train a model whose AUC measure plateaus around roughly 0.75 for both datasets. This finding is similar to the results of Kaufhold, Bayer, and Reuter (2020). In contrast to them, we also considered active learning with an RF classifier. In our evaluation setting, it performed best with an AUC in the range of 0.9. Therefore, we choose a RF classifier for our system.

Classification Model

In this subsection, we analyse whether the use of a different active learning algorithm-based sampling method is useful for an RF relevance classifier. We compare (1) kNN and (2) batchwise RF uncertainty sampling with (3) random sampling and (4) batchwise Random-RF-Hybrid Sampling. This hybrid approach picks 50% of tweets per batch by RF-based uncertainty sampling and 50% tweets at random. By determining a threshold of Random Trees, which is needed to classify an instance as positive, a classifier is instantiated from the learned RF. In the context of this contribution, we chose the F_1 metric for evaluation purposes, as it is suitable for imbalanced datasets.

We evaluated the performance of the RF instances based on the F_1 measure of the classifier instance with the highest F_1 measure for every 100 labelled tweets. The evaluation was conducted by leaving out 1,000 tweets and using them as a test set. In order to mitigate performance issues, the uncertainty sampling was performed on a randomly chosen subsample of size 200 (500 for active batch RF), which changed in every iteration, rather than on the complete data pool. The results of this evaluation are illustrated in Figure 15.2.

The experimental results show that every examined type of uncertainty sampling leads to classifier out-performance compared to random sampling. For every experiment, the classifier instance that used a randomly sampled dataset was not able to achieve the performance of uncertainty sampled classifier with 300 or more labelled tweets, even if it was trained based on 1,000 randomly sampled tweets. Furthermore, the results indicate that there are no significant performance differences between the tested uncertainty sampling classifiers.

---

[7] See the Appendix 16.7 in the electronic supplementary material.

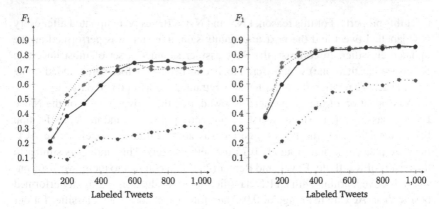

Figure 15.2 Performance Comparison of RF Classifier trained on dataset S1 (left) and S2 (right) with uncertainty sampling by different classifiers: Random (loosely dotted]), RF Classifier (dotted), 50% RF and 50% Random (dashed) and by kNN classifier with k = 50 (solid). Average over 5 Executions using a 1,000 tweet holdout set measured in F_1

Due to the fact that there are no substantial classification quality implications, we opted for the kNN based uncertainty sampling because it can be executed in an online manner. Additionally, the results suggest that the overall classification performance suffered for datasets with higher class imbalance. Nevertheless, the results indicate that after around 600 labelled tweets the classifier achieved its best classification quality and therefore did not show significant improvements for a bigger training dataset. This constituted a reduction of manual tweet annotation of up to 90% compared to a randomly sampled approach, which makes it necessary to label the whole dataset (roughly 6,000 tweets each).

15.3.3 Alert Generation

In this section, we jointly evaluate the clustering algorithm and the alert generation process. Therefore, we executed the combination of these modules using different parameters for *Similarity Threshold* and *Alert Tweet Count Threshold*. Even though there are multiple configurations for alert generation thresholds, the evaluation was performed based on the relevant tweet count per cluster metric only. Thereby, we received a list of clusters that represent a list of relevant events and their associated tweets. By comparing this list to the ground truth dataset (Section 15.3.1), the quality of the alert generation process could be estimated.

Therefore, clusters that were found by the clustering algorithm and flagged as alerts are classified as *topic related*, *mixed* or *duplicate*. A cluster was regarded as *topic* related if more than half of its tweets belong to the same topic of the ground truth topic list. If a *topic related* cluster that discussed this topic had been found before, the cluster was marked as *duplicate*. If there was no major topic in the cluster, it was defined as *mixed*. *Topic related* clusters were marked as positive, while *mixed* and *duplicate* clusters were marked as negative. Combining this information we derived a calculation for precision and recalled measures as follows:

$$Precision = \frac{\#truepositives}{\#truepositives + \#falsepositives} = \frac{\#topicrelated}{\#clusters} \qquad (15.1)$$

$$Recall = \frac{\#truepositives}{\#truepositives + \#falsenegatives} = \frac{\#topicrelated}{\#topics} \qquad (15.2)$$

In order to decouple the evaluation of clustering and alert generation from the performance of the relevance classifier, we tested the clustering-based alert generation algorithm on the set of *relevant* and *potentially relevant* tweets from our ground truth datasets S1 and S2. We used TF-IDF as tweet vectorization in order to avoid the formation of big clusters based on frequently used common words. The results show that an increase in the value of the used similarity threshold (in the observed range) decreases the recall[8]. Intuitively, this can be explained by the creation of more clusters due to similarity failing the threshold. Therefore, clusters are smaller on average and stay under the alert generation threshold, which leads to suppression of alert generation for relevant topics. In contrast, the influence of similarity threshold on cluster precision (which is the invert of the wrongful alert quote) is lower. This is the reason why operators should be advised to prefer lower values for the Cosine Similarity Threshold. Even though this configuration increases the wrongful alert rate, it increases the recall. Nevertheless, if the similarity threshold is chosen too low, this does not hold. For example, a similarity threshold of 0 led to every tweet being part of one giant cluster. This led to a low recall as well. The alert generation instance with the best performance regarding the F1 score resulted in a precision of 96.08% and a recall of 96.23%.

Our experiment shows that the value of the *Cosine Similarity Threshold* leading to an optimal F1-measure depends on the *Alert Tweet Count Threshold*. Furthermore, the results indicate that minor changes in *Alert Tweet Count Threshold* have no significant effect on the Alert Generation System's performance. Comparing the

---

[8] The details regarding the similarity threshold can be found in the Appendix 16.7 in the electronic supplementary material.

best performing configurations for every examined *Alert Tweet Count Threshold* (similarity threshold of 0.3 for 3, similarity threshold of 0.25 for 5) shows that the performance differences are lower than 5%. Therefore, the system operator is advised to choose the *Alert Tweet Count Threshold* based on an alert frequency, that s/he is willing to process.

15.3.4 System Performance

This section examines the performance of the overall system combining Uncertainty Sampling, Relevance Classification, and Alert Generation. The evaluation is conducted based on the datasets S1 and S2. After data preprocessing, an RF classifier was trained based on 600 tweets that were chosen by Uncertainty Sampling using a kNN classifier. Every tweet in the dataset that the resulting classifier deemed relevant was passed to the Alert Generation System which is configured according to the findings in Section 15.3.3: *Alert Tweet Count Threshold*=5, *Cosine Similarity Threshold*=0.25. The evaluation of the clusters was performed analogous to the procedure in Section 15.3.3 with *irrelevant* clusters as additional cluster class. A cluster was thereby considered *irrelevant* if it contained at least 50% tweets that are labelled as irrelevant. The experimental results (Table 15.2) suggest that the system is capable of detecting 90% of the events occurring in the ground truth data while 15% of reported alerts were not part of the ground truth data (false alert rate).

Table 15.2 Combined Performance of Relevance Classifier, Clustering Algorithm and Alert Generation for datasets S1 and S2

Dataset	S1	S2
Precision	95%	85.19%
Recall	90.48%	93.88%
F_1	92.68%	89.32%

15.3.5 (Near-)Real-Time Capability

The run-time tests were performed on a computer with an *AMD Phenom II X6* CPU and 12 GB DDR3 RAM running Windows 10. We divided the alert generation system into two stages and measured their execution time separately: (TU1) the Relevance Classifier and (TU2) combining the clustering process with the alert generation process. We conducted the experiments using dataset S1. Since individual tweet frequency is highly volatile, we conducted our simulation assuming the following worst-case scenario: Every user sends twice his/her average daily tweet count in the same one our frame: 2.5 Tweets per user per 15 minute time-frame.

Sabottke et al. (2015) suggest that the cyber security community on Twitter consists of about 32,000 accounts. Assuming that the system is used to issue alerts based on the tweets of 25% of these accounts, 20,000 have to be processed in a 15-minute time frame in order to allow near real-time execution. Our experiments show that the execution of (TU1) takes 17.5 seconds for 20,000 Tweets. Based on the class distribution, we determined in Section 15.3.1, $\approx 2,000$ of these tweets are going to be labelled as positive. Assuming that tweets that are older than 14 days are discarded, the clusters of the clustering service contain about 112,000 tweets at any time in this scenario. Extrapolation of the experiment on the execution time for the proposed clustering algorithm suggests that the clustering of 500 tweets takes about 210 seconds in this case. That corresponds to around 840 seconds (or 14 minutes) for the given 2,000 tweets. Adding the execution times of (TU1) and (TU2) up shows that an execution in the given 15-minute time frame is possible. An execution in a timely manner for more accounts or accounts that are more active is possible using a more powerful machine.

15.4   Related Work and Discussion

To use Twitter as an OSINT source for CERTs, we conducted a comparative analysis of existing tools and approaches which are suitable to complete this task (15.4.1). Based on our contributions (15.4.2), we identified limitations and potentials for future work (15.4.3).

15.4.1 Cyber Security Event and Hot Topic Detection

Previous work has examined the possibilities of Twitter as an information source for cyber security event detection (overview in Table 15.3). As the techniques for event detection using Twitter differ, Atafeh and Khreich (Atafeh & Khreich, 2015) offer a systematic approach that allows a comparison based on the of the necessary parts. Most previous work (Bose et al., 2019; Concone et al., 2017; Dionisio et al., 2019; Sapienza et al., 2018; Trabelsi et al., 2015) examines the detection of generic cyber security threats. The majority of these publications (Bose et al., 2019; Concone et al., 2017; Trabelsi et al., 2015) employs some kind of clustering algorithm on a Term Frequency-Inverse Document Frequency (TF-IDF) represen-

Table 15.3 An overview of event detection techniques with application to the cyber security domain, categorized by Retrieval Method (RM, [A]ccount-based or [K]eyword-based (* is filtering)), Detection Method (DM, [S]upervised or [U]nsupervised), as well as Pivot Technique (PT, [D]ocument- or [F]eature-based) and Detection Technique (DT) and Model, based on Atefeh and Khreich (2015)

Work	RM		DM		PT		Application	DT	Model
	A	K	S	U	D	F			
Alves et al., 2021	✓	*	✓		✓		Summarization	CluStream, SVM, NN	TF-IDF
Bose et al., 2019		✓		✓		✓	Threats	DBSCAN	TF-IDF
Concone et al., 2017		✓		✓	✓		Novel Malware	Counting, K-Means	#, TF-IDF
Dionísio et al., 2019	✓	*	✓		✓		Threats	NER by NN	Word Emb.
Dionísio et al., 2020	✓	*	✓		✓		Threats	NER by MTL	Word Emb.
Fang et al., 2020		✓	✓		✓		Threat Events	MTL	Word Emb.
Ji et al., 2019		✓	✓		✓	✓	Cur. Incidents	Prob. Learning	TF
Khandpur et al., 2017		✓		✓	✓		Attacks	Clustering	Exp. Queries
Lee et al., 2017	✓			✓	✓		Topics	Clustering	TF, Corr.
Le Sceller et al., 2017		✓		✓	✓	✓	Classification	Clustering	TF-IDF
Mittal et al., 2019		✓			✓		IT-Sec. Alerts	Rule-Based Reason.	Graph(VKG)
Ritter et al., 2015		✓	✓				IT-Sec. Events	Expect. Reg.	Diff. feat.
Sapienza et al., 2018	✓			✓	✓		Ident. Attacks	Term Filtering	TF
Simran et al., 2019		✓			✓		Threat Indicators	CNN-GRU	Random Emb.
Trabelsi et al., 2015		✓		✓		✓	0-day Exploits	K-Means	Documents
CySecAlert	✓	✓	✓		✓		IT-Sec Events	Rel. Filter, Clustering	TF-IDF

tation of single tweets compared by the cosine similarity distance. Even though the publications' core approach is related, they differ in details concerning the preprocessing of tweets and usage of the detected clusters. On closer inspection, most methodologies use human-generated input that serves as a filter for user-generated content and automatically expands these filters configuration by utilizing Twitter data (Le Sceller et al., 2017). These filters are either represented by lists of relevant keywords (Le Sceller et al., 2017) or a set of credible experts (Lee et al., 2017). To our knowledge, the scientific literature has not discussed the advantages and disadvantages of either approach extensively. This is especially true for the performance of machine learning algorithms on the respective databases. While a keyword-based retrieval approach is less prone to miss relevant tweets regarding a certain objective, it may attract a lot of tweets that contain a relevant keyword in a different semantic. Account-based approaches reduce the number of tweets that have to be processed and therefore reduce performance requirements for the underlying hardware. However, these accounts have to be known beforehand.

15.4.2 Contributions

For the **CySecAlert concept (C1)**, we opted for an account-based retrieval approach, that retrieves tweets based on a list of credible cyber security experts' accounts. Active learning using uncertainty sampling has shown to be beneficial for training supervised classifiers with limited data in other domains (Bernard et al., 2018; Imran et al., 2016; ; M.-A. Kaufhold, Bayer, & Reuter, 2020; Settles, 2010). Literature of crisis informatics in combination with our evaluation suggests that an incremental kNN classifier outperforms a Naive Bayes classifier and an active batch sampling version of an RF classifier if they are used as uncertainty sampling classifier for a batch RF classifier. Therefore, they allow high-quality classifiers with a smaller training set. This is valuable for the privacy by design principle of data minimization (B. -J. Koops et al., 2013). This means that fewer accounts and tweets are needed. In detail, our **evaluations (C2)** show that a training set containing only 600 tweets gathered by Uncertainty Sampling (10% of ground truth database) is suited to build a sufficient classifier. A classifier based on a training set consisting of 1,000 randomly sampled tweets is outperformed by a set of 200 uncertainty sampled tweets. The evaluation shows that *CySecAlert* scores a maximal F_1 measure of 92.68% (Precision: 95%, Recall: 90.48%) (Section 15.3.4). In **comparison to other approaches (C3)**, this exceeds the performance of Bose et al. (2019) with an F_1 measure of 78.26% (Precision: 81.82%, Recall: 75%) and is comparable to the results of Dionísio et al. (2020) with an F_1 measure of 95.1%, who have examined a related task. Although these papers are most comparable as they conduct similar experiments, a direct comparison of the evaluation results is nevertheless impractical because they refer to datasets of different time periods gathered from different sets of accounts. Regarding the real-time capability to our knowledge, only Le Sceller et al. (2017) included a simple evaluation in their experiments. We extend the research in this direction as we perform a more in-depth analysis also incorporating the usage behavior. The near real-time of the system is not only supported by its capability to analyse the real-time Twitter stream (Concone et al., 2017; Le Sceller et al., 2017; Sapienza et al., 2018), it also performs almost as fast as the SONAR system (Le Sceller et al., 2017) (17.5 seconds for 20,000 tweets compared to 12 seconds).

15.4.3 Limitations and Future Work

As the *CySecAlert* system is designed to support CERTs, further improvements and evaluations as part of larger-scale incident monitoring are planned, such as the deployment on other social media platforms and longitudinal testing with larger datasets. The tests will include further studies regarding the security of the system against hacked or fake accounts as well as the risk of model poisoning. Further, controlled experiments will be conducted to exclude the impact of the dataset. Additionally, in recent times more sophisticated clustering algorithms have been proposed. For instance, Alves et al. (2021) extends a greedy clustering approach by offline re-clustering if the cluster affiliation of a new tweet is unclear. This approach may be suited to avoid *duplicate* clusters in our clustering algorithm but may have a negative impact on the real-time properties. Furthermore, re-clustering, in general, interferes with the used online event selection process by changing cluster affiliation of past tweets. Future work should examine streaming clustering algorithms that are suited to enhance the proposed system's overall performance without strongly influencing the capability of processing tweets of many users in a timely manner and the need for re-clustering.

Following the proposed system by Kaufold, Bayer & Reuter (2020), we used the bag-of-word approach to represent text. However, recent contributions suggest that *Word Embeddings* can have relevant performance advantages over a multitude of other textual representation methods, including the bag of word approach applied in this contribution (Mikolov et al., 2013). Future research should examine if the application of Word Embeddings is suited to further improve the proposed alert generation system's performance without the negative influence of the system's timing constraints. Furthermore, NNs in general and in the domain of cyber security related event detection enjoy increasing popularity and show high performance in relevance classification tasks (Dionisio et al., 2019). While the current state of the system with its real-time, low-resource, and robust applicability is only suited for classical machine learning algorithms, future work should examine the influence of different uncertainty sampling classifiers on the performance of NNs as relevance classifiers.

15.5 Conclusion

This work proposes a framework for timely detection of novel and relevant cyber security related events based on data from the social media platform Twitter (*CySecAlert*). *CySecAlert* is capable of collecting tweets based on a list of trusted user accounts, filtering them by relevance, dividing them into clusters by topic similarity, and issuing alerts if one such topic surpasses a predefined significance threshold. The system further aims to support data minimization for OSINT by focussing on a network of expert accounts. Further, it is easy for an expert community, such as CERTs, to adopt as well as quick to train with little labelling and runs in near real-time. Our study based on manually labelled ground truth data shows that the amount of labelled data to train a classifier can be substantially reduced by the application of uncertainty sampling for training set generation in contrast to random sampling. The proposed classifier achieves a precision of 87.18% and a recall of 84.12%, while the cluster-based alert generation subsystem achieves a false alert rate of 3.77% and detects 96.08% of relevant events in the ground truth dataset. An evaluation of the overall system shows that it is able to detect up to 93.88% of relevant events in a ground truth dataset with a false alert rate of 14.81%.

Bibliography

Abdalla, M., Bellare, M., & Neven, G. (2018). Robust Encryption. *Journal of Cryptology*, *31*(2), 307–350. https://doi.org/10.1007/s00145-017-9258-8

AbuTaha, M., Farajallah, M., Tahboub, R., & Odeh, M. (2011). Survey paper: Cryptography is the science of information security. *International Journal of Computer Science and Security (IJCSS)*, 5, 298–309.

Acosta, M., Coronado, D., Ferrandiz, E., Marin, M. R., & Moreno, P. J. (2017). Patents and dual-use technology: An empirical study of the world's largest defence companies. *Defence and Peace Economics*, *29*(7), 821–839. https://doi.org/10.1080/10242694.2017.1303239

Acosta, M., Coronado, D., Ferrandiz, E., Marin, M. R., & Moreno, P. J. (2019). Civil-military patents and technological knowledge flows into the leading defense firms. *Armed Forces and Society*, *46*(3), 454–474. https://doi.org/10.1177/0095327X18823823

Acosta, M., Coronado, D., & Marin, R. (2011). Potential dual-use of military technology: Does citing patents shed light on this process? *Defence and Peace Economics*, *22*(3), 335–349. https://doi.org/10.1080/10242694.2010.491681

Acosta, M., Coronado, D., Marin, R., & Prats, P. (2013). Factors affecting the diffusion of patented military technology in the field of weapons and ammunition. *Scientometrics*, *94*(1), 1–22. https://doi.org/10.1007/s11192-012-0857-8

Adams, S. M., & Friedland, C. J. (2011). A Survey of Umanned Aerial Vehicle (UAV) Usage for Imagery Collection in Disaster Research and Management. *Proceedings of the Ninth International Workshop on Remote Sensing for Disaster Response*, 8, 1–8. https://doi.org/10.1037//0022-0167.35.3.298

Adamson, G., Havens, J. C., & Chatila, R. (2019). Designing a Value-Driven Future for Ethical Autonomous and Intelligent Systems. *Proceedings of the IEEE*, *107*(3), 518–525. https://doi.org/10.1109/JPROC.2018.2884923

Aghion, P., & Jaravel, X. (2015). Knowledge spillovers, innovation and growth. *Economic Journal*, *125*(583), 533–573. https://doi.org/10.1111/ecoj.12199

Agrawal, A., Gans, J., & Goldfarb, A. (2018). Economic Policy for Artificial Intelligence. In J. Lerner & S. Stern (Eds.), *Innovation policy and the economy* (pp. 139–159). National Bureau of Economic Research. https://doi.org/10.1086/699935

Ahmad, A., Hadgkiss, J., & Ruighaver, A. (2012). Incident response teams—Challenges in supporting the organisational security function. *Computers & Security*, *31*(5), 643–652. https://doi.org/10.1016/j.cose.2012.04.001

Akhgar, B., Fortune, D., Hayes, R. E., Guerra, B., & Manso, M. (2013). Social media in crisis events: Open networks and collaboration supporting disaster response and recovery. *2013 IEEE International Conference on Technologies for Homeland Security*, 760–765. https://doi.org/10.1109/THS.2013.6699099

Alam, F., Ofli, F., & Imran, M. (2020). Descriptive and visual summaries of disaster events using artificial intelligence techniques: case studies of Hurricanes Harvey, Irma, and Maria. *Behaviour & Information Technology (BIT)*, *39*(3), 288–318. https://doi.org/10.1080/0144929X.2019.1610908

Alavi, H., & Khamichonak, T. (2017). EU and US export control regimes for dual use goods: An overview of existing frameworks. *Romanian Journal of European Affairs*, *17*(1), 59–74.

Albers, A., Trautmann, S., Howard, T., Nguyen, T. A., Frietsch, M., & Sauter, C. (2010). Semi-autonomous flying robot for physical interaction with environment. *2010 IEEE Conference on Robotics, Automation and Mechatronics, RAM 2010*, 441–446. https://doi.org/10.1109/RAMECH.2010.5513152

Aldehoff, L., Dankenbring, M., & Reuter, C. (2019). Renouncing Privacy in Crisis Management? People's View on Social Media Monitoring and Surveillance. *Proceedings of the International Conference on Information Systems for Crisis Response and Management (ISCRAM)*.

Aldewereld, H., Dignum, V., & Tan, Y.-H. (2015). Design for values in software development. In J. van den Hoven, P. E. VermaasIbo, & I. van de Poel (Eds.), *Handbook of ethics, values, and technological design: Sources, theory, values and application domains* (pp. 831–845). Springer Netherlands. https://doi.org/10.1007/978-94-007-6970-0_26

Alger, C. F. (2014). Peace studies as a Transdisciplinary Project. In *Peace Research and Peacebuilding* (pp. 69–90). Springer.

Allan, J. (2012). *Topic detection and tracking: Event-based information organization* (Vol. 12). Springer Science & Business Media.

Allan, J., Lavrenko, V., & Jin, H. (2000). First story detection in TDT is hard. *Proceedings of the ninth international conference on Information and knowledge management*, 374–381.

Al-Ramahi, M., Alsmadi, I., & Davenport, J. (2020). Exploring hackers assets: Topics of interest as indicators of compromise. *Proceedings of the 7th Symposium on Hot Topics in the Science of Security*, 1–4. https://doi.org/10.1145/3384217.3385619

Al-rimy, B. A. S., Maarof, M. A., & Shaid, S. Z. M. (2018). Ransomware threat success factors, taxonomy, and countermeasures: A survey and research directions. *Computers & Security*, *74*, 144–166. https://doi.org/10.1016/j.cose.2018.01.001

Altmann, J. (2019). Natural-Science/Technical Peace Research. In C. Reuter (Ed.), *Information Technology for Peace and Security—IT-Applications and Infrastructures in Conflicts, Crises, War, and Peace* (pp. 39–60). Springer.

Altmann, J., & Sauer, F. (2017). Autonomous Weapon Systems and Strategic Stability. *Survival: Global Politics and Strategy*, *59*(5), 117–142. https://doi.org/10.1080/00396338.2017.1375263

Alves, F., Andongabo, A., Gashi, I., Ferreira, P. M., & Bessani, A. (2020). Follow the blue bird: A study on threat data published on twitter. *European Symposium on Research in Computer Security*, 217–236. https://doi.org/10.1007/978-3-030-58951-6_11

Alves, F., Bettini, A., Ferreira, P. M., & Bessani, A. (2021). Processing tweets for cybersecurity threat awareness. *Information Systems*, *95*, 1–18. https://doi.org/10.1016/j.is.2020.101586

Alves, F., Ferreira, P, M., & Bessani, A. (2019). Design of a classification model for a twitter-based streaming threat monitor. *49th Annual IEEE/IFIP International Conference on Dependable Systems and Networks Workshops*, 9–14. https://doi.org/10.1109/DSN-W. 2019.00010

Ames, M. (1996). Saving dollars makes sense of crypto export controls. In E. Dawson & J. Golić (Eds.), *Cryptography: Policy and algorithms* (pp. 90–97, Vol. 1029). Springer, Berlin, Heidelberg. https://doi.org/10.1007/BFb0032348

Amoroso, D., & Tamburrini, G. (2019). *What makes human control over weapons systems "meaningful"?* (Tech. rep.). Retrieved September 15, 2022, from https://www.researchgate.net/publication/335224146_WHAT_MAKES_HUMAN_CONTROL_OVER_WEAPON_SYSTEMS_MEANINGFUL

Anderson, K. (2016). Why the Hurry to Regulate Autonomous Weapon Systems-But Not Cyber-Weapons? *Temple International and Comparative Law Journal, 30*(1), 17–41.

Anderson, K., Reisner, D., & Waxman, M. (2014). Adapting the Law of Armed Conflict to Autonomous Weapon Systems. *International Legal Studies, 90*, 386–411.

Anderson, K., & Waxman, M. C. (2013). Law and Ethics for Autonomous Weapon Systems: Why a Ban Won't Work and How the Laws of War Can. *Jean Perkins Task Force on National Security and Law*. https://doi.org/10.2139/ssrn.2250126

Anderson, R. J. (1996). Crypto in Europe — Markets, Law and Policy. In E. Dawson & J. Golić (Eds.), *Cryptography: Policy and Algorithms* (pp. 75–89, Vol. 1029). Springer. https://doi.org/10.1007/BFb0032347

Andriole, S. (2018). *Apple, Google, Microsoft, Amazon And Facebook Own Huge Market Shares = Technology Oligarchy*. Retrieved August 23, 2022, from https://www.forbes. com/sites/steveandriole/2018/09/26/apple-google-microsoft-amazon-and-facebook-own-huge-market-shares-technology-oligarchy/?sh=42da55b12318

Arbeitsgruppe Kritische Infrastrukturen. (2020). *The Cyber Relief Agency: Concept for Increasing the Response Capabilities in Major Cyber Incidents*. Retrieved September 15, 2022, from https://ag.kritis.info/wp-content/uploads/2020/02/chw-konzept_v1.0.pdf

Arkin, R. C. (2010). The case for ethical autonomy in unmanned systems. *Journal of Military Ethics, 9*(4), 332–341. https://doi.org/10.1080/15027570.2010.536402

Arkin, R. C., Lyons, D., Shu, J., Nirmal, P., & Zafar, M. (2012). Getting it right the first time: predicted performance guarantees from the analysis of emergent behavior in autonomous and semi-autonomous systems. Proc. SPIE 8387, *Unmanned Systems Technology XIV*. https://doi.org/10.1117/12.918128

Arkin, R. C., Ulam, P., & Wagner, A. R. (2012). Moral decision making in autonomous systems: Enforcement, moral emotions, dignity, trust, and deception. *Proceedings of the IEEE, 100*(3), 571–589. https://doi.org/10.1109/JPROC.2011.2173265

Asaro, P. M. (2009). Modeling the moral user. *IEEE Technology and Society Magazine, 28*(1), 20–24. https://doi.org/10.1109/MTS.2009.931863

Atefeh, F., & Khreich, W. (2015). A survey of techniques for event detection in twitter. *Computational Intelligence, 31*(1), 132–164. https://doi.org/10.1111/coin.12017

Audretsch, D. B., & Keilbach, M. (2005). The Mobility of Economic Agents as Conduits of Knowledge Spillovers. In D. Fornahl, C. Zellner, & D. B. Audretsch (Eds.), *The Role of Labour Mobility and Informal Networks for Knowledge Transfer* (pp. 8–25). Springer. https://doi.org/10.1007/b100571

Audretsch, D. B., & Vivarelli, M. (1996). Firms size and R&D spillovers: Evidence from Italy. *Small Business Economics*, *8*(3), 249–258. https://doi.org/10.1007/BF00388651

Aupetit, M., & Imran, M. (2017). Interactive monitoring of critical situational information on social media. *Proceedings of the International Conference on Information Systems for Crisis Response and Management (ISCRAM)*, 673–683.

Australia. (2019). *Australia's System of Control and applications for Autonomous Weapon Systems* (tech. rep.). Geneva.

Australian Cyber Security Growth Network. (2018). *Global cyber security software market share by company domicile*. Retrieved September 15, 2022, from https://www.austcyber. com/tools-and-resources/sector-competitiveness-plan-2018

Azevedo, R., Medeiros, I., & Bessani, A. (2019). PURE: Generating Quality Threat Intelligence by Clustering and Correlating OSINT. *2019 18th IEEE International Conference On Trust, Security And Privacy In Computing And Communications/13th IEEE International Conference On Big Data Science And Engineering*, 483–490. https://doi.org/10. 1109/TrustCom/BigDataSE.2019.00071

Azmi, R., Tibben,W., & Win, K. T. (2016). Motives behind Cyber Security Strategy Development: A Literature Review of National Cyber Security Strategy. *Australasian Conference on Information Systems (ACIS)* 2016.

Babbage, S., Catalano, D., Cid, C., de Weger, B., Dunkelman, O., Gehrmann, C., Granboulan, L., Güneysu, T., Hermans, J., Lange, T., Lenstra, A., Mitchell, C., Näslund, M., Nguyen, P., Paar, C., Paterson, K., Pelzl, J., Pornin, T., Preneel, B., . . . Ward, M. (2012). *D.SPA.20: ECRYPT II Yearly Report on Algorithms and Keysizes (2011–2012)* (N. Smart, Ed.; tech. rep.). Retrieved September 15, 2022, from https://www.ecrypt.eu.org/ecrypt2/documents/ D.SPA.20.pdf

Backfried, G., Schmidt, C., Pfeiffer, M., Quirchmayr, G., Glanzer, M., & Rainer, K. (2012). Open source intelligence in disaster management. *2012 European Intelligence and Security Informatics Conference*, 254–258. https://doi.org/10.1109/EISIC.2012.42

Badsha, S., Vakilinia, I., & Sengupta, S. (2019). Privacy Preserving Cyber Threat Information Sharing and Learning for Cyber Defense. *2019 IEEE 9th Annual Computing and Communication Workshop and Conference (CCWC)*, 0708–0714. https://doi.org/10.1109/CCWC. 2019.8666477

Ball, J., Borger, J., & Greenwald, G. (2013). *Revealed: how US and UK spy agencies defeat internet privacy and security*. Retrieved August 23, 2022, from http://hdl.handle.net/11401/ 9864

Banisar, D., & Davies, S. (1998). The code war. *Index on Censorship*, *27*(1), 162–168. https:// doi.org/10.1080/03064229808536306

Bansal, G., Nushi, B., Kamar, E., Weld, D. S., Lasecki, W. S., & Horvitz, E. (2019). Updates in human-ai teams: Understanding and addressing the performance/compatibility tradeoff. *Proceedings of the AAAI Conference on Artificial Intelligence*, *33*(01), 2429–2437. https:// doi.org/10.1609/aaai.v33i01.33012429

Banta, D. (2009). What is technology assessment? *International journal of technology assessment in health care*, *25*(S1), 7–9. https://doi.org/10.1017/S0266462309090333

Barbé, E., & Badell, D. (2020). The European Union and Lethal Autonomous Weapons Systems: United in Diversity? In E. Johansson-Nogués, M. C. Vlaskamp, & E. Barbé (Eds.), *European Union Contested* (pp. 133–152). Springer.

Bardzell, S., & Bardzell, J. (2011). Towards a Feminist HCI Methodology: Social Science, Feminism, and HCI. *Proceedings of the SIGCHI Conference on Human Factors in Computing Systems*, 675–684. https://doi.org/10.1145/1978942.1979041

Barker, E., & Roginsky, A. (2019). *Transitioning the use of cryptographic algorithms and key lengths (tech. rep.)*. National Institute of Standards and Technology. Gaithersburg, MD. https://doi.org/10.6028/NIST.SP.800-131Ar2

Barnes, S. B. (2006). A privacy paradox: Social networking in the United States. *First Monday*, *11*(9). https://doi.org/10.5210/fm.v11i9.1394

Baruffaldi, S., Beuzekom, v. B., Dernis, H., Harhoff, D., Roa, N., Rosenfeld, D., & Squicciarini, M. (2020). *Identifying and measuring developments in artificial intelligence: Making the impossible possible* (tech. rep. No. 5). Paris, OECD Publishing. https://doi.org/https://doi.org/10.1787/5f65ff7e-en

Bates, O., Thomas, V., & Remy, C. (2017). Doing Good in HCI: Can we Broaden our Agenda? *Interactions*, *24*(5), 80–82. https://doi.org/10.1145/3121386

Bauman, Z. (1990). Modernity and ambivalence. *Theory, Culture & Society*, *7*(2–3), 143–169.

Bauman, Z., Bigo, D., Esteves, P., Guild, E., Jabri, V., Lyon, D., & Walker, R. B. J. (2014). After Snowden: Rethinking the impact of surveillance. *International Political Sociology*, *8*(2), 121–144. https://doi.org/10.1111/ips.12048

Becattini, G. (2002). From Marshall's to the Italian "Industrial Districts". A Brief Critical Reconstruction BT—Complexity and Industrial Clusters. In A. Q. Curzio & M. Fortis (Eds.), *Complexity and industrial clusters. contributions to economics* (pp. 83–106). Physica-Verlag HD.

Beck, U. (2004). *A critical introduction to risk society*. Pluto Press.

Behzadan, V., Aguirre, C., Bose, A., & Hsu,W. (2018). Corpus and deep learning classifier for collection of cyber threat indicators in twitter stream. *2018 IEEE International Conference on Big Data*, 5002–5007.

Belderbos, R., & Mohnen, P. (2013). *Intersectoral and international R&D spillovers*.

Belussi, F., & Pilotti, L. (2002). Knowledge creation, learning and innovation in Italian industrial districts. *Geografiska Annaler, Series B: Human Geography*, *84*(2), 125–139. https://doi.org/10.1111/j.0435-3684.2002.00118.x

Bennett, C. H., Bernstein, E., Brassard, G., & Vazirani, U. (1997). Strengths and Weaknesses of Quantum Computing. *SIAM Journal on Computing*, *26*(5), 1510–1523. https://doi.org/10.1137/S0097539796300933

Bernard, J., Zeppelzauer, M., Lehmann, M., Müller, M., & Sedlmair, M. (2018). Towards user-centered active learning algorithms. *Computer Graphics Forum*, *37*(3), 121–132. https://doi.org/https://doi.org/10.1111/cgf.13406

Bernard, R., Bowsher, G., Milner, C., Boyle, P., Patel, P., & Sullivan, R. (2018). Intelligence and global health: assessing the role of open source and social media intelligence analysis in infectious disease outbreaks. *Journal of Public Health*, *26*(5), 509–514. https://doi.org/10.1007/s10389-018-0899-3

Bigo, D. (2006). Security, exception, ban and surveillance. In D. Lyon (Ed.), *Theorizing Surveillance: The Panopticon and Beyond* (pp. 46–68). Routledge.

Bigo, D. (2011). Pierre Bourdieu and International Relations: Power of Practices, Practices of Power. *International Political Sociology*, *5*(3), 225–258. https://doi.org/10.1111/j.1749-5687.2011.00132.x

Black, S. K. (2002). Encryption. In R. Adams (Ed.), *Telecommunications law in the internet age* (1st ed., pp. 327–387). Morgan Kaufmann Publishers, San Francisco (USA).

Blaze, M., Diffie, W., Rivest, R. L., Schneier, B., Shimomura, T., Thompson, E., & Wiener, M. (1996). *Minimal Key Lengths for Symmetric Ciphers to Provide Adequate Commercial Security—A Report by an Ad Hoc Group of Cryptographers and Computer Scientists.*

Bode, I. (2019). Norm-making and the Global South: Attempts to Regulate Lethal Autonomous Weapons Systems. *Global Policy, 10*(3), 359–364. https://doi.org/10.1111/1758-5899.12684

Bode, I. (2020). Weaponised artificial intelligence and use of force norms. *The Project Repository Journal, 6*, 140–143. Retrieved September 15, 2022, from https://findresearcher.sdu.dk/ws/portalfiles/portal/173957438/Open_Access_Version.pdf

Bode, I., & Huelss, H. (2018). Autonomous weapons systems and changing norms in international relations (2018/02/19). *Review of International Studies, 44*(3), 393–413. https://doi.org/10.1017/S0260210517000614

Bode, I., & Watts, T. (2021). *Meaning-less human control: Lessons from air defence Systems on meaningful human control for the debate on AWS* (tech. rep.). Syddansk Universitet. https://dronewars.net/wp-content/uploads/2021/02/DW-Control-WEB.pdf

Boden, A., Liegl, M., & Büscher, M. (2018). Ethische, rechtliche und soziale Implikationen (ELSI). *Sicherheitskritische Mensch-Computer-Interaktion*, 163–182. https://doi.org/10.1007/978-3-658-19523-6_9

Boeke, S. (2018). National cyber crisis management: Different European approaches. *Governance, 31*(3), 449–464. https://doi.org/10.1111/gove.12309

Boersma, K., Büscher, M., & Fonio, C. (2022). Crisis management, surveillance, and digital ethics in the covid-19 era. *Journal of Contingencies and Crisis Management, 30*(1). https://doi.org/10.1111/1468-5973.12398

Boon, F., Derix, S., & Modderkolk, H. (2013). *NSA infected 50,000 computer networks with malicious software.* Retrieved August 23, 2022, from https://www.nrc.nl/nieuws/2013/11/23/nsa-infected-50000-computer-networks-with-malicious-software-a1429487

Booth, K. (1991a). Security and emancipation. *Review of International Studies, 17*(4), 313–326.

Booth, K. (1991b). Security in anarchy: Utopian realism in theory and practice. *International Affairs (Royal Institute of International Affairs 1944-), 67*(3), 527–545. https://doi.org/10.2307/2621950

Bordin, G., Hristova, M., & Luque-Perez, E. (2020). *JRC horizon scanning on dual-use civil and military research.* Publications Office of the European Union.

Bornmann, L., Haunschild, R., & Mutz, R. (2021). Growth rates of modern science: A latent piecewise growth curve approach to model publication numbers from established and new literature databases. *Humanities and Social Sciences Communications, 8*(224), 1–15. https://doi.org/10.1057/s41599-021-00903-w

Bose, A., Behzadan, V., Aguirre, C., & Hsu, W. H. (2019). A novel approach for detection and ranking of trendy and emerging cyber threat events in Twitter streams. *Proceedings of the 2019 IEEE/ACM International Conference on Advances in Social Networks Analysis and Mining*, 871–878. https://doi.org/10.1145/3341161.3344379

Boulanin, V. (2016). *Mapping the Innovation Ecosystem Driving the Advance of Autonomy in Weapon Systems* (tech. rep. No. December). SIPRI. https://www.sipri.org/sites/default/files/Mapping-innovation-ecosystem-driving-autonomy-in-weapon-systems.pdf

Boulanin, V., & Verbruggen, M. (2017). *Article 36 Reviews: Dealing with the Challenges posed by Emerging Technologies* (tech. rep.). Stockholm. https://www.sipri.org/publications/2017/other-publications/article-36-reviews-dealing-challenges-posed-emerging-technologies

Bourdieu, P. (1990). *The Logic of Practice*. Stanford University Press.

Bradbury, D. (2011). Data mining with LinkedIn. *Computer Fraud & Security, 2011*(10), 5–8. https://doi.org/10.1016/S1361-3723(11)70101-4

Branstetter, L., Gandal, N., & Kuniesky, N. (2017). *Network-Mediated Knowldedge Spillovers: A Cross-Country Comparative Analysis of Informaiton Security Innovations* [NBER Working Paper No. 23808]. Retrieved September 15, 2022, from https://www.nber.org/system/files/working_papers/w23808/w23808.pdf

Braun, B., Schindler, S., & Wille, T. (2019). Rethinking agency in International Relations: performativity, performances and actor-networks. *Journal of International Relations and Development, 22*(4), 787–807. https://doi.org/10.1057/s41268-018-0147-z

Brennan, R. L., & Prediger, D. J. (1981). Coefficient Kappa: Some Uses, Misuses, and Alternatives. *Educational and Psychological Measurement, 41*(3), 687–699. https://doi.org/10.1177/001316448104100307

Brown, I., & Korff, D. (2009). Terrorism and the proportionality of internet surveillance. *European Journal of Criminology, 6*(2), 119–134. https://doi.org/10.1177/1477370808100541

Brundage, M., Avin, S., Clark, J., Toner, H., Eckersley, P., Garfinkel, B., Dafoe, A., Scharre, P., Zeitzoff, T., Filar, B., Anderson, H., Roff, H., Allen, G. C., Steinhardt, J., Flynn, C., Heigeartaigh, S. O., Beard, S., Belfield, H., Farquhar, S., . . . Amodei, D. (2018). *The malicious use of artificial intelligence: Forecasting, prevention, and mitigation* (tech. rep. No. February). Oxford. https://arxiv.org/ftp/arxiv/papers/1802/1802.07228.pdf

Brzoska, M. (2006). Trends in global military and civilian research and development (R&D) and their changing interface. *Proceedings of the International Seminar on Defence Finance and Economics, 19*, 289–302.

BSI. (2019). *The State of IT Security in Germany 2018*. Retrieved September 15, 2022, from https://www.bsi.bund.de/SharedDocs/Downloads/DE/BSI/Publikationen/Lageberichte/Lagebericht2018.pdf?__blob=publicationFile%5C&v=1

BSI. (2020). *Die Lage der IT-Sicherheit in Deutschland 2019*. Retrieved September 15, 2022, from https://www.bsi.bund.de/SharedDocs/Downloads/DE/BSI/Publikationen/Lageberichte/Lagebericht2021.pdf?__blob=publicationFile%5C&v=3

BSI. (2021). *BSI warnt: Kritische Schwachstellen in Exchange-Servern*. Retrieved August 23, 2022, from https://www.bsi.bund.de/DE/Service-Navi/Presse/Pressemitteilungen/Presse2021/210305_Exchange-Schwachstelle.html

Buchanan, T., Paine, C., Joinson, A. N., & Reips, U.-D. (2007). Development of measures of online privacy concern and protection for use on the internet. *Journal of the American society for information science and technology, 58*(2), 157–165. https://doi.org/10.1002/asi.20459

Buchler, N., Rajivan, P., Marusich, L. R., Lightner, L., & Gonzalez, C. (2018). Sociometrics and observational assessment of teaming and leadership in a cyber security defense competition. *Computers & Security, 73*, 114–136. https://doi.org/10.1016/j.cose.2017.10.013

Bühner, M., & Ziegler, M. (2007). *Statistik für Psychologen und Sozialwissenschaftler [Statistics for Psychologists and Social Scientists]*. Pearson.

Burget, M., Bardone, E., & Pedaste, M. (2017). Definitions and conceptual dimensions of responsible research and innovation: A literature review. *Science and Engineering Ethics*, *23*(1), 1–19. https://doi.org/10.1007/s11948-016-9782-1

Burmeister, O. K. (2016). The development of assistive dementia technology that accounts for the values of those affected by its use. *Ethics and Information Technology*, *18*(3), 185–198. https://doi.org/10.1007/s10676-016-9404-2

Burrell, J. (2016). How the machine 'thinks': Understanding opacity in machine learning algorithms. *Big Data & Society*, *3*(1), 1–12. https://doi.org/10.1177/2053951715622512

Büscher, M., Becklake, S. J., Easton, C. R., Kerasidou, C. X., Oliphant, R. S., Petersen, K. G., Jasmontaite, L., & Paterour, O. (2016). ELSI Guidelines for networked collaboration and information exchange in PPDR and risk governance. *Proceedings of the ISCRAM 2016 Conference*, 1–12.

Büscher, M., Easton, C., Kerasidou, C., Escalante, M. A. L., Alter, H., Petersen, K., Bonnamour, M. C., Lund, D., Baur, A., Quinn, R. A., et al. (2018). The isitethical? exchange responsible research and innovation for disaster risk management. *15th International Conference on Information Systems for Crisis Response and Management (ISCRAM)*, 254–267.

Butler, J. (2011). *Bodies that matter: On the discursive limits of sex*. Routledge.

Buzan, B. (2008). *People, states & fear: an agenda for international security studies in the post-cold war era*. Ecpr Press.

Buzan, B., Wæver, O., De Wilde, J., et al. (1998). *Security: A new framework for analysis*. Lynne Rienner Publishers.

Cabrero-Holgueras, J., & Pastrana, S. (2021). SoK: Privacy-preserving computation techniques for deep learning. *Proceedings on Privacy Enhancing Technologies (PoPETs)*, *2021*(4), 139–162. https://doi.org/10.2478/popets-2021-0064

Cady, F. (2017). *The Data Science Handbook*. John Wiley Sons. https://doi.org/10.1002/9781119092919

Callari, F. G., Durand, J.-G. D., Yarlagadda, P. K. K., & Glozman, T. (2021, December 1). *Techniques for Managing Processing Ressources*. Seatle. https://patentimages.storage.googleapis.com/64/43/f2/7b8b2e6efe325b/US10893107.pdf

Callon, M. (1999). The role of lay people in the production and dissemination of scientific knowledge. *Science, Technology and Society*, *4*(1), 81–94. https://doi.org/10.1177/097172189900400106

Canellas, M. C., & Haga, R. A. (2016). Toward meaningful human control of autonomous weapons systems through function allocation. *IEEE International Symposium on Technology and Society, Proceedings (ISTAS)*, *2016-March*, 1–7. https://doi.org/10.1109/ISTAS.2015.7439432

Carbonara, N. (2018). Competitive Success of Italian Industrial Districts: A Network-based Approach. *Journal of Interdisciplinary Economics*, *30*(1), 78–104. https://doi.org/10.1177/0260107917700470

Carvin, S. (2017). Conventional Thinking? The 1980 Convention on Certain Conventional Weapons and the Politics of Legal Restraints on Weapons during the Cold War. *Journal of Cold War Studies*, *19*(1), 38–69. https://doi.org/10.1162/JCWS_a_00717

Casanovas, P. (2014). Open Source Intelligence, Open Social Intelligence and Privacy by Design. *Proceedings of the European Conference on Social Intelligence*, 174–185.

Casanovas, P. (2017). CyberWarfare and Organised Crime. A Regulatory Model and Meta-Model for Open Source Intelligence (OSINT). In M. Taddeo & L. Glorioso (Eds.), *Ethics and Policies for Cyber Operations* (pp. 139–167). Springer. https://doi.org/10.1007/978-3-319-45300-2

Casanovas, P., Arraiza, J., Melero, F., Gonzalez-Conejero, J., Molcho, G., & Cuadros, M. (2014). Fighting Organized Crime Through Open Source Intelligence: Regulatory Strategies of the CAPER Project. *The 27th International Conference on Legal Knowledge and Information Systems*, 189–198.

Castillo, C. (2016). *Big Crisis Data: Social Media in Disasters and Time-Critical Situations.* Cambridge University Press.

Castro, D. (2020). *Why New Calls to Subvert Commercial Encryption Are Unjustified* (tech. rep.). https://itif.org/publications/2020/07/13/why-new-callssubvert-commercial-encryption-are-unjustified/

Cath, C. (2018). Governing artificial intelligence: Ethical, legal and technical opportunities and challenges. *Philosophical Transactions of the Royal Society A: Mathematical, Physical and Engineering Sciences.* https://doi.org/10.1098/rsta.2018.0080

Cayford, M., van Gulijk, C., & van Gelder, P. (2014). All swept up: An initial classification of NSA surveillance technology. In T. Nowakowski, M. Mlyńczak, A. Jodejko-Pietruczuk, & S.Werbińska-Wojciechowska (Eds.), *Safety and Reliability: Methodology and Applications* (pp. 643–650). CRC Press. https://doi.org/10.1201/b17399-90

Cayford, M., & Pieters,W. (2018). The effectiveness of surveillance technology: What intelligence officials are saying. *The Information Society, 34*(2), 88–103. https://doi.org/10.1080/01972243.2017.1414721

Cerulli, G., & Potì, B. (2009). Measuring intersectoral knowledge spillovers: An application of sensitivity analysis to Italy. *Economic Systems Research, 21*(4), 409–436. https://doi.org/10.1080/09535310903569216

Chao, H., Cao, Y., & Chen, Y. (2010). Autopilots for small unmanned aerial vehicles: A survey. International *Journal of Control, Automation and Systems, 8*(1), 36–44. https://doi.org/10.1007/s12555-010-0105-z

Chitkara, A., Singh, D., Gupta, A., & Varshney, G. (2020). IntelliSpect: Personal Information Search Tool. *2020 International Conference on Information Networking*, 556–561. https://doi.org/10.1109/ICOIN48656.2020.9016488

Chmielewski, P. (2018). Ethical Autonomous Weapons?: Practical, Required Functions. *IEEE Technology and Society Magazine, 37*(3), 48–55. https://doi.org/10.1109/MTS.2018.2857601

Chouldechova, A., Benavides-Prado, D., Fialko, O., & Vaithianathan, R. (2018). A case study of algorithm-assisted decision making in child maltreatment hotline screening decisions. *Conference on Fairness, Accountability and Transparency*, 134–148.

Christen, M., Gordijn, B., Weber, K., van de Poel, I., & Yaghmaei, E. (2017). A Review of Value-Conflicts in Cybersecurity. *The ORBIT Journal, 1*(1), 1–19. https://doi.org/10.29297/orbit.v1i1.28

Chyung, S., Roberts, K., Swanson, I., & Hankinson, A. (2017). Evidence-based survey design: The use of a midpoint on the likert scale. *Performance Improvement, 56*, 15–23. https://doi.org/10.1002/pfi.21727

Cichonski, P., Millar, T., Grance, T., & Scarfone, K. (2012). NIST Special Publication 800-61 Revision 2: Computer Security Incident Handling Guide Recommendations. *NIST Special Publication.* https://doi.org/10.6028/NIST.SP.800-61r2

Clayton, J. (2021). *Apple sues Israeli spyware firm NSO Group.* Retrieved August 23, 2022, from https://www.bbc.com/news/business-59393823

Cobb, C., McCarthy, T., Perkins, A., Bharadwaj, A., Comis, J., Do, B., & Starbird, K. (2014). Designing for the deluge: understanding & supporting the distributed, collaborative work of crisis volunteers. *Proceedings of the 17th ACM Conference on Computer Supported Cooperative Work & Social Computing*, 888–899. https://doi.org/10.1145/2531602.2531712

Coeckelbergh, M. (2020). Artificial Intelligence, Responsibility Attribution, and a Relational Justification of Explainability. *Science and Engineering Ethics*, *26*(4), 2051–2068. https://doi.org/10.1007/s11948-019-00146-8

Collier, J. (2017). Strategies of Cyber Crisis Management: Lessons from the Approaches of Estonia and the United Kingdom. In *Ethics and Policies for Cyber Operations* (pp. 187–212). Springer International Publishing. https://doi.org/10.1007/978-3-319-45300-2_11

Collingridge, D. (1980). *The social control of technology.* St. Martins Press.

Comey, J. B. (2014). *Going Dark: Are Technology, Privacy, and Public Safety on a Collision Course?* Retrieved August 23, 2022, from https://www.fbi.gov/news/speeches/going-dark-are-technology-privacy-and-public-safety-on-a-collision-course

Computing Research and Education Association of Australasia. (2022). *Welcome to core.* Retrieved September 6, 2022, from https://www.core.edu.au

Concone, F., De Paola, A., Re, G. L., & Morana, M. (2017). Twitter analysis for real-time malware discovery. *2017 AEIT International Annual Conference*, 1–6. https://doi.org/10.23919/AEIT.2017.8240551

Costantini, V., Mazzanti, M., & Montini, A. (2013). Environmental performance, innovation and spillovers. Evidence from a regional NAMEA. *Ecological Economics*, *89*, 101–114. https://doi.org/10.1016/j.ecolecon.2013.01.026

Cottrell, M. P. (2009). Legitimacy and Institutional Replacement: The Convention on Certain Conventional Weapons and the Emergence of the Mine Ban Treaty. *International Organization*, *63*(2), 217–248. https://doi.org/10.1017/S0020818309090079

Cousins, K., Subramanian, H., & Esmaeilzadeh, P. (2019). A Value-sensitive Design Perspective of Cryptocurrencies: A Research Agenda. *Communications of the Association for Information Systems*, *45*(1), 511–547. https://doi.org/10.17705/1CAIS.04527

Coyne, L. (2018). Responsibility in practice: Hans Jonas as environmental political theorist. *Ethics, Policy & Environment*, *21*(2), 229–245. https://doi.org/10.1080/21550085.2018.1509487

CPC. (2019). *G06n: Computer systems based on specific computational models.* Retrieved August 23, 2022, from https://www.uspto.gov/web/patents/classification/cpc/html/cpc-G06N.html

Craig Timberg. (2014). *Newest Androids will join iPhones in offering default encryption, blocking police.* Retrieved August 23, 2022, from https://www.washingtonpost.com/news/the-switch/wp/2014/09/18/newest-androids-will-join-iphones-in-offering-default-encryption-blocking-police/

Croasdell, D. (2019). The Role of Transnational Cooperation in Cybersecurity Law Enforcement. *Proceedings of the 52nd Hawaii International Conference on System Sciences*, 5598–5607.

Crootof, R. (2016). A Meaningful Floor for "Meaningful Human Control". *Temple International & Comparative Law Journal*, *30*(1), 53–62.

Csernatoni, R. (2019). The EU's Technological Power: Harnessing Future and Emerging Technologies for European Security BT—Peace, Security and Defence Cooperation in Post-Brexit Europe: Risks and Opportunities. In C.-A. Baciu & J. Doyle (Eds.). Springer International Publishing. https://doi.org/10.1007/978-3-030-12418-2_6

Cuijpers, C. (2013). Legal aspects of open source intelligence—Results of the VIRTUOSO project. *Computer Law & Security Review, 29*(6), 642–653. https://doi.org/10.1016/j.clsr.2013.09.002

Cummings, M. L. (2004). Creating moral buffers in weapon control interface design. *IEEE Technology and Society Magazine, 23*(3), 28–33. https://doi.org/10.1109/MTAS.2004.1337888

Cummings, M. L. (2019). Lethal Autonomous Weapons: Meaningful Human Control or Meaningful Human Certification? *IEEE Technology and Society Magazine, 38*(4), 20–26. https://doi.org/10.1109/MTS.2019.2948438

Cummings, M. L. (2006). Integrating ethics in design through the value-sensitive design approach. *Science and Engineering Ethics, 12*(4), 701–715. https://doi.org/10.1007/s11948-006-0065-0

Dalton, A., Dorr, B., Liang, L., & Hollingshead, K. (2017). Improving cyberattack predictions through information foraging. *2017 IEEE International Conference on Big Data,* 4642–4647. https://doi.org/10.1109/BigData.2017.8258509

Dam, K. W., & Lin, H. S. (1996). *Cryptography's Role in Securing the Information Society.* National Academies Press. https://doi.org/10.17226/5131

Datenethikkommission. (2019). *Gutachten der Datenethikkommission.* https://www.bmi.bund.de/SharedDocs/downloads/DE/publikationen/themen/it-digitalpolitik/gutachten-datenethikkommission.pdf?__blob=publicationFil%5C&=6

Davis, J., & Nathan, L. P. (2015). Value Sensitive Design: Applications, Adaptations, and Critiques. In J. van den Hoven, P. E. Vermaas, & I. van de Poel (Eds.), *Handbook of Ethics, Values, and Technological Design. Sources, Theory, Values and Application Domains* (pp. 11–40). Springer.

Davis II, J. S., Boudreaux, B., Welburn, J. W., Aguirre, J., Ogletree, C., McGovern, G., & Chase, M. S. (2017). *Stateless Attribution: Toward International Accountability in Cyberspace.* RAND Corp Arlington VA United States.

Dean, P. (1999). A Right to Private Digital Communication? Updating the Debate. *Convergence: The International Journal of Research into New Media Technologies, 5*(3), 8–14. https://doi.org/10.1177/135485659900500302

Debatin, B., Lovejoy, J. P., Horn, A.-K., & Hughes, B. N. (2009). Facebook and online privacy: Attitudes, behaviors, and unintended consequences. *Journal of computer-mediated communication, 15*(1), 83–108. https://doi.org/10.1111/j.1083-6101.2009.01494.x

Decker, M., Ladikas, M., Stephan, S., & Wütscher, F. (2004). *Bridges between Science, Society and Policy: Technology Assessment-Methods and Impacts.* Springer.

Degli Esposti, S., & Santiago Gómez, E. (2015). Acceptable surveillance-orientated security technologies: Insights from the surprise project. *Surveillance and Society, 13*(3–4), 437–454. https://doi.org/10.24908/ss.v13i3/4.5400

de Sio, F. S., & van den Hoven, J. (2018). Meaningful human control over autonomous systems: A philosophical account. *Frontiers Robotics AI, 5,* 1–14. https://doi.org/10.3389/frobt.2018.00015

Deutscher Bundestag. (2009). *Gesetz zur Änderung des Grundgesetzes (Artikel 91c, 91d, 104b, 109, 109a, 115, 143d)*. Retrieved August 23, 2022, from https://dip.bundestag.de/vorgang/.../19041

Deutscher CERT-Verbund. (2021). *Überblick*. Retrieved September 2, 2021, from https://www.cert-verbund.de/

Diekmann, L., Fritsch, J., & Krätzner-Ebert, A. (2020). *Gemeinsamer Ausschuss zum Umgang mit sicherheitsrelevanter Forschung von DFG und Leopoldina*. Retrieved September 11, 2022, from https://www.leopoldina.org/uploads/tx_leopublication/2020_GA_Taetigkeitsbericht_Dual_Use.pdf

Dienlin, T., & Metzger, M. J. (2016). An extended privacy calculus model for SNSs: Analyzing self-disclosure and self-withdrawal in a representative US sample. *Journal of Computer-Mediated Communication, 21*(5), 368–383. https://doi.org/10.1111/jcc4.12163

Dillon, M. S. (2002). Network Society, Network-Centric Warfare and the State of Emergency. *Theory, Culture and Society, 19*(4), 71–79. https://doi.org/10.1177/0263276402019004005

Dinev, T., Masssimo, B., Hart, P., Christian, C., Vincenzo, R., & Ilaria, S. (2005). Internet users, privacy concerns and attitudes towards government surveillance-an exploratory study of cross-cultural differences between italy and the united states. *BLED 2005 Proceedings*, 1–13.

Dinev, T., Hart, P., & Mullen, M. R. (2008). Internet privacy concerns and beliefs about government surveillance-an empirical investigation. *The Journal of Strategic Information Systems, 17*(3), 214–233. https://doi.org/10.1016/j.jsis.2007.09.002

Dionisio, N., Alves, F., Ferreira, P. M., & Bessani, A. (2019). Cyberthreat Detection from Twitter using Deep Neural Networks. *2019 International Joint Conference on Neural Networks*, 1–8. https://doi.org/10.1109/IJCNN.2019.8852475

Dionisio, N., Alves, F., Ferreira, P. M., & Bessani, A. (2020). Towards end-toend cyberthreat detection from Twitter using multi-task learning. *2020 International Joint Conference on Neural Networks (IJCNN)*, 1–8. https://doi.org/10.1109/IJCNN48605.2020.9207159

Dix, A. (2017). Human-computer interaction, foundations and new paradigms. *Journal of Visual Languages & Computing, 42*, 122–134. https://doi.org/10.1016/j.jvlc.2016.04.001

Dombrowski, L., Harmon, E., & Fox, S. (2016). Social justice-oriented interaction design: Outlining kd Diendesign strategies and commitments. *Proceedings of the 2016 ACM Conference on Designing Interactive Systems*, 656–671. https://doi.org/10.1145/2901790.2901861

Domingo-Ferrer, J., & Blanco-Justicia, A. (2020). Ethical Value-Centric Cybersecurity: A Methodology Based on a Value Graph. *Science and Engineering Ethics, 26*(3), 1267–1285. https://doi.org/10.1007/s11948-019-00138-8

Donegan, K., & Sullivan, P. (n.d.). *Computer Security Incident Response Team (CSIRT)*. Retrieved August 23, 2022, from https://www.techtarget.com/whatis/definition/Computer-Security-Incident-Response-Team-CSIRT

Dunn Cavelty, M., & Wenger, A. (2020). Cyber security meets security politics: Complex technology, fragmented politics, and networked science. *Contemporary Security Policy, 41*(1), 5–32. https://doi.org/10.1080/13523260.2019.1678855

Duvillard, A., & Friedli, M. (2018). Nationale Cyber-Strategie: Einbezug der lokalen Ebene in einem föderalen Staat. In *Cybersecurity Best Practices* (pp. 117–123). Springer Fachmedien Wiesbaden. https://doi.org/10.1007/978-3-658-21655-9_10

Dzindolet, M. T., Peterson, S. A., Pomranky, R. A., Pierce, L. G., & Beck, H. P. (2003). The role of trust in automation reliance. *International journal of human-computer studies*, *58*(6), 697–718. https://doi.org/10.1016/S1071-5819(03)00038-7

Eames, M., & Egmose, J. (2011). Community foresight for urban sustainability: Insights from the citizens science for sustainability (suscit) project. *Technological Forecasting and Social Change*, *78*(5), 769–784. https://doi.org/10.1016/j.techfore.2010.09.002

Edler, J., & James, A. D. (2015). Understanding the emergence of new science and technology policies: Policy entrepreneurship, agenda setting and the development of the European Framework Programme. *Research Policy*, *44*, 1252–1265. https://doi.org/10.1016/j.respol.2014.12.008

Edwards, M., Larson, R., Green, B., Rashid, A., & Baron, A. (2017). Panning for gold: Automatically analysing online social engineering attack surfaces. *Computers & Security*, *69*, 18–34. https://doi.org/10.1016/j.cose.2016.12.013

Ehrenfeld, J. M. (2017). WannaCry, Cybersecurity and Health Information Technology: A Time to Act. *Journal of Medical Systems, 41*. https://doi.org/10.1007/s10916-017-0752-1

Eichler, R. R. (2018). Cybersecurity, Encryption, and Defense Industry Compliance with United States Export Regulations. *Texas A&M Journal of Property Law*, *5*(1), 5–36. https://doi.org/10.37419/JPL.V5.I1.2

Eijkman, Q., & Weggemans, D. (2012). Open source intelligence and privacy dilemmas: Is it time to reassess state accountability. *Sec. & Hum. Rts.*, *23*, 285–296. https://doi.org/0.1163/18750230-99900033

Ekelhof, M. (2019). Moving Beyond Semantics on Autonomous Weapons: Meaningful Human Control in Operation. *Global Policy*, *10*(3), 343–348. https://doi.org/10.1111/1758-5899.12665

Ekelhof, M. (2018). Lifting the Fog of Targeting: "Autonomous Weapons" and Human Control through the Lens of Military Targeting. *Naval War College Review*, *71*(3), 61–95.

Ekelhof, M. (2017). Complications of a common language: Why it is so hard to talk about autonomous weapons. *Journal of Conflict and Security Law*, *22*(2), 311–331. https://doi.org/10.1093/jcsl/krw029

Electronic Frontier Foundation. (1998). *Cracking DES: Secrets of Encryption Research, Wiretap Politics, and Chip Design*. O'Reilly. https://web.archive.org/web/20080731155316/http://cryptome.org/cracking-des/cracking-des.htm

ENISA. (2014). *Algorithms, Key Sizes and Parameters Report—2014*. Retrieved September 15, 2022, from https://www.enisa.europa.eu/publications/algorithms-key-size-and-parameters-report-2014

ENISA. (2016). *ENISA's Opinion Paper on Encryption—Strong Encryption Safeguards our Digital Identity*. Retrieved September 15, 2022, from https://www.enisa.europa.eu/publications/enisa-position-papers-and-opinions/enisas-opinion-paper-on-encryption/view

ENISA. (2018). Cyber Europe 2018: After Action Report. https://doi.org/10.2824/369640

ENISA. (2020). *CSIRTs by Country—Interactive Map*. Retrieved August 23, 2022, from https://www.enisa.europa.eu/topics/csirts-in-europe/csirt-inventory/certs-by-country-interactive-map

Esposti, S. D., & Santiago-Gomez, E. (2015). Acceptable surveillance-orientated security technologies: Insights from the surprise project. *Surveillance & Society*, *13*, 437–454.

EU Commission Rejects U.S. Plan on Encryption. (1997). Retrieved August 23, 2022, from
https://www.wsj.com/articles/SB876322992856833000

European Commission. (2013, July). *Towards a more competitive and efficient European defence and security sector.* Retrieved January 19, 2022, from https://ec.europa.eu/commission/presscorner/detail/en/IP_13_734

European Commission. (2015). *Eu funding for dual use—a pratical guide to accessing eu funds for european regional authorities and smes.* Retrieved August 23, 2022, from https://ec.europa.eu/docsroom/documents/12601/attachments/1/translations

European Commission. (2018). *Dual-use Export Controls.* Retrieved August 23, 2022, from https://policy.trade.ec.europa.eu/help-exporters-and-importers/exporting-dual-use-goods_en

European Commission. (2019). *Ethics Guidelines for trustworthy AI.* Retrieved August 23, 2022, from https://digital-strategy.ec.europa.eu/en/library/ethics-guidelines-trustworthy-ai

European Patent Office. (2021a). 3.3.1 artificial intelligence and machine learning. In *Guidelines for examination.* Retrieved January 19, 2022, from https://www.epo.org/law-practice/legal-texts/html/guidelines/e/g_ii_3_3_1.htm

European Patent Office. (2021b). Part G Patentability. In *Guidelines for examination.* Retrieved January 19, 2022, from https://www.epo.org/law-practice/legal-texts/guidelines.html

Evans, N. G. (2014). Dual-use decision making: relational and positional issues. *Monash bioethics review, 32*(3–4), 268–283. https://doi.org/10.1007/s40592-015-0026-y

Fallmann, H., Wondracek, G., & Platzer, C. (2010). Covertly probing underground economy marketplaces. *International Conference on Detection of Intrusions and Malware, and Vulnerability Assessment,* 101–110. https://doi.org/10.1007/978-3-642-14215-4_6

Fang, Y., Gao, J., Liu, Z., & Huang, C. (2020). Detecting cyber threat event from twitter using idcnn and bilstm. *Applied Sciences, 10*(17), 5922. https://doi.org/10.3390/app10175922

Fathi, R., Thom, D., Koch, S., Ertl, T., & Fiedrich, F. (2020). VOST: A case study in voluntary digital participation for collaborative emergency management. *Information Processing & Management, 57*(4). https://doi.org/10.1016/j.ipm.2019.102174

Favaro, M. (2021). *Weapons of Mass Distortion. A new approach to emerging technologies, risk reduction, and the global nuclear order* (tech. rep.). Centre for Science & Security Studies. Retrieved September 15, 2022, from https://www.kcl.ac.uk/csss/assets/weapons-of-mass-distortion.pdf

Feigh, K. M., & Pritchett, A. R. (2013). Requirements for Effective Function Allocation: A Critical Review. *Journal of Cognitive Engineering and Decision Making, 8*(1), 23–32. https://doi.org/10.1177/1555343413490945

Feinerer, I., & Hornik, K. (2018). *tm: Text Mining Package. R package version 0.7–6.* Retrieved August 23, 2022, from https://cran.r-project.org/web/packages/tm/tm.pdf

Feng, S., & Boyd-Graber, J. (2019). What can AI do for me? evaluating machine learning interpretations in cooperative play. *Proceedings of the 24th International Conference on Intelligent User Interfaces,* 229–239.

Fergusson, I. F., & Kerr, P. K. (2018). *The U.S. Export Control System and the Export Control Reform Initiative (Version 44).*

Figas, L. (2020). *USA: Der EARN IT Act—Analyse und Kritik.* Retrieved August 23, 2022, from https://www.boxcryptor.com/de/blog/post/earn-it-act-a-threat-to-end-to-end-encryption/

Fleurant, A., Kuimova, A., Tian, N., Wezeman, P., & Wezeman, S. (2017). The SIPRI Top 100 arms-producing and military services companies, 2016. *SIPRI Fact sheet*, (December), 1–8.

Flick, U. (2014). *An introduction to qualitative research.* SAGE Publications.

Floridi, L., Cath, C., & Taddeo, M. (2019). Digital Ethics: Its Nature and Scope. In C. Öhman & D. Watson (Eds.), *The 2018 yearbook of the digital ethics lab* (pp. 9–17). Springer.

Floridi, L., Cowls, J., Beltrametti, M., Chatila, R., Chazerand, P., Dignum, V., Luetge, C., Madelin, R., Pagallo, U., Rossi, F., Schafer, B., Valcke, P., & Vayena, E. (2018). AI4People—An Ethical Framework for a Good AI Society: Opportunities, Risks, Principles, and Recommendations. *Minds and Machines*, *28*(4), 689–707. https://doi.org/10.1007/s11023-018-9482-5

Floyd, R. (2007). Towards a consequentialist evaluation of security: Bringing together the copenhagen and the welsh schools of security studies. *Review of International Studies*, *33*(2), 327–350. https://doi.org/10.1017IS026021050700753X

Forge, J. (2010). A note on the definition of "dual use". *Science and Engineering Ethics*, *16*(1), 111–118. https://doi.org/10.1007/s11948-009-9159-9

Foucault, M. (1982). The Subject and Power. *Critical Inquiry*, *8*(4), 777–795.

Franke, U., & Brynielsson, J. (2014). Cyber situational awareness—A systematic review of the literature. *Computers & Security*, *46*, 18–31. https://doi.org/10.1016/j.cose.2014.06.008

Fraunhofer IOSB. (2018). *Fraunhofer iosb: Annual report 2017/2018* (tech. rep.). Retrieved January 19, 2022, from https://www.energie.fraunhofer.de/content/dam/energie/en/documents/05_PDF_annual_reports/iosb_jb_2017_2018_en.pdf

Fraunhofer IOSB. (2020). *Fraunhofer iosb: Business units.* Retrieved August 23, 2022, from https://www.iosb.fraunhofer.de/servlet/is/12576/

Friedman, B. (1996). Value-Sensitive Design. *Interactions*, *3*(6), 17–23. https://doi.org/https://doi.org/10.1145/242485.242493

Friedman, B., & Hendry, D. G. (2019). *Value sensitive design: Shaping technology with moral imagination.* MIT Press.

Friedman, B., Hendry, D. G., Borning, A., et al. (2017). A Survey of Value Sensitive Design Methods. *Foundations and Trends in Human-Computer Interaction*, *11*(2), 69–101. https://doi.org/10.1561/1100000015

Friedman, B., & Kahn, P. (2002). Human Values, Ethics, and Design. In J. A. Jacko & A. Sears (Eds.), *The Human-Computer Interaction Handbook: Fundamentals, Evolving Technologies and Emerging Applications* (pp. 1177–1201). L. Erlbaum Associates Inc.

Friedman, B., Kahn, P. H., Borning, A., & Huldtgren, A. (2013). Value Sensitive Design and Information Systems. In N. Doorn, D. Schuurbiers, I. van de Poel, & M. E. Gorman (Eds.), *Early engagement and new technologies: Opening up the laboratory* (pp. 55–95). Springer Netherlands. https://doi.org/10.1007/978-94-007-7844-3_4

Friedman, B., & Nissenbaum, H. (1996). Bias in Computer Systems. *ACM Transactions on Information Systems*, *14*(3), 330–347. https://doi.org/10.1145/230538.230561

Friedman, B., Smith, I., H Kahn, P., Consolvo, S., & Selawski, J. (2006). Development of a privacy addendum for open source licenses: Value Sensitive Design in industry. *International Conference on Ubiquitous Computing*, 194–211.

Fritsch, J. (2019). Kommissionen für Ethik sicherheitsrelevanter Forschung entsprechend den Empfehlungen von Leopoldina und Deutscher Forschungsgemeinschaft (DFG). *Bundesgesundheitsblatt—Gesundheitsforschung—Gesundheitsschutz*, 62(6), 744–750.

Fujiwara, A. (2017). The knowledge spillover resulting from the mobility of knowledge workers. *2017 6th International Conference on Industrial Technology and Management, ICITM 2017*, 181–191. https://doi.org/10.1109/ICITM.2017.7917918

Furnham, A., & Swami, V. (2019). Attitudes toward surveillance: Personality, belief and value correlates. *Psychology*, 10(5), 609–623. https://doi.org/0.4236/psych.2019.105039

Gallagher, R., & Greenwald, G. (2014). How the NSA Plans to Infect 'Millions' of Computers with Malware. *The Intercept*. https://firstlook.org/theintercept/article/2014/03/12/nsa-plans-infect-millions-computers-malware/

Galtung, J. (1964). An Editorial: What is Peace Research. *Journal of Peace Research*, 1(1), 1–4. https://doi.org/10.1177/002234336400100101

Gedris, K., Bowman, K., Neupane, A., Hughes, A. L., Bonsignore, E.,West, R.W., Balzotti, J., & Hansen, D. L. (2021). Simulating Municipal Cybersecurity Incidents: Recommendations from Expert Interviews Kira. *Proceedings of the 54th Hawaii International Conference on System Sciences 2021*, 2036–2045.

Gellman, B., & Miller, G. (2013). *'Black budget' summary details U.S. spy network's successes, failures and objectives*. Retrieved August 23, 2022, from https://www.washingtonpost.com/world/national-security/black-budget-summary-details-us-spy-networks-successes-failures-and-objectives/2013/08/29/7e57bb78-10ab-11e3-8cdd-bcdc09410972_story.html

Gerber, N., Reinheimer, B., & Volkamer, M. (2019). Investigating people's privacy risk perception. *Proceedings on Privacy Enhancing Technologies (PoPETs)*, 2019(3), 267–288. https://doi.org/10.2478/popets-2019-0047

German Federal Ministry of Defense. (2017). *Military scientific research report annual report 2017: Defence research for the german armed forces* (tech. rep.). https://www.bmvg.de/resource/blob/30420/77e30d89b05169e3ca3d55b20abdbed9/g-03-military-scientific-research-annual-report-2017-data.pdf

German Patent and Trade Mark Office. (2017). *Patente und Gebrauchsmuster für Staatsgeheimnisse*. Retrieved September 15, 2022, from https://www.dpma.de/docs/patente/geheimschutz.pdf

Gerring, J., & Cojocaru, L. (2016). Selecting Cases for Intensive Analysis. *Sociological Methods & Research*, 45(3), 392–423. https://doi.org/10.1177/0049124116631692

Geyik, S. C., Guo, Q., Hu, B., Ozcaglar, C., Thakkar, K.,Wu, X., & Kenthapadi, K. (2018). Talent Search and Recommendation Systems at LinkedIn: Practical Challenges and Lessons Learned. *SIGIR '18: The 41st International ACM SIGIR Conference on Research & Development in Information Retrieval*, 1353–1354. https://doi.org/10.1145/3209978.3210205

Ghazi, Y., Anwar, Z., Mumtaz, R., Saleem, S., & Tahir, A. (2018). A Supervised Machine Learning Based Approach for Automatically Extracting High-Level Threat Intelligence from Unstructured Sources. *2018 International Conference on Frontiers of Information Technology*, 129–134. https://doi.org/10.1109/FIT.2018.00030

Giesen, B., & Seyfert, R. (2016). Collective identities, empty signifiers and solvable secrets. *European Journal of Social Theory, 19*(1), 111–126. https://doi.org/10.1177/1368431015573364

Gill, A. S. (2019). Artificial Intelligence and International Security: The Long View (2019/06/07). *Ethics & International Affairs.* https://doi.org/10.1017/S0892679419000145

Gläser, J., & Laudel, G. (2010). *Experteninterviews und qualitative Inhaltsanalyse: Als Instrumente rekonstruierender Untersuchungen* (4th). VS Verlag für Sozialwissenschaften.

Glassman, M., & Kang, M. J. (2012). Intelligence in the internet age: The emergence and evolution of Open Source Intelligence (OSINT). *Computers in Human Behavior, 28*(2), 673–682. https://doi.org/10.1016/j.chb.2011.11.014

Gong, S., Cho, J., & Lee, C. (2018). A Reliability Comparison Method for OSINT Validity Analysis. *IEEE Transactions on Industrial Informatics, 14*(12), 5428–5435. https://doi.org/10.1109/TII.2018.2857213

Gonzalez-Granadillo, G., Faiella, M., Medeiros, I., Azevedo, R., & Gonzalez-Zarzosa, S. (2019). Enhancing Information Sharing and Visualization Capabilities in Security Data Analytic Platforms. *49th Annual IEEE/IFIP International Conference on Dependable Systems and Networks Workshops,* 1–8. https://doi.org/10.1109/DSN-W.2019.00009

Gonzalez-Granadillo, G., Faiella, M., Medeiros, I., Azevedo, R., & Gonzalez-Zarzosa, S. (2021). ETIP: An Enriched Threat Intelligence Platform for improving OSINT correlation, analysis, visualization and sharing capabilities. *Journal of Information Security and Applications, 58,* 1–15. https://doi.org/10.1016/j.jisa.2020.102715

Goodfellow, I., Bengio, Y., & Courville, A. (2016). *Deep learning.* The MIT Press.

Gopalakrishnan, M. (2016). *German court's ruling on mass spying is a victory for the BND and NSA.* Retrieved August 23, 2022, from https://www.dw.com/en/german-courts-ruling-on-mass-spying-is-a-victory-for-the-bnd-and-nsa/a-36402749

Gray, P. S., Williamson, J. B., Karp, D. A., & Dalphin, J. R. (2007). *The research imagination: An introduction to qualitative and quantitative methods.* Cambridge Univeristy Press. https://doi.org/10.1017/cbo9780511819391

Greenberg, A. (2019). *Security Isn't enough. Silicon Valley needs 'Abusability' Testing.* Retrieved August 23, 2022, from https://www.wired.com/story/abusability-testing-ashkan-soltani/

Greenwald, G. (2013a). *NSA collecting phone records of millions of Verizon customers daily.* Retrieved August 23, 2022, from https://www.theguardian.com/world/2013/jun/06/nsa-phone-records-verizon-court-order

Greenwald, G. (2013b). *XKeyscore: NSA tool collects 'nearly everything a user does on the internet'.* Retrieved August 23, 2022, from https://www.theguardian.com/world/2013/jul/31/nsa-top-secret-program-online-data

Greenwald, G., MacAskill, E., Poitras, L., Ackerman, S., & Rushe, D. (2013). *Microsoft handed the NSA access to encrypted messages.* Retrieved August 23, 2022, from https://www.theguardian.com/world/2013/jul/11/microsoft-nsa-collaboration-user-data

Grimmett, J. J. (2001). *CRS Report for Congress: Encryption Export Controls (RL30273).* Retrieved September 15, 2022, from https://file.wikileaks.org/file/crs/RL30273.pdf

Grin, J., Grunwald, A., et al. (2000). *Vision assessment: Shaping technology in 21st century society: Towards a repertoire for technology assessment.* Springer.

Grispos, G., Glisson, W., & Storer, T. (2019). How Good is Your Data? Investigating the Quality of Data Generated During Security Incident Response Investigations. https://doi.org/10.24251/HICSS.2019.859

Grodzinsky, F. S., Miller, K. W., & Wolf, M. J. (2011). Developing artificial agents worthy of trust: "Would you buy a used car from this artificial agent?". *Ethics and Information Technology, 13*(1), 17–27. https://doi.org/10.1007/s10676-010-9255-1

Grunwald, A. (2011). Responsible Innovation: Bringing together Technology Assessment, Applied Ethics, and STS research. *Enterprise and Work Innovation Studies, 31*, 10.

Grunwald, A. (2018). *Technology assessment in Practice and Theory*. Routledge.

Grunwald, A. (2020). The objects of technology assessment. hermeneutic extension of consequentialist reasoning. *Journal of Responsible Innovation, 7*(1), 96–112. https://doi.org/10.1080/23299460.2019.1647086

Guston, D. H., & Sarewitz, D. (2002). Real-time technology assessment. *Technology in society, 24*(1–2), 93–109. https://doi.org/10.1016/S0160-791X(01)00047-1

Guthrie, G. (2019). Machine Learning as a Service (MLaaS) is the Next Trend No One is Talking About. *DataDrivenInvestor*. Retrieved September 15, 2022, from https://medium.datadriveninvestor.com/machine-learning-as-a-service-mlaas-is-the-next-trend-no-one-is-talking-about-e100973121c1

Haas, M. C., & Fischer, S. C. (2017). The evolution of targeted killing practices: Autonomous weapons, future conflict, and the international order. *Contemporary Security Policy, 38*(2), 281–306. https://doi.org/10.1080/13523260.2017.1336407

Habdank, M., Rodehutskors, N., & Koch, R. (2017). Relevancy assessment of tweets using supervised learning techniques: Mining emergency related tweets for automated relevancy classification. *2017 4th International Conference on Information and Communication Technologies for Disaster Management (ICT-DM)*, 1–8. https://doi.org/10.1109/ICT-DM.2017.8275670

Hagele, G., & Soffker, D. (2017). A simplified situational environment risk and system reliability assessment for behavior assurance of autonomous and semi-autonomous aerial systems: A simulation study. *2017 International Conference on Unmanned Aircraft Systems, ICUAS 2017*, 951–960. https://doi.org/10.1109/ICUAS.2017.7991415

Hagendorff, T. (2020). The ethics of ai ethics: An evaluation of guidelines. *Minds and Machines, 30*(1), 99–120. https://doi.org/10.1007/s11023-020-09517-8

Haggerty, K. D., & Ericson, R. V. (2000). The Surveillant Assemblage. *The British Journal of Sociology, 51*(4), 605–622. https://doi.org/10.1080/00071310020015280

Hansen, L., & Nissenbaum, H. (2009). Digital disaster, cyber security, and the copenhagen school. *International studies quarterly, 53*(4), 1155–1175.

Harris, E. D. (Ed.). (2016). *Governance of Dual-Use Technologies: Theory and Practice*. American Academy of Arts & Sciences.

Hasan, M., Orgun, M. A., & Schwitter, R. (2018). A survey on real-time event detection from the twitter data stream. *Journal of Information Science, 44*(4), 443–463. https://doi.org/10.1177/0165551517698564

Ha-Thuc, V., Venkataraman, G., Rodriguez, M., Sinha, S., Sundaram, S., & Guo, L. (2015). Personalized expertise search at LinkedIn. *Proceedings—2015 IEEE International Conference on Big Data, IEEE Big Data 2015*, 1238–1247. https://doi.org/10.1109/BigData.2015.7363878

Havakhor, T., Soror, A. A., & Sabherwal, R. (2018). Diffusion of knowledge in social media networks: effects of reputation mechanisms and distribution of knowledge roles. *Information Systems Journal, 28*(1), 104–141. https://doi.org/10.1111/isj.12127

Hayes, D. R., & Cappa, F. (2018). Open-Source Intelligence for Risk Assessment. *Business Horizons, 61*(5), 689–697. https://doi.org/10.1016/j.bushor.2018.02.001

Hayes, P., & Kelly, S. (2018). Distributed morality, privacy, and social media in natural disaster response. *Technology in Society, 54*, 155–167. https://doi.org/10.1016/j.techsoc.2018.05. 003

Hayes, P., van de Poel, I., & Steen, M. (2020). Algorithms and values in justice and security. *AI and Society, 35*(3), 533–555. https://doi.org/10.1007/s00146-019-00932-9

Heath, C., & Luff, P. (1992). Collaboration and control. Crisis management and multimedia technology in London Underground Line Control Rooms. *Computer Supported Cooperative Work (CSCW), 1*(1–2), 69–94. https://doi.org/10.1007/BF00752451

Hellström, T. (2013). On the Moral Responsibility of Military Robots. *Ethics and Inf. Technol., 15*(2), 99–107. https://doi.org/10.1007/s10676-012-9301-2

Hellwig, O. (2015). Organisation, Rahmenbedingungen und Kommunikation bei CERTs. In E. Huber (Ed.), *Sicherheit in cyber-netzwerken* (pp. 559–574). Springer VS.

Hevner, A. R. (2007). A Three Cycle View of Design Science Research. *Scandinavian Journal of Information Systems, 19*(2), 87–92. http://aisel.aisnet.org/sjis/vol19/iss2/4

Hewett, T. T., Baecker, R., Card, S., Carey, T., Gasen, J., Mantei, M., Perlman, G., Strong, G., & Verplank, W. (1992). *ACM SIGCHI Curricula for Human-Computer Interaction.* ACM.

Hiltz, S. R., Hughes, A. L., Imran, M., Plotnick, L., Power, R., & Turoff, M. (2020). Exploring the usefulness and feasibility of software requirements for social media use in emergency management. *International Journal of Disaster Risk Reduction (IJDDR)*, 42. https://doi. org/10.1016/j.ijdrr.2019.101367

Hocraffer, A., & Nam, C. S. (2017). A meta-analysis of human-system interfaces in unmanned aerial vehicle (UAV) swarm management. *Applied Ergonomics, 58*, 66–80. https://doi.org/ 10.1016/j.apergo.2016.05.011

Hodkowski, W. A. (1997). Future of Internet Security: How New Technologies Will Shape the Internet and Affect the Law. *Santa Clara High Technology Law Journal, 13*(1), 217–275.

Horowitz, M. C., Allen, G. C., Saravalle, E., Cho, A., Frederick, K., & Scharre, P. (2018). *Artificial intelligence and international security* (tech. rep.). Center for a New American Security. Retrieved September 15, 2022, from https://csdsafrica.org/wp-content/uploads/ 2020/06/CNAS_AI-and-International-Security.pdf

Hoser, B., & Nitschke, T. (2010). Questions on ethics for research in the virtually connected world. *Social Networks, 32*(3), 180–186. https://doi.org/10.1016/j.socnet.2009.11.003

Hourcade, J. P., & Bullock-Rest, N. E. (2011). HCI for Peace: A Call for Constructive Action. *Proceedings of the SIGCHI Conference on Human Factors in Computing Systems*, 443–452. https://doi.org/10.1145/1978942.1979005

Hove, C., Tarnes, M., Line, M. B., & Bernsmed, K. (2014). Information Security Incident Management: Identified Practice in Large Organizations. *2014 Eighth International Conference on IT Security Incident Management & IT Forensics*, 27–46. https://doi.org/10. 1109/IMF.2014.9

Hu, H., Ahn, G.-J., & Jorgensen, J. (2011). Detecting and resolving privacy conflicts for collaborative data sharing in online social networks. *Proceedings of the 27th Annual Computer Security Applications Conference*, 103–112. https://doi.org/10.1145/2076732.2076747

Huang, R. (2016). *RQDA: R-based Qualitative Data Analysis. R package version 0.2–8.* Retrieved August 23, 2022, from https://rdrr.io/rforge/RQDA/

Huang, S.-Y., & Ban, T. (2019). A Topic-Based Unsupervised Learning Approach for Online Underground Market Exploration. *2019 18th IEEE International Conference On Trust, Security And Privacy In Computing And Communications/13th IEEE International Conference On Big Data Science And Engineering*, 208–215. https://doi.org/10.1109/TrustCom/BigDataSE.2019.00036

Huang, S.-Y., Huang, Y.-W., & Mao, C.-H. (2019). A multi-channel cybersecurity news and threat intelligent engine—SecBuzzer. *Proceedings of the 2019 IEEE/ACM International Conference on Advances in Social Networks Analysis and Mining*, 691–695. https://doi.org/10.1145/3341161.3345309

Huber, E. (2015). *Sicherheit in Cyber-Netzwerken*. Springer Fachmedien Wiesbaden.

Hubig, C. (2014). Technik als Medium und "Technik" als Reflexionsbegriff. *30.* http://www.philosophie.tu-darmstadt.de/institut/mitarbeiterinnen%5C_1/professoren/a%5C_hubig/downloadbereich/downloadsprofhubig.de.jsp.

Hult, F. M. (2015). Making Policy Connections across Scales Using Nexus Analysis. In F. M. Hult & D. C. Johnson (Eds.), *Research methods in language policy and planning: A practical guide* (pp. 217–223).Wiley.

Humbert, M., Trubert, B., & Huguenin, K. (2019). A survey on interdependent privacy. *ACM Computing Surveys (CSUR)*, 52(6), 1–40. https://doi.org/10.1145/3360498

Hur, W. (2017). The patterns of knowledge spillovers across technology sectors evidenced in paten citation networks. *Scientrometrics*, *111*, 595–619. https://doi.org/10.1007/s11192-017-2329-7

Husák, M., Jirsík, T., & Yang, S. J. (2020). SoK: Contemporary Issues and Challenges to Enable Cyber Situational Awareness for Network Security. *Proceedings of the 15th International Conference on Availability, Reliability and Security.* https://doi.org/10.1145/3407023.3407062

IAEA. (2022). *Nuclear power capacity trend*. Retrieved September 15, 2022, from https://pris.iaea.org/PRIS/WorldStatistics/WorldTrendNuclearPowerCapacity.aspx

IEEE. (2016). *Reframing Autonomous Weapons Systems*. Retrieved August 23, 2022, from https://standards.ieee.org/wp-content/uploads/import/documents/other/ead_reframing_autonomous_weapons_v2.pdf

Imran, M., Castillo, C., Diaz, F., & Vieweg, S. (2015). *Processing Social Media Messages in Mass Emergency: A Survey* (Vol. 47). ACM. https://doi.org/10.1145/2771588

Imran, M., Meier, P., & Boersma, K. (2018). The use of social media for crisis management: a privacy by design approach. In *Big data, surveillance and crisis management*. Routledge.

Imran, M., Mitra, P., & Srivastava, J. (2016). Enabling rapid classification of social media communications during crises. *International Journal of Information Systems for Crisis Response and Management (IJISCRAM)*, 8(3), 1–17. https://doi.org/10.4018/IJISCRAM.2016070101

Ioannou, A., & Tussyadiah, I. (2021). Privacy and surveillance attitudes during health crises: Acceptance of surveillance and privacy protection behaviours. *Technology in Society*, *67*, 1–16. https://doi.org/10.1016/j.techsoc.2021.101774

Ioannou, M., Stavrou, E., & Bada, M. (2019). Cybersecurity Culture in Computer Security Incident Response Teams: Investigating difficulties in communication and coordination.

2019 International Conference on Cyber Security and Protection of Digital Services (Cyber Security). https://doi.org/10.1109/CyberSecPODS.2019.8885240

IRAC. (2019). *Autonomy, artificial intelligence and robotics: Technical aspects of human control* (tech. rep.). Geneva. https://doi.org/10.18356/b4ecd7ae-en

Isaac, M. (2019). *Zuckerberg Plans to Integrate WhatsApp, Instagram and Facebook Messenger*. Retrieved August 23, 2022, from https://www.nytimes.com/2019/01/25/technology/facebook-instagram-whatsapp-messenger.html

Ishmaev, G., Dennis, M., & van den Hoven, M. J. (2021). Ethics in the covid-19 pandemic: Myths, false dilemmas, and moral overload. *Ethics and Information Technology, 23*(1), 19–34.

IT-Planungsrat. (2013). *Leitlinie für die Informationssicherheit in der öffentlichen Verwaltung- Hauptdokument-*. Retrieved September 15, 2022, from https://www.it-planungsrat.de/fileadmin/beschluesse/2013/Beschluss2013-01_Leitlinie_Informationssicherheit_Hauptdokument.pdf

IT-Planungsrat. (2016). *Kooperation der CERTs im Verwaltungs-CERT-Verbund (VCV)*.

Jaffe, A. B., Trajtenberg, M., & Henderson, R. (1993). Geographic Localization of Knowledge Spillovers as Evidenced by Patent Citations. *The Quarterly Journal of Economics, 108*(3), 577–598. https://doi.org/10.2307/2118401

Ji, T., Zhang, X., Self, N., Fu, K., Lu, C.-T., & Ramakrishnan, N. (2019). Feature driven learning framework for cybersecurity event detection. *Proceedings of the 2019 IEEE/ACM International Conference on Advances in Social Networks Analysis and Mining*, 196–203.

Jo, H., Kim, J., Porras, P., Yegneswaran, V., & Shin, S. (2021). GapFinder: Finding Inconsistency of Security Information From Unstructured Text. *IEEE Transactions on Information Forensics and Security, 16*, 86–99. https://doi.org/10.1109/TIFS.2020.3003570

Joh, E. E. (2013). Privacy protests: Surveillance evasion and fourth amendment suspicion. *Ariz. L. Rev., 55*, 997.

Jonas, H. (1979). Toward a philosophy of technology. *Hastings Center Report, 9*, 34–43. https://doi.org/10.2307/3561700

Jonas, H. (1980). *Das Prinzip Verantwortung: Versuch einer Ethik für die technologische Zivilisation*. Insel-Verlag.

Jones, R. W., & Jones, R. L.W. (1999). *Security, Strategy, and Critical Theory*. Lynne Rienner Publishers.

Jones, R., Beach, M. W., McClure Haughey, M., Sutherland,W., & Lee, C. P. (2021). Construction of shared situational awareness in traffic management. *Proceedings of the ACM on Human-Computer Interaction, 5*(CSCW1), 1–27.

Jordan, K., Polk, R. (2020). The internet "just works": The EARN IT Act threatens that and more | internet society. Internet society. https://www.internetsociety.org/blog/2020/07/the-internet-just-works-the-earn-it-act-threatens-that-and-more/

Jørgensen, M., & Phillips, L. (2012). *Discourse Analysis as Theory and Method*. Sage. https://doi.org/10.4135/9781849208871

Kaiser, R. (2014). *Qualitative Experteninterviews. Konzeptionelle Grundlagen und praktische Durchführung*. Springer VS. http://dx.doi.org/10.1007/978-3-658-02479-6

Kaldor, M. (2011). *Human Security. Society and Economy, 33*(3), 441–448. https://doi.org/10.1556/SocEc.33.2011.3.1

Kallio, H., Pietilä, A.-M., Johnson, M., & Kangasniemi, M. (2016). Systematic methodological review: Developing a framework for a qualitative semistructured interview guide.
Journal of Advanced Nursing, 72(12), 2954–2965. https://doi.org/10.1111/jan.13031

Kandias, M., Gritzalis, D., Stavrou, V., & Nikoloulis, K. (2017). Stress level detection via OSN
usage pattern and chronicity analysis: An OSINT threat intelligence module. *Computers &
Security, 69*, 3–17. https://doi.org/10.1016/j.cose.2016.12.003

Kandias, M., Mitrou, L., Stavrou, V., & Gritzalis, D. (2013). Youtube user and usage profiling:
Stories of political horror and security success. *International Conference on E-Business and
Telecommunications*, 270–289.

Kandias, M., Stavrou, V., Bozovic, N., & Gritzalis, D. (2013). Proactive Insider Threat Detection Through Social Media: The YouTube Case. *Proceedings of the 12th ACM workshop
on Workshop on privacy in the electronic society*, 261–266.

Kandias, M., Stavrou, V., Bozovic, N., Mitrou, L., & Gritzalis, D. (2013). Can We Trust This
User? Predicting Insider's Attitude via YouTube Usage Profiling. *Proceedings of the 2013
IEEE 10th International Conference on Ubiquitous Intelligence & Computing and 2013
IEEE 10th International Conference on Autonomic & Trusted Computing*, 347–354. https://
doi.org/10.1109/UIC-ATC.2013.12

Kannavara, R., Vangore, J., Roberts, W., Lindholm, M., & Shrivastav, P. (2019). A Threat Intelligence Tool for the Security Development Lifecycle. *Proceedings of the 12th Innovations
on Software Engineering Conference*, 1–5. https://doi.org/10.1145/3299771.3299789

Kassim, S. R. B. M., Li, S., & Arief, B. (2022). How national csirts leverage public data, osint
and free tools in operational practices: An empirical study. *Cyber Security: A Peer-Reviewed
Journal, 5*(3), 251–276.

Kaufhold, M.-A., Rupp, N., Reuter, C., & Habdank, M. (2020). Mitigating information overload in social media during conflicts and crises: Design and evaluation of a cross-platform
alerting system. *Behaviour and Information Technology, 39*(3), 319–342. https://doi.org/
10.1080/0144929X.2019.1620334

Kaufhold, M.-A. (2021). *Information Refinement Technologies for Crisis Informatics: User
Expectations and Design Principles for Social Media and Mobile Apps*. Springer Vieweg.
https://doi.org/10.1007/978-3-658-33341-6

Kaufhold, M.-A., Basyurt, A. S., Eyilmez, K., Stöttinger, M., & Reuter, C. (2022). Cyber
Threat Observatory: Design and Evaluation of an Interactive Dashboard for Computer
Emergency Response Teams. *Proceedings of the European Conference on Information Sys-
tems (ECIS)*, 1–17. http://www.peasec.de/paper/2022/2022_KaufholdBasyurtEyilmezSt
%C3%B6ttingerReuter_CyberThreatObservatory_ECIS.pdf

Kaufhold, M.-A., Bayer, M., & Reuter, C. (2020). Rapid relevance classification of social
media posts in disasters and emergencies: A system and evaluation featuring active, incremental and online learning. *Information Processing & Management, 57*(1), 102132. https://
doi.org/10.1016/j.ipm.2019.102132

Kaufhold, M.-A., Fromm, J., Riebe, T., Mirbabaie, M., Kuehn, P., Basyurt, A. S., Bayer,
M., Stöttinger, M., Eyilmez, K., Möller, R., Fuchß, C., Stieglitz, S., & Reuter, C. (2021).
CYWARN: Strategy and Technology Development for Cross-Platform Cyber Situational
Awareness and Actor-Specific Cyber Threat Communication. *Workshop-Proceedings Men-
sch und Computer*. https://doi.org/10.18420/muc2021-mci-ws08-263

Kaufhold, M.-A., Rupp, N., Reuter, C., & Habdank, M. (2020). Mitigating Information Overload in Social Media during Conflicts and Crises: Design and Evaluation of a Cross-Platform

Alerting System. *Behaviour & Information Technology (BIT)*, *39*(3), 319–342. https://doi.org/10.1080/0144929X.2019.1620334

Kaufmann, S. (2016). Security Through Technology? Logic, Ambivalence and Paradoxes of Technologised Security. *European Journal for Security Research*, *1*(1), 77–95. https://doi.org/10.1007/s41125-016-0005-1

Kavouras, P., & Charitidis, C. A. (2020). Dual use in modern research: Taming the janus of technological advance (R. Iphofen, Ed.). *Handbook of Research Ethics and Scientific Integrity*, 181–200.

Kawaguchi, Y., Yamada, A., & Ozawa, S. (2017). AI Web-Contents Analyzer for Monitoring Underground Marketplace. *Neural Information Processing*, 888–896. https://doi.org/10.1007/978-3-319-70139-4_90

Keller, W. (2004). International Technology Diffusion. *Journal of Economnic Literature*, *42*(3), 752–782. https://doi.org/10.1257/0022051042177685

Kelman, H. C. (1981). Reflections on the history and status of peace research. *Conflict Management and Peace Science*, *5*(2), 95–110.

Kensing, F., & Blomberg, J. (1998). Participatory design: Issues and concerns. *Computer supported cooperative work (CSCW)*, *7*(3), 167–185. https://doi.org/10.1023/A:1008689307411

Kessler, G. (2020). Cryptography, Passwords, Privacy, and the Fifth Amendment. *The Journal of Digital Forensics, Security and Law*, *15*, 1–23. https://doi.org/10.15394/jdfsl.2020.1678

Khandpur, R. P., Ji, T., Jan, S.,Wang, G., Lu, C.-T., & Ramakrishnan, N. (2017). Crowdsourcing cybersecurity: Cyber attack detection using social media. *Proceedings of the 2017 ACM on Conference on Information and Knowledge Management*, 1049–1057.

Khurana, H., Basney, J., Bakht, M., Freemon, M., Welch, V., & Butler, R. (2009). Palantir: a framework for collaborative incident response and investigation. *Proceedings of the 8th Symposium on Identity and Trust on the Internet—IDtrust '09*, 38. https://doi.org/10.1145/1527017.1527023

Khurana, N., Mittal, S., Piplai, A., & Joshi, A. (2019). Preventing Poisoning Attacks On AI Based Threat Intelligence Systems. *2019 IEEE 29th International Workshop on Machine Learning for Signal Processing*, 1–6. https://doi.org/10.1109/MLSP.2019.8918803

Killcrece, G., Kossakowski, K.-P., Ruefle, R., & Zajicek, M. (2003). *State of the Practice of Computer Security Incident Response Teams (CSIRTs)* (tech. rep.). CMU/SEI. Pittsburgh, PA, USA. https://doi.org/10.1184/R1/6584396.v1

Kim, D. H., Lee, B. K., & Sohn, S. Y. (2016). Quantifying technology-industry spillover effects based on patent citation network analysis of unmanned aerial vehicle (UAV). *Technological Forecasting and Social Change*, *105*(100), 140–157. https://doi.org/10.1016/j.techfore.2016.01.025

Kindervater, K. H. (2017). The technological rationality of the drone strike. *Critical Studies on Security*, *5*(1), 28–44. https://doi.org/10.1080/21624887.2017.1329472

Kininmonth, J., Thompson, N., McGill, T., & Bunn, A. (2018). Privacy Concerns and Acceptance of Government Surveillance in Australia. *29th Australasian Conference on Information Systems (ACIS2018)*. https://doi.org/10.5130/acis2018.cn

Kirchgaessner, S., Holmes, O., & Walker, S. (2021). *Pegasus project turns spotlight on spyware firm NSO's ties to Israeli state.* Retrieved August 23, 2022, from 8 https://www.theguardian.com/world/2021/jul/20/pegasus-project-turns-spotlight-on-spyware-firm-nso-ties-to-israeli-state

Klinger, J., Mateos-Garcia, J., & Stathoulopoulos, K. (2018). Deep learning, deep change? Mapping the development of the Artificial Intelligence General Purpose Technology. *CoRR, abs/1808.0*.

Koblentz, G. D., & Mazanec, B. M. (2013). Viral warfare: The security implications of cyber and biological weapons. *Comparative Strategy, 32*(5), 418–434.

Kocksch, L., Korn, M., Poller, A., & Wagenknecht, S. (2018). Caring for IT security: Accountabilities, moralities, and oscillations in IT security practices. *Proceedings of the ACM on Human-Computer Interaction (CSCW), 2*. https://doi.org/10.1145/3274361

Koenig, N. (2020). Leading beyond civilian power: Germany's role re-conception in european crisis management. *German Politics, 29*(1), 79–96. https://doi.org/10.1080/09644008. 2018.1496240

Kokolakis, S. (2017). Privacy attitudes and privacy behaviour: A review of current research on the privacy paradox phenomenon. *Computers & security, 64*, 122–134. https://doi.org/ 10.1016/j.cose.2015.07.002

Kolini, F., & Janczewski, L. (2017). Clustering and Topic Modelling: A New Approach for Analysis of National Cyber security Strategies. *PACIS 2017 Proceedings, 126*. https://aisel. aisnet.org/pacis2017/126

Koops, B. -J., Hoepman, J. H., & Leenes, R. (2013). Open-source intelligence and privacy by design. *Computer Law and Security Review, 29*(6), 676–688. https://doi.org/10.1016/j. clsr.2013.09.005.

Koops, B.-J., & Kosta, E. (2018). Looking for some light through the lens of "cryptowar" history: Policy options for law enforcement authorities against "going dark". *Computer Law & Security Review, 34*(4), 890–900. https://doi.org/10.1016/j.clsr.2018.06.003

Korenberg, A., & Hamer, T. (2018, December 3). *Assessing the EPO's new guidelines on AI*. Retrieved August 23, 2022, from https://www.ipstars.com/NewsAndAnalysis/Assessing-the-EPOs-new-guidelines-on-AI/Index/3981

Kossakowski, K.-P. (2001). *Information technology incident response capabilities*. Books on Demand.

Kossakowski, K.-P., & Neufert, C. (2012). *CERT-Dienstleistungen für Land und Kommunen in Hessen*.

Krawczyk, H., Paterson, K. G., & Wee, H. (2013). On the Security of the TLS Protocol: A Systematic Analysis. *Annual Cryptology Conference*, 429–448. https://doi.org/10.1007/ 978-3-642-40041-4_24

Krstic, M., Cabarkapa, M., & Jevremovic, A. (2019). Machine Learning Applications in Computer Emergency Response Team Operations. *2019 27th Telecommunications Forum (TELFOR)*, 1–4. https://doi.org/10.1109/TELFOR48224.2019.8971040

Krueger, R. A., & Casey, M. A. (2015). *Focus Group: A Practical Guide for Applied Research* (5th). Sage Publications.

Kuckartz, U. (2016). *Qualitative Inhaltsanalyse. Methoden, Praxis, Computerunterstützung (3rd)*. Beltz Juventa.

Kühn, P., Riebe, T., Apelt, L., Jansen, M., & Reuter, C. (2020). Sharing of Cyber Threat Intelligence between States. *S+F (Security and Peace), 38*(1), 22–28. https://doi.org/10. 5771/0175-274X-2019-4-22

La Fleur, C., Hoffman, B., Gibson, C. B., & Buchler, N. (2021). Team performance in a series of regional and national us cybersecurity defense competitions: Generalizable effects of training and functional role specialization. *Computers & Security*, *104*, 1–18. https://doi.org/10.1016/j.cose.2021.102229

Landau, S. (2015). NSA and Dual EC_DRBG: Déjà Vu All Over Again? *The Mathematical Intelligencer*, *37*(4), 72–83. https://doi.org/10.1007/s00283-015-9543-z

Larson, J. (2013). Revealed: The NSA's secret campaign to crack, undermine internet security. ProPublica. https://www.propublica.org/article/the-nsas-secret-campaign-to-crack-undermine-internet-encryption

Latour, B. (2007). *Reassembling the Social: An Introduction to Actor-Network-Theory*. Oup Oxford.

Lawrence, H., Hughes, A., Tonic, R., & Zou, C. (2017). D-miner: A framework for mining, searching, visualizing, and alerting on darknet events. *2017 IEEE Conference on Communications and Network Security*, 1–9. https://doi.org/10.1109/CNS.2017.8228628

Layton, R. (2016). Relative Cyberattack Attribution. In R. Layton & P. A.Watters (Eds.), *Automating Open Source Intelligence. Algorithms for OSINT* (pp. 37–60). Syngress.

Le Dantec, C. A., Poole, E. S., & Wyche, S. P. (2009). Values as lived experience: Evolving value sensitive design in support of value discovery. *Proceedings of the SIGCHI Conference on Human Factors in Computing Systems*, 1141–1150. https://doi.org/10.1145/1518701.1518875

Le Sceller, Q., Karbab, E. B., Debbabi, M., & Iqbal, F. (2017). Sonar: Automatic detection of cyber security events over the twitter stream. *Proceedings of the 12th International Conference on Availability, Reliability and Security (ARES)*, 1–11. https://doi.org/10.1145/3098954.3098992

Leal, D. d. C., Strohmayer, A., & Krüger, M. (2021). On activism and academia: Reflecting together and sharing experiences among critical friends. *Proceedings of the 2021 CHI Conference on Human Factors in Computing Systems*, 1–18. https://doi.org/10.1145/3411764.3445263

LeClair, D. (2020). *New US Bill would require makers of encrypted devices to leave a backdoor*. Retrieved August 23, 2022, from https://www.androidauthority.com/lawful-access-to-encrypted-data-1132922

Lee, K.-C., Hsieh, C.-H., Wei, L.-J., Mao, C.-H., Dai, J.-H., & Kuang, Y.-T. (2017). Secbuzzer: Cyber security emerging topic mining with open threat intelligence retrieval and timeline event annotation. *Soft Computing*, *21*(11), 2883–2896. https://doi.org/10.1007/s00500-016-2265-0

Leistner, F. (2012).*Connecting Organizational Silos*. John Wiley & Sons, Inc. https://doi.org/10.1002/9781119205258

Levy, Y., & J. Ellis, T. (2006). A Systems Approach to Conduct an Effective Literature Review in Support of Information Systems Research. *Informing Science Journal*, *9*, 181–212. https://doi.org/10.28945/479

Lewis, D. D., & Catlett, J. (1994). Heterogeneous uncertainty sampling for supervised learning. In *Machine Learning Proceedings 1994* (pp. 148–156). Elsevier.

Ley, B., Ludwig, T., Pipek, V., Randall, D., Reuter, C., & Wiedenhoefer, T. (2014). Information and Expertise Sharing in Inter-Organizational Crisis Management. *Computer Supported Cooperative Work (CSCW)*, *23*(4–6), 347–387. https://doi.org/10.1007/s10606-014-9205-2

Liao, X., Yuan, K.,Wang, X., Li, Z., Xing, L., & Beyah, R. (2016). Acing the IOC Game: Toward Automatic Discovery and Analysis of Open-Source Cyber Threat Intelligence.

Proceedings of the 2016 ACM SIGSAC Conference on Computer and Communications Security, 755–766. https://doi.org/10.1145/2976749.2978315

Liebert, W. (2013). Dual-use-Forschung und -Technologie. In A. Grunwald & M. Simonidis-Puschmann (Eds.), *Handbuch Technikethik* (pp. 243–244). Springer Verlag.

Liebert, W., & Schmidt, J. C. (2010). Collingridge's dilemma and technoscience. *Poiesis & Praxis, 7*(1), 55–71.

Liebert, W., & Schmidt, J. C. (2018). Ambivalenzen im Kern der wissenschaftlichtechnischen Dynamik: Ergänzende Anforderungen an eine Theorie der Technikfolgenabschätzung. *TATuP-Zeitschrift für Technikfolgenabschätzung in Theorie und Praxis, 27*(1), 52–58. https://doi.org/10.14512/tatup.27.1.52

Liegl, M., Boden, A., Büscher, M., Oliphant, R., & Kerasidou, X. (2016). Designing for ethical innovation: A case study on ELSI co-design in emergency. *International Journal of Human Computer Studies, 95*, 80–95. https://doi.org/10.1016/j.ijhcs.2016.04.003

Light, A., Powell, A., & Shklovski, I. (2017). Design for existential crisis in the anthropocene age. *Proceedings of the 8th International Conference on Communities and Technologies*, 270–279.

Lin, H. (2016). Governance of Information Technology and CyberWeapons. In E. D. Harris (Ed.), *Governance of dual-use technologies: Theorie and practice* (pp. 112–157). American Academy of Arts & Sciences.

Linden, T., Khandelwal, R., Harkous, H., & Fawaz, K. (2020). The privacy policy landscape after the GDPR. *Proceedings on Privacy Enhancing Technologies (PoPETs), 2020*(1), 47–64. https://doi.org/10.2478/popets-2020-0004

LinkedIn. (2020). *About LinkedIn: Statistics*. Retrieved August 23, 2022, from https://news.linkedin.com/about-us#Statistics

Liu, R., Zhao, Z., Sun, C., Yang, X., Gong, X., & Zhang, J. (2017). A research and analysis method of open source threat intelligence data. In B. Zou, M. Li, H. Wang, X. Song, W. Xie, & Z. Lu (Eds.), *Data Science. Third International Conference of Pioneering Computer Scientists, Engineers and Educators* (pp. 352–363). https://doi.org/10.1007/978-981-10-6385-5_30

Liu, S. B. (2014). Crisis Crowdsourcing Framework: Designing Strategic Configurations of Crowdsourcing for the Emergency Management Domain. *Computer Supported Cooperative Work (CSCW), 23*(4–6), 389–443. https://doi.org/10.1007/s10606-014-9204-3

Liu, W., Tao, Y., Yang, Z., & Bi, K. (2019). Exploring and visualizing the patent collaboration network: A case study of smart grid field in china. *Sustainability, 11*. https://doi.org/10.3390/su11020465

Longo, L., Goebel, R., Lecue, F., Kieseberg, P., & Holzinger, A. (2020). Explainable artificial intelligence: Concepts, applications, research challenges and visions. In A. Holzinger, P. Kieseberg, A. Tjoa, & E. Weippl (Eds.), *International Cross-Domain Conference for Machine Learning and Knowledge Extraction* (pp. 1–16). https://doi.org/10.1007/978-3-030-57321-8_1

Lösch, A. (2012). Techniksoziologie. In *Handbuch wissenschaftssoziologie* (pp. 251–264). Springer.

Lösch, A. (2017). Technikfolgenabschätzung soziotechnischer Zukünfte: Ein Vorschlag zur wissenspolitischen Verortung des Vision Assessments. *TATuP-Zeitschrift für Technikfolgenabschätzung in Theorie und Praxis, 26*(1–2), 60–65.

Lösch, A., Böhle, K., Coenen, C., Dobroc, P., Heil, R., Grunwald, A., Scheer, D., Schneider, C., Ferrari, A., Hommrich, D., et al. (2019). Technology assessment of socio-technical futures—a discussion paper. In A. Lösch, A. Grunwald, M. Meister, & I. Schulz-Schaeffer (Eds.), *Socio-Technical Futures Shaping the Present* (pp. 285–308). Springer.

Luhmann, M. (2011). R *für Einsteiger Einfürhung in die Statistiksoftware für die Sozialwissenschaften*. Beltz Verlag.

Luhmann, N. (1979). Trust: A mechanism for the reduction of social complexity. In *Trust and power*. JohnWiley & Sons.

Lukosch, S., Lukosch, H., Datcu, D., & Cidota, M. (2015). Providing Information on the Spot: Using Augmented Reality for Situational Awareness in the Security Domain. *Computer Supported Cooperative Work (CSCW), 24*(6), 613–664. https://doi.org/10.1007/s10606-015-9235-4

Lupu, M., Mayer, K., Kando, N., & Trippe, A. J. (2011). Preface. In M. Lupu, K. Mayer, N. Kando, & A. J. Trippe (Eds.), *Current challenges in patent information retrieval* (pp. i–viii). Springer. https://doi.org/10.1007/978-3-642-19231-9

Lyon, D. (2001). *Surveillance society: Monitoring everyday life (mcgraw-hill education.* UK.

Lyon, D. (Ed.). (2006). Theorizing Surveillance: The Panopticon and Beyond. In *Theorizing surveillance: The panopticon and beyond*. Willan Publishing. https://doi.org/10.1177/009430610703600639

Mahfoud, T., Aicardi, C., Datta, S., & Rose, N. (2018). The limits of dual use. *Issues in Science and Technology, 34*(4), 73–78.

Manders-Huits, N. (2011). What Values in Design? The Challenge of Incorporating Moral Values into Design. *Science and Engineering Ethics, 17*(2), 271–287. https://doi.org/10.1007/s11948-010-9198-2

Marzi, T., Knappertsbusch, V., Marzi, A., Naumann, S., Deerberg, G., &Waidner, E. (2018). Fragen zu einer biologischen technik. *UMSICHT-Diskurs Heft*, (2).

Maurer, T., Omanovic, E., & Wagner, B. (2014). *Uncontrolled Global Surveillance—Updating Export Controls to the Digital Age*.

Mayring, P. (2000). Qualitative Content Analysis. *Forum: Qualitative Social Research, 1*(2). https://doi.org/10.17169/fqs-1.2.1089

Mayring, P. (2004). Qualitative content analysis. *A companion to qualitative research 1*(2004), 159–176.

Mendelson, K. A., Walker, S. T., & Winston, J. D. (1998). The evolution of recent cryptographic policy in the united states. *Cryptologia, 22*(3), 193–210. https://doi.org/10.1080/0161-119891886876

Mendonça, D., Beroggi, G. E., & Wallace, W. A. (2001). Decision support for improvisation during emergency response operations. *International Journal of Emergency Management, 1*(1), 30–38.

Mendonça, D., Jefferson, T., & Harrald, J. (2007). Collaborative adhocracies and mix-and-match technologies in emergency management. *Communications of the ACM, 50*(3), 44–49. https://doi.org/10.1145/1226736.1226764

Menn, J. (2013). *Exclusive: Secret contract tied NSA and security industry pioneer*. Retrieved August 23, 2022, from https://www.reuters.com/article/ususa-security-rsa-idUSBRE9BJ1C220131220

Meunier, F. X., & Bellais, R. (2019). Technical systems and cross-sector knowledge diffusion: an illustration with drones. *Technology Analysis and Strategic Management, 31*(4), 433–446. https://doi.org/10.1080/09537325.2018.1518522

Mikolov, T., Chen, K., Corrado, G., & Dean, J. (2013). Efficient estimation of word representations in vector space. *arXiv preprint* arXiv:1301.3781.

Misselhorn, C. (2020). Artificial systems with moral capacities? a research design and its implementation in a geriatric care system. *Artificial Intelligence, 278*, 103179. https://doi.org/10.1016/j.artint.2019.103179

Mitropoulos, S., Patsos, D., & Douligeris, C. (2006). On Incident Handling and Response: A state-of-the-art approach. *Computers & Security, 25*(5), 351–370. https://doi.org/10.1016/j.cose.2005.09.006

Mittal, S., Das, P. K., Mulwad, V., Joshi, A., & Finin, T. (2016). Cybertwitter: Using twitter to generate alerts for cybersecurity threats and vulnerabilities. *2016 IEEE/ACM International Conference on Advances in Social Networks Analysis and Mining (ASONAM)*, 860–867.

Mittal, S., Joshi, A., & Finin, T. (2019). Cyber-all-intel: An ai for security related threat intelligence. *arXiv preprint* arXiv:1905.02895.

Molas-Gallart, J. (1997). Which way to go? Defence technology and the diversity of 'dual-use' technology transfer. *Research Policy, 26*(3), 367–385. https://doi.org/10.1016/S0048-7333(97)00023-1

Monsees, L. (2019). *Crypto-Politics: Encryption and Democratic Practices in the Digital Era*. Routledge.

Monsees, L. (2020). Cryptoparties: empowerment in internet security. *Internet Policy Review, 9*(4). https://doi.org/10.14763/2020.4.1508

Moore, G. M. (1965). Cramming more components onto integrated circuits With unit cost. *Electronics, 38*(8), 114.

Morrison, A. (2008). Gatekeepers of knowledge within industrial districts: Who they are, how they interact. *Regional Studies, 42*(6), 817–835. https://doi.org/10.1080/00343400701654178

Mowery, D. C., & Simcoe, T. (2002). Is the Internet a US invention?—An economic and technological history of computer networking. *Research Policy, 31*(8–9), 1369–1387. https://doi.org/10.1016/S0048-7333(02)00069-0

Mtsweni, J., Mutemwa, M., & Mkhonto, N. (2016). Development of a cyber-threat intelligence-sharing model from big data sources. *Journal of Information Warfare, 15*(3), 56–68.

Mueller, M., & Heger, O. (2018). Health at any cost? Investigating ethical dimensions and potential conflicts of an ambulatory therapeutic assistance system through value sensitive design. *Proceedings of the 39th International Conference on Information Systems*, 1–17.

Mueller, M., Heger, O., & Niehaves, B. (2018). Exploring ethical design dimensions of a physiotherapeutic mhealth solution through value sensitive design. *Americas Conference on Information Systems 2018: Digital Disruption, AMCIS 2018*, (1), 1–5.

Murphy, C. C. (2020). The Crypto-Wars myth: The reality of state access to encrypted communications. *Common Law World Review, 49*(3–4), 245–261. https://doi.org/10.1177/1473779520980556

Mutschke, P. (2008). Zentralitäts- und Prestigemaße [Centrality and Prestige Measurement]. In C. Stegbauer & R. Häußling (Eds.), *Handbuch netzwerkforschung [handbook network research]* (pp. 365–378). VS Verl. für Sozialwiss.

Nadler, J., Weston, R., & Voyles, E. (2015). Stuck in the middle: The use and interpretation of mid-points in items on questionnaires. *The Journal Of General Psychology, 142*, 2. https://doi.org/10.1080/00221309.2014.994590

Nazarko, Ł. (2017). Future-Oriented Technology Assessment. *Procedia Engineering, 182*, 504–509. https://doi.org/10.1016/j.proeng.2017.03.144

Neil, L., Mittal, S., & Joshi, A. (2018). Mining Threat Intelligence about Open-Source Projects and Libraries from Code Repository Issues and Bug Reports. *2018 IEEE International Conference on Intelligence and Security Informatics*, 7–12. https://doi.org/10.1109/ISI.2018.8587375

NIS Directive. (2016). *Directive (EU) 2016/1148 of the European Parliament and of the Council of 6 July 2016 concerning measures for a high common level of security of network and information systems across the Union.* Retrieved September 15, 2022, from https://eur-lex.europa.eu/legal-content/EN/TXT/?uri=celex:32016L1148

Nisioti, A., Loukas, G., Laszka, A., & Panaousis, E. (2021). Data-Driven Decision Support for Optimizing Cyber Forensic Investigations. *IEEE Transactions on Information Forensics and Security, 16*, 2397–2412. https://doi.org/10.1109/TIFS.2021.3054966

Nissenbaum, H. (2018). Respecting context to protect privacy: Why meaning matters. *Science And Engineering Ethics, 24*, 831–852. https://doi.org/10.1007/s11948-015-9674-9

Nissenbaum, H. (2001). Securing trust online: Wisdom or oxymoron? *Boston University Law Review, 81*(3), 635–664.

Nissenbaum, H. (2004). Privacy as contextual integrity. *Wash. L. Rev., 79*, 119–158.

Nissenbaum, H. (2005). Where Computer Security Meets National Security. *Ethics and Information Technology, 7*(2), 61–73.

Nordmann, A. (2010). A forensics of wishing: technology assessment in the age of technoscience. *Poiesis & Praxis, 7*(1), 5–15. https://doi.org/10.1007/s10202-010-0081-7

Nordmann, A. (2014). Responsible innovation, the art and craft of anticipation. *Journal of Responsible Innovation, 1*(1), 87–98. https://doi.org/10.1080/23299460.2014.882064

Nordmann, A., & Vida, K. (2022). "The Responsibility of Engineers is Boundless"- Professional Reflections. In Z. Anikina (Ed.), *Proceedings of the Conference "Integrating Engineering Education and Humanities for Global Intercultural Perspectives"* (pp. 415–423). https://doi.org/10.1007/978-3-031-11435-9_45

Normark, M., & Randall, D. (2005). Local expertise at an emergency call centre. In H. Gellersen, K. Schmidt, M. Beaudouin-Lafon, & W. Mackay (Eds.), *Proceedings of the Ninth European Conference on Computer-Supported Cooperative Work* (pp. 347–366). Springer. https://doi.org/10.1007/1-4020-4023-7_18

NSABB. (2007). *Proposed Framework for the Oversight of Dual Use Life Sciences Research: Strategies for Minimizing the Potential Misuse of Research Information.* Retrieved September 15, 2022, from https://osp.od.nih.gov/wp-content/uploads/Proposed-Oversight-Framework-for-Dual-Use-Research.pdf

Nunes, E., Shakarian, P., & Simari, G. I. (2018). At-risk system identification via analysis of discussions on the darkweb. *2018 APWG Symposium on Electronic Crime Research*, 1–12. https://doi.org/10.1109/ECRIME.2018.8376211

Okakita, Y. (2019). *Patent examination practices regarding ai-related inventions: Comparison in the epo, uspto and jpo* [Doctoral dissertation]. MIPLC Master Thesis Series. Retrieved January 19, 2022, from https://papers.ssrn.com/sol3/papers.cfm?abstract_id=3652173

Olmstead, K., & Polk, R. (2020). *Latest U.S. 'Anti-Encryption' Bill Threatens Security of Millions*. Retrieved August 23, 2022, from https://www.internetsociety.org/blog/2020/07/latest-u-s-anti-encryption-bill-threatens-security-of-millions/

Olteanu, A., Vieweg, S., & Castillo, C. (2015). What to Expect When the Unexpected Happens: Social Media Communications Across Crises. *Proceedings of the 18th ACM Conference on Computer Supported Cooperative Work & Social Computing*, 994–1009. https://doi.org/10.1145/2675133.2675242

Oltmann, S. (2015). Dual use research: Investigation across multiple science disciplines. *Science and Engineering Ethics*, *21*(2), 327–341. https://doi.org/10.1007/s11948-014-9535-y

Onorati, T., Díaz, P., & Carrion, B. (2018). From social networks to emergency operation centers: A semantic visualization approach. *Future Generation Computer Systems*, *95*, 829–840. https://doi.org/10.1016/j.future.2018.01.052

OpenPGP. (2020). *About*. Retrieved August 23, 2022, from https://www.openpgp.org/about/

The ota lagacy. (2022). Retrieved March 29, 2022, from https://www.princeton.edu/~ota/

Owen, R., Macnaghten, P., & Stilgoe, J. (2012). Responsible research and innovation: From science in society to science for society, with society. *Science and Public Policy*, *39*(6), 751–760. https://doi.org/10.1093/scipol/scs093

Owen-Smith, J., & Powell, W. W. (2004). Knowledge Networks as Channels and Conduits: The Effects of Spillovers in the Boston Biotechnology Community. *Organization Science*, *15*(1), 5–21. https://doi.org/10.1287/orsc.1030.0054

Padayachee, K., & Worku, E. (2017). Shared situational awareness in information security incident management. *2017 12th International Conference for Internet Technology and Secured Transactions (ICITST)*, 479–483. https://doi.org/10.23919/ICITST.2017.8356454

Pal, J. (2017). Chi4good or good4chi. *Proceedings of the 2017 CHI conference extended abstracts on human factors in computing systems*, 709–721.

Palen, L., & Anderson, K. M. (2016). Crisis informatics: New data for extraordinary times. *Science*, *353*(6296), 224–225. https://doi.org/10.1126/science.aag2579

Panahi, S., Watson, J., & Partridge, H. (2013). Towards tacit knowledge sharing over social web tools. *Journal of Knowledge Management*, *17*(3), 379–397. https://doi.org/10.1108/JKM-11-2012-0364

Papastergiou, S., Mouratidis, H., & Kalogeraki, E. M. (2019). Cyber security incident handling, warning and response system for the european critical information infrastructures (cyberSANE). *Communications in Computer and Information Science*, *1000*, 476–487. https://doi.org/10.1007/978-3-030-20257-6_41

Pardo, T. A., Cresswell, A., Dawes, S., & Burke, G. (2004). Modeling the social & technical processes of interorganizational information integration. *37th Annual Hawaii International Conference on System Sciences, 2004. Proceedings of the*, 8 pp. https://doi.org/10.1109/HICSS.2004.1265307

Pardo, T. A., Cresswell, A. M., Thompson, F., & Zhang, J. (2006). Knowledge sharing in cross-boundary information system development in the public sector. *Information Technology and Management*, *7*(4), 293–313. https://doi.org/10.1007/s10799-006-0278-6

Pastor-Galindo, J., Nespoli, P., Gomez Marmol, F., & Martinez Perez, G. (2020). The not yet exploited goldmine of OSINT: Opportunities, open challenges and future trends. *IEEE Access*, *8*, 10282–10304. https://doi.org/10.1109/ACCESS.2020.2965257

Paterson, K. G. (2015). *Countering Cryptographic Subversion*. Retrieved September 15, 2022, from https://hyperelliptic.org/PSC/slides/paterson-PSC.pdf

Pauli, R., Sarwary, H., Imbusch, P., & Lukas, T. (2016). "Accepting the Rules of the Game": Institutional Rhetorics in Legitimizing Surveillance. *European Journal for Security Research, 1*(2), 115–133. https://doi.org/10.1007/s41125-016-0007-z

Pecotic, A. (2019). Whoever predicts the future will win the ai arms race. *Foreign Policy*. https://foreignpolicy.com/2019/03/05/whoever-predicts-the-future-correctly-will-win-the-ai-arms-race-russia-china-united-states-artificial-intelligence-defense/

Pereira, S. d. A., & Quoniam, L. (2017). Intellectual property and patent prospecting as a basis for knowledge and innovation—a study on mobile information technologies and virtual processes of communication and management. *RAI Revista de Administração e Inovação*. https://doi.org/10.1016/j.rai.2017.07.006

Perlroth, N., & Goel, V. (2013). *Internet Firms Step Up Efforts to Stop Spying*. Retrieved August 23, 2022, from https://www.nytimes.com/2013/12/05/technology/internet-firms-step-up-efforts-to-stop-spying.html

Petersen, L., Fallou, L., Reilly, P., & Serafinelli, E. (2017). Public expectations of social media use by critical infrastructure operators in crisis communication. *Proceedings of the 14th ISCRAM Conference*, 1–10.

Pethia, R. D., & van Wyk, K. R. (1990). Computer Emergency Response—An International Problem. *Pittsburgh, Pa.: CERT Coordination Center., Software Engineering Institute, Carnegie Mellon University.*

Pfefferkorn, R. (2020). *NoThe EARN IT Act: How to Ban End-to-End Encryption Without Actually Banning It*. Retrieved August 23, 2022, from http://cyberlaw.stanford.edu/blog/2020/01/earn-it-act-how-ban-end-end-encryption-without-actually-banning-it

Pimenta Rodrigues, G., de Oliveira Albuquerque, R., Gomes de Deus, F., de Sousa Jr., R., de Oliveira Júnior, G., García Villalba, L., & Kim, T.-H. (2017). Cybersecurity and Network Forensics: Analysis of Malicious Traffic towards a Honeynet with Deep Packet Inspection. *Applied Sciences, 7*(10), 1082. https://doi.org/10.3390/app7101082

Plotnick, L., & Hiltz, S. R. (2018). Software Innovations to Support the Use of Social Media by Emergency Managers. *International Journal of Human-Computer Interaction, 34*(4), 367–381. https://doi.org/10.1080/10447318.2018.1427825

Van de Poel, I. (2013). Translating values into design requirements. In D. P. Michelfelder, N. McCarthy, & D. E. Goldberg (Eds.), *Philosophy and engineering: Reflections on practice, principles and process* (pp. 253–266). Springer.

Pokorny, J., Norman, A., Zanesco, A., Bauer-Wu, S., Sahdra, B. and Saron, C. (2016). "Network analysis for the visualization and analysis of quali- tative data," Psychol. Methods, vol. 23, no. 1, Nov. 2016.

Porche, I. R. I., O'Connell, C., II, J. S. D., Wilson, B., Serena, C. C., Krueger, T. C., Johnson, E.-E., Wisniewski, B. D., & Vasseur, M. (2017). *Cyber power potential of the army's reserve component*. RAND Corporation. https://doi.org/10.7249/RR1490

Poscher, R. (2016). Tendencies in Public Civil Security Law. *European Journal for Security Research, 1*(1), 59–76. https://doi.org/10.1007/s41125-016-0003-3

Pournouri, S., & Akhgar, B. (2015). Improving cyber situational awareness through data mining and predictive analytic techniques. *International Conference on Global Security, Safety, and Sustainability*, 21–34. https://doi.org/10.1007/978-3-319-23276-8_3

Pournouri, S., Zargari, S., & Akhgar, B. (2019). An Investigation of Using Classification Techniques in Prediction of Type of Targets in Cyber Attacks. *2019 IEEE 12th International Conference on Global Security, Safety and Sustainability (ICGS3)*, 202–212. https://doi.org/10.1109/ICGS3.2019.8688266

Preece, J. (2016). Citizen science: New research challenges for human-computer interaction. *International Journal of Human-Computer Interaction, 32*(8), 585–612. https://doi.org/10.1080/10447318.2016.1194153

Pu, Y., & Grossklags, J. (2016). Towards a model on the factors influencing social app users' valuation of interdependent privacy. *Proceedings on Privacy Enhancing Technologies (PoPETs), 2016*(2), 61–81. https://doi.org/10.1515/popets-2016-0005

Pugliese, J. (2015). Drones. In M. B. Salter (Ed.), *Making Things International 1: Circuits and Motion* (pp. 222–242). University of Minnesota Press.

Purohit, H., Hampton, A., Bhatt, S., Shalin, V. L., Sheth, A. P., & Flach, J. M. (2014). Identifying seekers and suppliers in social media communities to support crisis coordination. *Computer Supported Cooperative Work (CSCW), 23*(4), 513–545. https://doi.org/10.1007/s10606-014-9209-y

Quan-Haase, A., & McCay-Peet, L. (2016). Building Interdisciplinary Social Media Research Teams: Motivations, Challenges, and Policy Frameworks. In L. Sloan & A. Quan-Haase (Eds.), *The SAGE Handbook of Social Media Research* (pp. 40–56). SAGE Publications Ltd.

Quick, D., & Choo, K.-K. R. (2018). Digital forensic intelligence: Data subsets and Open Source Intelligence (DFINT+OSINT): A timely and cohesive mix. *Future Generation Computer Systems, 78*, 558–567. https://doi.org/10.1016/j.future.2016.12.032

Rädiker, S., & Kuckartz, U. (2019). *Analyse qualitativer Daten mit MAXQDA*. Springer.

Rajamäki, J. (2019). Design Science Research towards Privacy by Design in Maritime Surveillance ICT Systems. *Information & Security: An International Journal, 43*(2), 196–214. https://doi.org/10.11610/isij.4316

Rajamäki, J., & Simola, J. (2019). How to apply privacy by design in OSINT and big data analytics. *Proceedings of the 18th European Conference on Cyber Warfare and Security*, 364–371.

Ramanath, R., Inan, H., Polatkan, G., Hu, B., Guo, Q., Ozcaglar, C., Wu, X., Kenthapadi, K., & Geyik, S. C. (2018). Towards Deep and Representation Learning for Talent Search at LinkedIn. *CIKM '18: Proceedings of the 27th ACM International Conference on Information and Knowledge Management*, 2253–2261. https://doi.org/10.1145/3269206.3272030

Ranade, P., Mittal, S., Joshi, A., & Joshi, K. (2018). Using Deep Neural Networks to Translate Multi-lingual Threat Intelligence. *2018 IEEE International Conference on Intelligence and Security Informatics*, 238–243. https://doi.org/10.1109/ISI.2018.8587374

Randall, D., Harper, R., & Rouncefield, M. (2007). *Fieldwork for design: Theory and practice*. Springer Science & Business Media.

Rath, J., Ischi, M., & Perkins, D. (2014). Evolution of different dual-use concepts in international and national law and its implications on research ethics and governance. *Science and Engineering Ethics, 20*(3), 769–790. https://doi.org/10.1007/s11948-014-9519-y

Raykov, T. (2001). Estimation of congeneric scale reliability using covariance structure analysis with nonlinear constraints. *British Journal of Mathematical and Statistical Psychology, 2*, 315–323. https://doi.org/10.1348/000711001159582

Reform Governement Surveillance (RSG) (2020). https://www.reformgovernmentsurveillance.com

Reppy, J. (2006). Managing dual-use technology in an age of uncertainty. *The Forum: A Journal of Applied Research in Contemporary Politics, 4*(1).

Resnik, D. B. (2009). What is "dual use" research? a response to miller and selgelid. *Science and Engineering Ethics, 15*(1), 3–5. https://doi.org/10.1007/s11948-008-9104-3

Resnik, D. B. (2010). Can scientists regulate the publication of dual use research? *Studies in Ethics, Law, and Technology, 4*(1). https://doi.org/10.2202/1941-6008.1124

Reuter, C. (Ed.). (2019). *Information Technology for Peace and Security—IT-Applications and Infrastructures.* Springer Vieweg.

Reuter, C. (2020). Towards IT Peace Research: Challenges at the Interception of Peace and Conflict Research and Computer Science. *S+F (Security and Peace), 38*(1), 10–16. https://doi.org/10.5771/0175-274X-2020-1-10

Reuter, C., Aldehoff, L., Riebe, T., & Kaufhold, M.-A. (2019). IT in Peace, Conflict, and Security Research. In C. Reuter (Ed.), *Information Technology for Peace and Security* (pp. 11–37). Springer.

Reuter, C., Heger, O., & Pipek, V. (2013). Combining Real and Virtual Volunteers through Social Media. In T. Comes, F. Fiedrich, S. Fortier, J. Geldermann, & T. Müller (Eds.), *Proceedings of the International Conference on Information Systems for Crisis Response and Management (ISCRAM)* (pp. 780–790). https://doi.org/10.1126/science.1060143

Reuter, C., Hughes, A. L., & Kaufhold, M.-A. (2018). Social media in crisis management: An evaluation and analysis of crisis informatics research. *International Journal of Human-Computer Interaction, 34*(4), 280–294. https://doi.org/10.1080/10447318.2018.1427832

Reuter, C., & Kaufhold, M.-A. (2018). Fifteen years of social media in emergencies: a retrospective review and future directions for crisis informatics. *Journal of Contingencies and Crisis Management, 26*(1), 41–57. https://doi.org/10.1111/1468-5973.12196

Reuter, C., Kaufhold, M.-A., Spielhofer, T., & Hahne, A. S. (2017). Social Media in Emergencies: A Representative Study on Citizens' Perception in Germany. *Proceedings of the ACM: Human Computer Interaction (PACM): Computer-Supported Cooperative Work and Social Computing, 1*(2), 1–19. https://doi.org/10.1145/3134725

Reuter, C., Ludwig, T., & Pipek, V. (2014). Ad Hoc Participation in Situation Assessment: Supporting Mobile Collaboration in Emergencies. *ACM Transactions on Computer-Human Interaction (TOCHI), 21*(5), 1–26. https://doi.org/10.1145/2651365

Reuter, C., Ludwig, T., & Pipek, V. (2018). Resilienz durch Kooperationstechnologien. In C. Reuter (Ed.), *Sicherheitskritische Mensch-Computer-Interaktion: Interaktive Technologien und Soziale Medien im Krisen- und Sicherheitsmanagement* (pp. 443–465). Springer Vieweg.

Rich, S., & Gellman, B. (2014). *NSA seeks to build quantum computer that could crack most types of encryption.* Retrieved August 23, 2022, from https://www.washingtonpost.com/world/national-security/nsa-seeks-to-build-quantum-computer-that-could-crack-most-types-of-encryption/2014/01/02/8fff297e-7195-11e3-8def-a33011492df2_story.html

Riebe, T., Bäumler, J., Kaufhold, M.-A., & Reuter, C. (2023). Values and Value Conflicts in the Context of OSINT Technologies for Cybersecurity Incident Response: A Value Sensitive Design Perspective. *JCSCW.* https://doi.org/10.1007/s10606-022-09453-4

Riebe, T., Biselli, T., Kaufhold, M.-A., & Reuter, C. (2023). Privacy Concerns and Acceptance Factors of OSINT for Cybersecurity: A Representative Survey. *Proceedings on Privacy Enhancing Technologies (PoPETs)*. https://doi.org/10.56553/popets-2023-0028

Riebe, T., Haunschild, J., Divo, F., Lang, M., Roitburd, G., Franken, J., & Reuter, C. (2020). Die Veränderung der Vorratsdatenspeicherung in Europa. *Datenschutz und Datensicherheit— DuD, 44*(5), 316–321. https://doi.org/10.1007/s11623-020-1275-3

Riebe, T., Kaufhold, M.-A., & Reuter, C. (2021). The impact of organizational structure and technology use on collaborative practices in computer emergency response teams: An empirical study. *Proceedings of the ACM on Human-Computer Interaction, 5*(CSCW2), 1–30. https://doi.org/10.1145/3479865

Riebe, T., Kühn, P., Imperatori, P., & Reuter, C. (2022). U.S. Security Policy: The Dual-Use Regulation of Cryptography and its Effects on Surveillance. *European Journal for Security Research*, 1–27. https://doi.org/10.1007/s41125-022-00080-0

Riebe, T., & Reuter, C. (2019). Dual-Use and Dilemmas for Cybersecurity, Peace and Technology Assessment. In *Information Technology for Peace and Security* (pp. 165–183). Springer Fachmedien Wiesbaden. https://doi.org/10.1007/978-3-658-25652-4_8

Riebe, T., Schmid, S., & Reuter, C. (2020). Meaningful Human Control of Lethal Autonomous Weapon System: The CCW-Debate and its Implications for Value-Sensitive Design. *IEEE Technology and Society Magazine, 39*(4), 36–51. https://doi.org/10.1109/MTS.2020.3031846

Riebe, T., Schmid, S., & Reuter, C. (2021). Measuring Spillover Effects from Defense to Civilian Sectors -A Quantitative Approach Using LinkedIn. *Defence and Peace Economis, 32*(7), 773–785. https://doi.org/10.1080/10242694.2020.1755787

Riebe, T., Wirth, T., Bayer, M., Kühn, P., Kaufhold, M.-A., Knauthe, V., Guthe, S., & Reuter, C. (2021). CySecAlert: An Alert Generation System for Cyber Security Events Using Open Source Intelligence Data. *International Conference on Information and Communications Security*, 429–446. https://doi.org/10.1007/978-3-030-86890-1_24

Ritter, A., Wright, E., Casey, W., & Mitchell, T. (2015). Weakly supervised extraction of computer security events from Twitter. *Proceedings of the 24th International Conference on World Wide Web*, 896–905. https://doi.org/10.1145/2736277.2741083

Roberts, H., Cowls, J., Morley, J., Taddeo, M., Wang, V., & Floridi, L. (2021). The chinese approach to artificial intelligence: An analysis of policy, ethics, and regulation. *AI & SOCIETY, 36*(1), 59–77. https://doi.org/10.1007/s00146-020-00992-2

Robertson, P. L., & Jacobson, D. (2011). Knowledge Transfer and Technology Diffusion: An introduction. In P. Robertson & D. Jacobson (Eds.), *Knowledge transfer and technology diffusion* (pp. 1–34). Elgaronline. https://doi.org/10.4337/9780857930552.00006

Robinson, S. L. (1996). Trust and breach of the psychological contract. *Administrative Science Quarterly, 41*(4), 574–599. http://www.jstor.org/stable/2393868

Roff, H. M., & Moyes, R. (2016). *Meaningful Human Control, Artificial Intelligence and Autonomous Weapons: Briefing paper for delegates at the Convention on Certain Conventional Weapons (CCW) Meeting of Experts on Lethal Autonomous Weapons Systems*. Retrieved September 15, 2022, from https://article36.org/wp-content/uploads/2016/04/MHC-AI-and-AWSFINAL.pdf

Rosert, E., & Sauer, F. (2020). How (not) to stop the killer robots : A comparative analysis of humanitarian disarmament campaign strategies strategies. *Contemporary Security Policy*, 1–26. https://doi.org/10.1080/13523260.2020.1771508

Rotolo, D., Hicks, D., & Martin, B. R. (2015). What is an emerging technology? *Research Policy, 44*(10), 1827–1843. https://doi.org/10.1016/j.respol.2015.06.006

Rozenheim, A. Z. (2018). Surveillance Intermediaries. *Stanford Law Review, 70,* 99–189.

Rubinstein, I., & van Hoboken, J. (2014). Privacy and Security in the Cloud: Some Realism About Technical Solutions to Transnational Surveillance in the Post-Snowden Era. *NYU School of Law, Public Law & Legal Theory Research Paper Series, 14*(46), 486–533.

Russel, M. A. (2018). *Mining the social web* (3rd ed.). Oreilly & Associates Inc.

Ryan, M. (2020). In AIWe Trust: Ethics, Artificial Intelligence, and Reliability. *Science and Engineering Ethics, 26*(5), 2749–2767. https://doi.org/10.1007/s11948-020-00228-y

Rychnovská, D. (2016). Governing dual-use knowledge: From the politics of responsible science to the ethicalization of security. *Security Dialogue, 47*(4), 310–328. https://doi.org/10.1177/0967010616658848

Rychnovská, D. (2020). Security meets science governance: The EU politics of dual-use research. In A. Calcara, R. Csernatoni, & C. Lavallée (Eds.), *Emerging Security Technologies and EU Governance* (pp. 164–176). Routledge.

Sabottke, C., Suciu, O., & Dumitras, , T. (2015). Vulnerability disclosure in the age of social media: Exploiting twitter for predicting real-world exploits. *24th USENIX Security Symposium USENIX Security 15,* 1041–1056.

Salter, M., & Mutlu, C. E. (2013). Research methods in critical security studies. *New York, NY.*

Santos de Carvalho, J. (2018). A 'Male' Future?: An Analysis on the Gendered Discourses Regarding Lethal Autonomous Weapons. *Amsterdam Law Forum, 10,* 41–61. https://doi.org/10.37974/ALF.320

Saper, N. (2013). International Cryptography Regulation and the Global Information Economy. *Northwestern Journal of Technology and Intellectual Property, 11*(7), 673–688. https://doi.org/10.1109/ICECENG.2011.6057249

Sapienza, A., Ernala, S. K., Bessi, A., Lerman, K., & Ferrara, E. (2018). Discover: Mining online chatter for emerging cyber threats. *Companion Proceedings of the The Web Conference 2018,* 983–990. https://doi.org/10.1145/3184558.3191528

Sauer, F. (2016). Stopping 'Killer Robots': Why Now Is the Time to Ban Autonomous Weapons Systems. *Arms Control Today, 46*(8), 8–13.

Savage, C. (2020). *N.S.A. Phone Program Cost $100 Million, but Produced Only Two Unique Leads.* Retrieved August 23, 2022, from https://www.nytimes.com/2020/02/25/us/politics/nsa-phone-program.html

Scavo, C., Kearney, R. C., & Kilroy, R. J. (2007). Challenges to Federalism: Homeland Security and Disaster Response. *The Journal of Federalism, 38*(1), 81–110.

Schafer, W. A., Ganoe, C. H., & Carroll, J. M. (2007). Supporting Community Emergency Management Planning through a Geocollaboration Software Architecture. *Computer Supported Cooperative Work (CSCW), 16*(4–5), 501–537. https://doi.org/10.1007/s10606-007-9050-7

Schäfer, M., Fuchs, M., Strohmeier, M., Engel, M., Liechti, M., & Lenders, V. (2019). Blackwidow: Monitoring the dark web for cyber security information. *2019 11th International Conference on Cyber Conflict: Silent Battle,* 1–21. https://doi.org/10.23919/CYCON.2019.8756845

Schaffer, J., O'Donovan, J., Michaelis, J., Raglin, A., & Höllerer, T. (2019). I can do better than your AI: expertise and explanations. *Proceedings of the 24th International Conference on Intelligent User Interfaces,* 240–251. https://doi.org/10.1145/3301275.3302308

Scharre, P. (2018). *Army of none : autonomous weapons and the future of war*. W.W. Norton & Company.

Schlag, G., Junk, J., & Daase, C. (2015). Transformations of security and security studies: An introduction to the volume. In J. Junk, C. Daase, & G. Schlagsps (Eds.), *Transformations of Security Studies* (pp. 1–32). Routledge.

Schmid, J. (2017). The Diffusion of Military Technology. *Defence and Peace Economics*, *29*(6), 1–19. https://doi.org/10.1080/10242694.2017.1292203

Schmid, S., Riebe, T., & Reuter, C. (2022). Dual-Use and Trustworthy? A Mixed Methods Analysis of AI Diffusion Between Civilian and Defense R&D. *Science and Engineering Ethics*, *28*(2), 1–23. https://doi.org/0.1007/s11948-022-00364-7

Schörnig, N. (2019). Unmanned Systems: The Robotic Revolution as a Challenge for Arms Control. In C. Reuter (Ed.), *Information Technology for Peace and Security* (pp. 233–265). Springer.

Schramowski, P., Turan, C., Jentzsch, S., Rothkopf, C., & Kersting, K. (2020). *The Moral Choice Machine. Frontiers in Artificial Intelligence*, *3*, 1–15. https://doi.org/10.3389/frai.2020.00036

Schulze, M. (2017). Clipper Meets Apple vs. FBI—A Comparison of the Cryptography Discourses from 1993 and 2016. *Media and Communication*, *5*(1), 54. https://doi.org/10.17645/mac.v5i1.805

Schulzke, M. (2019). Drone proliferation and the challenge of regulating dualuse technologies. *International Studies Review*, *21*(3), 497–517. https://doi.org/10.1093/isr/viy047

Schwartz, S., Guntrum, L., & Reuter, C. (2022). Vision or Threat—Awareness for Dual-Use in the Development of Autonomous Driving. *IEEE Transactions on Technology and Society*. https://doi.org/10.1109/TTS.2022.3182310

Schwechter, M. S. (2016). *Brief Export Controls for Software Companies—What You Need to Know*. https://www.bakerlaw.com/webfiles/Litigation/2016/Brief/09-01-2016-Schwechter-Brief.pdf

Sechser, T. S., Narang, N., & Talmadge, C. (2019). Emerging technologies and strategic stability in peacetime, crisis, and war. *Journal of Strategic Studies*, *42*(6), 727–735. https://doi.org/10.1080/01402390.2019.1626725

Sempere, C. M. (2018). What Is Known About Defence Research And Development Spill-Overs? *Defence and Peace Economics*, *29*(3), 225–246. https://doi.org/10.1080/10242694.2016.1239364

Settanni, G., Skopik, F., Shovgenya, Y., & Fiedler, R. (2016). A collaborative analysis system for crob-organization cyber incident handling. *ICISSP 2016—Proceedings of the 2nd International Conference on Information Systems Security and Privacy*, (Icissp), 105–116. https://doi.org/10.5220/0005688301050116

Settles, B. (2010). *Active learning literature survey. university of wisconsin*. Retrieved August 23, 2022, from https://minds.wisconsin.edu/handle/1793/60660

Sharkey, A. (2019). Autonomous weapons systems, killer robots and human dignity. *Ethics and Information Technology*, *21*(2), 75–87. https://doi.org/10.1007/s10676-018-9494-0

Sharkey, N. (2016). Staying in the loop: human supervisory control of weapons. In C. Kreβ, H.-Y. Liu, N. Bhuta, R. Geiβ, & S. Beck (Eds.), *Autonomous weapons systems: Law, ethics, policy* (pp. 23–38). Cambridge University Press. https://doi.org/10.1017/CBO9781316597873.002

Shearer, J., & Gutmann, P. (1996). Government, cryptography, and the right to privacy. *Journal of Universal Computer Science, 2*(3), 113–146. https://doi.org/10.3217/jucs-002-03-0113

Shibata, N., Kajikawa, Y., & Sakata, I. (2011). Detecting potential technological fronts by comparing scientific papers and patents. *Foresight, 13*(5), 51–60. https://doi.org/10.1108/14636681111170211

Shields, J. (2018). Smart machines and smarter policy: Foreign investment regulation, national security, and technology transfer in the age of artificial intelligence. *SSRN, 51*(2). https://doi.org/10.2139/ssrn.3147091

Simran, K., Balakrishna, P., Vinayakumar, R., & Soman, K. P. (2020). Deep Learning Approach for Enhanced Cyber Threat Indicators in Twitter Stream [Series Title: Communications in Computer and Information Science]. In S. M. Thampi, G. Martinez Perez, R. Ko, & D. B. Rawat (Eds.), *Security in Computing and Communications* (pp. 135–145, Vol. 1208). Springer Singapore. https://doi.org/10.1007/978-981-15-4825-3_11

Simran, K., Balakrishna, P., Vinayakumar, R., & Soman, K. (2019). Deep Learning Approach for Enhanced Cyber Threat Indicators in Twitter Stream. In S. Thampi, G. Martinez Perez, R. Ko, & D. Rawat (Eds.), *International Symposium on Security in Computing and Communication* (pp. 135–145). https://doi.org/10.1007/978-981-15-4825-3_11

Sircar, S. (2018). *The Crypto Wars: Interpreting the Privacy versus National Security Debate from a Standards Perspective* [Thesis]. Retrieved September 15, 2022, from https://repository.library.georgetown.edu/bitstream/handle/10822/1043831/Sircar_georgetown_0076M_13737.pdf?sequence=1%5C&isAllowed=y

Skopik, F., Páhi, T., & Leitner, M. (Eds.). (2018). *Cyber Situational Awareness in Public-Private-Partnerships.* Springer Berlin Heidelberg. https://doi.org/10.1007/978-3-662-56084-6

Skopik, F., Settanni, G., & Fiedler, R. (2016). A problem shared is a problem halved: A survey on the dimensions of collective cyber defense through security information sharing. *Computers and Security, 60*, 154–176. https://doi.org/10.1016/j.cose.2016.04.003

Slayton, R., & Clarke, B. (2020). Trusting Infrastructure: The Emergence of Computer Security Incident Response, 1989–2005. *Technology and Culture, 61*(1), 173–206. https://doi.org/10.1353/tech.2020.0036

Smith, H. J., Milberg, S. J., & Burke, S. J. (1996). Information privacy: Measuring individuals' concerns about organizational practices. *MIS quarterly*, 167–196. https://doi.org/10.2307/249477

Soden, R., & Palen, L. (2018). Informating crisis: Expanding critical perspectives in crisis informatics. *Proceedings of the ACM on human-computer interaction, 2*(CSCW), 1–22. https://doi.org/10.1145/3274431

Southard, L. S. (1997). Securing Information Technology Through Cryptography: An Analysis of United States Policy. *Policy Perspectives, 4*(1), 43. https://doi.org/10.4079/pp.v4i1.4190

Spruit, S. L., Hoople, G. D., & Rolfe, D. A. (2016). Just a cog in the machine? the individual responsibility of researchers in nanotechnology is a duty to collectivize. *Science and engineering ethics, 22*(3), 871–887. https://doi.org/10.1007/s11948-015-9718-1

St. Denis, L. A., Hughes, A. L., & Palen, L. (2012). Trial by Fire: The Deployment of Trusted Digital Volunteers in the 2011 Shadow Lake Fire. In L. Rothkrantz, J. Ristvej, & Z. Franco (Eds.), *Proceedings of the International Conference on Information Systems for Crisis Response and Management (ISCRAM)* (pp. 1–10). ISCRAM.

Starbird, K., & Palen, L. (2011). Voluntweeters: Self-Organizing by Digital Volunteers in Times of Crisis. In *Proceedings of the Conference on Human Factors in Computing Systems (CHI)*. ACM-Press. https://doi.org/10.1145/1978942.1979102

Stehr, N., & Mast, J. (2005). Knowledge Economy. In D. Rooney, G. Hearn, & A. Ninan (Eds.), *Handbook on the Knowledge Economy* (pp. 17–37). Edward Elgar.

Stevens, G., & Pipek, V. (2018). Making use: understanding, studying, and supporting appropriation. In *Socio-Informatics: A Practice-Based Perspective on the Design and Use of IT Artifacts* (pp. 139–176). Oxford University Press.

Stevens, G., Rohde, M., Korn, M., Wulf, V., Pipek, V., Randall, D., & Schmidt, K. (2018). Grounded Design. A Research Paradigm in Practice-Based Computing. In V. Wulf, V. Pipek, D. Randall, & M. Rohde (Eds.), *Socio-Informatics: A Practice-Based Perspective on the Design and Use of IT Artifacts* (pp. 139–176).

Stieglitz, S., Mirbabaie, M., Fromm, J., & Melzer, S. (2018). The Adoption of Social Media Analytics for Crisis Management—Challenges and Opportunities. *Proceedings of the 26th European Conference on Information Systems (ECIS)*. https://aisel.aisnet.org/ecis2018_rp/4

Stieglitz, S., Mirbabaie, M., Ross, B., & Neuberger, C. (2018). Social media analytics—Challenges in topic discovery, data collection, and data preparation. *International Journal of Information Management*, 39, 156–168. https://doi.org/10.1016/j.ijinfomgt.2017.12.002

Stiftung Neue Verantwortung. (2019). *Staatliche Cyber-Sicherheitsarchitektur Version 3*. Retrieved September 11, 2022, from https://www.stiftung-nv.de/de/publikation/deutschlands-staatliche-cybersicherheitsarchitektur

Stowsky, J. (2004). Secrets to shield or share? New dilemmas for military R&D policy in the digital age. *Research Policy*, 33(2), 257–269.

Sundaramurthy, S. C., McHugh, J., Ou, X. S., Rajagopalan, S. R., & Wesch, M. (2014). An Anthropological Approach to Studying CSIRTs. *IEEE Security & Privacy*, 12(5), 52–60. https://doi.org/10.1109/MSP.2014.84

Syed, R. (2020). Cybersecurity vulnerability management: A conceptual ontology and cyber intelligence alert system. *Information & Management*, 57(6), 103334. https://doi.org/10.1016/j.im.2020.103334

Taddeo, M. (2010). Modelling trust in artificial agents, a first step toward the analysis of e-trust. *Minds and Machines*, 20(2), 243–257. https://doi.org/10.1007/s11023-010-9201-3

Taddeo, M. (2017). Trusting digital technologies correctly. *Minds and Machines*, 27(4), 565–568. https://doi.org/10.1007/s11023-017-9450-5

Taddeo, M., McCutcheon, T., & Floridi, L. (2019). Trusting artificial intelligence in cybersecurity is a double-edged sword. *Nature Machine Intelligence*, 1(12), 557–560. https://doi.org/10.1038/s42256-019-0109-1

Taddeo, M., McNeish, D., Blanchard, A., & Edgar, E. (2021). Ethical principles for artificial intelligence in national defence. *Philosophy & Technology*, 34(4), 1707–1729.

Taddicken, M. (2014). The 'privacy paradox' in the social web: The impact of privacy concerns, individual characteristics, and the perceived social relevance on different forms of self-disclosure. *Journal of Computer-Mediated Communication*, 19(2), 248–273. https://doi.org/10.1111/jcc4.12052

Taebi, B., van den Hoven, J., & Bird, S. J. (2019). The Importance of Ethics in Modern Universities of Technology. *Science and Engineering Ethics*, 25, 1625–1632. https://doi.org/10.1007/s11948-019-00164-6

Tapia, A. H., & Moore, K. (2014). Good enough is good enough: Overcoming disaster response organizations' slow social media data adoption. *Computer Supported Cooperative Work (CSCW), 23*(4–6), 483–512. https://doi.org/10.1007/s10606-014-9206-1

Tappi, D. (2001). *The Neo-Marshallian Industrial District A Study on Italian Contributions to Theory and Evidence* (tech. rep.). Retrieved September 11, 2022, from https://citeseerx.ist.psu.edu/viewdoc/download?doi=10.1.1.329.6443%5C&rep=rep1&type=pdf

Tatnall, A., & Gilding, A. (1999). Actor-Network Theory and Information Systems Research. *Proceedings of 10th Australasian Conference on Information Systems*, 955–966.

Tavani, H. T. (2018). Can social robots qualify for moral consideration? Reframing the question about robot rights. *Information (Switzerland), 9*(4). https://doi.org/10.3390/info9040073

The White House. (1993). *White House Annoucement of the Clipper Initiative: Statement by the press secretary.* Retrieved August 23, 2022, from https://www.whitehouse.gov/briefing-room/statements-releases/2022/08/19/statement-by-press-secretary-karine-jean-pierre-on-the-whitehouse-united-we-stand-summit/

Thiebes, S., Lins, S., & Sunyaev, A. (2020). Trustworthy artificial intelligence. *Electronic Markets*, 447–464. https://doi.org/10.1007/s12525-020-00441-4

Thom, D., Krüger, R., & Ertl, T. (2016). Can twitter save lives? A broad-scale study on visual social media analytics for public safety. *IEEE Transactions on Visualization and Computer Graphics, 22*(7), 1816–1829. https://doi.org/10.1109/TVCG.2015.2511733

Thornton, S. M., Lewis, F. E., Zhang, V., Kochenderfer, M. J., & Gerdes, J. C. (2018). Value Sensitive Design for Autonomous Vehicle Motion Planning. *2018 IEEE Intelligent Vehicles Symposium (IV)*, 1157–1162. https://doi.org/10.1109/IVS.2018.8500441

Tiedrich, L. J., Discher, G. S., Argent, F., & Rios, D. (2020). 10 best practices for artificial intelligence- related intellectual property. *Intellectual Property & Technology Law Journal, 32*(7), 3–8.

Timberg, C. (2013). *NSA slide shows surveillance of undersea cables.* Retrieved August 23, 2022, from https://www.washingtonpost.com/business/economy/the-nsa-slide-you-havent-seen/2013/07/10/32801426-e8e6-11e2-aa9f-c03a72e2d342_story.html

Timberg, C., & Nakashima, E. (2013). *Agreements with private companies protect U.S. access to cables' data for surveillance.* Retrieved August 23, 2022, from https://www.washingtonpost.com/business/technology/agreemens-with-private-companies-protect-us-access-to-cables-data-for-surveillance/2013/07/06/aa5d017a-df77-11e2-b2d4-ea6d8f477a01_story.html

Trabelsi, S., Plate, H., Abida, A., Aoun, M. M. B., Zouaoui, A., Missaoui, C., Gharbi, S., & Ayari, A. (2015). Mining social networks for software vulnerabilities monitoring. *2015 7th International Conference on New Technologies, Mobility and Security (NTMS)*, 1–7.

Trüdinger, E.-M., & Steckermeier, L. C. (2017). Trusting and controlling? Political trust, information and acceptance of surveillance policies: The case of Germany. *Government Information Quarterly, 34*(3), 421–433. https://doi.org/10.1016/j.giq.2017.07.003

Tucker, J. B. (Ed.). (2012). *Innovation, Dual Use, Security: Managing The Risks of Emerging Biological and Chemical Technologies.* MIT Press.

Tundis, A., Ruppert, S., & Mühlhäuser, M. (2020). On the automated assessment of open-source cyber threat intelligence sources. *International Conference on Computational Science*, 453–467. https://doi.org/10.1007/978-3-030-50417-5_34

Turilli, M., & Floridi, L. (2009). The ethics of information transparency. *Ethics and Information Technology*, *11*(2), 105–112. https://doi.org/10.1007/s10676-009-9187-9

Umbrello, S. (2019a). Beneficial Artificial Intelligence Coordination by Means of a Value Sensitive Design Approach. *Big Data and Cognitive Computing*, *3*(5), 1–13. https://doi.org/10.17705/1CAIS.04527

Umbrello, S. (2019b). Imaginative Value Sensitive Design: Using Moral Imagination Theory to Inform Responsible Technology Design. *Science and Engineering Ethics*, *26*, 575–595. https://doi.org/10.1007/s11948-019-00104-4

Umbrello, S. (2021). Coupling levels of abstraction in understanding meaningful human control of autonomous weapons: A two-tiered approach. *Ethics and Information Technology*, *23*(3), 455–464. https://doi.org/10.1007/s10676-021-09588-w

Umbrello, S., & De Bellis, A. F. (2018). A Value-Sensitive Design Approach to Intelligent Agents. *Artificial Intelligence Safety and Security*, (January), 395–410. https://doi.org/10.13140/RG.2.2.17162.77762

Umbrello, S., & Van de Poel, I. (2021). Mapping value sensitive design onto AI for social good principles. *AI and Ethics*, *1*(3), 283–296. https://doi.org/10.1007/s43681-021-00038-3

UNIDIR. (2014). *The Weaponization of Increasingly Autonomous Technologies: Considering how Meaningful Human Control might move the discussion forward*. Retrieved September 15, 2022, from https://unidir.org/sites/default/files/publication/pdfs/considering-how-meaningful-human-controlmight-move-the-discussion-forward-en-615.pdf

UNOG. (2018). *2018 Group of Governmental Experts on Lethal AutonomousWeapons Systems (LAWS)*. Retrieved August 23, 2022, from https://meetings.unoda.org/meeting/ccw-gge-2018/

Urban, T., Große-Kampmann, M., Tatang, D., Holz, T., & Pohlmann, N. (2020). Plenty of Phish in the Sea: Analyzing Potential Pre-Attack Surfaces. In L. Chen, N. Li, K. Liang, & S. Schneider (Eds.), *European Symposium on Research in Computer Security* (pp. 272–291). https://doi.org/10.1007/978-3-030-59013-0_14

Urbina, F., Lentzos, F., Invernizzi, C., & Ekins, S. (2022). Dual use of artificialintelligence-powered drug discovery. *Nature Machine Intelligence*, *4*(3), 189–191. https://doi.org/10.1038/s42256-022-00465-9

Urquhart, Q. E., & Sullivan, L. (2020, April 27). *April 2020: The increasing importance of trade secret protection for artificial intelligence*. Retrieved August 23, 2022, from https://www.jdsupra.com/legalnews/april-2020-the-increasing-importance-of-64465/

U.S. Department of Commerce. (2010). Rules and Regulations. *Federal Register*, *75*(122), 36482–36503. Retrieved September 15, 2022, from https://www.govinfo.gov/content/pkg/FR-2010-06-25/html/2010-15072.htm

U.S. Department of Commerce. (2016). *U.S. Commerce Control List (CCL)—Cat. 5 Part 2*. Retrieved August 23, 2022, from https://www.bis.doc.gov/index.php/regulations/commerce-control-list-ccl

U.S. Department of Commerce. (2020). *Encryption and Export Administration Regulations (EAR)*. Retrieved August 23, 2022, from https://www.bis.doc.gov/index.php/policy-guidance/encryption

U.S. Department of Commerce & National Institute of Standards and Technology. (1994). Approval of Federal Information Processing Standards Publication 185, Escrowed Encryption Standard (EES). *Federal Register—Notices, 59(27)*. Retrieved September

15, 2022, from https://csrc.nist.gov/csrc/media/publications/fips/185/archive/1994-02-09/
documents/fips185.pdf

USA. (2019). *Implementing International Humanitarian Law in the Use of Autonomy in Weapon Systems* (tech. rep.). Geneva.

USPTO. (2019). *Cooperative patent classification: B64g cosmonautics; vehicles or equiment thereof.* Retrieved August 23, 2022, from https://www.uspto.gov/web/patents/classification/cpc/html/cpc-B64G.html

Uttley, M. (2019). Review of 'The Emergence of EU Defense Research Policy: From Innovation to Militarization'. *Defence and Peace Economics.* https://doi.org/10.1080/10242694.2019.1571826

Utz, L., Schickert, N., & Dutschka, S. (2019). Die Zivilklausel der TU Darmstadt im Vergleich [accessed 2022-09-11]. https://tix.cast.d120.de/files/2019/paper_utz.pdf

Vacas, I., Medeiros, I., & Neves, N. (2018). Detecting Network Threats using OSINT Knowledge-Based IDS. *2018 14th European Dependable Computing Conference,* 128–135. https://doi.org/10.1109/EDCC.2018.00031

Valentino, N., Neuner, F., Kamin, J., & Bailey, M. (2020). Testing Snowden's Hypothesis Does Mere Awareness Drive Opposition to Government Surveillance? *Public Opinion Quarterly,* 84, 4. https://doi.org/10.1093/poq/nfaa050

Valladares, P., Fuertes, W., Tapia, F., Toulkeridis, T., & Perez, E. (2017). Dimensional data model for early alerts of malicious activities in a CSIRT. *2017 International Symposium on Performance Evaluation of Computer and Telecommunication Systems (SPECTS),* 1–8. https://doi.org/10.23919/SPECTS.2017.8046771

van den Hoven, J. (2010). The Use of Normative Theories in Computer Ethics. In L. Floridi (Ed.), *The Cambridge Handbook of Information and Computer Ethics* (pp. 59–76). Cambridge University Press. https://doi.org/10.1017/CBO9780511845239.005

van den Hoven, J. (2013). Value Sensitive Design and Responsible Innovation. In R. Owen, J. Bessant, & M. Heintz (Eds.), *Responsible innovation* (pp. 75–83). Wiley Online Library. https://doi.org/10.1002/9781118551424.ch4

van den Hoven, J., & Manders-Huits, N. (2020). *Value-sensitive Design.* In K. Miller & M. Taddeo (Eds.). https://doi.org/10.4324/9781003075011-23

van de Poel, I. (2011). The Relation Between Forward-Looking and Backward-Looking Responsibility. In N. A. Vincent, I. van de Poel, & J. van den Hoven (Eds.), *Moral responsibility: Beyond free will and determinism* (pp. 37–52). Springer Netherlands. https://doi.org/10.1007/978-94-007-1878-4

van de Poel, I. (2020). Core Values and Value Conflicts in Cybersecurity: Beyond Privacy Versus Security. In M. Christen, B. Gordijn, & M. Loi (Eds.), *The Ethics of Cybersecurity* (pp. 45–71). Springer. https://doi.org/10.1007/978-3-030-29053-5_3

van de Poel, I., & Royakkers, L. (2011). *Ethics, Technology, and Engineering: An Introduction.* Wiley-Blackwell.

Van der Kleij, R., Kleinhuis, G., & Young, H. (2017). Computer Security Incident Response Team Effectiveness: A Needs Assessment. *Frontiers in Psychology,* 8. https://doi.org/10.3389/fpsyg.2017.02179

Van der Velden, M., Mörtberg, C., et al. (2015). Participatory design and design for values. In J. van den Hoven, P. E. Vermaas, & I. van de Poel (Eds.), *Handbook of Ethics, Values, and Technological Design: Sources, Theory, Values and Application Domains* (pp. 41–66). Netherlands: Springer.

van Der Hoven, J., & Manders-Huits, N. (2020). Value-sensitive Design. In *The Ethics of Information Technologies* (pp. 329–332). Routledge.

van Gorp, A. F. (2014). Integration of Volunteer and Technical Communities into the Humanitarian Aid Sector: Barriers to Collaboration. *Proceedings of the International Conference on Information Systems for Crisis Response and Management (ISCRAM)*, (May), 620–629.

van Oort, F. G., & Raspe, O. (2012). Firm productivity in innovative urban milieus. In K. I. Westeren (Ed.), *Foundations of the Knowledge Economy* (pp. 109–117). Edward Elgar Publishing.

Vella, V. (2017). Is There a Common Understanding of Dual-Use ?: The Case of Cryptography. *Strategic Trade Review*, *3*(4), 103–122.

Verbruggen, M. (2019). The Role of Civilian Innovation in the Development of Lethal Autonomous Weapon Systems. *Global Policy*, *10*, 338–343. https://doi.org/10.1111/1758-5899.12663

Verdiesen, I. (2017a). *Agency perception and moral values related to autonomous weapons: An empirical study using the value-sensitive design approach* [Doctoral dissertation]. Delft University of Technology.

Verdiesen, I. (2017b). How do we ensure that we remain in control of our autonomous weapons? *AI Matters*, *3*(3), 47–55. https://doi.org/10.1145/3137574.3137585

Verdiesen, I. (2019). The Design of Human Oversight in Autonomous Weapon Systems. *Proceedings of the Twenty-Eighth International Joint Conference on Artificial Intelligence (IJCAI-19)*, 6468–6469. https://doi.org/10.24963/ijcai.2019/923

Verdiesen, I., Dignum, V., & Rahwan, I. (2018). Design Requirements for a Moral Machine for Autonomous Weapons. In B. Gallina, A. Skavhaug, E. Schoitsch, & F. Bitsch (Eds.), *Computer Safety, Reliability, and Security: SAFECOMP 2018 Workshops* (pp. 494–506, Vol. 11094 LNCS). Springer. https://doi.org/10.1007/978-3-319-99229-7_44

Verspagen, B. (1997). Estimating international technology spillovers using technology flow matrices. *Review of World Economics*, *133*(2), 226–248. https://doi.org/10.1007/bf02707461

Vice Admiral Cebrowski, A. K., & Garstka, J. (1998). *Network-Centric Warfare: Its Origin and Future* (tech. rep.). https://www.usni.org/magazines/proceedings/1998/january/network-centric-warfare-its-origin-and-future

Vieweg, S., Hughes, A. L., Starbird, K., & Palen, L. (2010). Microblogging During Two Natural Hazards Events: What Twitter May Contribute to Situational Awareness. *Proceedings of the Conference on Human Factors in Computing Systems (CHI)*, 1079–1088.

Villodre, J., & Criado, J. I. (2020). User roles for emergency management in social media: Understanding actors' behavior during the 2018 Majorca Island flash floods. *Government Information Quarterly*, *37*(4), 101521. https://doi.org/10.1016/j.giq.2020.101521

vom Brocke, J., Simons, A., Riemer, K., Niehaves, B., Plattfaut, R., & Cleven, A. (2015). Standing on the Shoulders of Giants: Challenges and Recommendations of Literature Search in Information Systems Research. *Communications of the Association for Information Systems*, *37*(1), 205–224. https://doi.org/10.17705/1CAIS.03709

von Schomberg, R. (2011). Introduction. In R. von Schomberg (Ed.), *Towards Responsible Research and Innovation in the Information and Communication Technologies and Security Technologies Frields* (pp. 7–16). European Commission.

Wæver, O., et al. (1993). *Securitization and Desecuritization*. Centre for Peace; Conflict Research Copenhagen.

Wagner, A. R., & Arkin, R. C. (2011). Recognizing situations that demand trust. *Proceedings—IEEE International Workshop on Robot and Human Interactive Communication*, 7–14. https://doi.org/10.1109/ROMAN.2011.6005228

Walker Smith, B. (2016). Controlling Humans and Machines. *Temple International & Comparative Law Journal*, 30(1), 167–176.

Wallace, J. R., Oji, S., & Anslow, C. (2017). Technologies, methods, and values: Changes in empirical research at CSCW 1990–2015. *Proceedings of the ACM on Human-Computer Interaction, 1(CSCW)*. https://doi.org/10.1145/3134741

Walsh, J. I. (2015). Political accountability and autonomous weapons. *Research and Politics*, 2(4), 1–6. https://doi.org/10.1177/2053168015606749

Waltz, K. N. (1990). Realist Thought and Neorealist Theory. *Journal of International Affairs*, 44, 21–37.

Wang, D., Yang, Q., Abdul, A., & Lim, B. Y. (2019). Designing theory-driven user-centric explainable AI. In *Proceedings of the 2019 CHI Conference on Human Factors in Computing Systems* (pp. 1–15). Association for Computing Machinery.

Wassenaar Arrangement Secretariat. (2021). *Wassenaar Arrangement on Export Controls for Conventional Arms and Dual-Use Goods and Technologies*. Retrieved September 15, 2022, from https://www.wassenaar.org/app/uploads/2021/12/Public-Docs-Vol-II-2021-List-of-DU-Goods-and-Technologies-and-Munitions-List-Dec-2021.pdf

Wassenaar Arrangement Secretariat. (2022). *The Wassenaar Arrangement*. Retrieved September 15, 2022, from https://www.wassenaar.org

Weatherseed, M. (2018). Being More Effective Through Information Sharing and Cooperation. In M. Bartsch & S. Frey (Eds.), *Cybersecurity best practices* (pp. 517–521). Springer Vieweg. https://doi.org/10.1007/978-3-658-21655-9_5

Weber, J., & Suchman, L. (2016). Human-Machine Autonomies. In C. Kreß, H.-Y. Liu, N. Bhuta, R. Geiß, & S. Beck (Eds.), *Autonomous Weapons Systems: Law, Ethics, Policy* (pp. 75–102). Cambridge University Press. https://doi.org/10.1017/CBO9781316597873.004

Wells, H., & Wills, D. (2009). Individualism and identity: Resistance to speed cameras in the uk. *Surveillance & Society*, 6(3), 259–274. https://doi.org/10.24908/ss.v6i3.3284

Werlinger, R., Muldner, K., Hawkey, K., & Beznosov, K. (2010). Preparation, detection, and analysis: the diagnostic work of IT security incident response (S. M. Furnell, Ed.). *Information Management & Computer Security*, 18(1), 26–42. https://doi.org/10.1108/09685221011035241

Wester, M., & Giesecke, J. (2019). Accepting surveillance-an increased sense of security after terror strikes? *Safety Science*, 120, 383–387.

Westeren, K. I. (2012). *Foundations of the knowledge economy: Innovation, learning and clusters*. Edward Elgar Publishing. https://doi.org/10.4337/9780857937728

Westin, A. F. (1967). *Privacy and Freedom*. The Bodley Head.

WHO. (2020). *Dual Use Research of Concern (DURC)*. Retrieved September 15, 2022, from https://www.who.int/news-room/questions-and-answers/item/what-is-dual-use-research-of-concern

Wiik, J., Gonzalez, J. J., & Kossakowski, K.-P. (2006). Effectiveness of Proactive CSIRT Services. *FIRST Conference*, 2–11.

Wilcox, L. (2017). Embodying algorithmic war: Gender, race, and the posthuman in drone warfare. *Security Dialogue*, 48(1), 11–28. https://doi.org/10.1177/0967010616657947

Williams, H., & Blum, I. (2018). *Defining Second Generation Open Source Intelligence (OSINT) for the Defense Enterprise.* RAND Corporation. https://doi.org/10.7249/RR1964

Wilton, R. (2017). After snowden-the evolving landscape of privacy and technology. *Journal of Information, Communication and Ethics in Society, 15.* https://doi.org/10.1108/JICES-02-2017-0010

Winfield, A. F., & Jirotka, M. (2018). Ethical governance is essential to building trust in robotics and artificial intelligence systems. *Philosophical Transactions of the Royal Society A: Mathematical, Physical and Engineering Sciences, 376*(2133). https://doi.org/10.1098/rsta.2018.0085

Winkler, T., & Spiekermann, S. (2021). Twenty years of value sensitive design: A review of methodological practices in vsd projects. *Ethics and Information Technology, 23*(1), 17–21.

WIPO. (2019). *WIPO Technology Trends 2019: Artificial Intelligence.* World Intellectual Property Organization. https://www.wipo.int/publications/en/details.jsp?id=4386

Wobbrock, J. O., & Kientz, J. A. (2016). Research Contributions in Human- Computer Interaction. *Interactions, 23*(3), 38–44. https://doi.org/10.1145/2907069

Wright, D., & Friedewald, M. (2013). Integrating privacy and ethical impact assessments. *Science and Public Policy, 40*(6), 755–766. https://doi.org/10.1093/scipol/sct083

Wulf, V., Rohde, M., Pipek, V., & Stevens, G. (2011). Engaging with practices: Design case studies as a research framework in cscw. *Proceedings of the ACM 2011 Conference on Computer Supported Cooperative Work,* 505–512. https://doi.org/10.1145/1958824.1958902

Yang, W., & Lam, K.-Y. (2020). Automated Cyber Threat Intelligence Reports Classification for EarlyWarning of Cyber Attacks in Next Generation SOC. *International Conference on Information and Communication Systems (ICICS),* 145–164.

Zade, H., Shah, K., Rangarajan, V., Kshirsagar, P., Imran, M., & Starbird, K. (2018). From Situational Awareness to Actionability: Towards Improving the Utility of Social Media Data for Crisis Response. *Proceedings of the ACM on Human-Computer Interaction, 2*(November).

Zambetti, M., Sala, R., Russo, D., Pezzotta, G., & Pinto, R. (2018). A patent review on machine learning techniques and applications: Depicting main players, relations and technology landscapes. *Proceedings of the Summer School Francesco Turco, 2018-Septe,* 115–128.

Zhang, Q., Lee, M. L., & Carter, S. (2022). You Complete Me: Human-AI Teams and Complementary Expertise. *CHI Conference on Human Factors in Computing Systems,* 1–28. https://doi.org/10.1145/3491102.3517791

Zhang, S., Feng, Y., Bauer, L., Cranor, L. F., Das, A., & Sadeh, N. (2021). "Did you know this camera tracks your mood?": Understanding privacy expectations and preferences in the age of video analytics. *Proceedings on Privacy Enhancing Technologies (PoPETs).* https://doi.org/10.2478/popets-2021-0028

Zweig, K. A. (2019). Algorithmische Entscheidungen : Transparenz und Kontrolle. *Analysen & Argumente Digitale Gesellschaft, 338*(338). https://www.kas.de/documents/252038/4521287/AA338+Algorithmische+Entscheidungen.pdf/533ef913-e567-987d-54c3-1906395cdb81?version=1.0%5C&t=1548228380797%5C%3E,%5C%20%5C%5Baccessed

Zweig, K. A., Wenzelburger, G., & Krafft, T. D. (2018). On Chances and Risks of Security Related Algorithmic Decision Making Systems. *European Journal for Security Research, 3*(2), 181–203. https://doi.org/10.1007/s41125-018-0031-2

Printed in the United States
by Baker & Taylor Publisher Services

Printed in the United States
by Baker & Taylor Publisher Services